*Padamalai*

# *Padamalai*

## Teachings of Sri Ramana Maharshi

Recorded in Tamil verse by
Muruganar

Translated by
Dr T. V. Venkatasubramanian, Robert Butler
and David Godman

Edited and annotated by
David Godman

Other titles by David Godman

*Be As You Are*
*No Mind - I am the Self*
*Papaji Interviews*
*Living by the Words of Bhagavan*
*Nothing Ever Happened* (three volumes)
*Annamalai Swami: Final Talks*
*The Power of the Presence* (three volumes)

See www.davidgodman.org for more details



Cover design: Gloria Lee

ISBN 0-9711371-3-7

Published by
David Godman,
Avadhuta Foundation,
3245, Prairie Avenue,
Boulder, CO 80301
USA

Printed at
Sudarsan Graphics Pvt. Ltd.,
No.27, Neelakanta Metha Street,
T.Nagar, Madras - 600 017.
India.

# Contents

## The Guru and the *Jnani*

## The Mind and its Creations

## Practice

## The World and its Creator



## Right Knowledge, Right Behaviour, Right Attitude

Sri Ramana Maharshi

Sri Muruganar

# Introduction

Muruganar (1890-1973) is widely regarded as being one of the most eminent and influential of Ramana Maharshi's devotees. He was instrumental in persuading Bhagavan to compose both *Ulladu Narpadu* and *Upadesa Undiyar*, two of his most important philosophical works, and he also recorded and rendered into Tamil verse some of Bhagavan's spoken teachings. Over eight hundred of these verses were published under the title *Guru Vachaka Kovai* (*A Garland of the Guru's Sayings*) during Bhagavan's lifetime. Bhagavan himself thoroughly edited the first printing of this book, thereby making it one of the most authoritative works on his teachings.

Muruganar first met Bhagavan when he came to Tiruvannamalai in September 1923. Prior to this visit he had been working on a committee that was compiling a multi-volume Tamil dictionary. This encounter was a defining moment in Muruganar's life, for he experienced Bhagavan's power and grace on his very first meeting:

> In the same way that wax melts on encountering fire, on seeing his feet, my mind dissolved and lost its form. Like the calf finding its mother, my heart melted and rejoiced in his feet. The hairs on my body stood on end. Devotion surged in me like an ocean that has seen the full moon. Through the grace of *chit-sakti* [the power inherent in consciousness], my soul was in ecstasy.[1]

Muruganar had been composing poetry on a variety of topics for many years before he came to Bhagavan. His very first offering to Bhagavan had, in fact, been a sequence of verses he had composed while he was on his way to meet him for the first time. However, shortly after meeting Bhagavan and experiencing his power and grace, Muruganar took a vow that in future he would only compose verses that either recorded his Guru's teachings or extolled his greatness in some way. For the next fifty years he kept his promise, writing thousands upon thousands of verses on these subjects. Some of these poetical works were published in Bhagavan's lifetime but many of them remained in manuscript form even after Muruganar himself passed away in 1973.

When Muruganar was nearing the end of his life, he appointed Sadhu Om to be his literary executor and gave him all the trunks that contained his unpublished material. Sadhu Om spent much of the next decade diligently arranging and editing these manuscripts. Professor K. Swaminathan, a long-time admirer of Muruganar and his poetry, persuaded the Government of India to give a grant to the Delhi Ramana Kendra so that all these poems could be published. The result was a nine-volume Tamil series entitled *Sri Ramana Jnana Bodham*. Though these books have been in print for several years, very few of these verses have ever appeared in English.

What is the subject matter of this vast output? The majority of verses praise Bhagavan, express Muruganar's gratitude towards him, recount the experiences he had through Bhagavan's grace, or explain Bhagavan's teachings. In volume nine, though, there is a very long poem entitled *Padamalai* (*A Garland for Padam*) that records many of the teaching statements that Muruganar heard Bhagavan make.

Over half of the 3,059 verses that comprise *Padamalai* contain a direct quotation from Bhagavan. These teaching statements can be identified by the phrase '*en Padam*' that concludes each of these verses. '*En Padam*' can be translated as 'So says *Padam*'. The word *Padam* appears in each of the 3,059 verses. When it occurs in the phrase '*en Padam*', *Padam* refers to Bhagavan himself. It also denotes Bhagavan when Muruganar praises Bhagavan or extols his greatness. Throughout the remainder of the work, *Padam*, which literally means 'the foot', is used as a synonym for the Self.

## The structure of the work

When Muruganar composed *Padamalai,* it was not his intention to make a systematic presentation of Bhagavan's teachings. This is what he wrote in his own introduction to the poem:

> What is said early on [in the work] gets mentioned repeatedly later, making it appear that repetition is its theme. Unlike the work of great ones, this does not contain in large amounts an extensive and deep philosophy that would give the work solidity and subtlety. Even if a few subtle ideas have serendipitously appeared here, like the

> letters seen in snail tracks, they are not present in any orderly and connected sequence. Can the words uttered by the mad, the ignorant and the devout be subject to a critical analysis? Following on from this, I can say that this work has been sung as a peculiar expression of my mental inclinations. However, in its own way, it is a congenial support for the extremely purifying remembrance of the divine feet of the Lord, the reality. For this reason alone, let devotees, the wise ones who possess love, recognise and preserve this *Padamalai*, which has come into being through grace-madness, as an auxiliary means for remembrance, chanting it with the above-mentioned attitude.

Muruganar's attempt to minimise the importance of this work and its philosophical depth is a typical example of his self-deprecating nature. Overall, the work is a major statement of Bhagavan's teachings on a wide variety of topics. Though Muruganar never intended this work to be a systematic presentation of Bhagavan's teachings, the sheer volume of the *Padamalai* verses he composed means that almost all aspects of Bhagavan's teachings have been covered. However, the coverage is not even. On some topics there are huge numbers of verses, on others hardly any at all.

When I decided to edit and arrange selected verses from *Padamalai* for publication in English, I ended up adopting the following guidelines:

1 I would not utilise all the verses since many of the ideas and teaching statements appear in an almost identical form in several places throughout the work. I also decided to omit any verses whose translation or meaning was problematic in any way. About 1,750 of the 3,059 verses made it to the final draft.

2 I decided to arrange the verses thematically in such a way that they form a systematic presentation of Bhagavan's teachings on a wide variety of topics. I have, accordingly, grouped the verses into subjects such as 'The Self', 'Grace', 'Self-enquiry', and so on.

3 In order to clarify or amplify the teaching statements, I have added a substantial number of editorial explanations and supplementary quotations, mostly from Bhagavan himself. These primarily comprise comments by Bhagavan which explain in more detail some idea that has been presented in the verse. They also occasionally include comments and elaborations on allied topics.

4 Since many of the verses in *Padamalai* are statements by Muruganar himself on the nature of the Self, on the experiences he had through Bhagavan's grace, and on the greatness of Bhagavan, I have included chapters that deal exclusively with these topics. In the first chapter, 'Bhagavan *Padam*', Muruganar describes Bhagavan's method of teaching, his greatness and his characteristics; in the chapter entitled '*Padam*' he expounds on the nature of the Self; in the final chapter, '*Padam's* Grace Towards Muruganar', he speaks movingly of the transformations he underwent through Bhagavan's power and presence. All the remaining chapters record some of Bhagavan's spoken teachings.

5 Though most of Bhagavan's statements conclude with the phrase '*en Padam*', I decided to omit this phrase in the translation since its inclusion would make for a lot of tedious repetition. I have, though, left in variations of this phrase such as '*Padam*, consciousness, speaks...,' '*Padam* warns...' and so on since a sprinkling of these terms helps to give a flavour and a reminder of the original format.

6 I have included a number of verses in the sections on Bhagavan's teachings that do not conclude with the standard '*en Padam*' attribution. I have discussed this matter at length with the other translators and editors and we all feel that these are statements uttered by Bhagavan. Two significant aspects of the work led us to this conclusion:

> (a) In many parts of *Padamalai* there are sequences that develop a theme over several verses. Some of these verses that record Bhagavan's teachings end with an '*en Padam*', and some do not. This is akin to passages of direct speech in written English prose in which some paragraphs end with a 'he said' or 'she said', whereas others omit the attribution. Whether the attribution is there or not, it is all direct speech.
>
> (b) Many ideas and teachings are repeated in *Padamalai* in slightly different forms. In some places a particular statement will end with an '*en Padam*', whereas an identical idea elsewhere in the work will lack this ending.

We concluded that Muruganar omitted the '*en Padam*' attribution when the teaching statement by Bhagavan consumed all the available space in his two-line verse format, leaving no room for a 'So says *Padam*' ending. However, honesty dictates that we identify these verses in some way. Throughout the book, such 'unattributed' statements have an asterisk after the verse number.

7 I have not used the original verse numbers in the text. I have, instead, started each chapter with a fresh '1, 2, 3,...' sequence. The 'References' section at the end of the book shows the correspondence between these numbers and the original *Padamalai* verses.

8 Though most of the *Padamalai* verses have no connection with what precedes or succeeds them, in some places it is clear that Muruganar is developing an idea over two or more verses. When this happens, I have kept the verses together in my arrangement.

9 There are eight major divisions within the book, corresponding to different aspects of Bhagavan's teachings and Muruganar's experiences with him. At the beginning of each of these sections I have included a few verses by Muruganar that I have taken from other works. The sources of these citations, and of all other quotations used, can be found in the 'References' and 'Bibliography' sections that I have included at the end of the book.

10 My own editorial comments are printed in italics and, except for paragraph indents, extend over the full width of the page. Quotations from Bhagavan and from the literature about him are always indented.

## Acknowledgements

The verses of *Padamalai* were first brought to my attention by Dr Venkatasubramanian, a devotee who has been studying Muruganar's poetry for many years. Dr Venkatasubramanian has worked on several Muruganar projects, including a Tamil edition of *Guru Vachaka Kovai* that contains Muruganar's own commentary on the verses. We worked on this *Padamalai* project together for many months, translating and revising our initial selection of verses several times. In the middle of 2002 we invited Robert Butler to join us. Robert had already translated volume one of *Sri Ramana Anubhuti*, one of Muruganar's poetical works, into English, so he was familiar with Muruganar's style and the particular problems it presents to would-be translators. The three of us went through all the verses again, revising and improving the English rendering and also supplementing the text with many new verses. While all this was going on, I was arranging the completed material in a thematic way and adding supplementary comments and quotations. After I had completed a first draft of the book, Dr Venkatasubramanian went through it and made many suggestions about the ordering of the verses and the appropriateness or otherwise of the additional material I had attached to them. I accepted and incorporated many of his suggestions. The final version, then, was very much a joint collaboration between the three of us. I should like to express my gratitude here for the efforts of both Dr Venkatasubramanian and Robert Butler for their massive contributions and for their willingness to devote so much of their time to a project that has taken almost two years to bring to fruition.

Thanks are also due to both the Delhi Ramana Kendra for giving me permission to translate and publish a version of *Padamalai* and to the President of Sri Ramanasramam, Sri V. S. Ramanan, for allowing me to quote extensively from the Ramanasramam literature and for giving permission to use photos of both Bhagavan and Muruganar.

I wish to acknowledge and express my gratitude to a devotee, who wishes to remain anonymous, for contributing a substantial donation for the publishing costs of the first printing. This has allowed me to reduce by a large amount the sale price of the book in India. I also wish to acknowledge and thank Gloria Lee for designing the cover.

Several people went through the book prior to its publication, pointing out the occasional error and making useful comments about the presentation of the material. My thanks to Karen Kapadia, Anna Losardi, Chris Mohr, Daesung Sunim, Nadhia Sutara, and Viorica Weissman.

David Godman

Arunachala, March 2004

# Bhagavan *Padam*

Primal Lord!
Lord who is the beautiful radiance that shines
as 'I-I' within the Heart of devotees!
Lord who is the Self, beyond the reach
of the mind's objective knowledge!
Lord who possesses justice rooted in grace!
Lord who stands, his feet firmly planted
in the Self-abidance of his followers!
Lord who remains as that which is [after all else is discarded]!
Noble Ramana whose play is to hold me in his loving embrace![1]

Through the path of his grace that even the gods cannot know he came as a teacher in a form knowable to the senses and easily accessible to the hearts of men, setting upon the earth those holy feet that shine like bright jewels set in wisdom's dawn.[2]

Let us fix our thoughts on *Sadguru* Ramana, who abides as the Self, that inner awareness 'I-I' that dwells as the grace of the supreme within the 'I' of my own heart, so that I obtain in full measure the blessing of divine silence, free from the deluded self-conceit that leads to pride and attachment.[3]

# Bhagavan *Padam*

*In this first section Muruganar is extolling the greatness of his Guru. Since, in this chapter, he is referring to Bhagavan himself when he uses the word* Padam, *I have used personal pronouns wherever appropriate.*

## *Padam's* form

1 Blissful *Padam* is that form of Siva who sports, assuming a disguise and masking his truth.

Pizhambu, *translated here as 'form of Siva', may also be translated as 'column of fire', a reference to the original manifestation of Siva as Arunachala.*

2 Fair *Padam*, the unattainable supreme, took on the noble vestments of the Guru to redeem this world.

3 *Padam*, the supreme flame, assuming the form of the Guru, the embodiment of grace, moves amongst us as the destroyer of bondage.

4 *Padam* is Dakshinamurti, conferring the final emancipation of *mukti*, whose nature is pure consciousness.

5 Appearing outwardly with a comely form and as the Self within, *Padam* rules over his devotees.

6 Many are the devotees upon this earth, thousands upon thousands, whom *Padam* brings under his sway, sweetly granting them his grace.

7 *Padam* confounds the ignorant by showing himself as a human being while actually existing as the form of the space [of consciousness], the fullness of the supreme reality [*para-vastu*].

8 When he is seen [properly], *Padam* remains merged as the impartial sun of benevolent grace, but people of the world needlessly slander him as being hard-hearted.

9 To loving devotees, *Padam* has a pleasant smile that resembles a

water lily, but to deceitful people it is terrible and dreadful.

10 Having assumed a form, *Padam*, the unique, true *jnana*, moves [amongst us] to show the way of truth to men.

11 Adopting the form of grace, resplendent *Padam* causes true *jnana* to shine in a fitting manner in the hearts of devotees.

## *Padam's* teachings

12 By his spoken word, which is a ringing bell with *mauna* [silence] as its clapper, Guru *Padam* drives home the teachings of *jnana*.

Jnana *is true knowledge, the knowledge that one is the Self. The one who has this definitive experience is known as a* jnani. *This knowledge takes the form of a subjective awareness, rather than knowledge of an object. Since there is no one left in the state of* jnana *to 'know' the knowledge, Bhagavan once remarked, 'There are no* jnanis, *there is only* jnana'. *The state of* jnana *is consciousness being aware of nothing other than itself.*

13 Like an incorporeal voice emanating from the heavenly sphere, *Padam* utters in ringing tones words of surpassing Siva-*jnana*.

> Once, we were all listening to the radio in the Jubilee Hall. At the end of the programme the names of all the artistes were announced. Bhagavan said, 'See! The radio sings and gives speeches. It even announces the names of the performers. But there is nobody inside the radio. In the same way my existence is also like the sky. Though the body may appear to speak, like a radio there is no individual person [*asami*] inside. There is only God [*Sami*].'[1]

14 The extremely ingenuous *Padam* clearly tells the truth as it really is, without concealing anything at all.

*Bhagavan had no secret teachings, as the following exchange makes clear:*

> **Question:** May I believe that there is nothing more to be known now, so far as the technique of *sadhana* is concerned, than that which has been written in your books

from time to time? This question arises from the fact that, in all other systems of *sadhana*, the *Sadguru* unfolds some secret technique of meditation to his disciple at the time of initiation or *diksha*, as it is called.

**Bhagavan:** There is nothing more to be known than what you find in books. No secret technique. It is all an open secret in this system.[2]

**15** *Padam* abounds with the excellent skill of elucidating reality without being verbose, compressing it more and more, enabling [listeners] to attain a focused mind.

One result of the originality of Sri Bhagavan's Self-realisation was that his approach to problems addressed to him was equally original. His replies to questions were never recondite or bookish, but always simple and direct. Like Christ he spoke as a man of authority because his words came not from book learning or hearsay, but from first-hand knowledge and experience. He said what he knew; he knew what he said. He went to the root of any question and simplified its terms. There were no confusing technicalities when he spoke, for he would give homely, concrete illustrations along with his answers that always made his meaning crystal clear.[3]

**16** *Padam* distils and dispenses countless deep and subtle teachings on truth to those with minds lacking in wisdom.

**17** The extremely wonderful *Padam* made public the supreme truth of the *Vedas*, which is normally declared only to trustworthy persons.

*In ancient time disciples would sometimes undergo a long probationary period during which their teacher would assess their spiritual maturity and capabilities. If, after this period, the disciples were deemed to be worthy enough, the teacher would impart one of the key vedic statements of identity, such as* 'Tat tvam asi' *(You are That). Bhagavan never held back any of his teachings while he assessed the worthiness of those who approached him. If visitors asked for the highest knowledge or the most direct practice, he would tell them immediately.*

*In a more general sense, 'the supreme truth of the* Vedas*' denotes the experience of the Self, rather than a revelation of scriptural knowledge.*

*In some verses of* Padamalai *Muruganar writes about 'the experience of Vedanta'. This too indicates an experience of the Self, rather than a knowledge or an understanding of particular texts.*

*Bhagavan's attitude to preliminary teachings is exemplified by the following story:*

> Once, when Ganapati Muni was present in the hall, a group of villagers asked, 'How are we to control the mind?'
>
> In reply Bhagavan asked them to look into the origin of the mind and explained the path of self-enquiry. Soon they left and Bhagavan as usual went out for a walk.
>
> Remarking to the others [Ganapati] Muni said, 'The path of Self-knowledge which Bhagavan teaches is so difficult even for the learned, and Bhagavan advocated it to the poor villagers. I doubt whether they understood it and still less whether they can practise it. If Bhagavan had advised them to practise some *puja* or *japa*, that would have been more practical.'
>
> When this was conveyed to Bhagavan, he commented, 'What to do? This is what I know. If a teaching is to be imparted according to the traditional way, one must first see whether the recipient is qualified or not. Then *puja, japa* or *dhyana* are prescribed step by step. Later the Guru says that this is all only preliminary and one has to transcend all this. Finally, the ultimate truth that "*Brahman* alone is real" is revealed and to realise this, the direct path of self-enquiry is to be taught. Why this roundabout process? Should we not state the ultimate truth and direct path at the beginning itself rather than advocating many methods and rejecting them at the end?'[4]

**18** *Padam* emphatically declares the manifold births to be a tale of the mind that is possessed by the defect of forgetfulness.

### *Padam's* glance of grace

**19** Manifesting as the supreme reality, *Padam* came to exercise his rule over devotees in the form of the *jnana*-Guru, he who possesses the grace-bestowing gaze.

20 Through his divine glance *Padam* liberally bestows on his devotees the treasure of grace, the realisation of the nature of *Sivam*.

Sivam, *the consciousness of Siva, is a synonym for reality. It is the ultimate goal of all Saivas to become one with* Sivam.

21 Through his glance, *Padam* graciously establishes in the hearts of devotees the blessing of a divine life in the realm of *Sivam*.

22 Bringing them to maturity through his gaze, *Padam* enlightens them with the truth, the supreme transcendence.

23 Even to the celestial beings in the high heavens, the shining, gracious glance of *Padam* is alone great and abundant wealth.

***Padam's* power**

24 *Padam*, the supreme, possesses the power of Self-knowledge that consumes all visions in his fire, transmuting them into his own form.

25 Upon those who, dwelling upon death, resort to him in fear, *Padam* will bestow the immortal life that flourishes, transcending the death that is the delusion of the ego.

26 The effulgent, silent *Padam* destroys forgetfulness of the Self, the mind, which is the taproot for the succession of afflictions.

27 *Padam* is firmly established in the state of *mauna*, the power of the Self, before which all other powers fade away.

28 *Padam*, the Heart abiding motionless as peace, attracts everyone to himself like a magnet.

29 *Padam* unites with grace devotees who have taken shelter under him in such a way that they also become like *Padam*, gaining in abundance his magnetic property.

30 *Padam*, concentrated consciousness, is an adept at the great conjuring trick of delivering one from primal ignorance, the birthplace of the *triputis*.

*The* triputis *are the trinities such as knower, knowing and known, and seer, seeing and seen.*

31 *Padam* completely destroys the powerful mental imagination [*dehatma buddhi*] that grows up to form the obstacle to steadfast abidance in the real.

Dehatma buddhi *is the I-am-the-body idea, the concept that one is an individual person who inhabits a particular physical body.*

**32** Golden *Padam* transformed [his] mother into the avatar of *chit-para-sakti*, the bestower of *Sivam*.

*'The avatar of* chit-para-sakti*' can be translated as 'the embodiment of the grace of the divine'. Grace in Saivism is always channelled through the female form of the divine. The verse is saying that, after her enlightenment, Bhagavan's mother became one with the divine grace that bestows* Sivam.

**33** *Padam* possesses such great depth, it is not possible for others to fathom and know the contents mingled in his Heart.

**34** Banging on the mighty, thunderous drum of *mauna*, *Padam* possesses the liberality of abundantly bestowing the grace of Siva-*jnana*.

**35** Radiant *Padam* reveals with certitude the clear truth of *jnana* even in the hearts of the most stupid blockheads who amount to less than a lump of clay.

**36** *Padam*, the peaceful refuge, possesses the great renown that all that happens occurs only through the power of his presence.

*Many people had wonderful experiences in Bhagavan's presence. Others found that if they appealed to Bhagavan for help with their problems, satisfactory solutions, some of them seemingly miraculous, would follow. Bhagavan never claimed responsibility for any of these phenomena. Instead, he said that there was a* sannidhi*, a presence in the vicinity of enlightened beings that took care of all the problems that were brought to their attention. Bhagavan himself was quite adamant that he did nothing in these circumstances. Narayana Iyer elicited the following explanation from Bhagavan on this point. The word* sankalpa *that appears several times in the exchange means 'will' or 'intention'. It is the desire to follow a particular course of action.*

> One day when I was sitting by the side of Bhagavan I felt so miserable that I put the following question to him: 'Is the *sankalpa* of the *jnani* not capable of warding off the destinies of the devotees?'
>
> Bhagavan smiled and said: 'Does the *jnani* have a *sankalpa* at all? The *jivanmukta* [liberated being] can have no *sankalpas* whatsoever. It is just impossible.'

I continued: 'Then what is the fate of all of us who pray to you to have grace on us and save us? Will we not be benefited or saved by sitting in front of you, or by coming to you?...'

Bhagavan turned graciously to me and said: '...a person's bad karma will be considerably reduced while he is in the presence of a *jnani*. A *jnani* has no *sankalpas* but his *sannidhi* [presence] is the most powerful force. He need not have *sankalpa*, but his presiding presence, the most powerful force, can do wonders: save souls, give peace of mind, even give liberation to ripe souls. Your prayers are not answered by him but absorbed by his presence. His presence saves you, wards off the karma and gives you the boons as the case may be, [but] involuntarily. The *jnani* does save the devotees, but not by *sankalpa*, which is non-existent in him, only through his presiding presence, his *sannidhi*.'[5]

**37** The effulgent *Padam* purifies the mind with the splendour of grace such that its defilement is removed, infusing it with a consciousness that is the rarest ambrosia.

**38** *Padam*, the truth, shines in the Heart, stunning the attitude of mind that conducts itself by faith alone.

*The point being presented here is that Bhagavan gives devotees a direct experience so that they no longer need to depend on faith.*

**39** The grace bestowed by *Padam* on true devotees who are worthy of his love enables them to know and attain him without any effort.

*Bhagavan sometimes graded the maturity of spiritual aspirants by comparing them to gunpowder, charcoal and green wood. Gunpowder ignites when exposed to a single spark; charcoal burns after a preliminary period of heating; green wood has to be left for a long time to season before it can be used for firewood. Those few devotees who were ready for the divine spark often had an experience of the Self in Bhagavan's presence very early in their association with him, having done little or no* sadhana. *Muruganar has written about this in one of his other poems:*

Having obtained Self-realisation at a young age,

without having to take instructions from others, or even having to make any conscious effort, you are now bestowing the gift of Self-knowledge upon your devotees through the power of your presence alone. Your devotees are fortunate indeed, for they are granted the highest wisdom without having to undergo the rigours of spiritual exercises.[6]

40 Because the two [*jiva* and Iswara or Guru and disciple] really exist as one, *Padam* bestows the grace to annihilate the [sense of] separateness as mere imagination.

*Iswara is a generic term that denotes the personal God of Hinduism. It does not refer to any particular deity.*

41 The effulgent *Padam* casts out the delusion of 'I' and 'mine' from the hearts of those true devotees who remain still in his presence.
42 The ego rises and expands with the sole purpose of conquering [while] *Padam* proceeds with his sole duty of slaying it.
43 Effulgent *Padam* totally subdues the awareness of that which is other [than itself], making it powerless, and bestows the consciousness of reality, the natural state of consciousness.
44 *Padam* is the wind that joyfully enables a wisp of straw, adrift on the ocean, to reach the shore and gain salvation.

*The point of this analogy is that* Padam *makes the apparently impossible possible.*

45 With the key of *jnana*, *Padam* opens the treasure-chest, which is abundant forgetfulness, inside which is reality.

### *Padam's* characteristics

46 *Padam* lives and moves about here for the benefit of devotees who desire the supreme truth, *jnana*.
47 *Padam* will bear upon his own head the accumulated burdens of those who have performed the great offering [of giving up the mind].
48 By bestowing the true knowledge that destroys the infatuation

which operates in ignorance, *Padam* fulfils all the desires of those who take shelter under him.

For him that is established in the supreme state, desires do not arise because the desirer, the ego, has ceased to exist. The sage in that state is ever contented, as if he had obtained simultaneously enjoyment of all possible desires at one stroke.[7]

**49** Because *Padam*, the one Self, is devoid of mind, he exists without any company, in solitude, even in the midst of a great crowd.

**Question:** I have this desire to live in a place where nobody visits. I feel another desire to get food without any effort. I also want to meditate constantly with my eyes closed, without seeing the world at all. These desires often come to me. Are they good or bad?
**Bhagavan:** If you have desires such as these you will have to take another birth to fulfil them. What does it matter where you stay? Keep your mind always in the Self. Apart from the Self, there is no solitary place 'outside'. Wherever you exist keeping company with the mind, that place is, without doubt, a crowded place.[8]

**50** *Padam,* whose true nature is absolute liberation, does not slip from *mauna* even when all the *karanas* [the mind, the senses and the physical organs] are in operation.
**51** Through his compassionate nature, *Padam* functions as though he were closely associated with everything, whilst in reality remaining without any association whatsoever.
**52** The extremely wonderful *Padam* acts as though he too is under the control of the actions of *sakti* that were initiated by him.
**53** *Padam* speaks words as if they were mere play, but the more and more we listen to them, the heart, without being satiated, longs for more.

Sri Bhagavan's manner of speaking was itself unique. His normal state was silence. He spoke so little, casual visitors who only saw him for a short while wondered whether he ever spoke. To put questions to him and to elicit his replies was an art in itself that required an unusual exercise in self-control. A sincere doubt, an earnest question submitted to him never went without an answer, though sometimes his silence itself was the best answer to particular questions. A questioner needed to be able to wait patiently. To have the maximum chance of receiving a good answer, you had to put your question simply and briefly. Then you had to remain quiet and attentive. Sri Bhagavan would take his time and then begin slowly and haltingly to speak. As his speech continued, it would gather momentum. It would be like a drizzle gradually strengthening into a shower. Sometimes it might go on for hours together, holding the audience spellbound. But throughout the talk you had to keep completely still and not butt in with counter remarks. Any interruption from you would break the thread of his discourse and he would at once resume silence. He would never enter into a discussion, nor would he argue with anyone. The fact was, what he spoke was not a view or an opinion but the direct emanation of light from within that manifested as words in order to dispel the darkness of ignorance. The whole purpose of his reply was to make you turn inward, to make you see the light of truth within yourself.[9]

**54** Whoever they may be and whatever *sadhana* they may practise, *Padam* will lovingly bless that *sadhana* with his grace.

Everyone knows what great stress Sri Bhagavan lays on *atma vichara*, self-enquiry. He wrote in *Atma Vidya Kirtanam*, 'Self-knowledge is an easy thing, the easiest thing there is'.

Yet, surprisingly, not once of his own accord did he ever ask any devotee to follow this method. He could have ordered the practice of self-enquiry, and all the devotees would have blindly and willingly followed...

Sri Bhagavan's presence and teachings gave hope and strength to different classes of seekers at different levels...Sri Bhagavan gave help and guidance to all kinds of people on all kinds of paths and never demanded that devotees change from one *sadhana* to another.[10]

A lot of people are under the impression that Bhagavan

talked advaitic philosophy all the time and prescribed self-enquiry to everyone who asked for his advice. This is simply not so: Bhagavan gave out different advice to different people. He would see their level of development and their temperament and act accordingly. One devotee might ask a question and be given an answer. If another devotee asked the same question a few minutes later, he might be given a different answer, so different in fact that it would contradict the first one. If each of these devotees acted on Bhagavan's advice, with full faith in its efficacy, each would find that Bhagavan's grace was flowing into him.[11]

**55** Whoever they may be, and whatever they have set their mind upon, *Padam*, through his grace, lovingly grants to each according to his desire.

*The fourth verse of* Ulladu Narpadu Anubandham *speaks about the great benefits of having the* darshan *of enlightened beings:*

Heat will be removed by the cool moon, poverty by the celestial wish-fulfilling tree, and sin by the Ganga. But know that all these, beginning with heat, will be removed merely by having the *darshan* of incomparable *sadhus*.

*Annamalai Swami once asked Bhagavan about this verse:*

'We know where the moon is, and we know where the Ganga is, but where is this wish-fulfilling tree?'

'If I tell you where it is,' replied Bhagavan, 'will you be able to leave it?'

I was puzzled by this particular answer, but I didn't pursue the matter. A few minutes later I opened a copy of *Yoga Vasishta* which was lying next to Bhagavan. On the first page I looked at I found a verse which said, 'The *jnani* is the wish-fulfilling tree'. I immediately understood Bhagavan's strange answer to my question. Before I had a chance to tell Bhagavan about this, he looked at me and smiled. He seemed to know that I had found the right answer. I told Bhagavan about the verse but he made no comment. He just carried on smiling at me.[12]

**56** Though he appears to see things in front of him, *Padam* is that extremely pure expanse, the eye [of *jnana*] that sees no object whatsoever before it.

*Though Bhagavan sometimes transmitted the power and grace of the Self by looking at devotees, he also maintained that he did not 'see' objects or people in front of him in the way that ordinary people did. He called this state* jnana-drishti. *It is an awareness of the Self in which seeing takes place, but without the false separation between the one who sees and the objects that are seen.*

*A visitor once asked Bhagavan if he had ever thought of travelling around India:*

> **Bhagavan:** I have never had any such idea, though several devotees have proposed it. Rajeswarananda once said he would arrange for a special train to take me all over India. But what is the use of my going anywhere? I am not able to see anything. (I [Devaraja Mudaliar] took this to refer to Bhagavan only seeing the Self in everything.)[13]

> **Question:** It is said that the eyes of a *jnani* appear to look at things, but in reality they see nothing.
> **Bhagavan:** Yes, the eyes of a *jnani* are likened to the eyes of a dead goat; they are always open, never closed. They glitter but they see nothing, though it seems to others that they see everything.[14]

*The state and experience of* jnana-drishti *will be elaborated on in a later chapter.*

**57** Even *Padam* [Bhagavan] cannot describe in words *Padam*, the pure expanse [of consciousness] that can only be recognised through the vision brought about by grace.

**58** Because his true nature is non-dual consciousness, fullness, there is no room in *Padam* to slander anyone.

> Whenever we heard that someone had died, we would make a point of going to sit before Sri Bhagavan because we were all keen to hear Sri Bhagavan compliment the departed person. Even when he talked about people who were, to the rest of us, inveterate scoundrels, he would

always find something good to say about them.

There was a rich man called Kandaswami who lived in town. Although he occasionally used to come to the ashram for Sri Bhagavan's *darshan*, the local people detested him because of his bad behaviour. During his last days, which he spent in the *mantapam* opposite the ashram, he suffered from both poverty and disease. While he was lying in this *mantapam*, he sent word through a messenger that he would like some gruel prepared in the Malayalam way. Immediately Sri Bhagavan arranged for this gruel to be prepared and sent to him. On the following day Kandaswami's condition became serious, so serious in fact that we were speaking among ourselves, wondering which of his good qualities Sri Bhagavan would speak about when he passed away. A day later, Sri Kandaswami died.

We immediately went and informed Sri Bhagavan and sat before him, thinking that even Sri Bhagavan would not be able to think of anything good to say about this man. What a disappointment!

Sri Bhagavan told us, 'No one could keep his body and clothes as clean as Kandaswami. He used neither oil nor soap. He would come at 8 a.m. in the morning and start washing his *dhoti*. Then he would hang it up to dry. By the time he had completed his bath it would be twelve noon. His hair and beard were always extremely clean.'

We hung our heads in shame. Who could equal Sri Bhagavan in seeing only the good qualities in all people?[15]

**59** *Padam* declares that the following is true for everyone: other than the life of [abiding as] the Self, free of forgetfulness, there is no other worthy attainment.

**60** *Padam*, who possesses the munificence of grace, has given the assurance that his greatest duty is that of affording protection [to devotees].

**61** *Padam* gets caught in the net of love spread out by devotees, and ensnares them in turn in his grace.

**62** Removing the weariness of some amongst his devotees with playful, softly spoken words, *Padam* is filled with a child-like delight.

**63** *Padam* possesses the wondrous, extraordinary power of bringing delight to his devotees through his gentle, laughing smile.

64 With his sweet smile, which graciously bestows the grace of his teachings, shining *Padam* dispels the deep sorrow wherein [we] languish in fear and torment in the pain of our ignorance.

> There is no way of describing the radiance of his smile. One who might appear a hardened businessman would leave Tiruvannamalai with a lilt in his heart from that smile. A simple woman said, 'I don't understand the philosophy but when he smiles at me I feel safe, just like a child in its mother's arms.' I had never yet seen him when I received a letter from my five-year-old daughter: 'You will love Bhagavan. When he smiles everyone must be so happy.'[16]

65 *Padam* bestows only the thought of itself [the Self] as the excellent *sat-achara*, and not religious observances.

*Though* achara *generally denotes external religious observances,* sat-achara *here signifies abiding as being, the reality.*

66 *Padam* has the righteousness of not interfering even slightly in divinely ordained events, which themselves do not deviate from righteousness.

*Bhagavan's teachings on free will and destiny were extremely deterministic in so far as he taught that all activities are pre-ordained and unchangeable. He made a classic statement on this topic in 1898 when his family discovered that he was living at the foot of Arunachala. When his mother begged him to return home, Bhagavan, who was only eighteen at the time, wrote her the following note:*

> The Ordainer controls the fate of souls in accordance with their past deeds – their *prarabdha* karma. Whatever is destined not to happen will not happen, try how hard you may. Whatever is destined to happen will happen, do what you may to stop it. This is certain. The best course, therefore, is for one to be silent.[17]

*Bhagavan's non-interference could occasionally take extreme forms, as the following anecdote from Kunju Swami reveals:*

Once, when Sri Bhagavan's brother, Niranjanananda Swami, was being physically lifted and carried away by a group of people who were threatening to kill him, he [Bhagavan] was absolutely unperturbed. He did not even turn his head in their direction. In the evening when Niranjanananda Swami came back unharmed and sat in front of Sri Bhagavan, he took no notice of his safe return. Of course, it was his grace that saved Niranjanananda Swami that day – but that is a different matter.[18]

**67** *Padam* demonstrates in his conduct that remaining calm and composed, without agitation and excitement, should be observed [by all].

*In 1924 a gang of thieves came to Ramanasramam and physically attacked Bhagavan during the course of their attempted robbery:*

Bhagavan received a severe blow on his leg during the robbery, but in a characteristic response he told the robbers, 'If you are not satisfied, you may strike the other leg also'.

Ramakrishna Swami, one of the devotees present, was so outraged by the assault on Bhagavan's person, he took up an iron bar with the intention of attacking the intruders.

Bhagavan restrained him, saying, 'Let these robbers play their role. We shall stick to ours. Let them do what they like. It is for us to bear and forbear. Let us not interfere with them.'[19]

**68** Not disdaining inferior creatures, *Padam*, caresses them and protects them.

**Bhagavan:** Any living being that comes to me [comes] only to work out the balance of its karma. So don't prevent anyone from coming to me.[20]

**69** *Padam* possesses in abundance the powerful vigour of undivided *mauna* such that even wild animals will not rouse themselves in anger and attack him.

> When a new animal was brought to the ashram, Bhagavan would usually decline to accept it unless a devotee volunteered to look after it. Bhagavan at first was unwilling to accept even Lakshmi and the white peacock. It was only when devotees assured him that they would be well looked after he agreed to let them stay in the ashram. Some animals which failed to find favour with anyone were returned to the donors. I remember a baby tiger that fell into this category. A devotee from North India brought it to Bhagavan. Even though it was small, it was already rather ferocious. It got angry with everyone except Bhagavan who tried to go near it. Bhagavan put it on his knee and had a photo taken but no one else could control it. After one week, when it became clear that the tiger was not going to settle down, Bhagavan told the owner to take it away.[21]

**70** *Padam* nods his head, indicating 'Good, good', to devotees who repeatedly approach, offering all kinds of information.

*Though Bhagavan seemed to like being informed of all the events that were happening in devotees' lives and in the running of the ashram, he had little or no inclination to take decisions on matters where there were differences of opinion between devotees:*

> **Question**: As we hold two different opinions, we are enquiring in order to find out what Bhagavan would like best.
> **Bhagavan**: Oh, I see. You want to know what Bhagavan would like best! What Bhagavan likes best is to remain silent without doing anything. If people with different opinions give up their *mauna*, which is the embodiment of love, and come to me and say, 'We will do this,' and 'We will do that,' and enquire of me which I like better of the two, what can I say? If you all agree upon a course of action, and then ask me for my opinion, I would then say that it is all right. But when you are of two opinions, why do you come to me and ask me which I like the better?

What I like is to know who I am and to remain as I am with the knowledge that what is to happen will happen and what is not to happen will not happen. Is that not right? Do you now understand what Bhagavan likes best?[22]

**71** When his devotees sometimes get angry with each other, *Padam* does not even utter the words 'What is all the fuss?'

*Though Bhagavan generally ignored disputes and quarrels among his devotees, he did occasionally show his displeasure in subtle ways:*

> One night, after the evening meal, there was a big quarrel in the dining room that resulted in Subramaniam Swami hitting Krishnaswami in the face. Krishnaswami immediately went and complained to Bhagavan but Bhagavan appeared to take no interest in the matter.
>
> Some one had paid for a big *bhiksha* [feast] for the following day, which meant a lot of work for everyone in the kitchen. Ordinarily, Bhagavan would have come to the kitchen at 3 a.m. to help Subramaniam to cut the vegetables but that morning he remained in the hall and made Subramaniam do all the work by himself. Subramaniam spent the first two hours wondering why Bhagavan was late but eventually he realised that he was being punished for attacking Krishnaswami.[23]

**72** Dwelling for long aeons upon this earth, *Padam* bestows on individual souls the longing for true *jnana*, which establishes them in the state of liberation.

**73** *Padam's* mode of behaviour is such that those who come to him realise that curtailing food intake is good for the stomach.

> Yesterday I wrote to you what Bhagavan told us about moderation in sleep, diet and movements. He teaches this in various ways by his own practical example. He does not take milk and is nowadays eating only one iddli for breakfast daily saying that a man who sits without doing any physical work does not require two. So also with his midday meal. Mixed with curry etc, each meal amounts only to about a handful. Even [with] that he does not eat

each dish separately as we do for taste. He makes a ball of the vegetable, chutney, soup etc. and then mixes it with rice and eats. In the course of the conversation one day, he said, 'It would be more tasty to eat the rice with only one dish instead of so many. Why so many dishes? We used to cat only a single dish in the olden days. I have not given up that practice even now. While I was on the hill many people used to bring rice, fruit and sweets. Whatever they brought I used to eat only as much as could be lifted with three fingers. I used to eat some of whatever they brought so that the whole day's intake of the food eaten did not amount to a handful. That method of eating used to give me more than happiness. Nowadays they spread a leaf and serve several things on it. As I cannot waste anything, I eat them and feel heavy thereafter.'[24]

**74** *Padam* has the habit of eating in moderation, since this is conducive to well being, making those who eat excessively feel ashamed.

Although Bhagavan was willing to spend hours each day ensuring that ashram food was properly cooked, he disliked elaborate meals consisting of many dishes. He was quite satisfied with rice, sambar and one vegetable dish. A lady from Kerala, who was accustomed to preparing a lot of dishes for each meal, once came for *darshan* and insisted on cooking for everyone. After a great expenditure of time and effort, she succeeded in preparing and serving thirty-two separate dishes. Bhagavan allowed her to serve each item separately on his banana leaf, but when the serving was over he mixed up all the offerings into a single homogenized lump.

By way of explanation he told her, 'You had to expend a lot of energy preparing all this food. Just collecting the materials must have been very time consuming. One vegetable – which is enough to clean the stomach and keep one free of constipation – is enough. Why make all this? Then there is another trouble: if you prepare thirty-two dishes, the mind is always thinking, "Shall I eat this one or that one?" So the mind is also dissipated while eating. If there is one dish there is no trouble. We can eat it very simply. Also, meals like this set a bad example to people who have no food. Poor people will get to hear that we are serving luxurious meals and think, "We are hungry, but these people, who are supposed to be simple *sadhus*, are eating so many dishes". Thoughts like these will cause unnecessary jealousy.'[25]

**75** *Padam* is an outstanding testimony [to the fact that] those who have put their trust in God alone have never been known to have been forsaken.

One morning, when there was virtually no food in the ashram, I saw him [Bhagavan] take what little food we had and begin to cook a meal. He had enough faith to begin the meal in the expectation that God would send more food before the cooking was over. It was about 5.30 in the morning when Bhagavan began to clean a handful of broken rice. He washed it in a pot, took all the stones out, and then started cooking it on a charcoal brazier. I found these activities rather perplexing.

'This rice,' I thought, 'is not even sufficient for me. How are all these people going to eat?'

As the rice came to the boil a devotee appeared with two litres of milk. When the rice was cooked, Bhagavan put a larger vessel on the fire and began cooking the rice and milk together. A few minutes later another devotee came with an offering of raisins and sugar candy. Bhagavan washed the offering and put it in the pot. At about 6.30, when the cooking was nearly finished, a party of devotees arrived from Kumbakonam. They brought with them a big pot containing iddlies, vadai, chutney, special hill bananas and some cups which had been made out of banana leaves. These banana-leaf cups [*tonnai*] were just what we needed to serve Bhagavan's homemade payasam. ...At about 7 a.m., after Bhagavan had taken his bath, we all sat down and ate a sumptuous meal.[26]

**76** Remaining in the Heart, *Padam* smiles at the ignorance of those who think they are deceiving him by being clever.

*Bhagavan generally knew if devotees were doing things that he disapproved of, or which he had specifically asked them not to do. He would mostly ignore these transgressions, but once in a while he would do something that indicated to devotees that they could not always get away with these indiscretions. The narrator of the following story is Annamalai Swami:*

> When I had been an attendant for about two weeks the Collector from Vellore [the senior-most civil servant from the district headquarters] came to have Bhagavan's *darshan*. He was called Ranganathan and he brought a large plate of sweets as an offering to Bhagavan. Bhagavan asked me to distribute the sweets to everyone in the ashram, including those who were not then present in the hall. While I was distributing the sweets to the people outside the hall, I went to a place where no one could see me and secretly helped myself to about double the quantity that I was serving to everyone else. When the distribution was completed I went back to the hall and put the plate underneath Bhagavan's sofa.
>
> Bhagavan looked at me and said, 'Did you take twice as much as everyone else?'
>
> I was shocked because I was sure that no one had seen me do it.
>
> 'I took it when no one was looking. How does Bhagavan know?'
>
> Bhagavan made no answer. The incident made me realise that it is impossible to hide anything from Bhagavan. From that time on I automatically assumed that Bhagavan always knew what I was doing. This new knowledge made me more alert and more attentive to my work because I didn't want to commit any similar mistakes again.[27]

77 It is the dancer *Padam* who, naturally established in the contemplative state of realisation wherein the Self is firmly embraced, performs all worldly activities well.

> Whenever there was a shortage of rice we used to go to the forest and collect a variety of green leaves. While we were cleaning them prior to cooking, Sri Bhagavan would explain the characteristics and medical properties

of each one of them – for example, how one produced cold in the body while another produced heat. We used to fill a large vessel of cleaned greens and cook them in whatever way Sri Bhagavan suggested. At eating time Sri Bhagavan would ask us to have the dish of greens as the main dish and rice as the side dish. These meals, tasting like nectar, would fill us up completely. It is not known how Sri Bhagavan came to acquire his knowledge of the special qualities of various leaves. He came to Arunachala as a schoolboy and immediately engaged himself in intense *tapas*. It is therefore amazing how Sri Bhagavan, who did not take up any other activities after coming to Arunachala, came to know cooking, the stitching of leaf plates, the making of flower garlands, the preparation of pickles and many other activities. There was seemingly nothing that Sri Bhagavan, who was perfection itself, did not know how to do. Sometimes we used to bring leaves to make leaf plates. Echammal, her sister and a few others, who knew how to stitch them properly, used to stitch along with Sri Bhagavan. Sri Bhagavan would stitch the leaves more beautifully, more neatly and more quickly than those who were very experienced in the art. The leaves he stitched always appeared beautiful and perfect.[28]

### *Padam,* the beneficent

**78** *Padam* bestows on devotees an endowment, the heaven of the Self, feeling that everything else is entirely disgusting.

**79** *Padam*, the mountain of supreme bliss that abides and shines, brings joy to the hearts of those who, having completely given up all desires, worship him.

**80** Abiding *Padam* bears on his head, as though it is his fate, the burden present in the hearts of those who have sought refuge in him.

**81** *Padam* confers all benefits on those noble-minded people who think that everyone should attain joy.

**82** Though *Padam* bestows everything, to those true devotees who have no desire for those things, he gives grace, the truth of oneself, Self-knowledge, as his loving present.

**The refrain**

**83** The bondage-free state in which the feet [the Self] and the head [the ego] merge and become one is the *Padam* of Guru Ramana, which shines at the summit of the *Vedas*.

*When Muruganar composed* Padamalai, *he had the idea of composing a work that would be chanted by devotees who would sing it in order to increase their 'remembrance of the divine feet of the Lord'. This verse is the refrain he composed, intending it to be chanted after each verse.*

# Bhagavan's Promises and Declarations

## Knowing and experiencing me

1 *Padam* tells and reveals: 'Instead of knowing with certainty by enquiry that I myself am present as your "I", why do you despair?'

2 To become established as the Self within the Heart is to experience my real nature, which is pure bliss.

3 Know me as the true essence of *jnana* that shines uninterruptedly in your Heart. Destroy the objectifying awareness of the ego-mind that arrogantly cavorts as 'I'.

4 When I am shining in your Heart as 'I-I', your own real nature, your attempt to 'attain' me is indeed a great marvel!

5 To meditate on my *swarupa* [true nature], which possesses the light that is the source of life, all that is needed is your one-pointedness of mind.

6 Whether you retire to the forest or remain in the midst of everyday life, attain my *swarupa* in the home that is the Heart.

7 Your search to attain me is like searching all over the world, ceaselessly straining to find the necklace around your own neck.

8 Just as you know that the necklace is there by feeling your neck, seek the treasure of the Self, your real nature, within the Heart, and know it.

9 Those who have come to my feet with love, and without delaying, are those whose birth has been graced by God. [Theirs is] an eminent and true life.

10 Through the thought of the feet of the Guru who has reigned over devotees, the intense darkness of ignorance [present in the] hearts of devotees will perish and ultimate liberation will be attained here and now.

## Give me your burdens

11 *Padam* lovingly said: 'It will be a duty well done if you place all your duties upon me.'

**12** For the cruel disease of burning *samsara* to end, the prescribed diet is to entrust all your burdens to me.

*'Prescribed diet' is a translation of* pattiyam, *an ayurvedic term. Ayurvedic practitioners say that their medicine will not work unless the* pattiyam, *the prescribed diet, is also followed. The implication in this verse is that the medicine is one's* sadhana, *such as enquiry or surrender, while the accompanying prescribed diet is entrusting all of one's burdens to Bhagavan.*

*This explanation is supported by Lakshman Sarma's Tamil commentary on verse 17 of* Ulladu Narpadu Anubandham. *Lakshman Sarma received this explanation directly from Bhagavan while he was having private lessons on the meaning of this work:*

> One should, with faith, hand over to Iswara all of the burdens, such as the family and the body, which naturally appear, and then remain without anxiety. Otherwise one cannot perform, with a one-pointed mind, either devotion or self-enquiry.[1]

**13** In order that your needless anxieties cease, make sure that all your burdens are placed on me through the courageous act of depending totally on grace.

*Devaraja Mudaliar once sang two of Muruganar's songs to Bhagavan. Bhagavan immediately asked him to translate parts of them for the benefit of the Maharani of Baroda who had come to the ashram in need of some consolation because she was separated from her husband, who had gone abroad. The portions that Bhagavan asked him to translate are as follows:*

> May all those devotees with great love also live long, who, coming to Ramana, get their desires fulfilled and, planting his feet in their heart, set all their troubles at rest and attain peace.

> The gist of it [the second verse that Bhagavan asked him to translate] is that Ramana bears upon his head, because it is his fate, the burdens of all those who throw themselves at his feet and regard him as their sole refuge, that peace comes naturally to all those who live with him,

that whatever dangers may threaten his devotees they need have no fear, and that Bhagavan had saved him, Muruganar, bidding him not to fear.[2]

**14** If you completely surrender all your responsibilities to me, I will accept them as mine and manage them.

**15** When bearing the entire burden remains my responsibility, why do you have any worries?

**16** Why do you still retain this attachment to the mental concepts of 'I' and 'mine' when, on that day, you had offered up all those things to me, avowing them to be mine?

*Guru Vachaka Kovai*, verse 317: After surrendering one's body and possessions to the *jnana*-Guru, to regard the body as 'I' and the possessions as 'mine' constitutes the sin of stealing back what has been given away as a gift. You should know that avoiding this fault is the impeccable worship of the *Sadguru*.

**17** If you enquire and know me, the Self within, in that state there will be no reason for you to worry about the world.

**Question:** Before and after meditation I get many thoughts about the unhappy people of the world.
**Bhagavan:** First find out whether there is an 'I' in you or not. It is this ego 'I' [*ahamkara*] that gets these thoughts and, as a result, you feel weakness. Therefore find out how identification with the body takes place. Body consciousness is the cause of all misery. When you conduct the enquiry into the ego 'I', you will find out its source and you will be able to remove it. After that there will be no more questions of the type you are asking.[3]

**18** Abandon the drama [of the world] and seek the Self within. Remaining within, I will protect you, [ensuring] that no harm befalls you.

**19** Seek my grace within the Heart. I will drive away your darkness and show you the light. This is my responsibility.

**20** Like the children of an emperor, my devotees are heirs to abundant rejoicing.

**Meditating on me**

**21** Splendorous *Padam* declares: 'Meditating on me with no sense of difference [between us] is accepting my grace and offering yourself to me. This in itself is enough.'

**22** If you worship me by meditating well on the excellence of my true nature, the greatness of your own true nature will well up in your Heart.

**23** Knowing that what abides in your Heart is the Self, my true and real nature, you should search for it there. Only this can be regarded as meditating on me with devotion.

**24** *Padam* advises: 'Keeping one's attention on the subtle consciousness that is experienced by the extremely subtle mind is personal service to me.'

*The following story is narrated by Kunju Swami:*

> In 1932, after spending about twelve years in personal attendance on Sri Bhagavan, I began to feel an urge to devote myself entirely to *sadhana*. I wanted to spend all my time alone. However, I could not easily reconcile myself to the idea of giving up my personal services to Sri Bhagavan. I had been debating the matter for some days when the answer came in a strange way. As I entered the hall one day I heard Sri Bhagavan explain to others who were there that real service to him did not mean attending to his physical needs; it meant following the essence of his teachings. That is, concentrating on realising the Self. Needless to say, that automatically cleared my doubts.
>
> I had heard Sri Bhagavan speak like this before. Once I had heard him say, 'It is no use saying to oneself, "I am doing personal service to Sri Bhagavan; I am dusting his bed; I have served him for so many years". In addition to serving the Guru physically, it is also important to follow the path shown by the Guru. The best service to the Guru is engaging in *vichara*, *dhyana* and other practices with a purity of body, speech and mind.'
>
> When Sri Bhagavan spoke like this he would often point out verse eighty-seven of *Kaivalyam, Part One,* in which the disciple asks the Guru how he can repay him for the grace he has received. The Guru replies that the

highest return the disciple can render to the Guru is to remain fixed in the Self without being caught by the three kinds of obstacles that obstruct it. Hearing Sri Bhagavan speak like this made me resolve to find a new attendant so that I could devote myself full-time to meditation.[4]

*Sadhu Natanananda has also recorded Bhagavan's views on this topic:*

Some of the devotees coming to the ashram from far off places to spend their holidays had a tendency to engage in ashram service. They were always directing their attention towards various activities. They would seize even the smallest opportunity to get immersed in activities throughout the day. They felt satisfied that such service would alone be sufficient for their salvation. Whenever Bhagavan happened to notice their attitude, he would refer to them by saying:

'In the name of service to the Guru, they should not waste their time in activities and become disappointed later. Such people will have cause to regret their ignorance in their last days. One should not forget, even for a moment, the aim of satsang. Having the belief that residence in the ashram will make realisation, which is most difficult to achieve in other places, easy to attain, one should always remain intent upon the realisation of one's true nature. There is no meaning in people who are not interested in that [Self-realisation] taking this place to be a special place. The spiritual service that devotees render to themselves by exerting themselves on the spiritual path for the attainment of their goal – that alone is sacred service to the Guru.'

Through these words he made it clear that he cannot be pleased by anything other than stilling the mind. The real benefit of coming to him was the subsidence of the mind. Because of this, he would exhort devotees to try to attend to the Self all the time.[5]

**25** The compassionate heart that flows from me to you will never fail except when you cease to have remembrance of 'me', who command and conduct everything.

26 You can know and experience my grace, which is my nature, if you remember me with no forgetfulness in your heart.

### Union with me

27 Seeking my true nature in your Heart, discovering it and rejoicing in it by bathing in the bliss of my *jnana swarupa* – this is union.
28 Only *bhakti sadhana* performed continuously with love will facilitate easily, in a gradual way, this union.
29 Enter with love the temple that is your own Heart and experience the bliss of being absorbed in my *swarupa*, becoming one with it.
30 I myself will command and control a mind that has died by the sacrifice of the ego.

### Give me your mind

31 'You should offer up to me the bright ruby of your mind. That is the gift that will bring me delight.'
32 'The sweet love I have for such a mind I do not have for anything else.' *Padam* desires this.
33 *Padam* receives the minds of loving devotees as an offering, swallowing them through a ruby-red light.
34 *Padam* accepts only the mind as a fitting offering, rejecting everything else as being incompatible.

> Many visitors came on one occasion and they all saluted Sri Bhagavan with the single prayer, 'Make me a *bhakta*. Give me *moksha*.' After they left Sri Bhagavan said, thinking aloud: 'All of them want *bhakti* and *moksha*. If I say to them, "Give yourself to me," they will not. How then can they get what they want?'[6]

### Bhagavan's *darshan*

35 Why do you pointlessly find fault with me, saying that I no longer look at you?
36 If you would only fix your gaze upon me, you would know that, established in the Heart, my gaze is ever fixed upon you.

> **Bhagavan:** Bhagavan is always bestowing grace. To regard the real as unreal and the unreal as real is alone ignorance.

> You yourself are always shining naturally as 'I', 'I'. Does Bhagavan exist apart from that being-consciousness? It is the attention turned towards the body that causes the distinctions between 'you' and 'I'. If, through Self-attention, it [attention to the body] is itself transformed into being-consciousness, and if one realises that the reality is only one, where, then, is the scope for saying 'you' or 'I'? Remaining still, having realised the truth as it is, is the Guru's grace.[7]

**37** Looking at you from within the Self, I never leave you. How can this fact be known to your externalised vision?

*Many of the ideas that Muruganar records in this work can be found in a more expanded form in* Guru Vachaka Kovai, *his Tamil-verse presentation of Bhagavan's teachings. The* Guru Vachaka Kovai *verses have four lines, whereas the* Padamalai *verses have only two. Muruganar also wrote prose versions of some of the* Guru Vachaka Kovai *verses that occasionally expand on the original text to bring out fully the implications of the verse. These prose renderings, known as* Pozhippurai, *have been published in Tamil by Sri Ramanasramam. Sometimes Muruganar wrote brief notes underneath the* Pozhippurai *that explain the significance of either the philosophy or key words used in the text. He entitled these explanatory notes 'Vilakkam'. I have utilised many of these prose-renderings and commentaries in my own notes since I feel that Muruganar, the author of these verses, is the best person to explain some of the more abstruse points.*

*When I give citations from* Guru Vachaka Kovai, *I will write* Pozhippurai *after the verse number if Muruganar's prose explanation has been translated. If that word is absent, what follows is a translation of the original four-line verse. If there is a* Vilakkam, *it will be given after the translation of the verse.*

*The first example, a commentary on the preceding* Padamalai *verse, is a* Pozhippurai.

> *Guru Vachaka Kovai* verse 966, *Pozhippurai*: The reality, the perfect One, exists in the state of supreme truth [*paramartha*] as 'I alone exist as the indivisible illumination in every discrete being'. It possesses the nature of the Heart that exists and shines as *Atma-swarupa*, the soul of the soul. It is verily the form of divine grace

[*tirvarul*] that dances on high, subduing everything else. Therefore, the fault of slighting it by not even thinking about it [lies] only with the beings who ought to think of that reality all the time and to such an extent that their minds soften and melt at such supreme love from reality. How can the blame for God not bestowing his sweet grace on them be attributed to God, the reality that exists?

*Vilakkam*: Feeling that the *jivas* should not suffer in the least in knowing and reaching Him, God, without remaining different from them, exists and shines as the *Atma-swarupa*, the reality of every being. This indeed is the greatness of the supreme compassion that God has towards *jivas*. It has therefore been said: 'It [reality] ... is verily the form of divine grace that dances on high, subduing everything else.'

God is perpetually bestowing His grace on all beings in the form of the illumination that is shining unceasingly as I-I in the Heart. It has therefore been said, 'How can the fault of not bestowing His sweet grace be attributed to God?'

Unless they [*jivas*] turn within, in His direction, and put attention on Him, the truth that God is continuously bestowing His grace on them all the time will not be known to them. Therefore, for the beings – who, through the individual self, do not enquire into Him who is the very form of grace – to say that He is not bestowing His grace on them, even slightly, is a grave mistake. This is why it has been said: 'the fault of slighting it by not even thinking about it [lies] only with the beings who ought to think of that reality all the time to such an extent that their minds soften and melt with supreme love from reality.'

The one reality, *Atma-swarupa*, exists and shines in the Heart, one without a second. Appearing as if it is many, it shines as 'I-I' in every individual being, who seem to be many because of *upadhi* [limiting ideas and associations]. Therefore, the plural term *ullam* [meaning] 'we exist' is appropriate. Because the Heart is the place for the existing and shining of the *Atma-swarupa*, in Tamil the Heart is known as *ullam*. The word *ullam* here gives both meanings simultaneously.

# The Self

The radiance of consciousness-bliss in the form of one awareness shining in the same way within and without is the supreme and blissful primal reality whose form is silence and which is declared by *jnanis* to be the final and incontrovertible state of true knowledge.[1]

Let us fix our thoughts only upon the perfection of *Sivam*,
formless, motionless, free of all attributes,
flourishing as the form of true *jnana*
that possesses in abundance a unique excellence
which may never be thwarted
by the unreal bondage of the world's illusion,
as the fullness whose nature is *mauna*,
and as that whose majesty shall never be dimmed.[2]

Let us fix our thoughts upon the absolute perfection
whose nature is the *mauna* that never perishes,
that exists as the surpassing purity of grace's expanse,
as the truth of the Self that shines within the Heart
as indestructible *jnana* for those who, entering the Heart,
know the 'I', having abandoned the pathways of the five senses.[3]

# *Padam*

*In this chapter Muruganar describes various properties, aspects and characteristics of* Padam, *the formless Self.*

## The nature of *Padam*

1 That which is known as *Padam* is never limited. It is complete perfection, the form of pure consciousness.
2 *Padam*, the very form of the real, stands united with, and undifferentiated from, the multitude of living beings, whether they realise it or not.
3 The special quality of reality, *Padam*, is that it exists universally within all things, shining its light.
4 *Padam*, whose equal disposition to all is unfailingly pure, is the harmony underlying all contradictions.
5 *Padam*, remaining solitary, is the shining of truth, the possessor of the victory that has nothing standing in opposition to it.
6 *Padam*, one's true nature, shines without becoming the body as the fiery flame of *jnana*, the [real] import of 'I'.
7 *Padam* is the extremely commonplace *swarupa* that exists as one's own nature. It is wrong even to say that it is easy to attain.

*The word 'commonplace' here indicates that* swarupa, *one's real nature, is not something rare, special or elevated. It is one's ordinary, natural state.* Padam *is not therefore something to be 'reached' or 'attained'; it is one's true and already existing state of being.*

8 The effulgent *Padam* is pure *jnana*, the *Atma-swarupa* that is devoid of *jiva*-nature, the mental delusion that thinks, 'I am bound'.

Swarupa *and* Atma-swarupa *are key terms in* Padamalai. Atma *denotes the Self and* swarupa *can be translated as 'real nature' or 'real form'. The word* swarupa *also occurs frequently by itself, not qualified by* Atma. *The two terms are mostly interchangeable, since they both denote the reality of the Self, but if a distinction is to be made, I would say that* Atma-swarupa *denotes the Self shining as 'I', whereas* swarupa *denotes the underlying reality that pervades and supports all manifestation. One should not pursue this difference too far, though, since Muruganar would often allow the metre or contents of the poem, rather than philosophical exactitude, to determine which of the two terms he used. Bhagavan himself often did not make distinctions between the various words that denote the Self (*mauna, *the Heart,* Brahman, *and so on), preferring instead to see them all as synonyms for the same fundamental reality.*

Jiva, *sometimes translated as 'soul', is the individual self. When it associates with the mind and identifies with it, it loses the knowledge that its true nature is the underlying reality, the Self.*

**9** *Padam*, the real, exists and shines as the ever-present void without arising from anything and without giving rise to anything.
**10** *Padam* is the form of the true Self, existing so firmly that it can neither be lost nor gained.
**11** Though *Padam* exists, pervading each and every [object] within and without, none of [them] ever exists in it.

## *Padam*, the Heart

*The Heart, a translation of the Tamil word* ullam, *is a synonym for the Self. When it is used, it denotes the Self as the centre of one's being, as the place where reality shines, and the place from where all manifestation, whether physical or mental, arises. It does not denote a particular location.*

**12** *Padam's* abode is the Heart that shines, pervading the whole world with its light.
**13** *Padam* is the consciousness, the Self that shines in the Heart as the motionless magnetic mountain.
**14** The Heart is the holy sanctum sanctorum in which *Padam* resides. Those with deceptive minds cannot bow down and see it.

*Entrances to the inner shrines of temples have very low roofs. Those who cannot bend low, an action that is equated with humility or with a general subsidence of the mind, cannot pass through the entrance.*

**Bhagavan:** Only humility can destroy the ego. The ego

keeps you far away from God. The door to God is open, but the lintel is very low. To enter one has to bend.[1]

**15** *Padam* shines as the supreme light in the Heart when the light of the [individual] self is merged inseparably in the Self, the supreme, which is the source of that light.
**16** Effulgent *Padam* dwells within the Heart in such a way that for its devotees the deluding agitation that rises for those with minds is entirely absent.
**17** *Padam*, the Heart, the expansive abode, possesses such great strength that the six baneful enemies cannot [even] approach.

*The six enemies are lust, anger, greed, delusion, intoxication and envy.*

**18** The effulgent *Padam* wells up within the Heart of every *jnani* as the centre that has no circumscribing circumference.
**19** Remaining in the Heart, *Padam* causes the minds of each and every one to act in accordance with his *vasanas.*

Vasanas *are the habits or tendencies of the mind, such as likes and dislikes, that make it behave the way it does. The term is usually translated as 'latent tendencies'.*

*At a more fundamental level* vasanas *are the cause of both manifestation and rebirth. According to Bhagavan, it is the* vasanas *that impel the mind to project and witness an illusory world. At the time of death, the uneradicated* vasanas *withdraw into the Heart where they remain latent for a while before bringing into existence a new body and a new world. The destruction of all* vasanas *is equated with Self-realisation since, in that state, there is no rebirth and no illusory, projected world.*

## *Padam* and knowledge

**20** *Padam,* the non-dual light of truth, abides neither knowing nor being known.
**21** True *Padam,* the expanse of consciousness, abides, shining out as pure consciousness, beyond both knowledge and ignorance.
**22** *Padam,* pure consciousness, demands that everything that has been learned as knowledge has to be completely forgotten as ignorance.

*Guru Vachaka Kovai* verse 147, *Pozhippurai*: Through one's great love of learning one may, with great enthusiasm, learn the *jnana* scriptures, thinking, 'These books, which are the basis for attaining the clarity of immaculate *jnana*, are certainly worth knowing'. Later, when one attains maturity and attempts to sink into the source, one will definitely have to forget completely the scriptural knowledge which, with great effort, one previously learned and mastered.

23 *Padam*, the perfect treasure of true *jnana*, is the truth that cannot be known by the false manliness, the ego that arrogantly cavorts about.

24 Beauteous *Padam*, which is true knowledge, the exalted *tapas* of *mauna*, will destroy empirical knowledge, which is multifarious.

Tapas *is generally defined as being 'an intense spiritual effort, often involving some sort of bodily mortification, whose aim is to burn off spiritual impurities'. Bhagavan sometimes remarked that abidance in* mauna, *though it may look like a state of effortless quietude, is in fact a state of intensely focused activity. The 'exalted* tapas *of* mauna' *is explained in the following extract:*

> **Question:** Is the state of 'being still' a state involving effort or effortless?
> **Bhagavan:** It is not an effortless state of indolence. All mundane activities, which are ordinarily called effort, are performed with the aid of a portion of the mind and with frequent breaks. But the act of communion with the Self [*Atma vyavahara*] or remaining still inwardly is intense activity which is performed with the entire mind and without break.
>
> *Maya*, which cannot be destroyed by any other act, is completely destroyed by this intense activity which is called '*mauna*'.[2]

25 Clarifying doubt and wrong understanding through direct knowledge, *Padam* comes forward and shines, making the world recede.

## The light of *Padam*

26 *Padam*, the truth, shines in the Heart by its own light, with no

other light whatsoever existing apart from it.

**27** Only *Padam*, the light of consciousness, knows the true import of *aham*, which shines as that light.

*The Sanskrit word* aham *is usually translated as 'I', but in Tamil the word is also sometimes used to denote the Heart, the source of the 'I'. Bhagavan generally used the Tamil word* ullam *when he spoke or wrote about the Heart as a synonym for the Self. When other words are used, they can sometimes be translated as 'mind'. Occasionally, these alternative words imply 'heart' in a general sense, implying the centre of emotions and feelings.*

**28** The light of *Padam* is the supreme light, the truth that reveals all other lights as illusory, and causes them to disappear.

> **Bhagavan:** To know an object an ordinary light inimical to darkness is needed. To know the Self a light is needed, which lights both light and darkness. This light is neither light nor darkness. But it is called light, because by it they are known. This light is the Self, the infinite consciousness, of which no one is unaware.[3]

**29** Lustrous *Padam*, Siva-*jnana*, shines in such a way that the yoga *siddhi* that is associated with the whirling confusion of the mind is revealed as false and ceases to be.

*Bhagavan taught that yogic attainments (yoga* siddhis*) can only be attained and sustained by effort, and that when the effort lapses, the 'attainment' disappears. True* jnana*, on the other hand, is the natural and effortless state that remains when the mind and all its activities have been eradicated. Siva-*jnana *is the mind-free natural state, whereas yoga* siddhi *is an unreal mental state. This distinction will be further elaborated on in the chapter entitled 'Advice on* Sadhana*'.*

**30** That good and great light is *Padam*, the utter perfection with which the mind that experiences the non-dual Self has coalesced.

**31** The hearts of true devotees that have been permeated by the light of *Padam* will surge in the form of blissful consciousness.

**32** *Padam*, the effulgent light of perfect silence, strikes, shattering the foolish argument that [the nature of] consciousness is twofold.

**33** Effulgent *Padam* is like a dense darkness [to those who] through delusion, become like the owl, blind during the day.

*Unlike in the West where the owl is perceived to be a wise bird, in India it is deemed to be stupid. Owl-like, deluded people are not aware of the shining light of* Padam, *even though it is present all the time.*

> **Bhagavan:** If the light of the sun is invisible to the owl, it is only the fault of that bird and not of the sun. Similarly, can the unawareness by ignorant persons of the Self, which is always of the nature of awareness, be other than their own fault?[4]

**34** *Padam* is the true light that shines as the unique basis for all that is seen as sentient and insentient.

**35** *Padam* is the wondrous illumination of the real that shines within the faculties, such as the mind and the intellect, lending them its light.

**36** *Padam* is the mind-transcending light of the Heart in which the manifold religions merge harmoniously, with their discordant verbiage ended.

## *Padam*, the support of the world appearance

**37** All things exist depending on *Padam*, but *Padam* has no desire whatsoever for any of those things.

**38** *Padam*, the surging brilliance of the real, is the centre for the spinning of the seven worlds, which revolve like a millstone [around its axis].

**39** *Padam*, the supporting screen, is the true light that projects this entire [universe] as a host of shadows, and then rotates them.

*The rotation of the crowd of shadows is a cinematic metaphor that explains the appearance of the world in terms of a projector whose film spools rotate, causing images of lights and shadows to be projected on a screen. The same model of creation was used by Bhagavan in* Arunachala Ashtakam, *verse six:*

> You, the Heart, the light of consciousness, the one reality, alone exist! A wonderful *sakti* [power] exists in you, which is not other than you. From [this *sakti* rise] a

series of atom-like shadow thoughts which, by means of consciousness in the whirl of *prarabdha*, are seen as shadowy world pictures, both inside on the mirror of the thought-light, and outside through the senses, such as the eyes, in the same way that a cinema picture comes into existence via a lens. O Hill of Grace! Whether they stop or whether they continue, they do not exist apart from you.[5]

**40** Whilst being the unique support that sustains the whole world, *Padam*, the ever-present Self, is without any support [whatsoever].
**41** Since the entire world appearance is founded in due order upon it, *jnanis* praise the effulgent *Padam,* the truth, as *Padam* [the feet, the ultimate support].
**42** Because it bears and sustains the whole world, the completely perfect being-consciousness is termed *Padam.*
**43** The splendid, effulgent *Padam* is the source not only for things seen [*idam*] but also for the false 'I' that is indispensable for the *idam*.

*Bhagavan sometimes spoke of* idam *and* aham, *the things that are seen and the 'I' that sees them. Here he is saying that* Padam *is the source that underlies them both.*

### *Padam*, moving and unmoving

**44** *Padam* remains within as the imperishable, unmoving axle that spins this world like a wheel.
**45** *Padam* is the Self Supreme, the perfect truth. Activity is possible only at the conceptual level.

**Question:** In the third mantra of the *Isavasyopanishad* it says: '*Brahman* moves and *Brahman* does not move.' How can these two contradictory truths both be within *Brahman*?
**Bhagavan:** The truth of not doing anything is the truth of one's real nature. Action or doing can only be seen from a relative point of view.[6]

**Question:** You have often said, and the books also say, that *Brahman* is immobile. Now you say it is all-powerful.

Does it not then move?

**Bhagavan:** Power implies movement. Though Iswara moves by his own power [*sakti*], which is movement, he transcends the movement. He is *achala* [motionless], *atita* [transcendent].[7]

46 *Padam* confounds the eye of those who lack true understanding of reality by appearing to be in rapid motion, whilst [in fact] it steadfastly abides without moving at all.

Sri Ramana Gita, *chapter 12, verse 15:*

> Though the supreme moves because of his own supreme *sakti*, he is in reality unmoving. Only the sage can understand this profound mystery.

47 *Padam* performs unreal activities with such great skill that they appear to be real.

48 The extremely wonderful *Padam* performs all activities just like the mind does, without swerving from its nature as consciousness.

*In the verse from* Arunachala Ashtakam *that I cited in the preceding section, Bhagavan explained how* sakti, *the dynamic aspect of the Self, brings manifestation into existence and sustains it.* Padam, *the unmanifest Self, is the support and ground for this manifestation, but it plays no direct part in creation. However, as this verse indicates, since* sakti *cannot be regarded as being different or apart from* Padam, *it is also true to say that* Padam *performs all the activities of the world. This same paradox was also brought out in the final line of* Arunachala Ashtakam, *verse six: 'Whether they stop or whether they continue, they do not exist apart from you.'*

## *Padam* and creation

49 The extremely wonderful *Padam* has fashioned the entire world from the clay of shining consciousness, the Self.

50 It is the extremely skilful *Padam* that, having manifested everything that appears, remains as the foremost, supreme witness.

51 The insurgent mind imagines that *Padam*, the reality, has forsaken

its real nature for the appearance of the world.

*This is a critique of the idea, espoused by some of Bhagavan's early devotees, that* Brahman *undergoes some manner of change when it manifests as the world.*

**52** Like a magician with his astonishing show, full of secrets, *Padam*, being-consciousness, performs the wonderful five divine functions through mere imagination.

*The five divine functions are creation, preservation, destruction, veiling and grace. In several schools of Indian philosophy God brings the world into existence, maintains it, and destroys it at the time of cosmic dissolution. While it exists, its true nature is hidden or veiled by the power of maya, illusion. To remove that veiling or illusion, God bestows grace on* jivas, *enabling them to understand who they really are.*

*The word translated as 'imagination' is the Tamil equivalent of the Sanskrit term* kalpana, *which means 'concept' or 'idea'. Creation is not a real event; it merely appears to take place. Bhagavan expressed the same idea when he said, in a reply to Kapali Sastri, 'This whole movement, the creation, called a play of* sakti, *is a formulation [*kalpana*] of the Lord. If this* kalpana *is transcended, what remains is* swarupa.*'*[8]

*The idea that creation has no intrinsic reality will be explored in more detail later.*

**53** In the wonderful *Padam*, universes become atoms and atoms become universes.

*In the* Arunachala Ashtakam *verse that I have twice recently cited Bhagavan wrote: 'From [this* sakti *rise] a series of atom-like shadow thoughts which, by means of consciousness in the whirl of* prarabdha, *are seen as shadowy world pictures, both inside on the mirror of the thought-light, and outside through the senses, such as the eyes, in the same way that a cinema picture comes into existence via a lens.' This part of the verse encapsulates Bhagavan's teachings on how the world comes into being as a projection of the mind that sees it.*

*In this verse Bhagavan uses the word* anu, *which means 'atom' to describe the microscopically small entity that comprises the ego and its inherent* vasanas. *In* Talks with Sri Ramana Maharshi, *talk no. 323, he explained this verse by saying, 'In the present stanza [*Arunachala

Ashtakam *verse six] the tiny dot [*anu*] equals the ego; the tiny dot made up of darkness equals the ego consisting of latent tendencies'.*

*The* anu, *the microscopic dot of ego and* vasanas, *acts as a 'film' when the light of the Self falls on it. As the verse goes on to say, the projected image becomes the world picture and the mind of the person who perceives it. The whole universe, therefore, is an expansion of this original atom. At the time of physical death the* vasanas *and the ego withdraw into the Heart, becoming atom-like again. After some time the ego and the* vasanas *manifest in a new form, a new body, and a new universe is projected through the light of the Self. These cycles of birth and rebirth, physical creation and dissolution, continue endlessly until the moment of liberation. Until then, 'universes become atoms and atoms become universes'.*

*The same process of expansion and contraction also occurs whenever the mind wakes and sleeps. In the moment of waking, the whole universe is created by an act of projection that simultaneously brings into being both the objects that are seen and the observer of them.*

**54** Having manifested in the world the ridiculous dance of all the five divine operations, *Padam* shines secretly as the sacred hall of *chitrambalam*.

*In Saivism, Siva is not directly responsible for the five divine functions. These are all performed by* sakti, *the divine energy that he brings into being, who is then personified as his female consort. While* sakti *performs all the five divine functions, Siva himself remains actionless and motionless, abiding as the still centre of consciousness.*

Chitrambalam *is the 'expanse of consciousness', and the 'sacred hall' is a reference to the main shrine of the Saiva temple at Chidambaram where the principal deity is an* akasa lingam, *an empty space that denotes or symbolises this expanse of consciousness. On a more metaphorical level, the sacred hall is the Heart in which* Padam *abides as motionless consciousness.*

## *Padam* and the gods

**55** *Padam* is God to those who are caught in concepts, but to the true *jnani*, who is without falsity and who has separated from all concepts, it is his own Self.

**56** Since even those who say that [God] does not exist do not [say] that they do not exist, *Padam* abides, acceptable to everyone.

**57** *Padam* possesses the authority that makes the Sun, Yama, Agni, Vayu and so on perform their duties fearfully, in an orderly way, without transgressing.

*Yama, Agni and Vayu are, respectively, the gods of death, fire and wind. The verse is a reference to an upanishadic text which states that all these minor deities perform their functions fearfully, through the power of the Self. Bhagavan referred to this scriptural passage in one of his answers in* Talks with Sri Ramana Maharshi, *talk no. 467.*

**58** In conformity with the imaginings of worshippers, *Padam* parades as the various gods who are renowned as liberators from bondage.

*Though the verb 'parades' can refer to any kind of activity, it may also specifically refer to the practice of taking gods out in processions on festival days.*

### Arunachala *Padam*

**59** *Padam* is the great pillar that manifested by itself as the lofty and noble flame of grace in the form of Annamalai.

*Annamalai is the most common Tamil name for Arunachala. According to the* Skanda Purana, *Siva manifested as a column of light at Arunachala in order to settle a dispute between Brahma and Vishnu, and to teach them humility.*

**60** On this earth all the learned men praise the lofty red mountain [Sona] as *Padam*, the light of the consciousness of being.

*Many saints and learned men have praised Arunachala, but Bhagavan was particularly fond of Jnanasambandhar's verse in which he praised Arunachala as 'a dense mass of* jnana, *capable of removing the I-am-the-body idea from your devotees'.*[9]

**61** *Padam* is the supernal light that manifested in the asterism of Ardra [in the month of Margazhi] as the mountain *lingam*, Lord Siva's very form.

*According to the* Arunachala Mahatmyam, *the Sanskrit work that describes Arunachala's greatness, Siva originally manifested as a column of light (that later condensed into Arunachala) on the star-day of Ardra in the month of Margazhi, which runs from mid-December to mid-January. The Sanskrit verse that records the manifestation of Arunachala was translated into Tamil by Bhagavan and included in his* Collected Works *in a selection of verses that have been taken from the same work. These are the first two verses in the selection:*

> Nandi said: 'That is the holy place! Of all, Arunachala is the most sacred! It is the heart of the world! Know it to be the secret and sacred Heart-centre of Siva! In that place he always abides as the glorious Aruna Hill!'
>
> 'That day on which the ancient and wonderful *lingam* of Arunachala took shape is the asterism of Ardra in the month of Mrigasira [Margazhi]. And the day on which Vishnu and the other *devas* worshipped the Lord in the form of the effulgence is the day of Mahasivaratri.[10]

*The last four words of the* Padamalai *verse, 'Lord Siva's very form,' refer to the belief that Arunachala is the physical form of Lord Siva, and not merely a representation of him, or a place where he resides. Bhagavan supported this belief by saying, 'Other sacred hills are described as the abodes of some deity, but Arunachala is God Himself in the shape of the hill'.*[11]

*Elsewhere Bhagavan has said, 'Kailas is in the Himalayas; it is the abode of Siva. Whereas this hill is Siva himself.'*[12]

### *Padam* is mind-free

**62** In the Self, *Padam*, whose nature is the true *jnana* that [merely] exists and shines, association with the mind, the intellect and all the rest is totally absent.

**63** Though *Padam* exists merged with the mind, not even the name 'mind' is present in it.

**64** *Padam*, the state of *Brahman* transcending the mind, is such that when one sleeps in *swarupa*, even the word '*turiya*' leaves.

*'Sleeps in* swarupa*' does not denote physical sleep; it implies abidance in one's real state.* Turiya, *meaning 'the fourth', is the fourth state that underlies the three states of waking, dreaming and sleeping. Since these three states are all states of mind, when the mind is transcended in*

Brahman, *the impersonal and transcendent reality, the idea that there is a fourth state that underlies the other three disappears. Only the one true and abiding state remains.*

> **Bhagavan:** What there is is one state only; you may call it *turiya* or *turiyatita* [beyond the fourth] or what you like. The wakeful state [*jagrat*], the dream state [*swapna*] and the state of deep sleep [*sushupti*] – these three states go on changing like the scenes in a cinema. All the three are ideas of the mind. That which is beyond these three, and which is real and permanent, is the Self itself. That is the state called the fourth, the *turiya* state. In common parlance, people talk of the fourth state and of beyond the fourth state, and so on, but strictly speaking, there is only one state.[13]

**65** In a Heart in which the mind is dead the lustrous *Padam* excels as the transcendent, non-dual *mauna*.

**66** Though one may run and run to the ends of the earth seeking it, *Padam*, one's true Self, never comes within the grasp of the ego mind.

### *Padam*, the destroyer of the mind

**67** *Padam* destroys the perversity of *samsara* that gives rise to the discord in which remembering is birth and forgetting is death.

Samsara *is the continuous cycle of birth and death to which the* jiva *is subjected prior to its liberation. In a more general sense* samsara *also denotes the empirical world of names and forms, especially as it appears to the unenlightened mind.*

**68** Effulgent *Padam* kills and annihilates the mind-illusion that causes bewilderment by making the reflection appear to be real.

*Bhagavan taught that the appearance of the world is a reflection in consciousness (*chidabhasa*) that is projected by the mind and then assumed to be real. This idea will be explored in more detail in the section on creation.*

**69** Splendorous *Padam* steals away the ego, the identification with the body, that which is the subject for discussions about birth, disease, old age and death.

70 The gracious *Padam*, the great silence, swallows the mind, conquering all the religions that exist as a consequence of mind.

### *Padam* and righteous behaviour

71 By virtue of the greatness of *Atma-swarupa*, which transcends the mind, *Padam* shines without any kind of do's and don'ts.

72 *Padam* is the supreme reality, the ultimate truth that makes *dharma*, *artha* and *kama* appear as mere reflections.

*Four legitimate lifestyle goals or practices have been approved by Hindu scriptures:*

> Dharma: *fulfilling one's social and family obligations according to the laws laid down in the scriptures.*
> Artha: *the acquisition of wealth, providing that it is done by morally acceptable means.*
> Kama: *the satisfaction of socially sanctioned desires.*
> Moksha: *liberation, the state of abiding as the Self.*

*The implication of these two verses is that* moksha, *liberation, is alone the true and abiding state of* Padam. Dharma, artha *and* kama *are relevant and approved courses of conduct for the unenlightened who still feel that choices and decisions have to be made about future courses of action, but for the one who abides as* Padam, *these issues do not arise because the one who chooses and decides has vanished.*

73 Religious observances are entirely concerned with the mind alone. The ever-silent *Padam* is always free from such religious practices.

### The grace of *Padam*

74 *Padam*, the grace-consciousness that is the supreme, is such that no one can realise the greatness of grace except through grace itself.

75 Only grace-bestowing *Padam*, which is full of the light of true *jnana*, the beautiful light, will chase away the darkness of the false life of the world.

76 *Padam* will not reveal the lofty state of authentic divine

consciousness until individualised consciousness has been totally annihilated.

**77** If one turns one's face steadfastly towards grace, the dark ignorance of infatuation with the ego will be dispelled, and true *Padam* will shine.

**78** *Padam*, the pure light of infinitely subtle being-consciousness, *swarupa*, rises to humble the mischief of mind and speech.

**79** Like removing dirt with dirt, *Padam* whitens the impure and dirty *maya* with the sublime light of beneficial *maya*.

*In rural India pots and plates are sometimes cleaned by rubbing dirt on the unclean surfaces of the vessels. The idea that 'pure'* maya *can eradicate 'impure'* maya *can be found in* Kaivalya Navaneeta*, part one, verse fifty-seven:*

> Just as poison is commonly antidoted with another poison, an iron spike is extracted with another [piece of] iron, arrows are turned aside by others, and dirt is washed away with other dirt [e.g. fuller's earth], so ignorance, which is weak in itself, can be eradicated by methods which are themselves of the same *maya*; later this also perishes like the pole used to turn a corpse that is burnt.

**80** Effulgent *Padam* abounds in joy in the hearts of true devotees such that they do not desire anything other than the life of dwelling under the grace-bestowing feet of the Lord.

**81** *Padam* comes swiftly bounding to see those devotees who are genuinely struggling to see it.

**82** *Padam*, the extremely intense, true and supreme grace, takes ten steps [towards the devotee] when the devotee takes one step [towards *Padam*].

> *Guru Vachaka Kovai*, verse 965: If you, thinking of God, take one step towards Him, in response, He, who is greater than a mother, thinking of you, takes nine steps – such a long distance – and accepts you. So great is His grace!
> *Vilakkam*: The essential point of the verse is: 'There is no need to have doubt about His grace.'

**Question:** Does God bestow grace on *jivas* or not?

**Bhagavan:** However much you remember God, God remembers you much more.[14]

**Question:** Has God or the Guru any solicitude for me?
**Bhagavan:** If you seek either – they are not really two but one and identical – rest assured that they are seeking you with a solicitude greater than you can ever imagine.[15]

### The power of *Padam*

83 *Padam*, the attainment of true *jnana*, has become worthy of being desired even by those who are accomplished yogis because of the greatness of its capacity [to grant] salvation.
84 *Padam* burns and consumes the 'yesterday, today and tomorrow' of time, and the 'here and there' of space, along with the binding chain of karma.
85 *Padam* is the eternally non-dual expanse of the supreme truth that reveals as false even the 'now' in which this dualistic scene appears.
86 *Padam* is that which removes the power of speech from those who, seeing [it], say nothing. *Padam* is that extremely wondrous illumination which those who speak have not seen.
87 The *Vedas* and *Agamas*, despite elaborating in greater and greater detail, are eventually compelled by *Padam* to lament, 'This [*Padam*] is beyond us'.
88 The divine *Padam* is that in which those who have known mental anxiety to be the cause of sorrow have found bliss by the cessation of anxiety.
89 For the mind that has secured the life of the supreme *Sivam*, *Padam* will banish the majesty of the reign of earthly monarchs as though it were a wisp of straw.
90 For those whose thoughts have been merged and transmuted into love as they chant 'Siva, Siva,' *Padam*, the truth, will shine so that they want for nothing more.

### *Padam's* games

91 *Padam*, despite remaining as the unique experience of one's own inherent nature, gets veiled by the concepts, the *triputis*.
92 *Padam* torments the *jiva* through *pramada*, which makes it forget

its real and excellent nature and pay attention to that which is alien [to the Self].

Pramada *is a term that will appear many times in* Padamalai. *It denotes forgetfulness or inattentiveness, and more specifically, forgetfulness of the Self. Bhagavan taught that we are all aware of the Self all the time, but we somehow lose this knowledge by permanently keeping our attention on the activities of the mind, the body and the world.*

**93** *Padam* is the Self, the pure consciousness, the infinite expanse that ignorant folks get frightened of and mentally recoil from, thinking it to be a void.

**94** *Padam* torments those whose hearts harbour attachments, but brings delight to those whose hearts possess the generosity [of not clinging to anything].

*Muruganar occasionally uses the Tamil word* udaram *or the phrase* udara gunam, *which is usually translated as 'generosity'. It is not restricted to the usual meaning of physical liberality because it also implies giving up or giving away all ideas and concepts. As such, it implies complete renunciation of the mind, rather than a willingness to dispose freely of one's physical possessions. In some places in* Padamalai *the phrase has been translated as 'munificence', since it indicates a very extreme form of generosity. Elsewhere, where it is appropriate, the word 'renunciation' is used.*

**95** Through their desire for the eight great *siddhis, Padam* orchestrates many yogis, giving them dancing lessons and making them dance.

Siddhis *are superhuman powers or attainments that can be acquired by various yogic practices. Eight are listed in classical yoga texts. Like most other teachers, Bhagavan taught that pursuing* siddhis *was a pointless, egotistic activity. However, as this verse indicates, if desires for* siddhis *exist in the hearts of yogis, the power of* Padam *will make such people waste a vast amount of energy pursuing them.*

**96** The crowd of *siddhis* bow to the eminent *Padam*, but *Padam* makes those *siddhis* appear as a wisp of straw to the minds of those who have become established in true service.

**97** *Padam* has invented many arts, full of illusory concepts, for those with insignificant intellects to know and delight in.

**98** The effulgent *Padam* becomes veiled in the same way that fire becomes veiled by the smoke that billows out from it and envelops it.

**99** So long as the seer does not see his real nature, the effulgent *Padam* ensnares him in concepts, in the power of delusion.

## Experiencing *Padam*

**100** *Padam* is the expanse of grace, the truth, the excellence of *ajata* that is realised in the hearts of those who are eminent in *sahaja nishta*, one's own true experience.

Ajata *means 'non-creation'. It is a philosophical or experiential standpoint that declares or knows that neither the physical world nor the* jivas *in it have ever been created. Questions about the liberation or bondage of* jivas *are therefore inadmissible and hypothetical since the* jivas *themselves do not really exist. They are all a complete fiction brought about by the power of defective imagination. This was Bhagavan's own experience and position, a point that Muruganar brought out in the* Pozhippurai *of verse 100 of* Guru Vachaka Kovai*:*

> Though Guru Ramana, who appeared as God incarnate, expounded various doctrines, depending on the beliefs of the devotees who resorted to his feet, what we have heard him say in private, as his own true experience, is only *ajata*.

*When one is established in one's true state, one knows the truth of* ajata *by direct experience. Such a one is* sahaja nishta, *one who is established in the natural state of the Self.*

**101** If they who desire *Atma-swarupa*, being-consciousness, abandon everything else as being false, then *Padam* is directly experienced.

**102** The lustrous *Padam* comes to be attained as the enduring, undecaying, supremely blissful grace only by the true *jnanis* who have completely rooted out desires.

**103** *Padam*, pure, free of all attributes, will gloriously arise through [divine] dispensation, something that cannot be clearly known and gained other than by renunciation.

**104** Only in the hearts of those who have offered themselves up as a sacrifice does *Padam*, the reality, merge and shine perpetually as the spotless temple.

Padam *is the deity who shines in the spotless temple of the Heart. This idea appears several times in* Padamalai.

**105** Since the nature of being is consciousness, *Padam* is the directly experienced pure enjoyment of *Sivam*. It is not like the [dualistic] enjoyment of sugar.

> **Bhagavan:** Some contend that the sugar cannot taste its own sweetness and that a taster must taste and enjoy it. Similarly, an individual cannot be the Supreme and enjoy the bliss of that state; therefore the individuality must be maintained on the one hand and Godhead on the other so that enjoyment may result! Is God insentient like sugar? How can one surrender oneself and yet retain one's individuality for supreme enjoyment?[16]

**How to reach *Padam***

**106** That which should be earnestly sought after by the *jiva* that desires to win liberation, so that the poverty of spiritual ignorance is destroyed, is auspicious *Padam*, consciousness, the supreme.

**107** *Padam* manifests when the heart is churned vigorously, with enquiry as the rope, and love as the churning rod.

*Some of the words in this verse are taken from a famous poem (*Tevaram, 5th Tirumurai, Patigam *90, verse 10) by Appar, an early Saiva saint. Appar's poem was developed over time into an elaborate analogy that equates the processes of grinding, churning and polishing with different degrees of spiritual maturity. Three substances are mentioned in the analogy: wood, milk and an uncut gem. You get fire from wood by rubbing it vigorously, butter from milk by churning it, and lustre from a jewel by polishing it. Devotees in the wood category have the maximum amount of impurities, devotees in the milk category have less, and those in the jewel category hardly any at all. Of the three processes, it is supposedly hardest to get fire by friction, second hardest to get butter from milk, and easiest to get the lustre out of a jewel. In all three categories the impurities are being removed.*

*Bhagavan alluded to this well-known analogy in* Arunachala Ashtakam, *verse five, when he wrote: 'If like a gem that is cut and polished, the mind is whetted on the grindstone of the mind to free it of its flaws, it will take on the light of your grace and shine like a ruby whose brightness is not flawed by any other object.'*

*Muruganar is saying in this verse that the impurities in the heart can be removed by two parallel processes: enquiry and love. When the churning is complete,* Padam *manifests.*

*Bhagavan referred to this process in his introduction to* Vivekachudamani*:*

> *Atmanusandhana* [constancy in the Self] has been likened to churning the curd to draw forth butter, the mind being compared to the churning rod, the heart to the curd and the practice of constancy in the Self to the process of churning. Just as by churning the curd butter is extracted and by friction fire is kindled, even so, by unswerving, vigilant constancy in the Self, ceaseless like the unbroken filamentary flow of oil, is generated the natural and changeless trance or *nirvikalpa samadhi*, which readily and spontaneously yields that direct, immediate, unobstructed and universal perception of *Brahman*, which is at once knowledge and experience, and which transcends time and space.[17]

**108** Whoever one may be and whatever *sadhana* one may do, *Padam* will not shine except through the enquiry of knowing one's real nature in the Heart.

**109** *Padam*, the nature of *mauna*, can only be experienced in the pure tranquillity where there is neither remembering nor forgetting, and not by the rising, objectifying consciousness.

**110** *Padam*, the highest of the high, can only be gained through a profound yearning in which one loses oneself, and not by mere imagination.

**111** *Padam*, the perfect first cause, cannot be gained in full measure unless the ego, the counterfeit consciousness, is destroyed.

**112** If one awakes from the whirling dream of ignorance, only the effulgent *Padam* remains as the pure expanse of consciousness.

**113** *Padam* is the supreme reality that is obtained when consciousness, abandoning attachment to sense objects, settles within the Self.

**114** One does not unite and merge with *Padam* by any kind of effort, but rather through the loss of ego, which is profound peace.

**115** Since *Padam*, as the storehouse of compassion, dispels the anxieties [of those who have surrendered to it], no other *sadhana* except surrender to it [exists for dispelling them].

**116** *Padam* cannot be gained except through the method of *dana* [offering]. Other than through *mauna*, *Padam* is entirely unattainable.

Dana *is the offering that a disciple gives to his teacher. The second half of this verse makes it clear that Bhagavan is saying that the only effective* dana *is giving the mind to the teacher, and remaining in silence thereafter. Bhagavan himself never encouraged or accepted any other form of* dana *in return for his teachings.*

> **Bhagavan:** It is mere delusion to think of *arpana* [offering] so lightly. *Arpana* means that the mind gets merged in the Self and becomes one with it. It means that it should become devoid of all *vasanas*. And that will not come about unless there is self-effort and God's grace. God's force cannot get hold of you and drag you into itself unless you surrender completely. But where is the question of our surrendering? The self itself is to be surrendered. Until one can accomplish that, one should go on struggling unceasingly. It is only after trying again and again that one may, finally, succeed in the effort. Once you succeed, there is no going back. That is the proper course. What is the use of merely repeating the word '*Arpana, arpana*'? Except that you give some money while repeating the word *arpana*, what is the effect on the mind?[18]

**117** To those who pay attention to nothing other than *nishta*, *Padam* awards as a prize the bright sword of *jnana*.

Nishta *means 'steady abidance', or more specifically, 'steady abidance in the Self'. Bhagavan is here prescribing continuous attention to the Self until one becomes wholly and continuously absorbed in it.*

**118** In a mind that holds exclusively onto *Padam*, the Self, without leaving it, not a single desire will thereafter be born.

> Later, while we [Bhagavan and Rangan] were walking

on the hill together, he pointed out one of the main differences between us: 'You always have a desire for something or other. I never desire anything.'[19]

**119** Noble *Padam* gets caught by genuine and limitless devotion, which was the religion of Sabari and Kannappa.

*Kannappa is a Tamil saint whose story is featured in the* Periyapuranam. *He was so in love with Siva, he gouged out one of his eyes and offered it to Siva when he was under the impression that Siva had damaged one of his own eyes. Kannappa was about to offer his second eye when Siva intervened and prevented him. Siva had set up the whole scene in order to demonstrate to a priest how great Kannappa's devotion was.*

*Sabari, whose story appears in the* Ramayana, *was a* gandarva, *an inhabitant of the celestial realms, who was cursed by her husband to be a hunter on earth because she had had an affair with a hunter in the* gandarva *realm. However, it was stated that the curse would be lifted if she met Rama. Sabari manifested on earth as a female hunter near the sage Matanga's ashram. She served him and his devotees faithfully for many years, mostly looking after the flowers in the sage's ashram. Before Matanga's devotees died they all blessed her, saying that she would have* darshan *of Rama and receive absolution from him. Rama did eventually visit Matanga's ashram. Sabari picked out the best fruit to present to them by personally nibbling a small portion of all the potential offerings. When Rama ate the ones she had selected, he declared that they tasted like nectar. Sabari, who had attained some* siddhis *during her period of* tapas *at the ashram, went into a trance and had a vision in which she saw how Rama would eventually be reunited with Sita. She passed on the information to Rama. Having earned the* darshan *of Rama by her selfless devotion to Matanga and his devotees, the curse was lifted. Her erstwhile husband descended from the* gandarva *realm and took her back there in his chariot.*

### Obstacles to reaching *Padam*

**120** *Padam* is much too far away to be seen by dark-minded deceitful people who roam around posing as *jnanis*.

**121** *Padam*, whose nature is transcendental peace, comes only within the grasp of a consciousness that has melted, but it will subtly evade a mind that indulges in disputation.

**122** Effulgent *Padam* recoils within itself from accepting, even slightly, the homage of dark, hypocritical minds that are filled with deceit.

**123** Leaving *Padam*, the sweet, luscious fruit, the ignorant will go off in all directions, pining for the [bitter] fruit of the nux vomica tree.

**124** Being non-dual, *Padam* cannot be thought of; hence, so long as one is thinking, it will not shine.

> *Guru Vachaka Kovai*, verse 1237, *Pozhippurai*: The eminent, non-dual experience will uninterruptedly shine only in the Heart of the *jnani* who has enquired into and known the *Atma-swarupa* – which remains without mingling with anything, despite pervading everything – in which the illusory appearance of the *triputis* has perished. It is not attainable for those who know it through *suttarivu*, [as they know] the sordid, falsely appearing sense objects that appear to be distinct from them.

> *Guru Vachaka Kovai*, verse 1238: The thought-free *Sivam*, whose very nature is being-consciousness, is known only by the heroic one whose mind has died, who abides in the source of the mind through being-consciousness, and who has a thought-free mind. It is not known by those whose minds are associated with thoughts.

Suttarivu, *referred to in the first quotation, is a key word in* Padamalai. *It denotes the false consciousness that divides itself into an external world and an internal perceiver who witnesses and interacts with it.*

**125** As soon as the *chit-jada* knot, the deluding connection, is undone, *Padam* shines as the one reality [*eka-swarupa*] everywhere.

*The* chit-jada *knot is the connection between consciousness (*chit*) and the insentient (*jada*) body. When the 'I am this body' idea vanishes, only* Padam *remains.*

### The bliss of *Padam*

**126** One should not procrastinate in reaching *Padam*, the extremely auspicious *Sivam*, the bliss of peace.

**127** To those who have truly achieved the goal of firmly establishing their hearts within the Self, *Padam* will bring such bliss, it will be as if they had obtained their every desire.

**128** *Padam* exists and shines as that about which it can be said: 'True bliss is that in which the dualistic pair of joy and misery has perished.'

**129** *Padam*, bliss, transforms those who are immersed in the bliss of *Padam* into being blissful *Padam* alone.

# The Self

*With the exception of the final chapter, in which Muruganar will relate the experiences he had through* Padam's *grace, all the remaining* Padamalai *verses will be direct teaching statements by Bhagavan.*

## Self-knowledge

1 The Self is not something that is either known or not known. The Self is knowledge [*jnana*] itself.

Ulladu Narpadu, *verse 33:*

It is a matter of ridicule to say either 'I have not realised myself,' or 'I have realised myself'. Why? Are there two selves, one self to become an object known [by the other]? 'I am one' is the truth that is the experience of everyone.[1]

**Bhagavan:** The Self is not something of which *jnana* [knowledge] or *ajnana* [ignorance] can be predicated. It is beyond *ajnana* and *jnana*. The Self is the Self; that is all that can be said of it.[2]

2 He who is struggling with a complete absence of knowledge about himself, what will he know, and even if he knows something, what use will it serve?

3 Only knowledge of the Self possesses the excellence of true knowledge. All other kinds of knowledge are erroneous.

Ulladu Narpadu, *verses 10, 12, 13:*

Without ignorance, which is dense and abundant like darkness, knowledge cannot exist, and without knowledge, that ignorance cannot exist. Only the knowledge that knows that self which is the base [of knowledge and ignorance by enquiring] 'To whom are that knowledge and ignorance?' is true knowledge.

That which is completely devoid of knowledge and ignorance is [true] knowledge. That which knows [objects] cannot be true knowledge. Since Self shines without another to know or be known by, it is [true] knowledge. It is not a void. Know thus.

Self, which is clear knowledge, alone is real. Knowledge of multiplicity is ignorance. Even this ignorance, which is unreal, cannot exist apart from the Self, which is knowledge...[3]

4 Knowledge and ignorance can only pertain to objects, the non-Self. They are not appropriate to the Self, whose form is pure consciousness.

**Question:** Does the absolute know itself?
**Bhagavan:** The ever-conscious is beyond both knowledge and ignorance. Your question presupposes subject and object but the absolute is beyond both. It is knowledge itself.[4]

5 True *jnana* is only the removal of wrong knowledge. Only this is useful for liberation.

**Bhagavan:** It is false to speak of realisation. What is there to realise? The real is as it is, ever. How to real-ise it? All that is required is this. We have real-ised the unreal, i.e., regarded as real what is unreal. We have to give up this attitude. That is all that is required for us to attain *jnana*. We are not creating anything new or achieving something which we did not have before. The illustration given in books is this. We dig a well and create a huge pit. The space in the pit or well has not been created by us. We have just removed the earth which was filling the space there. The space was there then and is also there now. Similarly, we have simply to throw out all the age-long *samskaras* [mental tendencies] which are inside us; and when all of them have been given up, the Self will shine, alone.[5]

6 *Padam* says: 'To call the truth of the Self, which is natural to everyone, a mystery is a great joke.'

> **Question:** How is it that *Atma vidya* [Self-knowledge] is said to be the easiest?
> **Bhagavan:** Any other *vidya* requires a knower, knowledge and the object to be known, whereas this does not require any of them. It is the Self. Can anything be so obvious as that? Hence it is the easiest. All that you need do is to enquire, 'Who am I?'[6]

7 Effulgent *Padam* poses the question: 'Who is the blind one who does not perceive the Self that exists as unerring wisdom?'

8 The weeping of those who come to this world-stage, who play their role and depart, is due to poverty, a lack of *jnana*.

9 *Jnana*, the supreme reality, is the truth of the four-fold objectives – *dharma*, *artha*, *kama* and *moksha* – that are the sanctioned goals of human beings.

Dharma, artha, kama *and* moksha *were explained on page 46. Bhagavan is saying here that* jnana *is the true* dharma, *the true* artha, *the true* kama *and the true* moksha.

10 *Jnana*, the Self with which one should merge, is the complete cessation of the addiction of the mind towards the non-Self.

11 In the godly state of *jnana*, the pure state, there are neither external indications [such as horripilation or shaking] nor ecstasy.

> **Question:** Horripilation, sobbing voice, joyful tears, etc. are mentioned in *Atma Vidya Vilasa* and other works. Are these found in *samadhi*, or before or after?
> **Bhagavan:** All these are symptoms of exceedingly subtle modes of mind [*vrittis*]. Without duality they cannot remain. *Samadhi* is perfect peace where these cannot find a place. After emerging from *samadhi* the remembrance of the state gives rise to these symptoms. In *bhakti marga* [the path of devotion] these are the precursors to *samadhi*.
> **Question:** Are they not so in the path of *jnana*?
> **Bhagavan:** May be. There is no definiteness about it. It depends on the nature of the individual. Individuality entirely lost, these cannot find a place. Even the slightest

trace of it being present, these symptoms become manifest.[7]

12 Only when the nature of reality is clearly known will false understanding perish, along with the delusion it brings with it.

**The Self is ever-attained**

13 Through *sadhana* [spiritual practice] one can attain things that are other than oneself. But with what *sadhana* can the Self be attained, and who is to attain it?

**Bhagavan:** *Knowing* the Self is *being* the Self, and being means existence – one's own existence – which no one denies, any more than one denies one's eyes, although one cannot see them. The trouble lies with your desire to objectify the Self, in the same way that you objectify your eyes when you place a mirror before them. You have become so accustomed to objectivity that you have lost the knowledge of yourself, simply because the Self cannot be objectified.[8]

14 There is nothing new to be attained. That 'attainment' is merely the *jnana* experience, free from ignorance.

**Bhagavan:** People ask: 'How did ignorance arise at all?' We have to say to them: 'Ignorance never arose. It has no real being. That which is, is only *vidya* [knowledge].'[9]

**Bhagavan:** *Brahma-jnana* [true knowledge of *Brahman*] is not a knowledge to be acquired, so that acquiring it one may attain happiness. It is one's ignorant outlook that one should give up. The Self you seek to know is verily yourself. Your supposed ignorance causes you needless grief, like that of the ten foolish men who grieved the 'loss' of the tenth man who was never lost.[10]

15 The non-dual truth is realised in the experience of pure, supreme consciousness. It is not attained afresh.

**Question:** If 'I' am always, here and now, why do I not feel so?

**Bhagavan:** That is it. Who says it is not felt? Does the real 'I' say it or the false 'I'? Examine it. You will find it is the wrong 'I'. The wrong 'I' is the obstruction. It has to be removed in order that the true 'I' may not be hidden. The feeling that I have not realised is the obstruction to realisation. In fact it is already realised; there is nothing more to be realised. Otherwise, the realisation will be new; it has not existed so far, it must take place hereafter. What is born will also die. If realisation be not eternal it is not worth having. Therefore what we seek is not that which must happen afresh. It is only that which is eternal but not now known due to obstructions; it is that we seek. All that we need to do is to remove the obstruction. That which is eternal is not known to be so because of ignorance. Ignorance is the obstruction. Get over this ignorance and all will be well.[11]

**16** From time immemorial you have been existing only as That which you are struggling hard to know.

**Bhagavan:** The Self is ever-attained [*nityasiddha*]. Each one wants to know the Self. What kind of help does one require to know oneself? People want to see the Self as something new. But it is eternal and remains the same all along. They desire to see it as a blazing light, etc. How can it be so? It is not light, not darkness (*na tejo, na tamah*). It is only as it is. It cannot be defined. The best definition is 'I am that I am'. The *srutis* [scriptures] speak of the Self as being the size of one's thumb, the tip of the hair, an electric spark, vast, subtler than the subtlest, etc. They have no foundation in fact. It is only being, but different from the real and the unreal; it is knowledge, but different from knowledge and ignorance. How can it be defined at all? It is simply being.[12]

**17** The ultimate state of supreme liberation is one's own real nature. It is always attained. Knowing this, be still.

**18** Your job is to enquire into and know the Self that is in an 'already prepared' state. There is no reason for you to make an effort to prepare anything from scratch.

**Question:** How shall I reach the Self?
**Bhagavan:** There is no reaching the Self. If the Self were to be reached, it would mean that the Self is not now and here, but that it should be got anew. What is got afresh, will also be lost. So, it will be impermanent. What is not permanent is not worth striving for. So, I say, the Self is not reached. You are the Self. You are already That. The fact is that you are ignorant of your blissful state. Ignorance supervenes and draws a veil over the pure bliss. Attempts are directed only to remove this ignorance. This ignorance consists in wrong knowledge. The wrong knowledge consists in the false identification of the Self with the body, the mind, etc. This false identity must go and there remains the Self.
**Question:** How is that to happen?
**Bhagavan:** By enquiry into the self.[13]

19 Why are you unnecessarily languishing by closing your eyes and thinking when the truth of oneself is shining in a self-evident way?

The existence of their own Self is inferred by some from mental functioning, by the reasoning 'I think therefore I am'. These men are like those dull-witted ones who ignore the elephant when it goes past and become convinced afterwards by looking at the footprints.[14]

**Bhagavan:** As an example of direct perception everyone will quote the simile of the *nellikai* placed in the palm of the hand. The Self is even more directly perceivable than the fruit on the palm. To perceive the fruit there must be the fruit, the palm to place it on and the eyes to see it. The mind should also be in the proper condition [to process the information]. Without any of these four things, even those with very little knowledge can say out of direct experience, 'I am'. Because the Self exists just as the feeling

'I am', Self-knowledge is very easy indeed. The easiest path is to see the one who is going to attain the Self.[15]

*A* nellikai *resembles a gooseberry except that it grows on a tree not a bush. If something is self-evident, people in many parts of India will often say, 'It's as clear as a gooseberry on the palm of the hand'.*

**20** Open your eyes! Know the light that shines through your eyes; shine in the Heart as the greatest of all lights, which transcends all thought.

**21** Remaining always as the Self and realising it is like the pilgrimage to Pandharpur that is performed while staying in Pandharpur itself.

*Pandharpur is a town in Maharashtra that has a very famous Krishna temple. The verse refers to a song and ritual that is performed by devotees of this shrine. Bhagavan mentioned it in the following exchange:*

**Question:** Where can we see the soul? How can we know it?

**Bhagavan:** Where can we see the soul? This question is like staying in Ramanasramam and asking 'Where is Ramanasramam?' The soul is at all times in you and everywhere, and to imagine that it is somewhere far off and to search for it is like performing Panduranga *bhajan*. This *bhajan* commences in the first quarter of the night with tinkling bells tied to the feet of the devotees, and with a brass lamp-stand placed in the centre of the house. The devotees go round and round the lamp-stand, dancing rhythmically to the tune, 'Pandharpur is thus far! Pandharpur is thus far! Come on, proceed!', but as they go round and round, they actually do not proceed even half a yard further. By the time the third quarter of the night is reached, they will begin to sing, 'See! See! There is Pandharpur! Here is Pandharpur! See, See!'

During the first quarter of the night they were going round the same lamp as they were in the third quarter. It dawns and they sing, 'We have arrived in Pandharpur. This is Pandharpur.' So saying, they salute the lamp-stand and end the *bhajan*. It is the same with this also. We go round and round in search of *Atma*, saying, 'Where is *Atma*? Where is *Atma*?' till at last the dawn of *jnana-drishti* [the vision of knowledge] is reached and we say, 'This is *Atma*. This is me.'[16]

**22** The Self, that object of supreme value, is always attained. One 'attains' it by knowing it well and by getting firmly convinced that one is That.

**The state of the Self**

**23*** Even ascetics and sages cannot formulate a definition of the Self, the real, except in negative terms.
**24*** What is that one thing that nobody has the power to reject or accept? That one thing is the *Atma-swarupa, Padam*.
**25** How wonderful that the experience of the Self, which is so obvious, becomes illusory!
**26** That Self which is intimately united with all beings is the unerring, pure, supreme reality.
**27** The state of the Self alone has the noble distinction of being the state of sublime reality. Distinct from this, all the other states that are experienced as different from oneself are alien to truth.
**28** Only Self-nature is worthy of being embraced; there is no union with any other nature.
**29** As a comparison to the Self, which shines as both the dwelling-place and that which dwells within it, the space of the physical universe is poor indeed.

*Guru Vachaka Kovai*, verse 426: If one enquires into the reason for repeatedly saying that for all things consciousness is the foundation, [it is because] consciousness, which is the excellent foundation for everything that rises, is the foundation even for itself.

*The physical universe rests within consciousness, but the true space of consciousness, the underlying, empty substratum, which contains nothing other than itself, is always greater:*

**Bhagavan:** *Chidakasa* [the expanse of consciousness] is pure knowledge only. It is the source of the mind. Just at the moment of rising up, the mind is only light; only afterwards the thought 'I am this' rises up; this 'I'-thought forms the *jiva* and the world.

The first light is the pure mind, the mind-ether [*manokasa*] or Iswara. Its modes manifest as objects. Because it contains all these objects within itself, it is called the 'mind-ether'. Like ether [space] containing objects, it contains the thoughts; therefore, it is the mind-ether.

Again, just as the physical ether through accommodating all the gross objects (the whole universe) is itself the content of the mind-ether, so also the latter is itself the content of the *chit*-ether [*chidakasa*]. The last one is *chit* itself. There are no things contained within it. It remains as pure knowledge only.[17]

**30** The triumphant revelation of the truth of oneself is eternally constant and never decays.

**31*** All changes are only for the non-Self. For one's own nature, the Self, the supreme, there is never any change.

**[Bhagavan:]** 'They say I gained realisation in twenty-eight minutes, or half an hour. How can they say that? It just took a moment. Why even a moment? Where is the question of time at all?'

I then asked Bhagavan if there was ever any change in his realisation after his experience in Madurai. He said, 'No. If there is a change, it is not realisation.'[18]

**32*** The Self that is in the beginning and is in the end exists in the intervening time also, as that which is.

**33** If a state is being experienced as something new, because that state is not one's own, it will definitely go away.

*Guru Vachaka Kovai,* verse 887: If that state is non-existent now and comes to be attained later, then that state, not being the natural state that exists as one's own, is bound to depart. It will not abide permanently.

*Vilakkam*: Irrespective of how great an experience is, and irrespective of how much bliss it bestows, if it remains for some time and leaves later, it is impermanent and not the ultimate state. It is only natural and proper that any state that is not the natural state should, at some point, leave.

**34*** Going and coming only exist in the mind. They do not exist in the Self, consciousness of being.

**35** When the ego dies and ceases to exist in the manifestation of grace that is the non-dual experience – this is the attainment of one's true nature.

**36** All objects appear and flourish in the Self only. Is there anything, therefore, that has the power to act independently of that Self?

## The light of the Self

**37** That which projects the images [in waking and dream], which are the concepts of the false mind, is reality, the light of blissful consciousness.

> **Bhagavan:** The Self is in the Heart. The Heart is self-luminous. Light arises from the Heart and reaches the brain, which is the seat of the mind. The world is seen with the mind, that is, by the reflected light of the Self. It is perceived with the aid of the mind. When the mind is illumined it is aware of the world. When it is not itself so illumined, it is not aware of the world. If the mind is turned in towards the source of light, objective knowledge ceases and Self alone shines forth as the Heart.
>
> The moon shines by the reflected light of the sun. When the sun has set, the moon is useful for revealing objects. When the sun has risen, no one needs the moon, although the pale disc of the moon is visible in the sky.
>
> So it is with the mind and the Heart. The mind is useful because of its reflected light. It is used for seeing objects. When it is turned inwards, the source of illumination shines forth by itself, and the mind remains dim and useless like the moon in daytime.[19]

**38** The effulgence of the perfectly pure Self alone is real; the vision of the impure mind is false.

> **Bhagavan:** The nature of the Self or 'I' must be illumination. You perceive all modifications and their absence. How? To say that you get the illumination from another would raise the question how he got it and there would be no end to the chain of reasoning. So you yourself

are the illumination. The usual illustration of this is the following: You make all kinds of sweets of various ingredients and in various shapes and they all taste sweet because there is sugar in all of them and sweetness is the nature of sugar. And in the same way all experiences and the absence of them contain the illumination, which is the nature of the Self. Without the Self they cannot be experienced, just as without sugar not one of the articles you make can taste sweet.[20]

**39** Reality has no name and no form. Amongst all that is subtle, that light is the most subtle.

**40*** This world that is seen in many ways is all the light of *swarupa*.

**41** Only the light of consciousness that abides with its focus on itself is true *jnana*, the reality. The *suttarivu* that knows the non-Self is utter ignorance.

**42** If one were not the form of reality, the light of consciousness, the experience of knowing objects would not be possible.

**43*** The light that exists when the appearance of the world and body has ceased exists equally even when the world and the body appear.

**44** Only the light of *jnana* is the light of grace, the feet of the Lord. All other lights are lights of an opposing kind.

**Question:** How are we to conceive of supreme consciousness [*chaitanya Brahman*]?

**Bhagavan:** As that which is.

**Question:** Should it be thought of as self-effulgent?

**Bhagavan:** It transcends light and darkness. An individual [*jiva*] sees both. The Self enlightens the individual to see light and darkness.[21]

**45** Those who know these other lights as objects and who believe them to be real are those who are caught up in the entanglements of the gross physical body.

**46** Within those noble hearts that are illuminated by the real, that most valuable thing of all, the light of liberation will shine forth even here upon the earth.

**47** *Padam* marvels: 'In this world the defect of ignorance, darkness, is indeed a great wonder!'

## The non-duality of the Self

**48** That which is, is only one, not two; and even that does not exclude you. Indeed, it is not different from you.

**49** In your true *swarupa* you alone exist without any second entity.

**50*** The reality that is non-dual and which is one's own nature is not compatible with the objectifying consciousness that has become two.

**51** In true *jnana* there truly never arises the slightest opposition to any other thing.

> **Bhagavan:** Whenever something has to be controlled, some obstacle removed or some change is necessary, the use of *sakti* is required. But in the supreme experience of *Atman*, meaning *stitha prajna* [the state of being established in wisdom], or the state that is beyond the *gunas* [the qualities of the mind], the only experience is that of non-duality. In that state there is no other principle that remains arrayed against it. For a *jnani* established in the Self there is nothing that remains in opposition to him. It is not therefore necessary [for him] to conquer any external things because in that state there is no remnant of anything that is separate. When the Self becomes all-pervasive, the physical world is totally absent. Therefore, in spite of the *sakti* being in the *Atman,* it does not become necessary to use it. If one is in a state in which opposition is felt, then to work on that opposition, *Atma sakti* is required.[22]

**52** The Self, the source of all beings, is not different from the indivisible consciousness that does not split itself into 'I' and 'this'.

> **Question:** Is it not that the 'I' exists only in relation to a 'this' [*aham – idam*]?
> **Bhagavan:** 'I', 'this' appear together now. But 'this' is contained in the 'I' – they are not apart. 'This' has to merge into and become one with 'I'. The 'I' that remains over is the true 'I'.[23]

## The Self has no associations

**53*** The Self, the single all-pervading consciousness, is eternally free of the twin attributes, association and non-association.

**54*** In the intellect of one who has clearly known himself to be consciousness there is no other thing to associate with.

**55** No concepts, which are just the appearance of differences, will attach to the peerless, pure, non-dual *swarupa*, which is self-shining.

## The Self is *upadhi*-free

**56*** Except from the viewpoint of *upadhis* [limiting adjuncts], truly, no division ever arises in the Self, whose nature is consciousness.

Upadhis, *usually translated by the phrase 'limiting adjuncts', are false and limiting identifications that are superimposed on consciousness, the one reality. Identification with a body or with any other form or idea is an* upadhi, *as Bhagavan explains in the following answer:*

> **Bhagavan:** The pure being is the reality. The others are mere associations. The pure being cannot be otherwise than consciousness. Otherwise you cannot say that you exist. Therefore consciousness is the reality. When that consciousness is associated with *upadhis* you speak of self-consciousness, unconsciousness, sub-consciousness, super-consciousness, human-consciousness, dog-consciousness, tree-consciousness and so on. The unfaltering common factor in all of them is consciousness.[24]

**57*** None of the defects arising through *upadhis* inhere in the lofty purity of that consciousness which is the Self.

## The Self as *swarupa*

Swarupa *can be variously translated as 'real form', 'real nature', 'own form', or 'own nature'. When this term is used as a synonym for the Self, it indicates that the ultimate nature of reality is not an alien or mediated experience; it is, rather, one's true and inherent state.*

**58** The true *jnana* is not something that is 'attained'. It exists as one's own *swarupa*.

59 *Swarupa*, which shines as consciousness, the supreme, is the substratum for everything that is present everywhere.
60 Describing *swarupa* with words is like trying to cross the sea, using a wisp of straw as a raft.
61* It is impossible to think of *swarupa-rasa* [the savour of reality], the enjoyment of which goes beyond concepts and transcends them, and to declare that its nature is such and such.
62 The greatness of the flourishing *swarupa* is that, being one's own true nature, it leaves no scope for even saying that it is easy to attain.
63 In that *swarupa* one can only abide as That. There is no scope for thinking in this state.
64 The certainty of one's unceasing true *swarupa* is the imperishable essence, the ambrosia that bestows immortality.
65 All else that remains apart from the real is a mental construct, to which there is no definitive and incontestable finality.
66 *Jnana-swarupa*, one's real nature, which is entitled to your love, never suffers, gets bewildered or decays.

> **Question:** Love postulates duality. How can the Self be the object of love?
> **Bhagavan:** Love is not different from the Self. Love of an object is of an inferior order and cannot endure. Whereas the Self is love, in other words, God is love.[25]

67 Ah! Ah! Your greatness will indeed be beyond measure if you have comprehended the truth of your own deathless *swarupa*.

## Abiding as *swarupa*

68 The source of all faults and mistakes is not realising one's true nature. It is a most egregious mistake. This is the first thing you should know.
69 Investigate and realise that from the very beginning you possess as your very own nature the *swarupa* you are journeying to attain.
70 The reason why consciousness loses clarity and rushes towards the world is that it forsakes the Self, the reality.
71 Except for abidance as *Atma-swarupa*, the enduring state, all other states are defective because they are associated with the mind.
72 Those who think of other forms, forgetting their real form that

remains merged with them as *jnana swarupa*, are strangers [to *jnana*].

73 The life of those deluded ones who doubt even their own *swarupa* is completely illusory.

74 Why have you not yet known the *swarupa* that by nature shines always realised and which is incontrovertible?

75 The state of union, *samadhi*, is your real *swarupa*; the many *sadhanas* performed are false pretences.

76 Whatever leaves you, let it leave; whatever comes to you, let it come. [Irrespective of what happens] remain merged in your auspicious *swarupa*.

77 Do not let your mind dwell on anything other than your *swarupa*, for apart from this, there is no other truth.

78 Only the *swarupa* that obliterates and makes the non-Self non-existent is described as the emptiness, *nirvana*.

> **Bhagavan:** Your real nature [*swarupa*] is always there. Your meditation, etc., come only temporarily. Reality being your Self, there is nothing for you to realise. All that is required is that you should give up regarding the unreal as real, which is what all are doing. The object of all meditation, *dhyana* or *japa* is only that, to give up all thoughts regarding the 'not Self', to give up many thoughts and to keep to the one thought.[26]

*Bhagavan's interpretation of the term* nirvana *was a little different from the traditional Buddhist one:*

> **Bhagavan:** *Nirvana* is perfection. In the perfect state there is neither subject nor object; there is nothing to see, nothing to feel, nothing to know. Seeing and knowing are the functions of the mind. In *nirvana* there is nothing but the blissful pure consciousness 'I am'.[27]

## Desire for the Self

79 Through a longing for the *swarupa* that waxes more and more as abundant bliss, infatuation for the false world will slip away.

80 The glory of Self-realisation is not experienced except in the hearts of those who are very zealous about sinking into the Self.

**Bhagavan**: Long for it intensely so that the mind melts in devotion. After the camphor burns away no residue is left. The mind is the camphor; when it has resolved itself into the Self without leaving even the slightest trace behind, it is realisation of the Self.[28]

**81** Those who greatly desire the Self, the state of mere being that transcends all concepts, will not desire anything else.
**82*** Devotion to the Self, the best of desires, yields the true *jnana* sight in which all names and forms are names and forms of the Self.
**83** If you wholeheartedly desire and realise the truth, that truth itself will liberate you.

## *Pramada* [forgetfulness of the Self]

**84** The compassionate *Padam* declares: 'There is no other mistake like *pramada* that ruins your bliss.'
**85*** Ignorance only exists in the vision of others. To the splendorous light, the nature of the Self, the obstacle of *pramada* never exists.
**86** Through forgetfulness the villainous mind will throw away the Self, that which is, and will get agitated.
**87*** In the state in which one has known the truth without any *pramada*, all names and forms are *Brahman*.
**88** The reason why the state of *Brahman* has become different from you is nothing other than your deceitful forgetfulness of the Self.

**Question:** As I go on thinking of it [the thought 'I am *Brahman*'] there is forgetfulness, the brain becomes heated and I am afraid.
**Bhagavan:** Yes, the mind is concentrated in the brain and hence you get a hot sensation there. It is because of the 'I'-thought. So long as there is thought there will be forgetfulness. There is the thought 'I am *Brahman*'; forgetfulness supervenes; then the 'I'-thought arises and simultaneously the fear of death also. Forgetfulness and thought are for 'I'-thought only. Hold it; it will disappear as a phantom. What remains over is the real 'I'. That is the Self. 'I am *Brahman*' is an aid to concentration. It keeps off other thoughts. That one thought alone persists. See whose is that thought. It will be found to be from 'I'.

Wherefrom is the 'I'-thought? Probe into it. The 'I'-thought will vanish. The supreme Self will shine forth of itself. No further effort is needed.[29]

**89** The removal of *pramada* is the attainment of one's own *swarupa*, the exalted and changeless essence.

**90** If you tightly grasp with your mind, without any forgetfulness, the Self that is *Padam*, you will attain the reality that shines at the summit of the *Vedas*.

*'The summit of the* Vedas' *refers to the* Upanishads *and to the direct experience of the Self that they expound.*

**91** Is it not because one forgets the truth of the Self, which always abides changelessly, that one gets involved in endless disputations?

**92** The agitation of the mind that is associated with *pramada* will be destroyed by the mental attitude that regards all actions as being those of Siva.

**93** Unless consciousness becomes firm and still, the powerful birth that associates [with you] through forgetfulness will not cease to be.

## Self-attention

**94** Only attention directed towards the Self, a seeking without seeking, will unite you with that primal entity whose nature never changes.

**95** Stop seeking the path that leads you to the forest, abandoning your home. A better course of action is to reverse [the] direction [of your search], turning your attention inwards.

**96** If anything disturbs your inward focus, whatever it may be, reject it without a second thought.

**97** Though one may gain any amount of greatness in worldly life, there is no peace except through turning towards the Self [*ahamukham*].

**98** What is termed 'being turned towards the Self' [*ahamukham*] is the state in which the mind, abandoning sense objects, which are alien [to the Self], shines as pure, unalloyed consciousness.

*Turning towards the Self (*ahamukham*) instead of looking outwards towards the world is fundamental to the process of doing* *self-enquiry properly. Bhagavan described how this could be done in* Who am I?:

> What does it matter if ever so many thoughts arise? At the very moment that each thought rises, if one vigilantly enquires 'To whom did this appear?' it will be known 'To me'. If one then enquires 'Who am I?' the mind will turn back to its source and the thought that had arisen will also subside. By repeatedly practising in this way, the mind will increasingly acquire the power to abide at its source. When the mind, which is subtle, is externalised via the brain and the sense organs, names and forms, which are material, appear. When it abides in the Heart, names and forms disappear. Keeping the mind in the Heart, not allowing it to go out, is called 'turning towards the Self' [*ahamukham*] or 'facing inwards'. Allowing it to go out from the Heart is termed 'facing outwards' [*bahirmukham*]. When the mind abides in the Heart in this way, the 'I', the root of all thoughts, [vanishes]. Having vanished, the ever-existing Self alone will shine. The state where not even the slightest trace of the thought 'I' remains is alone *swarupa*.

**99** If, with a mind that possesses renunciation, you turn inward, union with the Heart will arise very easily and naturally.

### Self-abidance

**100** Attaining unceasing abidance is the merging of consciousness with the indestructible supreme.

**101** The state of steadfast abidance is alone the true state. It is not to think repeatedly of something or other and become fatigued.

> **Bhagavan:** The state of *Atmanishta* [being fixed in the Self], devoid of the individual feeling of 'I', is the supreme state. In this state there is no room for thinking of objects, nor for this feeling of individual being. There is no doubt of any kind in this natural state of being-consciousness-bliss.[30]

**102** If you desire the experience of *jnana nishta*, subdue, root out and destroy the ego-mind to the best of your ability.

103 So long as distinctions persist in your world-view, *nishta* [Self-abidance] is indispensable.

> *Guru Vachaka Kovai*, verse 765: So long as the differences that arise from the *triputis* are experienced, *sadhana* is absolutely indispensable. From the *triputis*, one can conclude that the ego, the deluding concept, has not perished.

104 You should know that absorption in the supreme state, which is the goal worthy of attainment by you, is simply to become one with the Self.

> **Question:** How is meditation to be practised?
> **Bhagavan:** Meditation is, truly speaking, *Atmanishta* [to be fixed as the Self]. But when thoughts cross the mind and an effort is made to eliminate them, the effort is usually termed meditation. *Atmanishta* is your real nature. Remain as you are. That is the aim.[31]

105 The whirling [of the mind] that arises through *suttarivu* [the consciousness that divides into seer and seen] will not be stilled other than through the continuous Self-abidance that comes from *vichara* [self-enquiry].

> **Question:** If I go on rejecting thoughts can I call it *vichara?*
> **Bhagavan:** It may be a stepping stone. But really *vichara* begins when you cling to your Self and are already off the mental movement, the thought-waves.[32]

106*If one abides clinging to the Self, then, through that state of peace, all other attachments will fall away, and only your natural state, liberation, will remain.

107 The heroic ones should attain and remain firmly established in Self-abidance in the Heart. Other than this, what is the point of practising many *sadhanas*?

108 Unsurpassed and perpetually abiding good fortune exists only in the deep peace wherein one remains as the Self, and in no other state of being whatsoever.

109 The occurrence of the true experience of Self-abidance will not

manifest in all its glory unless the ego is totally destroyed.

**110** The deception of the mind that roams around without any restraints is extremely wicked. Expel the conceptualising tendencies of the mind through Self-abidance.

**111** Those who, instead of recognising the Self, try to know [it] with their minds will get choked and perplexed.

**112** Unless you clearly know your real nature by remaining firmly established in Self-abidance, you will get enmeshed in creation and become bewildered.

**113** Reach the Self, the land of consciousness, the reality, which is your own country. Shun residence in a foreign land.

## Self-remembrance

**114** Remembering the Self, one's real nature, without faltering even slightly, is the eminent victory of true *jnana*.

**115** With your consciousness hold fast to and never abandon the substratum, your own real nature, the supreme that can neither be held nor relinquished.

> **Bhagavan:** Is it [the Self] something far away that you have to touch it? The higher Self exists as one, but it is only your thoughts that make you feel that it is not. You can neither think about it nor forget it.[33]

**116** Only those supreme devotees who firmly stick to the remembrance of the Self as the foremost *sadhana* are great *tapasvins*.

Tapasvins *are those who perform* tapas, *which is arduous spiritual practice aimed at burning away all impurities.*

**117** Other than the thought of the Self, any other thought you may associate with is a mere mental construct, foreign to that Self.

*In* Who am I? *Bhagavan wrote, 'Remaining firmly in Self-abidance, without giving the least scope for the rising of any thought other than the thought of the Self [*Atma chintanai*], is surrendering oneself to God.' Since Bhagavan seems in* Who am I? *to be equating Self-abidance with 'thought of the Self', I think the same interpretation can be applied here. The same idea, and the same correspondence, also occurs in the next* Padamalai *verse.*

*The Self can never be an object of thought, a fact that Bhagavan confirms in the following quotation:*

> **Question:** How is one to think of the Self?
> **Bhagavan:** The Self is self-luminous without darkness and light, and is the reality which is self-manifest. Therefore, one should not think of it as this or as that. The very thought of thinking will end in bondage. The purport of meditation on the Self is to make the mind take the form of the Self. In the middle of the heart-cave the pure *Brahman* is directly manifest as the Self in the form 'I-I'. Can there be greater ignorance than to think of it in manifold ways, without knowing it as aforementioned?[34]

**118***Thinking of the Self is to abide as that tranquil consciousness. *Padam*, the true *swarupa* can neither be remembered nor forgotten.

### Holding onto the Self

**119** By holding on tightly to the motionless Self, taking it as one's support, the mind will become free of agitation.

> *Guru Vachaka Kovai*, verse 1192, *Pozhippurai*: The ego is the reflection of the Self in the water of the mind, which is constantly throwing out thought-waves. If one searches for the method to still its movement, the correct way is to cling to the Self, the true import of the ego, as the object, remaining determinedly still, paying no attention to that reflection which makes one slip away from one's true state.

> **Bhagavan:** Because we exist, the ego appears to exist too. If we look on the Self as the ego, then we are the ego, if as the mind, we are the mind, if as the body, we are the body. It is the thought that works up in many ways. Looking at the shadow on the water, it is found to be shaking. Can anyone stop the shaking of the shadow? If it should cease to shake, you should not look on the water. Look at your Self. Therefore, do not look to the ego. The ego is the 'I'-thought. The true 'I' is the Self.[35]

**120** Always practise holding tightly to the Heart, which is full of perfect peace, without abandoning it through desire or inattention.

**Question:** It is said '*Atma samstham manah krtva* [fixing the mind in the Self]'. But the Self is unthinkable.
**Bhagavan:** Why do you wish to meditate at all? Because you wish to do so you are told *Atma samstham manah krtva*. Why do you not remain as you are without meditating? What is that *manah* [mind]? When all thoughts are eliminated it becomes *Atma samstha* [fixed in the Self].[36]

**Question:** The mind does not sink into that state even for a second.
**Bhagavan:** A strong conviction is necessary that I am the Self, transcending the mind and the phenomena.
**Question:** Nevertheless, the mind proves to be a cork against attempts to sink it.
**Bhagavan:** What does it matter if the mind is active? It is so only on the substratum of the Self. Hold the Self even during mental activities.[37]

**121** Do not get spoiled by thinking about the non-Self with your mind. Hold tightly to yourself and attain peace.
**122** To shine as consciousness without thoughts is the *jnana samadhi* of holding tightly to *swarupa*.
**123** Hold onto the path of holding onto the one who has no attachments. By holding onto this path of holding on, you rid yourself of [those attachments] that hold you to the world.
**124***By holding tightly to the one who has no attachments, your attachment to the non-Self will go away. When that [attachment to the non-Self] has gone, holding on tightly to the one who has no attachments will also cease, and all attachments will come to an end.

## The bliss of the Self

**125** The deeper one subsides within the Heart, the greater will be the rising of the nature of the flood of supreme bliss.
**126***The true opening ceremony is the Heart opening and the Self,

the space of supreme bliss, rising.

**127** Why do you vainly lament, crying 'Where can the state of true bliss be found?' You yourself have happiness as your own true nature, and its location is the Heart.

**Bhagavan:** *Ananda* [supreme bliss] always exists. It is only the worldly things that have to be given up. If they are given up, what remains is only bliss. That which is, is the Self, Where is the question of catching that which is? That is one's own nature [*swabhava*].
**Question:** Is that nature also called *swarupa*?
**Bhagavan:** Yes. There is no difference between the two.
**Question:** If it is said that *ananda* is the Self itself, then who is it that experiences it?
**Bhagavan:** That is the point. So long as there is one who experiences, it shall have to be stated that *ananda* is the Self itself. When there is no one to experience, where is the question of a form of *ananda?* Only that which 'is' remains. That 'is' is *ananda.* That is the Self. So long as there is the feeling that the Self is different from oneself there will be one who enquires and experiences, but when one realises the Self there will be no one to experience. Who is there to ask? What is there to say? In common parlance, however, we shall have to say that bliss is the Self or is our real nature [*swarupa*].[38]

**Muruganar:** Unless the thought 'the bliss of the Self has not been experienced' is completely destroyed, the experience of the Self is not revealed. It is experienced as one's own nature. It is not experienced like a sense pleasure with the accompanying false and fake activity of the mind [*chitta vritti*]. Indeed, activity of the mind is the obstacle to it.[39]

**128** In a heart [*aham*] in which true love is overflowing, it will be known clearly that one's own real nature is nothing but bliss.

**129** Cherish as *Brahma-samadhi* the blissful state of the Self, the perfect contentment.

**130** Leaving the hot sun of samsaric misery, remain steadfastly in the shade of the tree of *jnana*, the blissful real nature of the Self.

*From the essay version of* Who am I?:

> The shade under a tree is very pleasant. Away from it the sun's heat is scorching. A person who is wandering around outside reaches the shade and is cooled. After a while he goes out again, but unable to bear the scorching heat, returns to the tree. In this way he is engaged in going from the shade into the hot sunshine and in coming back from the hot sunshine into the shade. A person who acts like this is an *aviveki* [someone who lacks discrimination], for a discriminating person would never leave the shade. By analogy, the mind of a *jnani* never leaves *Brahman*, whereas the mind of someone who has not realised the Self is such that it suffers by wandering in the world before turning back to *Brahman* for a while to enjoy happiness. What is called 'the world' is only thoughts. When the world disappears, that is, when there are no thoughts, the mind experiences bliss; when the world appears, it experiences misery.

**131** The true bliss of tranquillity does not exist in any state except in the state of the Self, which forever exists and shines as the very form of bliss.

> **Bhagavan:** There is happiness when agreeable things are presented to the mind. It is the happiness inherent to the Self, and there is no other happiness. And it is not alien and afar. You are diving into the Self on those occasions which you consider pleasurable; that diving results in self-existent bliss. But the association of ideas is responsible for foisting that bliss on other things or occurrences while, in fact, that bliss is within you. On these occasions you are plunging into the Self, though unconsciously. If you do so consciously, with the conviction that comes of the experience that you are identical with the happiness which is verily the Self, the one reality, you call it realisation. I want you to dive consciously into the Self, i.e., into the Heart.[40]

**132** Only the completely perfect *swarupa*, the pure consciousness that is devoid of objectification, is the life of unlimited true bliss.

**133** Only the consciousness that sinks into the Heart is the means for storing up the flood of true bliss.

**134** There will never be any dearth of bliss if you merge lovingly with the Self and become mind-free.

**135** Rid yourself of *pramada* and live forever, attaining the *jnana*-bliss of the one Self, a bliss whose nature can never be described.

### Real and spurious bliss

**136** If the mind, which rarely subsides, actually does subside, bliss will multiply many million-fold.

> **Question:** When I meditate I feel a certain bliss at times. On such occasions, should I ask myself 'Who is it that experiences this bliss?'
> **Bhagavan***:* If it is the real bliss of the Self that is experienced, i.e., if the mind has merged really in the Self, such a doubt will not arise at all. The question itself shows real bliss was not reached.[41]

> **Question***:* How to get bliss?
> **Bhagavan***:* Bliss is not something to be got. On the other hand you are always bliss. This desire is born of the sense of incompleteness. To whom is this sense of incompleteness? Enquire. In deep sleep you were blissful. Now you are not so. What has interposed between that bliss and this non-bliss? It is the ego. Seek its source and find you are bliss.
>
> There is nothing new to get. You have, on the other hand, to get rid of your ignorance which makes you think that you are other than bliss. For whom is this ignorance? It is to the ego. Trace the source of the ego. Then the ego is lost and bliss remains over. It is eternal.[42]

**137** The bliss of *jnana*, the Self, that manifests in the tranquil mind will disappear and cease to appear in the *ghora vritti* [rajasic mind].

> **Question:** *Brahman* is said to be *sat-chit-ananda swarupa* [the true nature of being-consciousness-bliss]. What does that mean?

**Bhagavan:** Yes. That is so. That which is, is only *sat*. That is called *Brahman*. The lustre of *sat* is *chit* and its nature is *ananda*. These are not different from *sat*. All the three together are known as *sat-chit-ananda*. It is the same in regard to attributes of the *jiva* – *sattvam, ghoram* and *jadam*. *Ghoram* means the quality of *rajas*, and *jadam* means the quality of *tamas*. Both these are parts of *sattvam*. If these two are removed, what remains is only *sattvam*. That is the truth which is eternal and pure. Call it *Atman, Brahman, sakti* or anything you like. If you know that that is yourself, everything is lustrous. Everything is *ananda*.[43]

**138** In those ignoble and ignorant people who wander in the ways of the illusory mind, the feeling of true bliss does not exist in any degree whatsoever.

**139** Those who fall under the spell of imagination will have no chance to obtain the bliss [of the Self], the true fruition of desire.

**140** *Padam* sternly warns: 'So long as you are seeking something other than yourself as the agent for gaining bliss, there is no bliss for you.'

*Guru Vachaka Kovai*, verse 1026, *Pozhippurai*: Though the *Atma-swarupa*, one's own nature, is supreme bliss, without realising this, the deceptive mind that has associated with delusion seeks sense objects, struggling and searching for bliss all the time as if that bliss were present in the non-Self. This is what causes one to lose the Self-experience, the enjoyment of bliss.

*Vilakkam*: One who has woken up from sleep declares the truth of his experience when he says, 'I slept happily'. It is a fact, acceptable to all, that in the natural state of deep sleep, wherein the mind remains thought-free, having no contact with sense objects, the Self is experienced as happiness. The bliss that was one's own nature in the state of sleep ceases and fails to manifest when one wakes because the desires that chase after sense-objects make one forget one's Self-nature, which is bliss, and separate one from the state of the Self. Therefore, one should attain the fortune of unsurpassed bliss, one's own true experience, by having a mind that does not, through the desires that arise from delusion, wander after sense-objects, that remains calm without forgetfulness of the Self in the waking state, just as it does in sleep.

**141** Those who have realised the truth that flourishes in the Heart will live eternally in the state of perfect bliss.

**142** The pleasures experienced through the senses are only spurious versions of bliss. Only the nature of the undivided *Atma-swarupa* is true bliss.

**Question:** Bhagavan, the *sastras* talk about so many different kinds of *ananda* [happiness or bliss]. Are there really so many different types?

**Bhagavan:** No, *ananda* is only one. That *ananda* is itself God. Our natural state is *ananda*. Because this is experienced externally through various sensual enjoyments, various names are given to it. However many varieties of happiness are enjoyed, many millions of varieties of misery will also have to be experienced. But this is not so for the *jnani*. He enjoys all the happiness enjoyed by everyone in the world as his own *Brahmananda* [bliss of *Brahman*]. *Brahmananda* is like an ocean. The external types of happiness are like waves, foam, bubbles and ripples.[44]

## The treasure of the Self

**143** The divine treasure trove that yields the ultimate benefit to the soul exists only in the Heart. Not even a trace of it exists [anywhere else].

**144** The nine treasures, beginning with *sanga*, are trivial when viewed from the perspective of the treasure that is the Self.

*The nine treasures are the property of Kubera, the god of wealth.*

**145** The benefit arising from that treasure trove, which is one's own *swarupa* and one's natural state, is beyond measure.

**146***The treasure trove, one's real nature, will be clearly revealed when *avarana* [veiling] and *vikshepa* [restlessness] depart.

*Bhagavan sometimes uses* vikshepa *to denote restlessness, rather than its more usual meaning, multiplicity:*

> **Bhagavan:** It is said that awaking from ignorance is like awaking from a fearful dream of a beast. It is thus. There are two taints of mind, veiling and restlessness [*avarana* and *vikshepa*]. Of the two, the former is evil; the latter is not so. So long as the veiling effect of sleep persists there is the frightful dream; on waking the veiling ceases, and there is no more fear. Restlessness is not a bar to happiness. To get rid of the restlessness caused by the world, one seeks the restlessness (activity) of being with the Guru, studying the sacred books and worshipping God with forms, and by these awakening is attained.[45]

# Consciousness

## Consciousness alone exists

1* Since everything is included in consciousness, consciousness is the ultimate, supreme truth [*paramartha*].

2 The nature of the Self is consciousness alone. Like gold jewellery [fashioned from gold], objective knowledge is an imaginary appearance within the Self.

3 Only consciousness abides as the supreme. The five senses and the perceptions of the five senses, which are not consciousness, are false deceptions.

4 All the objects perceived through the senses that adhere to you have nothing other than consciousness as their material cause.

5* Ignorance is an erroneous superimposition. The infinite, blissful consciousness is alone the one existing reality.

> *Guru Vachaka Kovai,* verse 547: If one abides as consciousness, there is no ignorance. Ignorance is false; only consciousness is real. If one really knows, it will be known that ignorance never existed. Know that one's real nature is pure consciousness.

6* No other consciousness exists to know or make known the Self, the pure consciousness.

7 Only consciousness is the life of the Self. The life associated with forms and attributes, which are defective, is the play of delusion.

## Knowing consciousness

8* One's own Self, consciousness, is different from all that is known [objectively] by consciousness.

9 Everything that is known through the mind and the senses, rather than by the light of consciousness, is *asat* [unreal].

10* When one knows one's real nature, consciousness, it will be known that ignorance never existed.

> **Bhagavan:** To know that there never was ignorance is the goal of all the spiritual teachings. Ignorance must be of one who is aware. Awareness is *jnana*. *Jnana* is eternal and natural. *Ajnana* is unnatural and unreal.[1]

**11** That which deserves to be known and attained is consciousness, the Self. Apart from this, there is no other blessing that deserves to be attained in this birth.

**12** Only when the truth that shines as mere consciousness is attained as your *swarupa* will duality cease.

**13** Knowing consciousness is not different from knowing reality. They are one and the same because reality is not different from consciousness.

**14** 'I have not known any God apart from consciousness.' [You will also know this] if you subside in the Heart where it resides.

**15** Only those who have known consciousness have known the truth. Those who have known things other than consciousness are, whatever else they might have known, ignorant.

**16** If you abide as consciousness by knowing consciousness, the profound delusion caused by the frenzied obsession with sense objects will come to an end.

**17** Out of all the *sadhanas* that are worth performing, knowing consciousness is the only excellent and definitive one.

**18** The child Murugan, concealing nothing, taught this state of pure being to Lord Siva, revealing it as the inner meaning of *Om*.

*Murugan, the second son of Siva, once revealed the meaning of the* Om *mantra to his father, thus earning him the title 'The Guru of Siva'.*

**19** To abide as the Self, pure consciousness, bereft of the *suttarivu* – this is the meaning of 'knowing consciousness through consciousness'.

**20** Know this statement to be the great and glorious meaning of the unique phrase [*summa iru*] that tells you to be still.

**21** Because in that state [of the Self] there is neither another self to know, nor are there any rapidly arising concepts.

**Obstacles to knowing consciousness**

**22** Until the thoughts agitating the mind cease, it is impossible to encounter the immaculate state of consciousness, the supreme.

**23** Unless the mind becomes clear by waking into consciousness, separation from ignorance, the base *samsara*, will not be possible.

**24** If you have forgotten the pure consciousness that shines as your *swarupa*, whatever else you do, how will it profit you?

**25** Those who have not learned to exercise sovereignty over consciousness through the power of grace will be thrown into confusion by forms and attributes.

**Enquiring into consciousness**

**26** The reason why one regards reality as different from oneself is that one has not known, through enquiry, the true nature of consciousness.

**27** The mind will only become firm if it dives within and subsides into the Self through the practice of [investigating] consciousness.

**28** *Padam* speaks mockingly: 'The intelligence of a supremely intelligent one who has not enquired and known the nature of consciousness is great indeed!'

**29** Consciousness will become replete when the knower enquires within and knows himself.

**30** If you enquire into consciousness and know it as it really is, then, for that truth-consciousness, there will never ever be any delusion.

**31** Without allowing the thinking mind to become scattered, concentrate it inwardly and merge with the wondrous light of consciousness.

**32** Abide bodiless as the space-like limitless consciousness.

**Being-consciousness**

**33** To realise that you yourself are the Self, why do you require any light other than being-consciousness, the light of the Self?

> *Guru Vachaka Kovai*, verse 759: Since reality shines radiantly within oneself as the Self, only that Self deserves to be known. For enquiry into one's real nature as it actually is in the Heart, the best guide is the unrejectable true light of the Self ['I am'].

34 Rather than remaining still, as being-consciousness, why do you sprout forth as 'I' and suffer miserably?

35 Unless the mind gets firmly established in being, it is impossible for the powerful and ignoble conceit, 'I', to be obliterated.

36 Those who do not possess in their hearts being-consciousness, the real attainment, will lose their lives and get ruined by infatuation for the false world.

37 When the mind attains clarity, the attainment of the bliss of *swarupa*, consciousness of being, will result, and your heart will attain fullness.

38 In one's real nature, being-consciousness, which is the light that outshines all other lights, concepts of name and form never exist.

39 *Swarupa* shines as being-consciousness, that which is perfect fullness. The mind becoming like that *swarupa* and uniting with it is yoga [union].

40 The splendour of being-consciousness – which is easy to know and which deserves to be known – is shining as pure being.

> **Question:** When a man realises the Self, what will he see?
> **Bhagavan:** There is no seeing, Seeing is only being. The state of Self-realisation, as we call it, is not attaining something new or reaching some goal which is far away, but simply being that which you always are and which you always have been. All that is needed is that you give up your realisation of the not-true as true. All of us are realising, i.e., regarding as real that which is not real. We have only to give up this practice on our part. Then we shall realise the Self as the Self. In other words, 'Be the Self'. At one stage one would laugh at oneself that one tried to discover the Self which is so self-evident. So, what can we say to this question? [2]

41 For those who have the strength to enquire diligently and know the real nature of the mind, it will shine as the pure being-consciousness.

42 Remain still, now itself, and in your experience of consciousness of being, which is *swarupa*, merge with peace.

43 That consciousness [*chit*], which is one's own being [*sat*], is that bliss [*ananda*] within the Heart, without beginning and end.

44* The Lord and the Lady, along with Kandan, merged together are respectively the obstruction-free *sat*, *chit* and *ananda*.

*The Lord and the Lady are Siva and Parvati, and Kandan (also known as Murugan and Subramania) is their second son.*

## The *sahaja* state of consciousness

'Sahaja' *means natural. In the Ramanasramam literature the term often appears as an adjective qualifying* nirvikalpa samadhi, *the direct experience of the Self in which no differences or distinctions arise.* Sahaja nirvikalpa samadi *is the definitive state of realisation in which one can live a normal ('natural') life fully aware of the Self at all times.*

**45** To remain in the state in which consciousness of the supreme reality is not lost even during activities is *sahaja*.

**Question:** Swami, *samadhi* is said to be of two sorts, *kevala nirvikalpa* and *sahaja nirvikalpa*. What are their attributes?

**Bhagavan:** One who accustoms himself naturally to meditation [*dhyana*] and enjoys the bliss of meditation, will not lose his *samadhi* state whatever external work he does, whatever thought may come to him. That is called '*sahaja nirvikalpa samadhi*'. It is these two states that are called complete destruction [*nasa*] and suppression [*laya*]; *nasa* is *sahaja nirvikalpa* and *laya* is *kevala nirvikalpa*. Those who are in the *laya* [suppressed] *samadhi* state will have to bring the mind back under control from time to time. If the mind is destroyed, it will not sprout again; the mind will then be something like a fried seed. Whatever is done by such people is just incidental; they will not slide down from their high state. Those that are in the *kevala nirvikalpa samadhi* state are not *siddhas* [realised beings]; they are mere *sadhakas* [spiritual practitioners]. Those who are in the *sahaja nirvikalpa* state are like a light in a windless place, or the ocean without waves; that is, there is no movement. They cannot find anything which is different from themselves. But those who do not reach that state, everything appears to be different from themselves.[3]

**Bhagavan:** In *sahaja samadhi* the activities, vital and

mental, and the three states are destroyed, never to reappear. However, others notice the *jnani* active e.g., eating, talking, moving, etc. He is not himself aware of these activities, whereas others are aware of his activities. They pertain to his body and not to his real Self, *swarupa*. For himself, he is like the sleeping passenger – or like a child interrupted from sound sleep and fed, being unaware of it. The child says the next day that he did not take milk at all and that he went to sleep without it. Even when reminded he cannot be convinced. So also is *sahaja samadhi*.[4]

**46** Unless the ego, the identification with the body, dies, it will be impossible for anyone to realise that natural and abiding state of absorption within the Heart.

**47** Until that state [of *sahaja*] merges in the Heart, there is no liberation for the *jiva*, irrespective of what other state it may experience.

**Bhagavan:** Why do you think, 'I didn't meditate but instead I worked'? If the thoughts 'I did' and 'I didn't' are given up, all actions will end up as meditation. Then meditation cannot be given up. Even if we give it up, it will not let go of us. This, indeed, is the state of *sahaja samadhi*.[5]

**48** If you know and abide in your natural state, which is the fullness of bliss, how will the thought of misery arise there?

**49** Reversing the outgoing nature of the mind, merge it with its source, and by so doing, attain the natural state of bliss.

### The happiness of consciousness

**50** In a heart that has not attained tranquillity of consciousness, the experience of the Self, the ambrosia of consciousness, cannot exist.

**51** The many different pleasures enjoyed through the mind are just the superficial bubbles on the sea of brahmic bliss.

Bhagavan explained how it is said in books that the highest possible happiness which a human being can attain or which the ten grades of beings higher than man, ending with gods like Brahma, can attain, is like foam in the deluging flood of the bliss of the Self.

Imagine a man in robust health, of vigorous adult age, endowed with unsurpassed wealth and power, with intellect and all other resources, and married to a fair and faithful wife, and conceive of his happiness.

Each higher grade of being above man is capable of hundredfold greater happiness than that of the grade below. But the highest happiness of all the eleven grades of being is only the foam in the flooding ocean of divine bliss.[6]

**52*** To the realised sage in the supreme state of Siva-consciousness that happiness of consciousness will become an abundant, permanent and uninterrupted experience.

**Question:** In what *asana* [seat or posture] is Bhagavan usually seated?

**Bhagavan:** In what *asana?* In the *asana* of the Heart. Wherever it is pleasant, there is my *asana*. That is called *sukhasana*, the *asana* of happiness. That *asana* of the heart is peaceful, and gives happiness. There is no need for any other *asana,* for those who are seated in that one.[7]

**Bhagavan:** You think that you can only get happiness when there is contact with something separate from you. But that is not the truth. *Ananda* [bliss] is the very nature of the Self. The happiness that you get from other things is part of the happiness of the *Atman,* but it is not the complete happiness. So long as an external object is required [for happiness], incompleteness is felt. When it is felt that the *Atman* alone is there, permanent happiness stays...

If you are in a state that is giving you the experience of *ananda*, at that time you are actually diving into the *Atman*. It is because of this diving into the *Atman* that you get the bliss of the *Atman*. However, because of your association with incorrect thoughts, you project [the cause of] the *ananda* on to external things. When you experience *ananda*, you are unknowingly diving into the *Atman*. The truth of one's own real nature, which is the *Atman,* is that it is an undivided oneness. One's own reality is *ananda.* That is what you are. If you were to dive knowingly into the *Atman,* with the conviction born of this experience, then the state of Self would be experienced.[8]

**53*** In the state wherein the mind-limitation is completely destroyed, the truth of the happiness of consciousness, which is beyond the reach of deductive thought, will become clear.

*Bhagavan taught that happiness is not something that can be pursued and attained. It is, instead, the natural and fundamental state of all human beings. He explained this position in the following extract from* Who am I? *His comments were prompted by the question 'What is happiness?'*

What is called happiness is merely the nature of the Self. Happiness and the Self are not different. The happiness of the Self alone exists; that alone is real. There is no happiness at all in even a single one of the [many] things in the world. We believe that we derive happiness from them on account of *aviveka* [a lack of discrimination, an inability to ascertain what is correct]. When the mind is externalised, it experiences misery. The truth is, whenever our thoughts [that is, our desires] get fulfilled, the mind turns back to its source and experiences Self-happiness alone. In this way the mind wanders without rest, emerging from and abandoning the Self and [later] returning within.

### The worship of consciousness

**54*** Worship of consciousness is getting firmly established in consciousness, with the mind disconnecting itself from other things.

**55** The state in which consciousness does not desire the non-Self is worship of the Self without being separate from it.

**56** Other than consciousness, the pure clarity in which excellence flourishes, there is no God who is worthy of being worshipped.

*Guru Vachaka Kovai*, verse 417: Only those who, through

consciousness, know Siva as the form of extremely pure consciousness in the Heart, the golden temple of consciousness, are worshipping truth, because consciousness is indeed the supreme reality.

**57** Only the pure being-consciousness is the true God who is worthy of being worshipped by the vast assembly of *jivas*.

**58** As consciousness is the real nature of Siva, only enquiry into consciousness is the true worship of Siva.

> *Guru Vachaka Kovai*, verse 204: The state of profound peace is remaining inseparably in harmony with *Atma-swarupa*, the fullness, the reality that is consciousness, through the thought-free thought. Know well that this is the immaculate Siva-*puja*.

**59** In a mind that worships by praising the feet of the Lord, pure consciousness, the addiction to knowing things as separate objects will be totally destroyed.

### Consciousness, the support of the world appearance

**60** The world has as its unmatched and tightly held support the consciousness, the supreme, which shines without needing to hold on to any support.

**61** The world shines through your existence, but your being does not depend on the existence of the world.

**62** Keep this in your mind: you are the being-consciousness that shines as the stage for the drama; you are not the actor.

**63** Only *Atma-swarupa*, pure consciousness, is the genuine support for the *jiva*. Everything that is conceived by the mind is a false reflection.

**64** Realise that all these [dualities and trinities] that fall within the play of consciousness have consciousness as their real nature.

**65** Know that the world that rises, persists and then sets is wholly the play of *chit-sakti* [the power of consciousness].

**66** Know that the [categories of] sentience and insentience, which are distinguished by the mind, are merely the natural play of pure being-consciousness.

**67** The imperfect body and the world arise in consciousness as consciousness, remain in consciousness, [and subside in consciousness].

68 As it is consciousness that appears as everything, those who have known the truth of consciousness have known the truth of everything.

69 To a *muni* [a sage], all the multifarious scenes that appear before him will shine merely as the ever-present pure consciousness.

# Other Synonyms for the Self

## *Mauna*

Mauna, *usually translated as 'silence', is not merely an absence of physical or even mental noise. It is the motionless and utterly silent centre of being upon which nothing ever impinges.*

1 True realisation is to cherish with one's understanding, without any obstruction, the first cause of all that is, that *mauna* which is liberation.

2 The perfect *mauna* in which the ego, the root, has been destroyed is the pure *swarupa*, which will never be vanquished.

> **Question:** What is *mauna* [silence]?
>
> **Bhagavan:** That state which transcends speech and thought is *mauna*. That which is, is *mauna*. How can *mauna* be explained in words?
>
> Sages say that the state in which the thought 'I' does not rise even in the least, alone is *swarupa*, which means *mauna*. That silent Self is alone God; Self alone is the *jiva*. Self alone is this ancient world.
>
> All other knowledges are only petty and trivial knowledges; the experience of silence is alone the real and perfect knowledge.[1]

3 The eminent and powerful state of *mauna* can be reached in the Heart only by attaining the Self-state, the unmoving axis.

4 Only *mauna*, which is the end point of *jnana*, is that true vision which is the profound truth of Vedanta.

5 In the state of *mauna* one merely abides as 'I-I'. Apart from this, there is neither thinking nor knowing.

6 *Mauna* will manifest itself when the clarity of Self-knowledge, which overflows with the exalted direct experience, causes the *triputis* to depart.

*The* triputis *are the trinities of knower, knowing and known, and seer, seeing and seen. Though they appear to be real and valid distinctions, the experience of the Self reveals them to be a false, mental superimposition on the underlying state of* mauna. Triputis *only manifest in* chidabhasa, *the reflected light of consciousness, not in pure consciousness itself.*

**7** If the *triputis* that have risen from *mauna* subside in *mauna*, then bliss will arise.

**8** A mind that has experienced the light of *mauna* will not readily accept the conceptual drama, consisting of the *triputis*, that appears in the other light [*chidabhasa*].

**9** It is the mind that is diminished when there is a feeling of deficiency. In the fullness of *mauna*, there is only consciousness, but no thoughts.

**10** That bliss that grows in the field of *mauna* is not attained and experienced in any other field.

**11** Those who have seen the light of *mauna* are without any attachment to the world, which is an infatuating snare that rises from *kartrutva*.

Kartrutva *is the I-am-the-doer idea, the feeling that there is a person who is performing the actions that the body engages in. This concept disappears in the state of* mauna.

**12** The feeling of remaining young forever is attained in nothing else other than *mauna*, the blossoming of truth.

**13** Since it is thought that creates a sense of deficiency, only thought-free *mauna* is fullness.

**14** In order to attain the supreme state of *mauna*, that which is worthy of attainment by *sadhakas* is the loss of individuality.

**15** You should know that the supreme state of liberation exists only in a mind that has attained the state of *mauna*, and nowhere else.

**16** The concept-free experience of the vast emptiness of *mauna* will rise, putting an end to the delusion of the ego, the deceiving fixation.

**17** The direct experience of the Self, *mauna*, is the axis [of everything]. This is the summit, the highest good.

**18** Those who have sunk deeply into the ocean of *mauna* and drowned will live on the summit of the supreme mountain, the expanse of consciousness.

## Peace

19 That which is cherished by the great ones [*jnanis*] as the matchless rapture of *Brahman* is the bliss of peace, the limitless contentment.
20 The *kaivalya* [oneness] that the distinguished ones experience and exult in as the bliss of the supreme state is peace alone.
21 Only peace, shining without the impediment of differentiation that is associated with the ego, is limitless *jnana*.
22 Joy and misery are not natural to humanity. Only peace, the life of bliss, is natural.

**Question:** What is the method to be adopted for securing peace?
**Bhagavan:** The conception that there is a goal and a path to it is wrong. We are the goal or peace always. To get rid of the notion that we are not peace is all that is required.[2]

23 Once absorption in the state of true realisation, in which no thoughts arise, becomes your natural state, peace will well up and firmly take hold of you.

*In Tamil, the implication in this verse is that to whatever extent thought-free abidance in the Self has become natural, to that extent peace will shine.*

**Bhagavan:** As I said already, that which is, is peace. All that we need to do is to keep quiet. Peace is our real nature. We spoil it. What is required is that we cease to spoil it. We are not going to create peace anew. There is space in a hall, for instance. We fill up the place with various articles. If we want space, all that we need do is remove all those articles, and we get space. Similarly if we remove all the rubbish, all the thoughts, from our minds, the peace will become manifest. That which is obstructing the peace has to be removed. Peace is the only reality.[3]

24 Peace in the Heart is the sign of true *jnana*; agitation in the mind is the sign of the false and delusory life.

**Question:** How to get peace?
**Bhagavan:** That is the natural state. The mind obstructs the innate peace. Our investigation is only in the mind. Investigate the mind; it will disappear.
There is no entity by name mind. Because of the emergence of thought we surmise something from which they start. That we term 'mind'. When we probe to see what it is, there is nothing like it. After it has vanished, peace will be found to remain eternal.[4]

## The Heart

25 'The Heart' and '*Atma-swarupa*' are not different from each other. The difference is only in the words used.

Sri Ramana Gita*, chapter five, verses 2, 3 and 5:*

**[Bhagavan:]** That from which all thoughts of embodied beings issue forth is called the Heart. All descriptions of it are only mental concepts.

The 'I'-thought is said to be the root of all thoughts. In brief, that from where the 'I'-thought springs forth is the Heart.

This Heart is different from the blood-circulating organ. '*Hridayam*' [the Heart] stands for *hrit*, 'the centre which sucks in everything', and *ayam* 'this', and it thus stands for the Self.

26 It is the conviction of sages who possess clear knowledge of reality that the *Atma-swarupa* exists as the Heart within the Heart.

**Question:** Sri Bhagavan speaks of the Heart as the seat of consciousness and as identical with the Self. What does the Heart exactly signify?
**Bhagavan:** The question about the Heart arises because you are interested in seeking the source of consciousness. To all deep-thinking minds, the enquiry about the 'I' and its nature has an irresistible fascination.

Call it by any name, God, Self, the Heart or the seat of consciousness, it is all the same. The point to be grasped is this, that 'Heart' means the very core of one's being, the centre, without which there is nothing whatever.[5]

27 Those are truly wise who drink the flooding honey of *Atma-swarupa*, which shines in the Heart as the Heart, and feel contented.

28 Only in the silence of the Heart, where the movement of mind and intellect ceases, will the unique light of pure consciousness blaze forth, radiating brightly.

29 Thinking is imagination. The Heart, thought-free *Atma-swarupa*, is the reality, pure consciousness.

30 When perfection exists as the nature of your Heart, why do you lose your composure by dwelling on imperfections?

31 The Heart is the *jiva-samadhi* where the soul of the true devotee resides forever with bliss-consciousness.

*At the end of their lives some yogis take* 'jiva-samadhi', *which means that they are buried alive in a* samadhi *pit, or permanently walled up inside some cave or similar structure. This verse is describing a state in which the* jiva *is permanently entombed within the Heart, where it perpetually enjoys the bliss of the Self.*

32 The Heart that has attained through diligent application the true awareness of the nature of reality will become a storehouse of deep and abiding joy.

33 It is impossible for a Heart that has realised itself to be the vast expanse of consciousness to be obscured by the thick black darkness of ignorance.

**Abiding in the Heart**

34 True *jnana*, which bestows the bliss of the Self, will reveal itself in a Heart that, having conquered the ego, remains utterly still.

35 Unless one reaches the Heart and remains established there, it is impossible to destroy agitation of the mind and attain peace.

36 Abiding in the neutral state of equilibrium is reaching and abiding in the Heart through firm awareness of the Self, which is the true *jnana-swarupa*.

37 To exist and shine in the Heart, without any thoughts holding onto you, is *mauna samadhi*, one's own [true] nature.

38 Those things that leave you, let them leave. Instead, know that

which abides permanently in the Heart and live in consciousness.

39 Let the good and wise ones embrace as true *tapas* the realisation of the truth in their Heart, and the steadfast abidance as That.

40* The supreme benefit of possessing consciousness is rejoicing in the Heart, experiencing union with the Self.

41 The benefit of true *tapas*, free from illusory appearances, is a Heart that remains uninterruptedly and perpetually full of the true life that abides as consciousness.

### Establishing the mind in the Heart

42 Only the Heart deserves to be conquered and possessed, for it gives sovereignty over a country whose produce is indescribable supreme bliss.

43 An unruffled mind established in the Heart is the fence that protects the field of liberation.

44 Mind abiding in the Heart, free of thoughts, is pure bliss, the *jnana* that is difficult to attain.

45 Restrain yourself in such a way that you reside steadfastly in the Heart, the heavenly expanse of grace whose form is consciousness.

46 Unless the mind is firmly established in the Heart, reality will become veiled by the falsehood that is the mind.

> **Question:** How long can the mind stay or be kept in the Heart?
> **Bhagavan:** The period extends by practice.
> **Question:** What happens at the end of the period?
> **Bhagavan:** The mind returns to the present normal state. Unity in the Heart is replaced by variety of phenomena perceived. This is called the outgoing mind. The Heart-going mind is called the resting mind.[6]

47 To attain the life of true bliss, which is your very nature, firmly establish yourself in the Heart and abide immovably there.

48 The truth of oneself that exists and shines in the Heart as one's own nature becomes veiled by a mind that is full of delusion.

49 Immerse yourself in the Heart and dwell there, so that you remain beyond reproach, untroubled by the crashing waves of the mind.

> **Bhagavan:** To see objects the reflected light of the mind

is necessary. To see the Heart it is enough that the mind is turned towards it. Then the mind loses itself and the Heart shines forth.[7]

**50** To whatever extent you dive with a one-pointed mind within the Heart, to that extent you will experience bliss.

**51** [In so doing] the vexation of the clamorous and exceedingly cruel ego ghost, the mind, will perish, leaving not a trace.

# God

## The state of God

**52** That which has the right to be loved is one's *Atma-swarupa*, the supremely blissful entity that is the state of God.

**53** The state of abiding as God is becoming clear and abiding in the Heart; it is a state to which no activity of any kind adheres.

**54** That which exists devoid of the ego-consciousness, the beginningless delusion, is the true state of God.

**55*** The state of God should be attained by seeking within oneself with a one-pointed mind.

**56** If the mind is purified and fixed in the state of God, the life of the *jiva* will attain total perfection.

**57** The unattainable state of God comes to be attained when there is the experience of Self-abidance.

## Seeing God, knowing God

**58** Even though you may see wonderful visions [of the gods] that are worthy of being adored, these visions you have obtained are actually of little importance.

Ulladu Narpadu, *verse 20:*

Seeing God without seeing oneself, the seer of the objects seen, is seeing but a mental image. He who, by losing the base [the ego] sees the Self, the source of himself, alone truly sees God, because Self is not other than God.[8]

**Question:** I once before told Sri Bhagavan how I had a

vision of Siva at about the time of my conversion to Hinduism. A similar experience recurred at Courtallam. These visions are momentary. But they are blissful. I want to know how they might be made permanent and continuous. Without Siva there is no life in what I see around me. I am so happy to think of him. Please tell me how his vision may be everlasting to me.

**Bhagavan:** You speak of a vision of Siva. Vision is always of an object. That implies the existence of a subject. The value of the vision is the same as that of the seer. That is to say, the nature of the vision is on the same plane as that of the seer. Appearance implies disappearance also. Whatever appears must also disappear. A vision can never be eternal. But Siva is eternal.

The *pratyaksha* [vision] of Siva to the eye signifies the existence of the eyes to see; the *buddhi* [intellect] lying behind the sight; the seer behind the *buddhi* and the sight; and finally the consciousness underlying the seer. This *pratyaksha* [vision] is not as real as one imagines it to be, because it is not intimate and inherent; it is not first-hand. It is the result of several successive phases of consciousness. Of these, consciousness alone does not vary. It is eternal. It is Siva. It is the Self.

The vision implies the seer. The seer cannot deny the existence of the Self. There is no moment when the Self as consciousness does not exist; nor can the seer remain apart from consciousness. This consciousness is the eternal being and the only being. The seer cannot see himself. Does he deny his existence because he cannot see himself with the eyes as *pratyaksha* [in vision]? No! So, *pratyaksha* does not mean seeing, but being.

'To be' is to realise. Hence, 'I am that I am' is Siva. Nothing else can be without him. Everything has its being in Siva and because of Siva.

Therefore, enquire 'Who am I?' Sink deep within and abide as the Self. That is Siva as being. Do not expect to have visions of him repeated. What is the difference between the objects you see and Siva? He is both the subject and the object. You cannot be without Siva. Siva is always realised here and now. If you think you have not realised him it is wrong. This is the obstacle for realising

Siva. Give up that thought also and realisation is there.[9]

**59** To completely abandon the illusory creations of the ego-mind is the true vision of God, who transcends all concepts.

Ulladu Narpadu, *verses 21 and 22:*

> When scriptures speak of 'seeing the Self' and 'seeing God', what is the truth they mean? How to see the Self? As the Self is one without a second, it is impossible to see it. How to see God? To see Him is to be consumed by Him.
>
> Without turning inwards and merging in the Lord, His light that shines within the mind and lends it all its light, how can we know the Light of Lights with the borrowed light of the mind?[10]

**Bhagavan:** There is no one who has not seen God. God-vision is natural to all. Ignorance consists in not being aware of this natural experience of truth. As wrong knowledge is only the ego, the I-am-the-body idea, loss of ego means gaining God. Knowing oneself is knowing God, and knowing God is only abiding as the Self. As Self-realisation is God-realisation, Self and God are not different.[11]

**60** Forgetting the perfect and truly joyful state of abiding as God and getting caught in the mouth of the crocodile, the false and useless ego – this is indeed pitiable.

**61** *Padam*, consciousness, says: 'The mistake of getting bewildered about one's nature as the Self is the reason for complaining about God or oneself, and for self-pity.'

**62** Those who ask 'Where is God? He is not visible,' should enquire 'Who am I? Where am I?' and meet God there [where the answer is found].

**63** That which appears and shines, without another, in the space of the Heart, and which is encountered there, is the form of God.

**64** Realise that the scenes that expand before you in the form of the world are just a concept of the mind. Otherwise, see the world as the form of God.

**65** If everything that appears is a form of the vast God, how can attraction and aversion be appropriate?

**Question:** In the fifth stanza of *Arunachala Pancharatna* reference is made to seeing 'Your form in everything'. What is the form referred to?
**Bhagavan:** The stanza says that one should completely surrender one's mind, turn it inwards and see 'you', the Self within, and then see the Self in 'you' in everything. It is only after seeing the Self within that one will be able to see the Self in everything. One must first realise there is nothing but the Self and that he is that Self, and then only he can see everything as the form of the Self.[12]

**66*** God-vision is merely seeing everything that is perceived and known as the play of God, and [as a consequence] becoming calm.

**Question:** How is God to be seen?
**Bhagavan:** Within. If the mind is turned inward, God manifests as inner consciousness.
**Question:** God is in all – in all the objects we see around us. They say we should see God in all of them.
**Bhagavan:** God is in all and in the seer. Where else can God be seen? He cannot be found outside. He should be felt within. To see the objects, mind is necessary. To conceive God in them is a mental operation. But that is not real. The consciousness within, purged of the mind, is felt as God.[13]

**67** *Mauna jnana*, true knowledge of God, is only one. It is only in the knowledge of objects that there are many differences.
**68** Only he who dwells in the resplendent residence [*parandama*] as God [*paradevata*] is a *paradesi*.

*A* paradesi *generally denotes a foreigner or a wandering, begging monk. However, in this verse Bhagavan uses the word in a completely different sense.* Para *means supreme;* desa *means country;* desi *means a citizen of that land.*

**69** Only the resplendent abode [*parandama*], whose nature is consciousness of being and which surges as *bhuma* [the immanent reality], is the non-dual Self, the Supreme.

**Bhagavan:** *Bhuma* alone is. It is infinite. There arises from it this finite consciousness taking on an *upadhi* [limiting adjunct]. This is *abhasa* or reflection. Merge this individual consciousness into the supreme One. That is what should be done.
**Question:** *Bhuma* is an attribute of supreme consciousness.
**Bhagavan:** *Bhuma* is the Supreme – *yatra naanyat pasyati yatra naanyat srunoti sa bhuma* [where one does not see any other, hears nothing, it is *bhuma*]. It is indefinable and indescribable. It is as it is.
**Question:** There is a vastness experienced. Probably it is just below *bhuma* but close to it. Am I right?
**Bhagavan**: *Bhuma* alone is. Nothing else. It is the mind which says all this.[14]

## *Sivam*

### The nature of *Sivam*

*Saivas distinguish between Siva, the anthropomorphic form of God, and* Sivam, *the reality, the formless consciousness that is the real nature of Siva.*

**70** To call him 'The Three-Eyed One who bears the three radiant entities [sun, moon and fire]', is insulting to *Sivam*, whose nature is pure consciousness.
**71** Only the subtle space of consciousness, existing in the Heart, is the form of Siva. Everything else, described by words, is a concept.
**72*** The one who has realised the truth as his own real nature is assuredly of the form of *Sivam*.
**73** The existing truth of oneself is the great apple of the eye that deserves to be remembered, without forgetfulness, as the auspicious *Sivam*.
**74** The extremely pure clarity of Siva-experience exists in the thought-free consciousness that is present in the Heart.
**75** The realisation of the Self, pure consciousness of being, is the state of Sivahood, free from the mind-impurity.

**76** The state of union with *Sivam*, which is difficult to reach, is shining alone as being.

**77** There is not the slightest difference between Siva, his devotees and the *Puranas* that describe their greatness.

*This is similar to the popular Vaishnava idea that Bhagavan (God), his* bhaktas *and the* Bhagavatam *are all the same. Bhagavan alluded to this when he answered a query about some of his own writings:*

> **Question:** I have been reading the *Five Hymns*. I find that the hymns are addressed to Arunachala. You are an advaitin. How do you then address God as a separate being?
> **Bhagavan:** The devotee, God and the hymns are all the Self.[15]

### Knowing and becoming *Sivam*

**78** Non-existent to the senses, but cognisable through consciousness, *Sivam* shines as the reality, as 'I'.

> **Bhagavan:** There is no being who is not conscious and therefore who is not Siva. Not only is he Siva but also all else of which he is aware or not aware. Yet he thinks in sheer ignorance that he sees the universe in diverse forms. But if he sees his Self he is not aware of his separateness from the universe; in fact his individuality and the other entities vanish although they persist in all their forms. Siva is seen as the universe. But the seer does not see the background itself. Think of the man who sees only the cloth and not the cotton of which it is made; or of the man who sees the pictures moving on the screen in a cinema show and not the screen itself as the background; or again the man who sees the letters which he reads but not the paper on which they are written. The objects are thus consciousness and forms. But the ordinary person sees the objects in the universe but not Siva in these forms. Siva is the being assuming these forms and the consciousness seeing them. That is to say, Siva is the background underlying both the subject and the object, and again Siva in repose and Siva in action, or Siva and

Sakti, the Lord and the Universe. Whatever it is said to be, it is only consciousness whether in repose or in action. Who is there that is not conscious? So, who is not realised? How then can questions arise doubting realisation or desiring it? If 'I' am not *pratyaksha* [directly experienced] to me, I can then say that Siva is not *pratyaksha.*[16]

**79** If you remain without the 'I', the experience of becoming *Sivam,* the true *jnana-swarupa,* will unite with you.

**80** The great enemy for the noble and abiding experience of *Sivam* is the rising of the ego known as 'I'.

**81** In one's real nature, in which life exists as *Sivam,* the light, the feeling of degradation is an error [due to] fickleness of the mind.

**82** The way to attain the clarity of grace is to perform the Siva worship of completely ignoring anything that is other [than Siva].

**83** For a mind that wanders around, without getting firmly rooted in consciousness, it is impossible to know the pure *Sivam,* the fullness of being.

**84*** That which constitutes contemplation of *Sivam* is the natural calm state of the *jiva's* mind, free from thoughts of other things.

**Bhagavan:** The *jiva* itself is Siva; Siva himself is the *jiva.* It is true that the *jiva* is no other than Siva. When the grain is hidden inside the husk, it is called paddy; when it is dehusked, it is called rice. Similarly, so long as one is bound by karma one remains a *jiva;* when the bond of ignorance is broken, one shines as Siva, the deity. Thus declares a scriptural text. Accordingly, the *jiva,* which is mind, is in reality the pure Self; but, forgetting this truth, it imagines itself to be an individual soul and gets bound in the shape of mind.[17]

**85** It is a calamity to waste one's life pointlessly instead of having the mind rejoice in *Sivam.*

**86** Those who do not sacrifice themselves in *Sivam* will be drowned in *samsara* and will suffer intensely.

**87** The flood of supreme *Sivam* will flow into and merge with a submissive mind, putting out the fire of mental anguish.

**Siva *jnana***

**88** The effulgent *Padam* gives out this secret clue: 'Except for the beneficial Siva-*jnana*, there is no other sword to cut off the powerful bond of *samsara*.'

**89** Siva-*jnana* is just realising within oneself that individuality, the ego, is useless knowledge.

**90** Do not get drowned in the evil infatuation for the world but attain that glorious treasure which is the lofty Siva-*jnana*.

**91** Regarding the state of *mauna* as supreme, become firmly established in the life of Siva-*jnana*.

**92** In the extreme tranquillity of mind that rises from abidance in Siva-*jnana* it is impossible for the infatuation for the evil, worldly life to approach.

**93** Only the life in which inner and outer are harmonised will dam up and store the clear light of Siva-*jnana*.

# The Guru and the *Jnani*

Lord Arunachaleswara, who stands as the grace-bestowing Supreme, assumed the form of the *Brahman*-knowing Guru. His only wish is to transform the life of devotees into a blissful life that possesses the surging *jnana* that is devoid of ignorance.[1]

However much one may study, whatever *tapas* one may practise, no one has the power to bring about the loss of one's own ego. If [you ask me] 'How was it possible for me?' [I would reply] 'This wonder was the accomplishment of the great and enduring Lion-Guru, brought about by his luminous eyes.'[2]

Though one has shaken off all vices, secured all virtues, renounced all relatives, and observed all the austerities prescribed by the *sastras*, can one reach eternal bliss unless one meets the *jnana* Guru?[3]

# The Guru

## The true form of the Guru

1 The true form of the Guru can be known only if one realises, through the grace of the Guru, one's own real form.

> **Question:** How is one to decide upon a proper Guru? What is the *swarupa* [the real form or true nature] of a Guru?
> **Bhagavan:** He is the proper Guru to whom your mind is attuned. If you ask, 'How to decide who is the Guru and what is his *swarupa*?' he should be endowed with tranquillity, patience, forgiveness and other virtues capable of attracting others even with the bare eye, like the magnetic stone, and with a feeling of equality towards all – he that has these virtues is the true Guru. If one wants to know the true Guru *swarupa,* one must know one's own *swarupa* first. How can one know the true Guru *swarupa* if one does not know one's own *swarupa* first? If you want to perceive the true Guru *swarupa,* you must first learn to look upon the whole universe as Guru *rupa* [the form of the Guru]. One must have the *Gurubhavam* towards all living beings [that is, seeing everything as the Guru]. It is the same with God. You must look upon all objects as God's *rupa.* How can he who does not know his own Self perceive Iswara *rupa* or Guru *rupa?* How can he determine them? Therefore, first of all know your own real *swarupa.*[1]

2 Do not imprison the true form of the Guru within a cage but seek inwardly and realise it to be the formless, omnipresent expanse of consciousness.

3 Only the divine grace that wells up in abundance in the form of

the Guru can very easily put a stop to the dizzying whirl of the infatuated mind.

> In the Saiva Siddhanta tradition there are three impurities – *anava* (ego), karma and *maya* (illusion) – that prevent devotees from attaining the ultimate goal, oneness with the consciousness of Siva. Those who have all three impurities (*malas*) need a human Guru to realise *Sadasivam*, consciousness of Siva. Those devotees who are only afflicted by *anava* and karma can reach *Sadasiva* by having Siva appear before them in a physical form. Many of the devotees from the *Periyapuranam* would come into this category. Those in the third category, whose only *mala* is *anava*, can get enlightenment through the power of the Self within, without needing either a human Guru or the *darshan* of an external God. Bhagavan would be a good example of someone who became enlightened through the power of the Self alone. Since devotees who fall into the second and third category are quite rare, the necessity of a human Guru is stressed.

*The above explanation has been taken from an editorial note on page 118 of* Sri Ramana Darsanam. *The implication of this threefold division is that the human Guru is the most powerful vehicle through which grace can operate. Muruganar subscribed to this Saiva philosophical view since he has written the following words on Bhagavan's enlightenment:*

> The fact that the enquiry 'Who am I?' spontaneously arose in his [Bhagavan's] heart as a result of practice in past [lives], and the fact that he attained the ultimate state of perfection very easily merely by that enquiry – from these [facts] the discerning ones can realise that only a trace of *anava* remained as a cause for his final birth.[2]

*Earlier in the same essay Muruganar made a similar comment about Bhagavan: 'As a result of* tapas *performed in the past, only a little of the* anava *impurity was left over, and this was as thin as the wing of a fly…'*

*Elsewhere Muruganar has written: 'God reveals the truth to most people by appearing physically, assuming a form which is the embodiment of grace. To a few he appears by shining within as the* Self, *the pure consciousness that supports the mind. The way he appears will depend on the fitness of the aspirant.'*[3]

**4*** That which dwells within as the supreme Self is indeed that which sports before [you] as the very visible form of the Guru.

*Guru Vachaka Kovai*, verse 656: Those who have not realised the truth declare that reality does not have any form. You should know that the form of the one who abides as truth, who has enquired into and realised the truth – the space of consciousness as it truly is – is indeed the form of truth.
*Vilakkam*: Bhagavan here denies the fact that truth has no form. How? One who is in the natural state, having known the truth as it really is, and who abides as That, will not differ from that truth, and hence he is indeed the form of truth. This verse is an elucidation of the statement that 'the *jnani* is himself the Self'.

**5** The form of the *jnana*-Guru that bestows an abundance of grace is *Sivam*, who abides within oneself as pure consciousness.

**Bhagavan:** *Jnana* is given neither from outside nor from another person. It can be realised by each and everyone in his own Heart. The *jnana* Guru of everyone is only the Supreme Self that is always revealing its own truth in every Heart through the existence-consciousness 'I am, I am'. The granting of being-consciousness by him is initiation into *jnana*. The grace of the Guru is only this Self-awareness that is one's own true nature. It is the being-consciousness by which he is unceasingly revealing his existence. This divine *upadesa* [teaching] is always going on naturally in everyone. As this *upadesa* alone is what reveals the natural attainment of the Self through one's own experience, the mature ones need at no time seek the help of external beings for *jnana upadesa*. The *upadesa* obtained from outsiders in forms such as sounds, gestures and thoughts are all only mental concepts. Since the meaning of the word *upadesa* (*upa* + *desa*) is only 'abiding in the Self' or 'abiding as the Self', and since this is one's own real nature, so long as one is seeking the Self from outside, Self-realisation cannot be attained. Since you are yourself the reality that is shining in the Heart as being-consciousness, abide always as a *sthita prajna* [one who is established in wisdom] having thus realised your own true nature. This firm abidance in the experience of the Self is described in the *Upanishads* by such terms as 'the import of the *mahavakyas*', 'Supreme silence', 'Being still', 'Quiescence of mind', and 'Realisation of one's true nature'.[4]

## Worship of and surrender to the Guru

6 Since the divine form, the form of the Guru assumed by Iswara, is actually a physical embodiment of grace, that form is worthy of being worshipped.

7 Siva-*jnana-yoga* is remaining still through the never-diminishing grace of the Guru who bestows true *jnana*.

**Question:** While sitting near you, what sort of mental state should we have so as to receive the transmission from your Self?

**Bhagavan:** Keep your mind still. That is enough. You will get spiritual help sitting in this hall if you keep yourself still. The aim of all practices is to give up all practices. When the mind becomes still, the power of the Self will be experienced. The waves of the Self are pervading everywhere. If the mind is in peace, one begins to experience them.[5]

8* Grace will freely flow in a heart that, meditating upon the Guru as the true form of Lord Siva, becomes lost in adoration.

**Question:** Is it possible to gain knowledge without the blessings of a Guru? Even Rama, who was like a dullard in his early life, became a realised soul only with the help of his Guru.

**Bhagavan:** Yes, how can there be any doubts? The grace of the Guru is absolutely necessary. That is why Thayumanavar praised his Guru in his hymns, and another said, 'O Gurudeva, your look falling upon it, a tiger becomes gentle like a goat, a snake like a squirrel, and a bad man like a good man. And what else may not happen? With your gracious look everything becomes good. How can I describe your greatness?' Thus he sang. The Guru's grace is extraordinary.[6]

**9*** The greatness of noble disciples is that they obtain clear knowledge by trusting and believing in their heart that the Guru's form is the embodiment of grace.

**10** It is not ordained that noble disciples who have obtained the grace of the Guru, and who are therefore rejoicing in the Heart, shall feel fear and despair.

**Question:** What is Guru-*kripa* [Guru's grace]? How does it lead to Self-realisation?
**Bhagavan:** Guru is the Self... Sometimes in his life a man becomes dissatisfied with it, and, not content with what he has, he seeks the satisfaction of his desires, through prayer to God etc. His mind is gradually purified until he longs to know God, more to obtain his grace than to satisfy his worldly desires. Then, God's grace begins to manifest. God takes the form of a Guru and appears to the devotee, teaches him the truth and, moreover, purifies his mind by association. The devotee's mind gains strength and is then able to turn inward. By meditation it is further purified and it remains still without the least ripple. That calm expanse is the Self.

The Guru is both 'external' and 'internal'. From the 'exterior' he gives a push to the mind to turn inward; from the 'interior' he pulls the mind towards the Self and helps in the quieting of the mind. That is Guru-*kripa*. There is no difference between God, Guru and the Self.[7]

**11** The disciple who completely surrenders himself to the Guru will attain the life of true *jnana*, the auspicious life.

**12** If, like the goddess Uma, you offer only a half of yourself to the Guru, that will not be sufficient for attaining *jnana*.

*I suspect that Bhagavan may be speaking ironically here. Uma surrendered so completely to Siva that he bestowed on her half of his physical form. Alternatively, Bhagavan may be suggesting that, for full surrender to be effective, one must cease to exist as a separate entity. Union with God is not the aim of true surrender; the real goal should be the complete extinction of the sense of being an individual who can unite with God.*

> **Bhagavan:** Complete surrender means that you have no further thought of 'I'. Then all your predispositions [*samskaras*] are washed off and you are free. You should not continue as a separate entity at the end of either course [enquiry or surrender].[8]

*This interpretation is supported by the following verses, which are a continuation of the previous one about Uma.*

**13** The immaculate true *jnana* will only shine if you renounce the ego, the sense of individuality, leaving no remnant behind.

**14** Know that the surrender of the ego is in no way commensurate with the immortal state of perfection that one then attains.

**15** Attaining the Self by sacrificing the ego is like a business transaction in which one receives the true, ancient, primal essence in return for the reflection, the ego.

> **Muruganar:** Unless one pays for a thing in worldly life, it is not possible to get it. In the same way, in the life of the spirit, unless one offers oneself, which is the support of everything, it will not be possible to attain the primal, whole, being-consciousness-bliss, which is the reality, the supreme Self. When one compares the price, self-surrender, with the greatness of the reality, the supreme Self that is attained by offering it, the price for this exchange is extremely small.
>
> > Sankara [Siva]! You gave me yourself and took me [in exchange]! Who is the cleverer? I got endless bliss, but what did you get from me? (Manikkavachagar)
>
> As the great saint has written in the above verse, this barter or exchange is extremely profitable.[9]

***Namaskaram***

**16** The true meaning of *namaskaram* is the ego bowing its head and getting destroyed at the feet of the Guru.

Namaskaram *is a gesture of obeisance, often a full-length prostration on the floor.*

> *Guru Vachaka Kovai*, verse 207: This is the significance of the *namaskaram*: when the *jiva*, the imperfect one, places his proud head beneath the divine feet of his possessor, he is subduing the ego consciousness that says 'I' and merging with the Siva consciousness, which then rises and flourishes.

> *Guru Vachaka Kovai*, verse 310, *Pozhippurai*: The ignorant ego is the cause of the appearance of the utter delusion, the profitless sense of difference that regards the non-dual supreme reality, the *Atma-swarupa*, the real nature of Guru and Siva, as split up into Guru-disciple, Siva-*jiva*, and so on. The true meaning of the *namaskaram* that one performs to them [Siva and the Guru], fully aware and in a fitting manner, is only the *mauna* in which the ignorant ego does not arise even slightly in the Heart.
> *Vilakkam*: As only the knowledge of differences is *ajnana*, it is said to be 'the profitless sense of difference'. 'Knowledge of multiplicity is ignorance,' says *Ulladu Narpadu*. Unless the ego mind first rises, there will be no room for the appearance of differences, which are many. Therefore, the ego is the basis of all differences. Since the rise of the ego differentiates Guru and Siva from oneself, only the *mauna* in which the ego ceases is the truth of the *upasana* that unites them [Guru and Siva] with the Heart. While saying that *mauna* alone is the meaning of *namaskaram*, in addition he [Bhagavan] has described [in this verse] the nature of that *mauna*. It is this *mauna* that is described as 'pure *mauna*' by Thayumanavar.

**17** When the ego is totally destroyed at the feet of the Guru, it will then shine as the unsurpassed sea of *mauna* [silence].

> **Bhagavan:** Only the Supreme Self, which is ever shining in your Heart as the reality, is the *Sadguru*. The pure awareness, which is shining as the inward illumination 'I', is his gracious feet. The contact with these [inner holy feet] alone can give you true redemption. Joining the eye of reflected consciousness [*chidabhasa*], which is your sense of individuality [*jiva bodha*], to those holy feet, which are the real consciousness, is the union of the feet and the head that is the real significance of the word '*asi*'. As these inner holy feet can be held naturally and unceasingly, hereafter, with an inward-turned mind, cling to that inner awareness that is your own real nature. This alone is the proper way for the removal of bondage and the attainment of the supreme truth.[10]

*The word* 'asi' *refers to the* mahavakya 'tat tvam asi' *(you are that).* Asi *means 'are'. Bhagavan's metaphor indicates that the inner state of being is revealed when individuality is merged in the 'holy feet' of pure consciousness.*

**18** *Padam* [Bhagavan] communicates this truth: 'The meaning of the word '*nama*' [obeisance] is abiding as the Self, with the ego destroyed.'

> **Question:** Swami, I have only one desire, namely to put my head on Bhagavan's foot and do *namaskar*. Bhagavan must grant me this favour.
> **Bhagavan:** Oh, is that the desire! But then which is the foot and which is the head?
> **Questioner:** [No reply.]
> **Bhagavan:** Where the self merges, that is the foot.
> **Question:** Where is that place?
> **Bhagavan:** Where? It is in one's own Self. The feeling 'I', 'I', the ego, is the head. Where that *aham vritti* [the 'I'-thought] dissolves, that is the foot of the Guru.[11]

### The primal Guru, Dakshinamurti

**19** The excellent teaching that the primal Guru Dakshinamurti gave to the great ascetics was *mauna,* his own unique method.

**Bhagavan:** Silence is never-ending speech. Vocal speech obstructs the other speech of silence. In silence one is in intimate contact with the surroundings. The silence of Dakshinamurti removed the doubts of the four sages. *Mauna vyakhya prakatita para brahma tattvam* ['Who expounds the knowledge of supreme *Brahman* through silence']. Silence is said to be exposition. Silence is so potent.

For vocal speech, organs of speech are necessary and they precede speech. But the other speech lies even beyond thought. It is, in short, transcendent speech or unspoken words, *para vak.*[12]

**Bhagavan:** Silence is ever-speaking; it is a perennial flow of language; it is interrupted by speaking. These words obstruct that mute language. There is electricity flowing in a wire. With resistance to its passage, it glows as a lamp or revolves as a fan. In the wire it remains as electric energy. Similarly also, silence is the eternal flow of language, obstructed by words.

What one fails to know by conversation extending to several years can be known in a trice in silence, or in front of silence – e.g., Dakshinamurti, and his four disciples.

That is the highest and most effective language.[13]

**20** That silent speech untied the *chit-jada* knot [the connection between the insentient body and consciousness] of the disciples and destroyed their minds that ramified with differentiating thoughts.

**21** If the doubts that could not be dispelled by the many oral instructions were dispelled by that *mauna*, what power that *mauna* has!

*In none of the traditional accounts of Dakshinamurti's life does Dakshinamurti ever speak. However, when Bhagavan narrated this story, he sometimes said that Dakshinamurti initially attempted to communicate his teachings verbally, but without success. It was only when he sat in silence that his four* rishi*-disciples understood what his teachings were and realised the Self. When Muruganar once remarked that he had never read this version of events in any book, and asked Bhagavan for the* *source of this story, Bhagavan replied , 'But this is exactly what happened'.*

*Muruganar concluded from this that Bhagavan was Dakshinamurti himself, and that his knowledge of this particular incident was a personal memory of having sat in silence in front of the four sages.*[14]

**22** No one has the ability to describe the power of the grace of the Guru abiding in *mauna*.

> **Question:** What are the marks of the Guru's grace?
> **Bhagavan:** It is beyond words and thoughts.
> **Question:** If that is so, how is it that it is said that the disciple realises his true state by the Guru's grace?
> **Bhagavan:** It is like the elephant which wakes up on seeing a lion in its dream. Even as the elephant wakes up at the mere sight of the lion, so too is it certain that the disciple wakes up from the sleep of ignorance into the wakefulness of true knowledge through the Guru's benevolent look of grace.[15]

### Unqualified teachers

**23** Some wicked people conceal deceit in their heart through their dress and their external conduct and pose as great *jnanis*.

> **Question:** How can one know whether a particular individual is competent to be a Guru?
> **Bhagavan:** By the peace of mind found in his presence and by the sense of respect you feel for him.
> **Question:** If the Guru happens to turn out incompetent, what will be the fate of the disciple who has implicit faith in him?
> **Bhagavan:** Each one according to his merits.[16]

**24** If one takes those who are fake *jnanis* to be genuine *jnanis* and suffers, this is merely the work of one's deluding *prarabdha*.

*'Deluding* prarabdha*' in this context means immaturity.*

**25** Those ignorant people with their proud minds will be greatly hurt by their half-baked understanding.

**26** You who set your heart on thriving and flourishing as a teacher [of others]! First become an enquirer, and enquire into your own self.

**27** Only he who has eradicated the disease of delusion within his own nature can be a *jnana* doctor who cures the disease of delusion in others.

**28** Before you embark on treating the disease of others, first completely destroy your own disease, and only then start your practice.

> *Guru Vachaka Kovai*, verse 804: O doctor! Since it is said that one must be the doctor for oneself, before you embark on giving us treatment, first treat your own disease, and then come.

**29** Indeed, how can he who does not know how to diagnose and dispel his own disease dispel the cruel disease of others?

# The *Jnani*

## The *jnani* is God himself

1 Upon thorough investigation, it will be known that those who possess the greatness of the immensely vast and noble Self are Iswara [God] himself, for their nature is divine.

> **Bhagavan:** The gods and the sages experience the infinite continuously and eternally, without their vision being obscured at any moment. Their minds are surmised by the spectators to function; but in fact they do not. Such surmise is due to the sense of individuality in those who draw inferences. There is no mental function in the absence of individuality. Individuality and mind functions are co-existent. The one cannot remain without the other.[1]

> **Bhagavan:** God and the *jnani* are identical. To know oneself as pure consciousness distinct from the body is to know God. God consciousness is not different from one's real nature, pure consciousness. Knowing God is only being the Self. The supreme spirit [*Parabrahman*] and the *jnani* who has the firm experience of the Self are identical because of the experience of adjunct-free being-consciousness. [2]

2 Because Iswara shines as their own *swarupa*, love for Iswara has become natural for true *jnanis*.

3 Any offering to a Siva-*jnani*, who shines having attained liberation, is an offering to Siva.

## The existence of *jnanis* benefits the whole world

4 Those great ones who have obtained as their right the state of oneness are indispensable not only for a life of grace but also for the life of the world.

**Bhagavan:** The sage helps the world merely by being the real Self. The best way for one to serve the world is to win the egoless state. [3]

**Question:** Some say that to make an effort for one's liberation is selfish, and that instead of that, one should do good to others by selfless service.
**Bhagavan:** Those people believe that *jnanis* are selfish and that they themselves are selfless, but this is not a true belief. The *jnani* lives in the experience of *Brahman* and the effect of this experience spreads all over the world. A radio transmission is done from one point but its effect can be felt all over the world. Those who would like to benefit from it can do so. Similarly, the Self-realisation of the *jnani* spreads everywhere and whosoever wants can tune into it. This is not a lesser service. [4]

5 If the mere existence of the *mauna jnanis* who have swallowed the mind is service to God, what else is there [for them] to do?
6 It is impossible to describe the greatness of a *jnani* who, by merely living on this earth, confers the greatest benefit on the world.

**Bhagavan:** A Self-realised being cannot help benefiting the world. His very existence is the highest good. [5]

**Bhagavan:** Realisation of the Self is the greatest help that can be rendered to humanity. Therefore, the saints are said to be helpful, though they remain in forests. But it should not be forgotten that solitude is not in forests only. It can be had even in towns, in the thick of worldly occupations.
**Question:** It is not necessary that the saints should mix with people and be helpful to them?
**Bhagavan:** The Self alone is the reality; the world and the rest of it are not. The realised being does not see the world as different from himself.
**Question:** Thus then, the saint's realisation leads to the uplift of humanity without the latter being aware of it. Is it so?
**Bhagavan:** Yes. The help is imperceptible but is still there. A saint helps the whole of humanity, unknown to the latter.

**Question:** Would it not be better if he mixed with others?
**Bhagavan:** There are no others to mix with. The Self is the one and only reality.
**Question:** If there be a hundred Self-realised men will it not be to the greater benefit of the world?
**Bhagavan:** When you say 'Self' you refer to the unlimited, but when you add 'men' to it, you limit the meaning. There is only one infinite Self.[6]

## Worship of *jnanis*

7 Because they have had their mental delusions removed and, as a result, have woken up from the sleep of *samsara*, you should honour *jnanis* as beings who are worthy of being worshipped.

8 Honour and cherish the *jnani* who lives in a walking temple more than a god who lives in a big temple surmounted by fluttering flags.

**Bhagavan:** Whatever outward shape they [*jnanis*] may have, *sishya* [disciple], *bhakta* [devotee] *udaseena* [the unconcerned] and *papatma* [sinner], all the people in these four categories are protected through the grace of the *jnanis.* The *sishyas* worship them as Gurus, ascertain the truth and attain *mukti* [freedom from bondage]. *Bhaktas* pray to them as the *swarupa* [real form] of God and get release from their sins. *Udaseenas* listen to what the Guru says, get enthused and become devotees. Sinners hear the stories from people that come and go and get release from their sins. People in these four categories are protected by the grace of *jnanis.*[7]

## Association with *jnanis*

9 Only by coming into contact with *jnanis* who are exalted by the goodness of *jnana* can the world associate with conduct that is full of the sanctity of love.

**Question:** It is said that one look of a *mahatma* [great soul] is enough; that idols, pilgrimages, etc. are not so effective. I have been here for three months, but I do not know how I have been benefited by the look of Maharshi.

**Bhagavan:** The look has a purifying effect. Purification cannot be visualised. Just as a piece of coal takes long to be ignited, a piece of charcoal takes a short time, and a mass of gunpowder is instantaneously ignited, so it is with grades of men coming in contact with *mahatmas*.[8]

**10** Those who have obtained the good fortune, the grace of the *jnani* who has destroyed infatuation, will bathe in the sorrow-free bliss of liberation.

**11** They are meritorious ones who have obtained association with *jnanis*, who enjoy bliss by remaining still as pure consciousness in the Heart.

**Bhagavan:** The opportunity to be in the company of a *Sadguru* comes effortlessly to those who have performed worship of God, *japa, tapas*, pilgrimages, etc. for long periods in their previous births. There is a verse by Thayumanavar which points out the same thing: 'O Lord of the first and last, those who properly start the worship of idols, holy places and sacred waters will meet the *Sadguru* who will tell them the words of truth.'

Only he who has done plenty of *nishkamya punyas* [meritorious actions performed without any thought of a reward or consequence] in previous births will get abundant faith in the Guru. Having faith in the Guru's words, such a man will follow the path and reach the goal of liberation.[9]

**12** Let the conduct of your life be such that it harmonises with that of *jnanis* whose nature manifests proper behaviour, and who are full of the light of *jnana*.

## Satsang

**13** Attachment to the mischievous and harmful ego is bad association [*dussanga*]. Satsang, which destroys that attachment, is abiding as the Self, the 'I am'.

**14** To remain in association with *Atma-swarupa*, consciousness, the supreme, is satsang. It is not proper to stay away from the Self, the supreme being.

**Question:** All that I want to know is whether satsang is necessary and whether my coming here will help me or not.
**Bhagavan:** First you must decide what is satsang. It means association with *sat* [being] or Reality. One who knows or has realised *sat* is also regarded as *sat*. Such association with *sat* or with one who knows *sat* is absolutely necessary for all. Sankara has said that in all the three worlds there is no boat like satsang to carry one safely across the ocean of births and deaths.[10]

**15** Only when you leave the Self, the cool shade, do all miseries approach and scorch you, tormenting your mind.
**16** It is fitting to remain in the company of those noble ones who have realised the truth, forsaking the path of those people who are deluded, degenerate and ignorant.
**17** If you come into the company of the most virtuous, the *jnanis*, that true relationship will bestow on you the supreme benefit of liberation.

Bhagavan once drew my [Devaraja Mudaliar's] attention to the statement in *Yoga Vasishta* that the place of *moksha* has four gate keepers, that one of these is satsang, and that if we make friends with any of the gatekeepers we can easily secure admittance. Bhagavan quoted to me on different occasions the following stanzas also:

> To stay where a *jnani*, who is none else but the supreme Self, stays is *mukti* [liberation]. He who serves a *jnani* is so great that I permanently bear on my head his feet. None can equal the spotless and supreme *jnani*, neither Siva, Vishnu nor I, Brahma. Who else then can equal him?
>
> The imperfect will become perfect, danger, good luck, inauspicious, auspicious by association with holy men. For those who have bathed in the Ganga of such company, *homam*, *yajna* [both of these are vedic rituals], penance, almsgiving, bathing in sacred rivers are all unnecessary. Seek

therefore by all means the company of the great and wise, which is a boat to carry one across the ocean of births.[11]

**18** If you have the society of true devotees who are established in the Self and who are therefore abiding forever in sorrow-free bliss, you yourself will reach the state of bliss.

### Behaviour of *jnanis*

**19** The actions of a *jnani* need not conform to any plans or schemes formulated by other people.

*Though* jnanis *often seem to act in response to the desires or pleas of their devotees, their behaviour can occasionally appear to be irrational. In the first of the following two quotations Bhagavan explains some of the factors that lie behind a* jnani's *behaviour, while in the second extract, Chalam describes some of the strange and inexplicable incidents he witnessed in Bhagavan's presence:*

> **Bhagavan:** *Prarabdha* [the actions the body has to perform in this life] is of three categories, *ichha, anichha, and parechha* [personally desired, without desire and due to others' desire]. For him who has realised his Self, there is no *ichha-prarabdha.* The two others, *anichha* and *parechha* remain. Whatever he does is for others only. If there are things to be done by him for others, he does them but the results do not affect him. Whatever be the actions that such people do, there is no *punya* [merit] and no *papa* [sin] attached to them.[12]
>
> Many different types of people came to see Bhagavan: high officials, lowly beggars, rich people, ascetics, devout pilgrims, pretty women, and many more besides. All of them wanted Bhagavan's attention, but none of them ever discovered a way of ensuring that they got it. Some, who came with many questions, could not manage to get even a single word from him. But while they were trying, Bhagavan might unexpectedly call out to someone else, enquire about his welfare and talk with him about many things. Sometimes Bhagavan would get irritated with

someone for no apparent reason and treat him very harshly. Some people would be scolded or made fun of in front of every one else till all present laughed at them.

Once, when a devotee went home after visiting Bhagavan, he had a dream in which Bhagavan asked him to come back to the ashram. It was not convenient for the devotee to return, but nevertheless he still rushed back to the ashram. He went straight to the hall but Bhagavan did not even bother to look at him. For several days Bhagavan neither smiled at him nor enquired about his welfare. During those days Bhagavan talked in an animated way to many other devotees. He spoke to them all with great love and made many enquiries about their well being, but the returning devotee was ignored.

Bhagavan would often give a lot of attention to people who, to my eyes, were merely showing off. I saw one man, who seemed to be filled with self-importance, holding a book and a pencil and paper in front of him. He put a question to Bhagavan and then looked around at the audience with an obvious show of great pride. Bhagavan, surprisingly, spoke to him at great length on quite an insignificant matter. But while this was going on, other people who had come from a distant place and who were in a hurry to go back there, had to wait for a number of days to have their doubts cleared.

The events, activities and dialogues in the hall often seemed, to uninformed observers, to have a bizarre or irrational character, but that was only because they were not aware that the power of Bhagavan orchestrated the scene in such a way that everything that needed to happen happened automatically. One inexplicable incident might be a message for one devotee in the hall. That devotee might understand the import of the message and consequently find his devotion or faith increasing. The rest of us, not knowing the full circumstances, would merely be bewildered. Or, in another case, Bhagavan might notice that the ego of a devotee sitting before him was rising and rebuke him in some way. The others in the hall might interpret this as an unprovoked attack, but from Bhagavan's point of view, it was what that devotee needed at that particular time.[13]

**20** Though a *jnani* may sometimes behave like a madman in the world, he will always be remembering his real nature, consciousness.

*Though Bhagavan himself lived an exemplary life, he readily admitted that socially acceptable behaviour was not necessarily a consequence of enlightenment. The following story, narrated by Bhagavan, provides a good example of this position:*

> 'Kaduveli Siddhar was famed as a very austere hermit. He lived on the dry leaves fallen from the trees. The king of the country heard of him, saw him, and offered a reward for the one who would prove this man's worth. A rich *dasi* [temple dancer] agreed to do it. She began to live near the recluse and pretended to attend on him. She gently left pieces of *poppadum* along with the dry leaves picked by him. When he had eaten them, she began to leave other kinds of tasty food along with the dry leaves. Eventually, he took good tasty dishes supplied by her. They became intimate and a child was born to them. She reported the matter to the king.
>
> 'The king wanted to know if she could prove their mutual relationship to the general public. She agreed and suggested a plan of action. Accordingly, the king announced a public dancing performance by that *dasi* and invited the people to it. They gathered there and she also appeared, but not before she had given a dose of physic to the child and left it in charge of the saint at home.
>
> 'The dance was at its height; the child was crying at home for the mother. The father took the babe in his arms and went to the dancing performance. She was dancing hilariously. He could not approach her with the child. She noticed the man and the babe. She contrived to kick her legs in the dance so as to unloosen one of her anklets just as she approached the place where the saint was. She gently lifted her foot and he tied the anklet. The public shouted and laughed, but he remained unaffected. To prove his worth he sang a Tamil song meaning:
>
>> 'For victory let go my anger! I release my mind when it rushes away. If it is true that I sleep day

and night quite aware of my Self, may this stone burst into two and become the wide expanse!

'Immediately a stone idol burst with a loud noise. The people were astounded.'

Sri Bhagavan continued, 'Thus he proved himself an unswerving *jnani*. One should not be deceived by the external appearance of a *jnani*.'[14]

**21** Only knowledge of reality is identical in all *jnanis*. All other things will be of many different natures.

**Question:** Though Janaka was a *jnani*, he was a ruling monarch, but his Guru, Yajnavalkya, who was also a *jnani*, renounced the world and went to the forest. Why was this so?

**Bhagavan:** All happens according to the destiny of each *jnani*. Krishna was an enjoyer of pleasures whereas Sukdev was an ascetic. Janaka and Rama were kings while Vasishta was a believer in activities. All of them were *jnanis*. Their inner experience was the same while their external lives were in accordance with their respective destinies.[15]

**22** Only duplicitous people who lack discrimination lead a life of secrecy. The lives of those who have obtained *jnana* will be an open book.

*For much of his life Bhagavan lived in places that were open to the public twenty-four hours a day. From 1928 till the early 1940s, a period when he was living in what is now called 'the old hall', the only time he was behind a locked door was when he went to the bathroom. Devotees who had problems had the freedom to go and see him even in the middle of the night.*

## Learning from *jnanis*

**23** Do not follow the path of the ignorant, those who know no better. Reach for and take as your most excellent refuge the feet of *jnanis*.

**24** It is proper to learn the truth only from those *jnanis*. If it is learned from anyone else, it will be known incorrectly.

**25** Other than by hearing and knowing it from the lips of those who have seen and known it, we know of no other 'royal road' to realising *jnana*.

*Guru Vachaka Kovai*, verse 1158, *Pozhippurai*: After careful investigation one must say that the *jnani* who has realised the truth and the scholar who has mastered the *jnana*-scriptures are quite different. Consequently, the proper course for those who are attempting to free themselves from the bondage of ignorance is to forsake those scholars and resort to those who, abiding as the Self, have realised the Supreme.

*Vilakkam*: Unless one resorts to someone who abides as the Self, the experience of *jnana* is not attained. This is why Bhagavan speaks in this way. The benefit that comes from mere scriptural knowledge is only fame and adulation in this world.

**26** Humility and self-restraint are the marks of those transformed and radiant beings who embody the quality of virtue.

*Guru Vachaka Kovai*, verse 332, *Pozhippurai*: Only those who have realised the truth are those who possess faultless virtues. Other than them, everyone else is only base-natured. Hence, he who longs for the fortune of liberation should redeem himself only by resorting to those already-mentioned meritorious ones, who shine as reality through the knowledge of reality, which is devoid of the world-delusion.

*Vilakkam*: All the rare virtues automatically seek and reach those who have realised the truth through purity of mind. Hence, in order to emphasise that only they deserve to be called virtuous who are naturally replete with all the noble traits, it has been said 'Only those who have realised the truth are those who possess faultless virtues'. In those people who do not have true *jnana*, even though they may be extremely virtuous in the external conduct they observe, the ego that is the source of all evil traits remains in their hearts without perishing. Therefore it was said: 'Everyone else is base-natured.' While all other things may be obtained from [these unenlightened] people, the knowledge of reality – that which bestows the bliss of peace, the redemption that is free of the mind – can only be obtained from these meritorious ones. Those who are fit to become Gurus have been indicated.

**27** The books speak of the characteristics of *jnanis* in order that you should cherish these [characteristics] appropriately in your heart and gain salvation.

**28** Therefore, approach a *jnani* and, strengthened by the knowledge that his is the fair form of the Lord himself, conduct yourself accordingly.

**29** Follow not the path of the many, but cleave to the way of those who are noble, great and good [*jnanis*].

**30** In order to become exalted, study and learn the magnificent *jnana-achara* in the company of sages who are established in being, and then practise it with devotion.

Achara *generally refers to conduct or behaviour. In this particular case it refers to the behaviour, or the spiritual practice, that will bring about* jnana.

**31** The teachings of true *jnanis* who are established in the experience [of the Self] will bestow the light of truth on those who meditate on them [the teachings] in their heart.

*Guru Vachaka Kovai,* verse 1159: For *jivas* who have fallen under the sway of darkness, and who have long been deluded, the words uttered by a *jnani*, he who has known the reality that sustains everything by the power of [its] grace, will always be a redeeming anchorage to cling to.

## *Siddhis* [supernatural powers] and *jnanis*

**32** The eight great *siddhis* will reach the presence of and will sport before those whose hearts are naturally established in Self-abidance.

**33** Those who rejoice, having subsided in *Sivam*, will not pay even the slightest attention to these [*siddhis*] that only cause sorrow.

*Guru Vachaka Kovai*, verse 221: In a heart that has caught fire through the spreading flames of the blazing fire of supreme devotion, the entire collection of *siddhis* accumulate simultaneously. However, because true devotees have the desire to become a complete prey to the feet of their Lord, they will not feel, even slightly, any desire for them.

**34** Before the self-effulgent attainment of Siva *jnana*, all other *siddhis* will slip away, being defective.

**35*** Even if many wonderful *siddhis* reach them, in the hearts of true *jnanis* there is no infatuation for them.

**36** Describing through [his] *siddhis* the realised state of a *jnani*, which surges, transcending the mind, is a delusion of the mind.

*Guru Vachaka Kovai*, verse 1168: Because *mukti* alone is the attainment of *swarupa*, the *jivanmukta* shines in the state of the Self either in association with *siddhis* or separated from them. The greatness of a *jivanmukta* will be underestimated when *siddhis* alone are used as the yardstick instead of the truth. You should know that those ignorant ones who esteem *siddhis* will not know the greatness of the *jivanmukta*.

*Guru Vachaka Kovai*, verse 1169: The world abounds in lunatics who trivialise the grandeur of a *jnani*, who rests and shines in the utter beyond, by imagining, through their unworthy, ignoble and deluded perspective, [that he has] many *siddhis*.

*Guru Vachaka Kovai*, verse 1170: This you should know: attributing greatness to a perfect one who shines as the Self because he has *siddhis* is like fulsomely praising the greatness of the perfectly effulgent sun by describing the greatness of the crowd of specks seen in a bright sun beam that enters a house.

## Enlightened Life

### The ego-free life

**37** Only in a sage who has vanquished the dishonourable delusion known as 'I' will all the actions that are performed become yoga.

*Yoga in this context does not imply any striving to accomplish anything. It implies abidance in the state of union with the Self. In a similar vein Bhagavan has said on other occasions that all the actions of* jnanis *are acts of worship.*

**38** Only those enlightened ones who have completely renounced the 'I' can act as benefactors, granting boons.

**39** When the ego that made one forget the Self has been destroyed, one rises resurrected as the *Atma-swarupa*. That life of the Self is imperishable.

> **Question:** In the *jnani* the ego subsists in the sattvic form and therefore it appears as something real. Am I right?
> **Bhagavan:** No. The existence of the ego in any form, either in the *jnani* or *ajnani,* is itself an appearance. But to the *ajnani* who is deluded into thinking that the waking state and the world are real, the ego also appears to be real. Since he sees the *jnani* act like other individuals, he feels constrained to posit some notion of individuality with reference to the *jnani* also.
> **Question:** How then does the *aham-vritti* [the 'I'-thought] function in the *jnani*?
> **Bhagavan:** It does not function in him at all.[16]

**40** Living in the world with the worthless ego destroyed is like witnessing a battle of rutting elephants from the vantage point of a mountain peak.

*The rutting elephants are the egos of the unenlightened. One implication of this image is that the* jnani *is safe and secure on his mountain vantage point, whereas the unenlightened are all in danger. The* jnani *stands aloof from all the fights and battles of the world, seeing them as a projection that is ultimately unreal:*

> **Bhagavan:** The external universe is a cinema show to the realised man. It is free and the performance goes on day and night. He lives and works in it knowing that its objects and bodies are illusory appearances, just as an ordinary man knows the scenes and characters on the cinema screen

at a theatre are illusions, and do not exist in real life. But the ordinary man takes the external objects of daily life as real, whereas the realised one sees them only as illusory cinema pictures.[17]

**41** Those who are abiding in *Padam*, with their egos destroyed, are true devotees, steadfast as a mountain.

**The enlightened perspective**

**42** In the natural life in which both inner and outer have become harmonious, worldly life and godly life will become one.

**Question:** What is the difference between the *baddha* and the *mukta,* the bound man and the one liberated?
**Bhagavan:** ...The ordinary man lives in the brain unaware of himself in the Heart. The *jnana siddha* [the one who has attained *jnana*] lives in the Heart. When he moves about and deals with men and things, he knows that what he sees is not separate from the one supreme reality, the *Brahman* that he realised in the Heart as his own Self, the real.
**Question:** What about the ordinary man?
**Bhagavan:** I have just said that he sees things outside himself. He is separate from the world, from his own deeper truth, from the truth that supports him and what he sees. The man who has realised the supreme truth of his own existence realises that it is the one supreme reality that is there behind him, behind the world. In fact, he is aware of the One, as the real, the Self in all selves, in all things, eternal and immutable, in all that is impermanent and mutable.[18]

**43*** Because of the majestic outlook of *Brahman*, karma [action, activity] is not different from *Brahman*.
**44** Living as the Self is the essence of all *dharmas*. All other *dharmas* merge there.

*Guru Vachaka Kovai*, verse 705: Since the impartite, non-dual, true *jnana*, abides and shines as the refuge for all *dharma*-observances, the *jnani* [alone] becomes the one

who has observed all the *dharmas*.
*Vilakkam*: Since non-dual *jnana* alone shines as the refuge for all the *dharmas*, the *jnani* who is established in that state [automatically] becomes the one who has observed all *dharmas* impeccably. There is no greater *dharma* than getting firmly established in the Self. All the actions of that *jnani* who possesses motionless consciousness are actions of God.

**45** Associating with the world in a harmonious way, householders will conduct themselves from the secure viewpoint of their own Self-nature.
**46** The great ones who stand triumphant in this world are those who have fully realised in their hearts the One, which is of the form of consciousness.
**47** That boundless existence attained by the great sages who know it as final liberation is the most fitting and excellent state.
**48*** For those who conduct themselves in such a way that they do not deviate from the noble path [the path of *sat*], every state is equally and pleasingly acceptable.
**49** In the hearts of *muktas* who delight in the sweet savour of *mauna*, none of the tastes of food and drink will find a hold.

*The phrase 'tastes of food and drink' in Tamil implies perceptions of all the other senses as well.*

**50** Conducting oneself in such a way that one sees even oneself as *anyan* [other, apart] is living the life of abiding in the Self, consciousness.

*The word* anyan*, here translated as 'other, apart', in this context means completely detached from the body.*

**Bhagavan:** Only that man has desires who identifies himself with the body. But the sage has become free from the thought 'I am the body'. The sage looks upon his own body as if it were the body of another.[19]

*The* jnani *knows himself to be the unmanifest Self, not just the body that it animates. From that perspective the body is sometimes seen to be something that is 'other', something that is not a real and fundamental part of his being. This was brought out by a verse Bhagavan composed in January 1946:*

> The body is impermanent. Whether it is at rest or moves about and whether by reason of *prarabdha* it clings to him or falls off from him, the Self-realised *siddha* is not aware of it, even as the drunken man blinded by intoxication is unaware whether his cloth is on his body or not.[20]

*On other occasions Bhagavan compared his body to a leaf-plate that could be discarded after the meal had been eaten, and to a load that a worker has carried a long distance. The worker, said Bhagavan, looks forward to discarding his load, knowing that it is something 'other', something he can happily live without. As the next verse indicates, the Self is the true reality that can never be destroyed or discarded.*

**51** Those who have realised the truth will subjugate and conquer even Yama [the god of death] through the power of their *jnana* that shines as a result of their *tapas*.

**52** The real is that which cannot be destroyed, and that which can be destroyed is not the real. One who knows this to be the truth is a wise one.

**53** Those who are established in consciousness, the Self, who have uprooted the ego, the infatuation, will live as glorious beings, born through the grace of God.

**54** That state in which peace abounds through the full attainment of Self-knowledge is a most exalted condition, the highest of the high.

**55** Only those who, as enquirers, have realised their true nature shining within their hearts, are brahmins, possessors of *jnana*.

**56** A brahmin is one who has a heart that possesses the true *jnana* experience and cool compassion in his mind.

*Though the word 'brahmin' generally denotes a member of a particular caste, the etymology of the word can also make it mean 'one who knows* Brahman*'.*

**57** Those who are struggling hard every day to flourish in the artificial life [of the world] have not thought about the natural life [of *jnana*] that bestows true contentment.

**58*** For the *jnani* who has become firm by his renunciation, everything is only good, and nothing is repugnant.

**59** The experience of the Self in which arises an exhilarating indifference that says: 'To me, what does it matter where the sun rises?' is truly a wonder.

**60** In this world appearance that shines as many differences, what the true *jnani* relishes is the light of consciousness.

# The Mind and its Creations

O Mind, it is not wise for you to come out. It is best to go within. Hide yourself deep within the Heart and escape from the tricks of *maya*, which tries to ruin you by drawing you outwards.[1]

[O Mind,] do not waste your life in roaming outside, pursuing wonders and wallowing in enjoyments. To know the Self through grace and to abide in this way firmly in the Heart is alone worthwhile.[2]

Even if the *jiva* gives up all other attachments, eminence is only [to be found] in the cessation of the attachment to the flawed mind. Only the mind, the great delusion, is the fetter. Nothing else can bind the *jiva* in the same way [that the mind can].[3]

If the mind is transcended, all else, which does not exist apart from the mind, is transcended also.[4]

# The Nature of the Mind

## The obdurate nature of the mind

1 The intrinsic purity of your own Self-nature was corrupted on account of your worthless mind.

2 It is the mind that deceives you and imprisons you within the body, deluding and tormenting you.

3 Those who are ensnared by the countless and endlessly diverse appearances of the mind have been caught in the net of bondage.

4 The very nature of the degraded mind that has been spinning endlessly since time immemorial is to distort one thing into another.

5 The defect of the mind is to connect [wrongly], making it appear as though the nature of one thing is the nature of another.

6 You can only experience joy if you first put an end to the mischief of the mind that rushes about continuously, grasping then letting go of one thing after another.

7 It is through the mask [of the mind], adhering in the form of infatuation, that the blissful enjoyment of salvation, the Self, has become hidden from view.

8 The mind that dishonours consciousness [by ignoring it] will be whirled around in a world of falsity and, as a consequence, will become confused.

9 Ignoble, ignorant and deluded people will get whirled around by the droll dance of the shrunken, limited and deceitful mind.

10 Those who revel in drinking the milk of the mind [indulging in fancies] will not have the wisdom to drink the milk of grace-bestowing Nandini.

*Nandini is a celestial cow, a divine being. In this analogy she signifies the Self.*

11 As mind itself is a defective entity, so long as the mind survives it will be impossible to gain the fullness of perfect contentment.

**Muruganar:** Human beings, who are, in reality, immortal get into a deluded state of consciousness through being intoxicated with the liquor known as mind. What a pity! They suffer and die as mortals. When they have got rid of this intoxication caused by the liquor, on that very day they will shine, attaining again their natural and immortal state. The mind is death and takes the form of forgetfulness of the Self. This is the truth discovered by our Maharshi. The first man and woman, Adam and Eve, were created by God as his own reflection, but ate the forbidden fruit, transgressing the command of God. Thus, not only they, but all their descendants lost their divine nature and were ruined forever. In this story, found in the Old Testament, it is the mind that is the forbidden fruit. It is the mind, the wonderful *maya sakti*, that makes the impossible appear as possible, confuses good with evil and evil with good. It is impossible for the mind to determine the eternal truth of one's true nature... The connection one has with the mind should be completely destroyed.[1]

**12*** A feeling of deficiency only arises because of the mind-deficiency. In truth, no one has any kind of lack.

**13** True *jnana* is completely incompatible with attachment to the world, which arises from delinquent delusion, the mind-defect.

**14** *Padam* warns: 'It is hard indeed for those who are deluded, taking mind-consciousness to be the truth, to discern the nature of the real.'

**15** How can one apprehend one's real nature that shines, transcending all concepts, with a mind that has spread out and expanded itself with concepts?

### Associating with mind, the demoness

**16** Do not associate with the mind that rises like the goddess who smites men with love. Destroy it by abiding in the Self.

**17** Should you succumb to its spell and embrace it, alas, it will destroy your life by drowning you in the intoxication of pride.

**18** That demoness, the mind, is extremely adept at amorously caressing you with false pretences.

**19** Heed this warning! From now on, stay away from that utterly sinful woman, without even mentioning her name.

20 That woman, the mind, is a great demoness whose embrace brings death to all.

21 She somehow deceives everyone and brings them under her spell. She is an extremely cunning woman, a thief who practises deception.

22 This murderess, this beautiful and seductive woman, is a despicable sinner who has totally ruined the lives of many a *sadhaka*.

23 She is an evil, low-born woman who hates and torments your lawfully wedded wife, peace.

## Understanding and transcending the mind

24 Since consciousness is reality, in order to know reality why is it necessary to associate with the movements of the mind?

25 Those who possess a mind that roams about in the false concept [the world] will not know the consciousness, the supreme, and even if they do know it, they will be perplexed [by it].

26 If one enquires into the matter, it will be known that remembering, forgetting, and so on, all belong to the mind. They do not exist in the Self.

27 Knowing and not knowing are only for the mind that experiences the non-Self. They do not belong to the Self.

28 Do not grieve, taking yourself to be the mind, but merge with the inner peace through the attainment of knowing yourself to be the reality.

29 Do not struggle with the mind, regarding it as something real. If you enquire within and know what it is, it will cease to exist.

> **Bhagavan:** To ask the mind to kill the mind is making the thief the policeman. He will go with you and pretend to catch the thief, but nothing will be gained. So you must turn inward and see where the mind rises from, and then it will cease to exist.
> **Question:** Is not asking the mind to turn inwards and seek its source also employing the mind?
> **Bhagavan:** Of course we are employing the mind. It is well known and admitted that only with the help of the mind [can the mind] be killed. But instead of setting about saying there is a mind, and I want to kill it, you begin to seek the source of the mind, and you find the mind does

not exist at all. The mind, turned outwards, results in thoughts and objects. Turned inwards, it becomes the Self.[2]

**Question:** What is the difference between the mind and the Self?
**Bhagavan:** There is no difference. The mind turned inwards is the Self; turned outwards, it becomes the ego and all the world. The cotton made into various clothes we call by various names. The gold made into various ornaments we call by various names. But all the clothes are cotton and all the ornaments gold. The one is real, the many are mere names and forms.

But the mind does not exist apart from the Self, i.e., it has no independent existence. The Self exists without the mind, never the mind without the Self.[3]

**Question:** How shall we discover the nature of the mind i.e., its ultimate cause, or the noumenon of which it is a manifestation?
**Bhagavan:** Arranging thoughts in the order of value, the 'I' thought is the all-important thought. Personality-idea or thought is also the root or the stem of all other thoughts, since each idea or thought arises only as someone's thought and is not known to exist independently of the ego. The ego therefore exhibits thought-activity. The second and the third persons do not appear except to the first person. Therefore, they arise only after the first person appears, so all the three persons seem to rise and sink together. Trace, then, the ultimate cause or 'I' or personality.[4]

**30** For those who do not realise their real nature as the unchanging supreme reality, the whirling [of their minds] will not be stilled.

### Merging the mind in the Heart

**31** Do not use your mind to enquire in the heart about anything other than your own real nature.

**32** If mind-consciousness subsides into the source from which it arose, the experience of being, absolute perfection, will unite with you here and now.

33 A mature mind that has managed to establish itself firmly in the extremely subtle state of pure being will not get enmeshed in the tangle of the world.

34 When mind exists holding onto the reality alone, which is consciousness, one's own nature, this constitutes true life.

**The dead mind**

35 The delusion-filled mind has caused *samsara* to merge with you. It will cease when that mind is completely destroyed.

> *Guru Vachaka Kovai*, verse 920, *Pozhippurai*: The ego will not die by any means other than Self-attention. Similarly, the misery-filled world appearance, which is seen like a dream, will not be destroyed by any means other than the total destruction of the mind.
> *Vilakkam*: The complete destruction of the false, illusory, body-ego will not be possible except through knowledge of reality, the undivided consciousness, the *Atma-swarupa* that abides as the substratum of everything. Similarly, since the world is wholly mind [*manomaya*], except by the destruction of the mind, the world concept will not cease.

36 Upon the destruction of the mind, the appearance of the world that adheres to you in the state of harmful delusion will stand illustrious as pure consciousness.

37 Even the gods in the heavens cannot stir those deeply peaceful ones who shine, having killed their minds.

> **Bhagavan:** It is in the mind that birth and death, pleasure and pain, in short, the world and ego exist. If the mind is destroyed all these are destroyed too. Note that it should be *annihilated,* not just made latent. For the mind is dormant in sleep. It does not know anything. Still, on waking up, you are as you were before. There is no end of grief. But if the mind be destroyed, the grief will have no background and will disappear along with the mind.[5]

38* The mind that has died in pure consciousness, mere being, will surge forth, resurrecting itself as *bhuma* [the all-pervasive reality].

**Muruganar:** That which frightens people into regarding the natural state as real death is false knowledge in the form of individuality. It is for this reason that ignorance has to be destroyed prior to liberation, which is pure consciousness, the reality. Know that it is this death that is praised by synonyms such as 'destruction of ego', 'self-surrender', 'loss of ego', *manonasam* [destruction of the mind] and *vasana kshaya* [destruction of *vasanas*], which is the final means of liberation. The decad lamenting 'I am not yet dead' in the *Tiruvachakam* also speaks of this same aspect. Saint Pattinathar also instructs, 'Wander around like a dead person'. The statements of the great ones expressing the same idea are innumerable.[6]

**39** Only when everything shines as consciousness alone can the mind-impurity be said to have perished.

**40** True *jnana*, the experience of *Sivam* that rises in a dead mind, will, extending to the very heavens, leap and surpass [everything].

## The Self is *guna*-free

*The next five verses in this chapter describe the enlightened state as being* guna*-free. The* gunas *are the three modes or qualities of mind –* sattva *(harmony or purity),* rajas *(excitement or activity) and* tamas *(sloth or torpor). The three* gunas *are held by several schools of Indian philosophy to be the fundamental components of physical manifestation as well as the mind. As some of the preceding verses make clear, one logical consequence of the mind dying is that the world too vanishes since they are both composed of the same fundamental* gunas.

*Some of the schools of thought that incorporate the interplay of the* gunas *in their theories about the mind and the world maintain that the state of* sattva *is the state of the Self, and that the fluctuating mind actually comprises only* rajas *and* tamas. *In some of his replies Bhagavan took this position himself. However, I suspect that he did so only when he was speaking to people who subscribed to this particular view, or to people who felt uncomfortable with the notion of a mind that was truly dead. I would take the following five verses to be a trenchant presentation of Bhagavan's real views on this subject.*

**41*** It is impossible for the attribute-free Self to abide except in the hearts of those in whom the mind, which takes the form of the three *gunas*, is dead.

42 He who has renounced the fraudulent mind has renounced the three *gunas*. He has emerged [into true vision] after completely ripping up the cataract of delusion.

43 He who has not seen and embraced the infinite expanse of *mauna* will be snared by the threefold *gunas* and suffer in the degraded world.

44 Only he who has destroyed the *guna*-mind that wells up, burying the *swarupa*, is a *gunatita* [one who has transcended the three *gunas*].

45 The magnificent nature of the life that has transcended the mind is not disturbed in any way whatsoever by any of the *gunas*.

### Killing the mind

46 Unless the mind is destroyed, it is not possible to attain the fortune of clarity, the life of living in God's grace.

47 The means for realising one's true nature as the Self is to kill off the base mind known as 'I'.

> **Bhagavan:** *Atman* is realised with the *mruta manas* [dead mind], that is, mind devoid of thoughts and turned inwards. Then the mind sees its own source and becomes that [the Self]. It is not as the subject perceiving an object.[7]

48 Know that the one direct path [*vichara*] that eliminates the despicable *pramada* is the means to destroy the mind.

49 Unless the force that activates thought is driven deeply within and destroyed, it is impossible to enjoy one's own experience of *jnana*.

> **Bhagavan:** By enquiry, you will drive the thought force deeper till it reaches its source and merges therein. It is then that you will have the response from within and find that you rest there, destroying all thoughts, once and for all.[8]

50 So long as you do not kill the harmful and illusory association, the prostituting mind, there will be neither bliss nor good conduct.

**Muruganar:** In having no settled principles, nothing else matches the mind. Its perception and evidence are completely unreliable. Its nature is to prostitute itself. At an opportune moment for deceiving the *sadhaka*, it will jump outwards towards sense objects. So long as the mind survives, its nature will not change. Hence, the mind should be destroyed at its roots by unceasing *dhyana* and *vichara*. Until the mind has been destroyed, no sensible aspirant should remain satisfied and think that he has accomplished all that needs to be done.[9]

**51** Only when the mind dies through discriminating enquiry, will it come to shine by itself as '*Sivoham* [I am Siva]'.

**52** There are no effective means other than *vichara* to chase out the ego from within you and kill it.

*Guru Vachaka Kovai*, verse 885: Except by the path of enquiring into the mysterious clue [the *aham-vritti*, the 'I'-thought], irrespective of how much effort one makes following all the other paths such as karma [*bhakti*, yoga and *jnana*], such effort cannot enable one to attain and enjoy the Self, the treasure shining in the Heart.

**53** Only if you enquire and realise the Self in the Heart will the bond, the mind that is the obsession for the false, be destroyed.

**Question:** How to destroy the mind?
**Bhagavan:** Seek the mind. On being sought, it will disappear.
**Question:** I do not understand.
**Bhagavan:** The mind is only a bundle of thoughts. The thoughts arise because there is the thinker. The thinker is the ego. The ego, if sought, will vanish automatically. The ego and the mind are the same. The ego is the root-thought from which all other thoughts arise.
**Question:** How to seek the mind?
**Bhagavan:** Dive within. You are now aware that the mind rises up from within. So, sink within and seek.[10]

**54** True life will only be attained if you destroy the degraded mind, which shamelessly dotes upon the fleshy body, by not showing any affection towards it.

55 The mind that has died in the experience of *Sivam*, which is true *jnana*, supreme consciousness, will of itself shine as the supreme being.

56 That exquisitely subtle mind which, in dying, has transcended all form, will come to shine as your own Self.

# *Suttarivu*

## *Suttarivu* is a false consciousness

*Suttarivu is a Tamil word that denotes the unreal consciousness that divides itself into objects of perception and a perceiver who sees them. It is sometimes translated here as 'objectifying consciousness', 'objectified consciousness', 'objective knowledge' or 'relative knowledge'. Usually, though, the original term is retained since there is no brief phrase in English that fully brings out all its connotations. It usually denotes knowledge by a knower of objects that are perceived either mentally or physically. When there is true knowledge,* jnana, *consciousness does not divide itself into knower and known, or seer and seen.*

1 *Suttarivu* is a fraudulent consciousness arising in the wicked ego-mind. It is the scheming of the conceptualising [mind].

2 Though the *Atma-swarupa* is one's own true nature, the reason why it appears difficult to attain is because of the powerful illusion wrought through *suttarivu*.

3 That which exists is only the one consciousness. The many conceptualised varieties of objectified consciousness are only an imaginary notion in that which is.

4 For those who conclude that *suttarivu* is real and immerse themselves in it, the Self will be violated, their consciousness will be bewildered, and their mind will gasp for breath.

5 That objective awareness which adheres to you, appearing to be distinct from consciousness, *Atma-swarupa*, is a deception.

6 If you imagine that reality is different from you, then the consciousness that thinks so is false.

7 To entertain the doubt that the supreme reality, which is devoid of all objectification, is a void, is indeed a deception perpetrated by the false, objectifying consciousness.

8 It is because of the infatuation with objective knowledge that the splendour of the boundless Self appears to be a void.

9 If Self-consciousness is unreal [*asat*] and insentient [*jada*] in nature, then tell me how objective knowledge [*suttarivu*] exists for you?

*Bhagavan is saying here that the false consciousness,* suttarivu, *is dependent on the real consciousness for its existence. He then propounds the notion that the mere existence of* suttarivu *is an indirect proof of a more abiding consciousness that supports and sustains it.*

### Seeking the Self through *suttarivu* is futile

10 It is foolishness to suffer by desiring and struggling to know the Self in the same way that sense objects are known by the *suttarivu*.
11 It is not possible to see the eye with the eye. [In the same way] it is not possible to see the Self with *suttarivu*.
12 One's real nature, which exists and shines beyond duality within the Heart, will not be revealed to the eye of the bewildered mind.
13 The struggle to know that non-dual Self through objective knowledge mediated by the senses, with its consequent delusion and distress, is indeed a wonder.
14 It is only because the Self shines as you, and as not different from you, that it has become impossible for you to attain it through your *suttarivu*.
15 Pray tell, how can the real nature of the Self reveal itself and shine to the *suttarivu*?

### The necessity of eliminating *suttarivu*

16 Until [objectified] consciousness subsides, having become a prey to the light of the Self, the misery of birth will never cease.
17 Unless you thoroughly burn up the objectifying tendency of the mind, destroying it utterly, you will not attain one iota of Self-knowledge.
18 Not reflecting upon one's true nature, the reality behind the objective knowledge that causes the non-Self to shine, is [spiritual] poverty.
19 The experience of the bliss of blemishless, true *jnana samadhi* will abide in a heart in which the *suttarivu* has perished.

### Ending *suttarivu*

20 If we enquire into the means for the destruction of bondage, it is

[through] the perfect wisdom in which the objectifying tendency of the mind is totally destroyed.

21 Knowledge of the reality of the knower terminates mind-consciousness, the *suttarivu* that knows the non-Self.

22 Confusion, the whirling of the mind that is *suttarivu*, will not cease except by internal renunciation.

23 Turning your face against the consciousness that binds, merge with that pure consciousness in which there is no bondage, and which is full of the light of truth.

24 The cavorting mind, *suttarivu*, will not die except by consciousness of the truth of the real nature of the thinker.

25 If the objectifying consciousness is brought under the spell of the Self, all that was formerly known [objectively] will become one with the *jiva*.

## *Triputis*

*The* triputis, *the trinities of seer, seeing and seen and knower, knowing and known are an inevitable consequence of* suttarivu, *the divided consciousness. When one abides in consciousness as consciousness alone, all these distinctions are recognised to be unreal.*

26 So long as you are confused, regarding yourself as the knower, you are not [experiencing] the truth of the [real] nature of the knower.

27 Listen to this secret: apart from consciousness, all the dualities and trinities are completely illusory.

Ulladu Narpadu, *verse 9:*

> 'Twos' and 'threes' depend upon one thing, the ego. If one asks in one's heart, 'What is this ego?' and finds it, they slip away. Only those who have found this know the truth, and they will never be perplexed.[1]

28* The supreme truth remains as the source not only for the objects seen but also for the seer and the seeing.

29 From the perspective of union with the Supreme, which is the state of pure being, the *triputis* have reality. However, seen apart from it, they are false.

30 The *triputis* appear as a reflection in the mirror of the mind like a sleight-of-hand conjuring trick.

31 Those who do not see the world as their own Self and become its support will get caught up and drown in the *triputis*, which adhere to them through ignoble delusion.

*'Become its support' means being the screen on which the world appears.*

32 Only in the false stupor, the darkness of ignorance, can the separated fragments of the *triputi*-scene occur.

> **Bhagavan:** The light must be dim in order to enable the ego to rise up. In broad daylight a rope does not look like a snake. The rope itself cannot be seen in thick darkness, so there is no chance of mistaking it for a snake. Only in dim light, in the dark, in light darkened by shadows or in darkness lighted by dim light does the mistake occur of a rope seeming [to be] a snake. Similarly, for the pure radiant being to rise up as the ego – it is only possible if its light is diffused by darkness.[2]

> **Bhagavan:** In a cinema show you can see the pictures only in a very dim light, or in darkness. But when all the lights are switched on, the pictures disappear. So also in the floodlight of the supreme *Atman*, all objects disappear... The world can be seen neither in the utter darkness of ignorance, as in deep sleep, nor in the utter light of the Self, as in Self-realisation or *samadhi*.[3]

33 All the *triputis* sprout and dance from the sordid delusion [*moha*], which is [the consequence of] ignorance, the absence of enquiry.

34 Being insubstantial reflections, they disappear in the very instant that the light of *jnana vichara* falls upon them.

35 [When] all sense objects are known to be consciousness alone and the confusion caused by the *triputis* has ceased, this is *jnana*.

### Distinctions and differences are unreal

*Distinctions and differences are only perceived when the* suttarivu *and its inherent* triputis *are functioning. When true knowledge causes them to disappear, distinctions and differences vanish.*

**36** The feelings arising from pairs of opposites [such as joy and misery], which result from the confusion of the distorted mind, cannot exist in the non-dual *jnana*.

**37** Once your consciousness has become clear, all differences will disappear and everything will appear as the nature of your own self [*tanmaya*].

**38** The distinctions, sentient [*chetana*] and insentient [*achetana*], are negated in the perspective of the resplendent consciousness of the Self.

> **Question:** There is differentiation made between the sentient and the insentient [*chit* and *jada*] in the opening verse of *Upadesa Saram*.
> **Bhagavan:** The *Upadesa* is from the standpoint of the hearer. There is no truth in the insentient [*jada*]. One whole consciousness prevails all alone.[4]

**39** Why do you regard yourself as the form of the mind, perceive all the differences and get frightened?

**40** Differences are only perceived by the ego. When the ego has departed, there is nothing that is seen as 'other'.

**41** The clarity in which the sense of difference [*bheda-buddhi*] does not arise is the extreme perfection [*paripurna*] that exists as consciousness of being.

## Perceiving and pursuing sense objects

**42** This world that appears so wonderful consists merely of names and forms. Transient as a bubble, it exists only at the level of the five senses.

**43** The impressions of the five senses that adhere to you are a monumental edifice created by the frenzied mind merely to ensure its own prosperous existence.

**44** Do not let your attention dwell on the concept [that is the world]. Stop perceiving sense objects and know that the world is merely a dream.

**45** Why give up the marvellous experience of peace by desiring imaginary and degraded [sense] enjoyments?

46* The mind is *Brahman* when the desire for the five sense objects, which arises through the expansion of the mind, has left.

47 The base form of consciousness always pays attention to the five sense perceptions, seeing them as objects. The superior consciousness attends to itself and remains merged with itself.

48 Those who are enjoying the excellent bliss of *samadhi*, knowing their real nature, will not get deluded by what is false and then seek objects perceived by the five senses.

> *Guru Vachaka Kovai*, verse 947, *Pozhippurai*: If one enquires, through the inward enquiry 'Who am I?', one knows authoritatively, through direct experience, that one is not the ego – which ceases, being a mere word – but *Atma-swarupa*, the real import of the 'I'. Afterwards, what can be desired, and for whom? Will that true supreme *jnani* experience mental anguish by desiring some enjoyment that is apart from himself?
>
> *Vilakkam*: Because he [the *jnani*] is the non-dual *Atma-swarupa*, the undivided bliss, neither any *jiva* nor any bliss exists apart from himself. This is why it was said, 'what can be desired and for whom?'
>
> The *Tirukkural* [368] states: 'To those without desires, misery ceases to exist; if desire is there, misery will arise increasingly and unceasingly.'
>
> Therefore, without desire, misery will not arise. Hence, it was stated above: 'Will that true supreme *jnani* experience mental anguish by desiring some enjoyment that is apart from himself?' The meaning is: the *jnani* has attained the state of perfection [*purna*] in which one does not know anything other than the Self.

49 For those who are enjoying in their Heart the bliss of *swarupa*, which is free from anxiety, there is nothing enjoyable in the objects perceived by the five senses.

**Time**

*It may seem curious to include a section on time at this point, but it should be remembered that in Bhagavan's teachings time and space, and the inevitable divisions that are inherent in them, are all part of the false consciousness, the* suttarivu *that projects a false world and simultaneously an observer who sees it.*

**50** That which exists is only the present. Past and future are encountered when the present is disregarded. They are opposed to the present.

Ulladu Narpadu, *verses, 15, 16:*

The past and future exist depending upon the present; they too, while occurring, were and will be the present. Therefore [among the three times] the present alone exists. Trying to know the past and the future without knowing the truth of the present is like trying to count without [the number] one.

On scrutiny, where is time and where is space, [where is anything] except 'we', the clearly known existing reality? If we are the body, we shall be involved in time and space, but are we the body? Since we are one now, then, and ever, one in space, here, there and everywhere, 'we', the timeless and spaceless 'we', alone are.[5]

*The pronoun 'we' in the second verse refers to the Self.*

**51** That which is perceived as time and space is nothing other than reality, the Self that is pure consciousness.

**52** Destruction is only for time and space. There is absolutely no movement for the Self, the supreme reality.

**Question:** It is said in the *Puranas* that the *kaliyuga* consists of so many thousands of years, and that so much of it has passed, and that so much yet remains, etc. May I know when this *yuga* is to end?

**Bhagavan:** I don't consider time real. So, I take no interest in such matters. We know nothing about the past or the *yugas* which were in the past. Nor do we know about the future. But we know the present exists. Let us know about it first. Then all other doubts will cease. [After a pause] Time and space always change. But there is something which is eternal and changeless. For example, the world and time, past or future, nothing exists for us during sleep.

But *we* exist. Let us try to find out that which is changeless and which always exists. How will it benefit us to know that the *kaliyuga* started in such and such a year and that it would end so many years after now?[6]

**53** Give up forever the 'tomorrow', which is false, and which never exists, and know the truth of today.

**54** Those who do not realise the present firmly in their heart, which is the truth, will be lost in the other [times, past and future] through joy [and misery].

# Individual Identity

## The nature of the *jiva*

1 *Jiva*-nature – the ignorant ego that does not remain in the pure, true, *jnana vichara* – is a non-existent entity.

*Jiva, the individual self, is an unreal entity that appears to come into existence by wrong association. The following sequence of verses, in which Lakshman Sarma summarises Bhagavan's teachings on this topic, makes this clear:*

> 396 Since it is settled that the one named *jiva* does not exist, how can we think of its bondage or deliverance? There is neither bondage nor deliverance for the real Self, who remains unswervingly whole and solitary.
>
> 397 The soul [the *jiva*] comes to be taken as real by the failure to discriminate rightly. This occurs when there is false identification between the body, which is limited in space and time, and the Self, who is only consciousness, unlimited by space and time.
>
> 398 First one assumes that one particular body is 'I'. Then one assumes that the body is real. Once this happens, the ignorant man sees other bodies as being real, and sees different *jivas* in them.
>
> 402 The man who has not experienced his own real Self, thinking 'I am this body', sees himself as 'I', the first person of grammar. He sees another person whom he calls 'you', and refers to third persons as 'he'.
>
> 403 These three distinct persons are not real. They are seen on account of the false notion 'I am the body'. When the ego-soul is lost as a result of the quest of the real Self, only that Self, consciousness alone, will shine.
>
> 404 To one who thinks himself to be a *jiva* or a body, a

plurality of *jivas* will appear. But to the sage who is freed from this ignorance, no *jiva* will appear.[1]

2* If the delusion of the *jiva*, the false I-am-the-body idea, is destroyed, the nature of the *jiva* will be the form of true bliss, *Sivam*.

Aksharamanamalai, *verse 73:*

With some magic powder you stupefied me, robbed me of my *jiva*-hood and revealed instead your Siva-hood.[2]

3 The *jiva* that has been parted from the ego will shine as the superlative space of consciousness, transcending the furthest extremities of the universe.

### *Jiva* associating with the mind

4 For your *jiva*, the only true connection is with the state of bliss. How, then, is there association with the miserable world?

**Question:** If the *jiva* is by nature identical with the Self, what is it that prevents the *jiva* from realising its true nature?
**Bhagavan:** It is forgetfulness of the *jiva's* true nature; this is known as the power of veiling.
**Question:** If it is true that the *jiva* has forgotten itself, how does the 'I'-experience arise for all?
**Bhagavan:** The veil does not completely hide the *jiva;* it only hides the Self-nature of 'I' and projects the I-am-the-body notion; but it does not hide the Self's existence which is 'I', and which is real and eternal.[3]

5 None of the adherents of the [different] faiths can explain how the delusion of association with the mind has arisen for the *jiva*.
6 Know that the *jiva* suffers like a fool because of its close association with that buffoon, the mind.
7 Unless the activity of the senses that operate through the consciousness of the *jiva* totally ceases, it will be extremely difficult to achieve union with that divine consciousness, which is the bliss of the Self.

8 The state of existing as a *jiva*, which makes its living by changing its form endlessly, is one of extreme shame.

9 Now that you have seen and become aware of this wonder, which is an injustice, from now on at least, it will be proper to embrace the life of truth.

10 Wasting away through failing to see the light that shines as the source of life is indeed the misfortune of the *jiva*.

## *Jiva* returning to its source

11 Until the *jiva* knows that its own essential nature is matchless bliss, it will, like the musk deer, be confused.

> *Guru Vachaka Kovai*, verse 1028: The musk deer carries the fragrant musk within itself. Not knowing this fact, and believing that the fragrance comes from a source outside itself, it wanders everywhere, searching for it. In the same way, only those who are not able to realise that their own *swarupa* is bliss will be bewildered, seeking sense objects, imagining that they are the source of their happiness. But those who are able to realise their *swarupa* properly will abide in their own state, without pursuing the world.

12 If the *jiva* parts company with the clarity of consciousness, it will not find intimacy anywhere else.

13 Only the unique truth of oneself can become the haven for the *jiva*. Other than this, no other truth exists anywhere at any time.

> The cause of all misery and evil, beginning with the birth experienced by *jivas*, is forgetfulness of the way they came. This is illustrated by the following story.
>
> In the hall where Bhagavan used to give *darshan* there was a chimney. The chimney was closed on all sides with steel mesh, except at the bottom. One day, a beautiful small bird somehow entered it and became trapped inside this chimney. The bird found itself trapped in conditions diametrically opposed to its natural environment: the vast space where it could fly freely. From the moment it entered the chimney, it was frantically struggling to escape, but all its efforts proved futile. Why? Because, forgetting the

way it came, it was repeatedly trying to escape through all the closed routes. Sri Bhagavan took this opportunity to reveal a great truth:

'This bird has given up the all-pervasive space, its natural place of residence. It has been caught in this limited space, which is opposed to its nature. Not knowing how to escape from this prison, it is agitated and afraid. Like this bird, *jivas* have also given up their natural place of residence, the vast space of consciousness. Through the delusion of ignorance they have become trapped in the prison of the body. Without knowing how to escape, they are tormented by various afflictions. The ceaseless efforts of this bird to reach its natural place of residence are unsuccessful because they are directed upwards, the way of bondage, instead of downwards, the way it came. Similarly, the reason why the *jiva's* ceaseless efforts to attain freedom are unsuccessful is because they too are directed outwards, the way of bondage, instead of inwards, the way they came. The natural tendency of the bird to go upwards asserts itself even in its attempt for freedom. Likewise, the natural tendency of *jivas* to roam outwards asserts itself even in their attempts at liberation. This is the *jiva's* natural tendency. If, through true discrimination and awareness, the *jiva* is made to turn back from outward-directed sight to inward sight, and if it remains fixed there, it is certain that it would attain liberation in an instant.'[4]

**14** For the *jiva* there is no refuge other than truth. Therefore, enquire and know your own truth, which is extremely close to you.

**15** Only when the life of the *jiva* blossoms into *Sivam* will it be possible for it to attain the true love that knows no misery.

**16** If the *jiva* is not filled with clarity, which is the *prasad* of the mind, what can other kinds of *prasad* do?

**17** If the *jiva* remains without the *suttarivu*, in that state it will clearly see itself as the immaculate, pure *swarupa*, free from limitations.

*Guru Vachaka Kovai*, verse 646: The revelation of grace, which does not shine when viewed through *suttarivu*, shines when that *suttarivu* perishes: 'When I stare hard at my beloved, she looks at the ground, but when I do not look at her, she looks at me and smiles.'

*The quoted material in the second half of the verse comes from* Tirukkural, *verse 1094.*

**18** Wherever the mind may roam, forgetting its own nature, its final destination is only the Self.

Arunachala Ashtakam, *verse eight:*

> The raindrops showered down by the clouds, risen from the sea, cannot rest until they reach, despite all hindrance, once again their ocean home. The embodied soul from you proceeding may through various ways self-chosen wander aimless for a while, but cannot rest till it rejoins you, the source. A bird may hover here and there and cannot in mid-heaven stay. It must come back the way it went to find at last on earth alone its resting place. Even so, the soul must turn to you, O Aruna Hill, and merge again in you alone, ocean of bliss.[5]

**19** The main obligation of the *jiva* is to absorb into the Self that objective consciousness [*suttarivu*] that knows the non-Self, so that ignorance is destroyed.

**20*** Except in *mauna*, wherein delusion has been completely cleared away, union with the Self is not possible for the *jiva*.

## The liberation of the *jiva*

**21*** The spiritual practice adopted by the *jiva* becomes complete upon the destruction of the ego at its source.

**22*** Like the moth [in the flame], a *jiva* on which the shining light of *swarupa* has fallen will be annihilated, becoming the supreme.

**23** The experience of *Atma jnana*, the realisation that one is bodiless, is the liberation of the *jiva* who regarded himself as the body.

**24** For the *jiva* who has realised the truth, that truth itself will help in uniting it with liberation.

**25** Only he in whom the 'I' is dead will know the union of the *jiva* with the supreme, which is the full, non-dual [experience].

**26*** The *jiva* that has succeeded in annihilating its ego-ridden mind in the Self, which is pure consciousness, will itself become consciousness, the supreme.

27* For the good *jiva* that has attained *jnana*, grace, there is never ever any *pramada* [forgetfulness of the Self], the darkness of ignorance.

28 In the *Atma-swarupa*, the supreme, *pramada* is always a complete folly for the *jiva*.

29 Drowning [the *jiva*] in the Heart in such a way that no thought arises for any reason – this is the grace, the power of the Self, who is the Lord of the *jiva*.

## The unreality of the ego

30 Neither in this world nor anywhere else does there exist for you a malevolent enemy like the ego.

31 Enquire within and know the source of the ego so that the ego departs and the experience of *Atma-swarupa* surges.

32 If you enquire within yourself and know the nature of the powerful ego-ghost, then, like the [presumed] best man, it will run away and disappear.

**Bhagavan:** In a Hindu marriage function, the feasts continue five or six days. A stranger was mistaken for the best man by the bride's party and they therefore treated him with special regard. Seeing him treated with special regard by the bride's party, the bridegroom's party considered him to be some man of importance related to the bride's party and therefore they too showed him special respect. The stranger had altogether a happy time of it. He was also all along aware of the real situation. On one occasion the groom's party wanted to refer to him on some point. They asked for him. He scented trouble and made himself scarce. So it is with the ego. If looked for, it disappears. If not, it continues to give trouble.[6]

**Bhagavan:** Reality is simply the loss of the ego. Destroy the ego by seeking its identity. Because the ego is no entity it will automatically vanish and reality will shine forth by itself. This is the direct method. Whereas all other methods are done, only retaining the ego. In those paths there arise so many doubts and the eternal question remains to be tackled finally. But in this method the final question is the only one and it is raised from the very beginning. No *sadhanas* are necessary for engaging in this quest.

There is no greater mystery than this – *viz.*, ourselves being the reality we seek to gain reality. We think that there is something hiding our reality and that it must be destroyed before the reality is gained. It is ridiculous. A day will dawn when you will yourself laugh at your past efforts. That which will be on the day you laugh is also here and now.[7]

**33** Like an onion, the ego-appearance is an unreal thing that consists of a combination [of many *tattvas*]. When enquired into, it will be found to have no *swarupa*.

*When every layer of an onion has been peeled away, there is no onion left.* Swarupa *here means 'ever-present and inseparable nature'.*

**34** As long as the ego exists, how can one see, with a ramifying mind, the truth of oneself?

**The ego-ghost**

**35** The ego that becomes embroiled in the multitude of moving pictures, which gets tossed about and suffers as a result, is a worthless phantasm.

**36** The droll dance of the ego-ghost, whose form is the body, the dirty vessel of filth, will ruin the immortal life.

**37** Binding one thing tightly to another is the profession of the ignoble ghost, the mind, the deceiving association.

Ulladu Narpadu*, verses 25, 26:*

What a wonder it is! This ghostly ego which is devoid of form comes into existence by grasping a form; grasping a form it endures; feeding upon forms which it grasps, it waxes more; leaving one form it grasps another; when sought for it takes to flight. Know thus.

If the ego, the root, comes into existence, all else will come into existence. If the ego does not exist, all else will not exist. Verily, the ego is all! Hence, scrutinizing 'What is it?' is indeed giving up all. Know thus.[8]

38 Those true devotees who have come under the sway of grace will not get deluded, becoming possessed by the ego-ghost.

39 There is nothing as insubstantial as the ego-ghost that remains firmly established, refusing to leave.

40 It is impossible to imagine the suffering experienced by this world through the sovereignty exercised by that ego ghost.

41 Only through the application of the *vibhuti* of *jnana vichara* will the ghost be exorcised.

*In India it is traditional in some places to use* vibhuti, *sacred ash, during exorcism rituals. Bhagavan is saying here that self-enquiry, enquiry into the nature of true consciousness, is the exorcism ceremony that will effectively banish the ego-ghost.*

42 Not only will it be exorcised, it will get beheaded and destroyed before your very eyes.

**Association with the ego**

43 What benefit have you gained by associating with an ego, which is just a thought that attaches itself to you?

44 To the ego-mind of ignoble people, the *Atma-swarupa* that is consciousness, the supreme, is very, very far away.

45 Seeing him, the ego, the degraded *chandala*, is defilement. Even hearing about him is defilement. He is an untouchable.

*A* chandala *is an outcaste. In Bhagavan's time such people were deemed to be 'untouchables', and were shunned by all caste Hindus. Bhagavan's advice here is to treat the ego in the same way that society treated outcastes, and by doing so avoid the degradation and defilement that comes from wrong association. In* Talks with Sri Ramana Maharshi, *talk no. 308, he remarked, 'The non-Self is untouchable. The social untouchability is man-made, whereas the other untouchability is natural and divine.'*

46 Unless one knows oneself as the witness, ignorance, which takes the form of the ego, will not be removed.

## Ego, the cause of suffering

**47** The ego that deludes you through forgetfulness will unsettle you, becoming the enemy of your stability.

**48** A life in which the ego-ghost, which possesses desire and attachment, dances is a desolate hell of corruption and ruin.

> **Bhagavan:** That bliss of the Self is always with you, and you will find it for yourself, if you would seek it earnestly. The cause of your misery is not in the life without; it is in you as the ego. You impose limitations on yourself and then make a vain struggle to transcend them. All unhappiness is due to the ego; with it comes all your trouble. What does it avail you to attribute to the happenings in life the cause of misery which is really within you? What happiness can you get from things extraneous to yourself? When you get it, how long will it last?
>
> If you would deny the ego and scorch it by ignoring it, you would be free. If you accept it, it will impose limitations on you and throw you into a vain struggle to transcend them. That was how the thief sought to 'ruin' King Janaka.
>
> To be the Self that you really are is the only means to realise the bliss that is ever yours.[9]

**49** In the certain knowledge of the Self, wherein the ego dies completely and is resurrected, mental anguish completely ceases.

**50*** If even a trace of the ego, 'I', exists, the experience of the Self will be obstructed.

**51** Other than getting ruined, what else can the ego accomplish when it loses the light of consciousness by getting enmeshed in the net of worldly life?

**52** A rutting elephant [the ego] will kill itself, trying to gore the mountain it takes to be its enemy, but which is in fact its own shadow.

**53** The upsurging ego-consciousness is the misery of *samsara*, the bondage of false, mental creations.

**54** Until you subjugate, root out and destroy that enemy, all manner of blame and sin will accrue to you.

**55** As long as that ego exists, innumerable obstacles will arise in succession, like winged white ants streaming out of an ant hill.

### Ego, the source of sin

56 Just as the source of all virtue is the real 'I', the source of the accumulation of sins is the false and deceitful 'I'.

57 The ego, which is the very personification of evil, is a great ocean in which all sins dwell together.

58 *Pudam* questions: 'What sin will the ego – the thief who habituates one to the erroneous belief that one is the body – not commit?'

59 Since the ego stands as the accumulation of all sins, its destruction constitutes all that is virtuous.

### Destruction of the ego

60 Only after the ego 'I' has been completely destroyed will Self-experience arise.

61 Unless you eradicate completely the obsession with the ego-mind, knowing it to be an extremely powerful poison, there will be no bliss in your heart.

62 For those who have attained the unique greatness of ego-loss, which is the greatest of all good fortunes, there is no other fortune to desire and attain.

63* Only the destruction of the false ego, which is a corruption of *dharma*, excels as the true Siva *dharma*.

64 True realisation is the assured state which has that steadfast strength which derives from the death of that source of forgetfulness, the deluding ego.

65 The moment you uproot and overthrow the mischievous ego, lordship over the world of liberation will flood your heart.

### Killing the ego

66 'Kill me. If you do not, I will kill you now.' Challenging in this way, the ego will rise.

67 Kill the cruel ego that rules tyrannically before it kills you.

> **Question:** What is the best way of killing the ego?
> **Bhagavan:** To each person that way is the best which appears easiest or appeals most. All the ways are equally good, as they lead to the same goal, which is the merging of the ego in the Self. What the *bhakta* calls surrender, the man who does *vichara* calls *jnana*. Both are trying

only to take the ego back to the source from which it sprang and make it merge there.[10]

**68** Unless you annihilate it completely, in such a way that it ceases to exist, you will not be able, in however small a measure, to experience the bliss of peace.

**69** While it is alive, the ego is death; the death of the ego is life. This riddle is indeed difficult to understand.

**70** The ego that has subsided and died in the Heart will attain the greatness of the Self and surge like a vast ocean.

**71** When the ego is destroyed, the truth of the Self will shine undivided, extending to the farthest extremities of the four quarters [of the universe].

**72** Why abuse God instead of killing the misery-inducing ego, which is ignorant pride?

### *Chit-jada*

Chit-jada *is a Sanskrit term that literally means 'consciousness-inert'. Bhagavan frequently used it to describe the unreal bond or knot that ties or limits consciousness to the otherwise inert physical body. As such,* chit-jada *is co-extensive with the ego or the 'I'-thought that, through false association, limits identity to a particular form.*

**73** The life of individualised existence, which is a combination of the two opposing entities [*chit* and *jada*], is just a manifestation of the mind [*manomaya*].

**74** The *chit-jada* ego, which is neither *sat* [real] nor *asat* [unreal], remains in your Heart like an enemy masquerading as a friend.

**75** That *chid-jada* ego known as 'I' is the founding ancestor of the lineage of the mind.

**76** That which liberates, cutting asunder the shackle of *chit-jada*, is the enquiry that leads to knowledge of the truth of one's real nature.

**Question:** While the one aim is to realise the unconditioned, pure being of the Self, which is in no way dependent on the ego, how can the enquiry pertaining to the ego in the form of *aham-vritti* [the 'I'-thought] be of any use?

**Bhagavan:** From the functional point of view, the ego has one and only one characteristic. The ego functions as the knot between the Self, which is pure consciousness, and the physical body which is inert and insentient. The ego is therefore called *chit-jada-granthi* [the knot between consciousness and the inert body]. In your investigation into the source of *aham-vritti*, you take the essential *chit* [consciousness] aspect of the ego. For this reason the enquiry must lead to the realisation of pure consciousness of the Self.[11]

**77*** There exists no path other than that of separating [the knot that joins] spirit and body, that lowly state of existing as the body.

**78*** The true birth celebration is when ego dies through the untying [of the *chit-jada* knot] and is born in *Brahma-swarupa*.

**79** Unlike a blossoming lotus that closes [during the night], the Heart-lotus, which has blossomed after the untying of the ignoble knot, will never close again.

*Guru Vachaka Kovai*, verse 1124, *Pozhippurai*: If at any time in the past the *chit-jada* knot, the source of all other [bonds], has been severed, then one will never again be caught in the bondage of *samsara*. The state of God, the possession of power, and profound peacefulness – all these are in truth only this state of shining as *swarupa*.
*Vilakkam*: The three aspects of *sat*, *chit* and *ananda* – all of which belong to the One – are respectively described here as the state of God, the possession of power, and profound peacefulness.

*The following commentary appears under verse one of* Arunachala Pancharatna *in Bhagavan's* Collected Works. *I do not know who the author is, but it is not Bhagavan himself:*

Just as the lotus bud, flourishing in marshy pools, blossoms at sunrise, so also the Heart, behind the soiled mind, shines forth by the grace of God who is the Self of all selves, and who is externally visible as Arunachala. But this sun, after rising up, never sets again and the Heart of the realised soul is in blossom once and for all.

**The I-am-the-body idea**

**80** The feeling of living in the body and the world is what destroys the life of firm *swarupa*, the being-consciousness.

**81** Taking the body to be 'I' is the error that murders *Brahman*, that which is merged with you as *Atma-swarupa*.

**82** Know the deceitful ego, a consummate impersonator, as a villainous murderer whose profession is death.

*Though* Brahman *is essentially indestructible, Bhagavan often spoke of devotees who 'killed' or 'murdered'* Brahman *by not being aware of it.*

**83** Only the ego, the delusion that spreads by identifying with the insentient *upadhi* [the body], is bondage.

**84** That which should be clearly known is the Self, mere consciousness. That which should be destroyed is attachment to the body.

Ulladu Narpadu*, verse 17:*

> To those who do not know the Self and to those who do, the body is the 'I'. But to those who do not know the Self the 'I' is bounded by the body; while to those who within the body know the Self the 'I' shines boundless. Such is the difference between them.[12]

**85** The delusive life of [living in] the body and the world is the product of the 'I' sense that cherishes the body, which is just a corpse.

> **Question:** Is there no *dehatma buddhi* [I-am-the-body idea] for the *jnani*? If, for instance, Sri Bhagavan be bitten by an insect, is there no sensation?
> **Bhagavan:** There is a sensation and there is also the *dehatma buddhi.* The latter is common to both *jnani* and *ajnani* with this difference, that the *ajnani* thinks *dehaiva Atma* [only the body is myself], whereas the *jnani* knows all is of the Self [*Atmamayam sarvam*], or all this is *Brahman* [*sarvam khalvidam Brahma*]. If there be pain let it be. It is also part of the Self. The Self is *poorna* [perfect].[13]

86 *Padam* questions: 'Why did you, who are in truth consciousness, consider your form to be a fleshy body and immerse yourself in misery?'

### The cause of the I-am-the-body idea

87 The I-am-the-body mistake arises when objectification causes one to see sordid sense objects before first seeing one's real nature.

88 Taking the body to be 'I' – an erroneous superimposition that is like calling mother-of-pearl 'silver' – is the confusion of the spinning mind.

89 The same confusion of the mind takes the perceptions of the five senses to be real. This results in an agitation of the mind that struggles with desires for them.

### The destruction of the I-am-the-body idea

90 Establish yourself in the complete perfection of your own real nature. Do not limit yourself to the [body] *upadhi*.

91 Except through the rare medicine of direct experience it is impossible to escape from the I-am-the-body disease.

92* Unless the belief 'I am the body' is completely destroyed, true knowledge of the one Self is not possible.

93 The disappearance of the I-am-the-body notion, the wrong understanding that causes infatuation, is the experience of the *Atma-swarupa*.

94 In the state wherein the ego, the I-am-the-body delusion, has ceased, both yoga and *bhoga* [enjoyment], without becoming two, merge together as one.

> *Guru Vachaka Kovai*, verse 62: He who has known the world appearance – an association that comprises the five sense perceptions – as his own Self, the consciousness that is the supreme, knows and experiences the same *swarupa* through his five senses as well.
> *Vilakkam*: This verse explains the little-known fact that the *sahaja* state is experienced even in external perceptions. For him who truly knows sense perceptions to be his own Self, the world is not an obstacle. He experiences and enjoys his own Self in all perceptions and rejoices identically both internally and externally,

without even a trace of the thought of bondage.

### 'I' and 'mine'

**95** Those whose tamasic minds are overspread with the darkness of worldly bondage [*pasam*], and whose nature is obsessed with 'I' and 'mine' are said to be stupid people.
**96** The thought 'I' that rises first in the Heart is the cause of the thoughts 'mine' and 'for me'.
**97** The ultimate reality, which is eternal, is just the being that exists devoid of 'I' and 'mine'.
**98** Since inner attachment will afflict you like a contagious disease through all the many births, relinquish it.

*In Tamil, 'inner attachment' refers to the inner, contracted feeling of being an 'I' that is limited to the body, while 'outer attachment' corresponds to 'mine', the idea that certain things belong to the 'I'.*

**99** If the experience of the Self merges with you, the base delusion of 'I' and 'mine' will be dead.

### Renunciation of individual identity

**100** The best kind of renunciation is remaining in the state in which the mind holds extremely tightly to the *swarupa*.
**101** Knowing one's real nature, the abiding truth, is merely renouncing one's infatuation for the *triputis* that veil it.
**102** If you attain perfect mastery of internal renunciation, external renunciation will have no importance.

*Internal renunciation is renunciation of the ego whereas external renunciation is giving up possessions. It is the former that results in enlightenment. Bhagavan sometimes illustrated this point by telling the story of King Sikhidhvaja who unnecessarily gave up his kingdom and retired to the forest to seek enlightenment:*

> **Bhagavan:** He [the king] had *vairagya* [non-attachment] even while ruling his kingdom and could have realised the Self if he had only pushed his *vairagya* to the point of killing the ego. He did not do it but came to the forest, had a timetable of *tapas* and yet did not improve even

after eighteen years of *tapas*. He had made himself a victim of his own creation. Chudala [his enlightened wife] advised him to give up the ego and realise the Self, which he did and was liberated.

It is clear from Chudala's story that *vairagya* accompanied by ego is of no value, whereas all possessions in the absence of ego do not matter.[14]

**103** For those who have abandoned their ego-mind, what other things besides that are left that are worthy of being renounced?

*Guru Vachaka Kovai*, verse 837: For those who have, with great difficulty, accomplished the renunciation of the ego, there is nothing else to renounce.

**104** Renunciation, glorious and immaculate, is the total extirpation of the impure ego mind.

**105** Only those who have renounced the ego-mind have truly renounced. What have all the others, who may have given up other things, really renounced?

### *Kartrutva* [the feeling of being the performer of actions]

**106** The ignoble infatuation *kartrutva* that associates with you is the confused attitude of mind that regards the instruments [of action and cognition] as 'you'.

**107** Deeds [karma] are not your enemy, only the sense of doership [*kartrutva*] is. Therefore, live your life, having completely renounced that enemy.

**108** If you perform all activities, relying primarily on grace, the delusion, the ego, will be completely destroyed.

**Bhagavan:** Only so long as you think that you are the worker are you obliged to reap the fruits of your actions. If, on the other hand, you surrender yourself and recognise your individual self as only a tool of the higher power, that power will take over your affairs along with the fruits of actions. You are no longer affected by them and the work goes on unhampered. Whether you recognise the power or not the scheme of things does not alter. Only there is a change of outlook. Why should you bear your load on the head when you are travelling in a train? It carries you and your load whether the load is on your head or on the floor of the train. You are not lessening the burden of the train by keeping it on your head but only straining yourself unnecessarily. Similar is the sense of doership in the world by individuals.[15]

**109** The proper course for a *sadhaka* is to practise *sadhana* at all times until the sense of being the doer ceases.

**110** 'Only the cessation of the sense of being the doer is self-surrender.' *Padam* emphatically declares this, imprinting it upon the mind.

**Question:** Without the sense of doership – the sense 'I am doing' – work cannot be done.
**Bhagavan:** It can be done. Work without attachment. Work will go on even better than when you worked with the sense that you were the doer.
**Question:** I don't understand what work I should do and what not.
**Bhagavan:** Don't bother. What is destined as work to be done by you in this life will be done by you, whether you like it or not...
**Question:** If, as Arjuna was told, there is a certain work destined to be done by each and we shall eventually do it, however much we do not wish to do it or refuse to do it, is there any free will?
**Bhagavan:** It is true that the work meant to be done by us will be done by us. But it is open to us to be free from the joys or pains, pleasant or unpleasant consequences of the work, by not identifying ourselves with the body or that which does the work. If you realise your true nature and know that it is not you that do any work, you will be unaffected by the consequences of whatever work the body may be engaged in according to destiny or past karma or divine plan, however you may call it. You are always free and there is no limitation of that freedom.[16]

**111** At the very moment that the sense of being the doer ceases one will be redeemed, becoming one who has done all that needs to be done. After this there is no more effort.

**Question:** It is an established rule that so long as there is the least idea of I-am the-doer, Self-knowledge cannot be attained, but is it possible for an aspirant who is a householder to discharge his duties properly without this sense?

**Bhagavan:** As there is no rule that action should depend upon a sense of being the doer, it is unnecessary to doubt whether any action will take place without a doer or an act of doing. Although the officer of a government treasury may appear, in the eyes of others, to be doing his duty attentively and responsibly all day long, he will be discharging his duties without attachment, thinking 'I have no real connection with all this money' and without a sense of involvement in his mind. In the same manner a wise householder may also discharge without attachment the various household duties which fall to his lot according to his past karma, like a tool in the hands of another. Action and knowledge are not obstacles to each other.[17]

**112** Those who have cast off *kartrutva* will feel exhilarated within themselves, having done all that needs to be done.

## Expecting results from actions

**113** That which veils your insight into the real is the attitude of desiring fruits from actions. Therefore, you should cultivate an understanding in which there is no expectation of results.

**114***Without exceedingly strong rectitude of mind, the performance of obligatory duties without desiring their fruits is impossible.

**115** Except for those who can perform karma as yoga, for everyone else karma will end up as *moha* [infatuation].

## Responsibility for actions performed

**116** So long as you have not renounced the belief 'I am the doer', keep in your mind the correct perspective that your responsibilities are yours alone.

*As long as the 'I am the doer' idea persists, new karma will accumulate and will be experienced by the one who thinks he is the doer. When this idea ends, no new karma is accumulated. Bhagavan is saying that one cannot evade responsibility for one's actions until one has the direct experience of the Self in which the sense of being an individual person has vanished.*

**Question:** Even though people commit adultery and theft and take alcoholic drinks and so on, can their sins be wiped out by doing *japa*... Or will the sins stick to them?
**Bhagavan:** If the feeling 'I am doing *japa*' is not there, the sins committed by a man will not stick to him. If the feeling 'I am doing *japa*' is there, why should not the sin arising from bad habits stick on?
**Question:** Will not this *punya* [the merit accumulated from performing the *japa*] extinguish that *papam* [the consequences of the sinful acts]?
**Bhagavan:** So long as the feeling 'I am doing' is there, one must experience the results of one's acts, whether they are good or bad. How is it possible to wipe out one act with another? When the feeling 'I am doing' is lost, nothing affects a man. Unless one realises the Self, the feeling 'I am doing' will never vanish.[18]

*Guru Vachaka Kovai*, verse 570, *Pozhippurai*: An ignorant person thinks, through the delusion I-am-the-body, that an individual 'I' exists separate from God, the complete and utter fullness. So long as he believes himself to be an individual, it has to be accepted that he will alternately perform good and bad actions through the ego-feeling I-am-the-doer and will necessarily receive and experience their results in the form of joy and misery.

*Guru Vachaka Kovai*, verse 668: If it is conceded that all the actions of the *jiva* are only Siva's actions, then the *jiva* should have become, by a perfect self-surrender in which independence and individuality are lost, not different from Siva. If he exists as different from Siva, all his actions are his actions and not Siva's, and he will be considered an independent agent.
*Vilakkam*: This is a very subtle point. When it is conceded that all the actions of the *jiva* are those of Siva, then *jiva* and Siva are not different. At that point the *jiva*, having lost the feeling that he is performing actions, becomes

Siva, the free One. Surrendering in this way is not yielding to the ego, but is the complete destruction of it. However, those who act with their ego nature, saying, 'Everything is Siva's doing,' have not really surrendered.

**117** The sense of responsibility, a false feeling, does not exist in the true state of realisation of the Self.
**118***When this ego-based sense of responsibility is destroyed, the bliss of the Self will surge and overflow.

## *Kartavya* [the feeling that there are activities that must be done]

**119** The notion of duties that need to be done [*kartavya*] will not cease as long as the sense of doership [*kartrutva*] exists in the heart.
**120** Why do you become mentally agitated, blindly believing there are things you have to do [*kartavya*]?
**121** The bondage called 'duty' will cease, [being known] as a delusion caused by the ego, when the firm knowledge of reality is attained.

**Question:** I want to know my *tattva* [my truth, my reality] and my duties.
**Bhagavan:** Know your *tattva* first and then you may ask what your duties are. You must exist in order to know and do your duty. Realise your existence and then enquire of your duties.[19]

**122** A mind that has dissolved in the state of God, and ceased to exist, will not be aware of any activity that needs to be performed,
**123** because, when the ego, which has the idea that it is the performer of actions, has been completely destroyed, the idea that something needs to be accomplished ends.
**124** Those who do not see anything as a duty that has to be done will attain the bliss of peace that yields limitless contentment.

# The *Avasthas*

*The* avasthas *are the three states of waking, dreaming and sleeping.*

## The mind and the *avasthas*

1 The reason for the mind becoming enmeshed in the *avasthas* is that the *jiva*, forsaking its own truth, Siva consciousness, enquires into the non-Self.

2 The mind, forgetting *Sivam*, gets deluded, puts its attention on the *avasthas* and causes great harm to itself.

> **Bhagavan:** For the *jnani* all the three states are equally unreal. But the *ajnani* is unable to comprehend this, because for him the standard of reality is the waking state, whereas to the *jnani* the standard of reality is reality itself. This reality of pure consciousness is eternal by its nature and therefore subsists equally during what you call waking, dreaming and sleep. To him who is one with that reality there is neither the mind nor its three states and, therefore, neither introversion nor extroversion.
>
> His is the ever-waking state, because he is awake to the eternal Self; his is the ever-dreaming state, because to him the world is no better than a repeatedly presented phenomenon of dream; his is the ever-sleeping state, because he is at all times without the 'body-am-I' consciousness.[1]

3 That which abides everywhere and in all *avasthas*, that consciousness alone is the truth.

> **Bhagavan:** There is only one state, that of consciousness or awareness or existence. The three states of waking, dream and sleep cannot be real. They simply come and go. The real will always exist. The 'I' or existence that

alone persists in all the three states is real. The other three are not real and so it is not possible to say they have such and such a degree of reality. We may roughly put it like this. Existence or consciousness is the only reality. Consciousness plus waking, we call waking. Consciousness plus sleep, we call sleep. Consciousness plus dream, we call dream. Consciousness is the screen on which all the pictures come and go. The screen is real, the pictures are mere shadows on it. Because by long habit we have been regarding these three states as real, we call the state of mere awareness or consciousness as the fourth. There is however no fourth state, but only one state.

**Question:** But why should these three states come and go on the real state or the screen of the Self?

**Bhagavan:** Who puts this question? Does the Self say these states come and go? It is the seer who says these states come and go. The seer and the seen together constitute the mind. See if there is such a thing as the mind. Then, the mind merges in the Self, and there is neither the seer nor the seen. So the real answer to your question is, 'Do they come and go? They neither come nor go.' The Self alone remains as it ever is. The three states owe their existence to *avichara* [non-enquiry] and enquiry puts an end to them. However much one may explain, the fact will not become clear till oneself attains Self-realisation and wonders how he was blind to the self-evident and only existence so long.[2]

## Waking and dreaming

4 Because it appears and disappears just as dreams do, the waking state that appears to be solid and full of differences is also imaginary.

*The following extract from the essay version of* Who am I? *was originally a response to the question, 'Is there no difference between waking and dream?'*

One should consider the universe to be like a dream. Except that waking is long and dreams are short, there is no difference [between the two states]. To the extent to which all the events which happen while one is awake appear to be real, to that same extent even the events that happen in dreams appear at that time to be real. In dreams, the mind assumes another body. In both the dream and the waking [states] thoughts and names-and-forms come into existence simultaneously.

*Guru Vachaka Kovai*, verse 553: Those possessing *jnana drishti* [the vision that comes from true knowledge] say that when enquiry is made, both the waking and dream states are identical in being defective. Does not the valued world of the waking state also slip away and leave, just like the dream world?

*Guru Vachaka Kovai*, verse 555: *Jnanis* declare that both the waking and dream states are the creation of the confused mind. One should conclude that in both dream and waking, association with thoughts and names-and-forms is the same.

5 The confusing waking and dream states do not appear except when one gets immersed in the stupor of ignorance.

6 Forget and forsake the waking state, regarding it as a dream concept that has taken shape merely as a manifestation of the obsessive behaviour of the mind.

7 Just as dreams cease on waking, the waking state will fade away in true *jnana*.

*The same idea appears in the next verse, but in a more metaphorical way: when one 'wakes up' to the Self, the sleep of ignorance is banished, and the delusive dream vision of the world fades away.*

8 Other than through the waking consciousness that arises when sleep vanishes, it is not possible to destroy the delusive dream-vision.

9 To lose one's chastity by desiring the waking state that has no immutability [*vyavastha*] is a mistake.

*Bhagavan and Muruganar often compare the mind or the* jiva *to a wife who needs to maintain her marital fidelity by keeping her attention on her husband, the Self. If her focus strays to the world, she becomes entangled in its unreal affairs and loses her chastity.*

## Existence and enquiry during sleep

*The first two verses in this section encapsulate replies that Bhagavan gave to people who claimed that they were unaware of their existence while they were asleep. Bhagavan taught that pure being was the one true reality and that this being was present and experienced as the substratum of all three states. Many questioners pointed out that they had no awareness at all during sleep:*

> **Question:** I am not aware in my sleep.
> **Bhagavan:** True, there is no awareness of the body or of the world. But you must exist in your sleep in order to say now, 'I was not aware in my sleep'. Who says so now? It is the wakeful person. The sleeper cannot say so. That is to say, the individual who is now identifying the Self with the body says that such awareness did not exist in sleep.
> ... The sleep state appears dull because you were not there as an individual and therefore these things [the world] were not. But what is the fact? There is the continuity of being in all the three states, but no continuity of the individual and the objects.[3]

**10** You have to accept your own existence even in the state of unconscious sleep where the scenes involving the *triputis* cease to exist.

> *Guru Vachaka Kovai*, verse 356: The being in which the thought 'I' does not rise even slightly is the Self, the supreme reality that is known as *tan*, [the real 'I']. Whoever became non-existent in sleep, just because the thought 'I' did not rise?

**11** If you do not accept the fact of your existence [in sleep], how did that knowledge come to you?

**12** Since sleep is that splendid, pure consciousness, devoid of mind and intellect, that mysterious experience cannot be enquired into by the mind and intellect.

**_Suddha_ [the pure state]**

'Suddha' *means 'pure'. In Tamil it also means 'the pure state', the underlying state of the Self that is covered up by the* avasthas. *Bhagavan sometimes said that this* suddha *state manifested very briefly in a very short interval between the end of sleep and the beginning of the waking state. It can also occasionally be experienced as the underlying reality in the gap that exists between the end of one thought and the beginning of another. Bhagavan taught that these brief gaps were windows of opportunity through which one can discern the nature of the Self.*

**13** Know the pure state [*suddha*], your own real nature, by keenly observing the interval between two thoughts.

> *Guru Vachaka Kovai*, verse 760: Having enquired and known that the nature of the abiding, supreme, true *swarupa* is identical to the nature of the mind in the interval between two thoughts, abiding firmly in the Heart in this way is the unsurpassed state.
>
> **Bhagavan:** The ego in its purity is experienced in the intervals between two states or between two thoughts. The ego is like the worm which leaves one hold only after it catches another. Its true nature is known when it is out of contact with objects or thoughts. You should realise this interval as the abiding, unchangeable reality, your true being, through the conviction gained by the study of the three states, *jagrat* [waking], *swapna* [dreaming] and *sushupti* [sleeping].[4]
>
> If that mind-free consciousness, which is at the meeting point of deep sleep and waking somehow becomes continuous, then the state that then dawns is declared by sages to be the state of deliverance.[5]

**14** This pure state [*suddha*] of being-consciousness, the one Self that shines as the underlying source [of the *avasthas*], abides whole and undivided.

**15** Remaining still [*summa iruttal*] is the state of truth, also known as the pure state [*suddha*]. Realise this eminent experience by keen enquiry.

**Sleep and waking sleep**

**16*** It is the void-like sleep that shines as one's nature, abiding in the Heart devoid of the delusion 'I'.

*Bhagavan sometimes compared the state of the Self to the state of sleep since the mind and the world are absent in both. However, as Bhagavan explains in the following dialogue, there are crucial differences between them:*

> **Question:** Is one nearer to pure consciousness in deep sleep than in the waking state?
> **Bhagavan:** The sleep, dream and waking states are mere phenomena appearing on the Self which is itself stationary and also a state of simple awareness. Can any one remain away from the Self at any moment? This question can arise only if that were possible.
> **Question:** Is it not often said that one is nearer pure consciousness in deep slumber than in the waking state?
> **Bhagavan:** The question may as well be: Am I nearer to myself in my sleep than in my waking state? ...
> **Question:** Relatively speaking, is not the sleep state nearer to pure consciousness than the waking state?
> **Bhagavan:** Yes, in this sense: When passing from sleep to waking the 'I' thought must start; the mind comes into play; thoughts arise; and then the functions of the body come into operation; all these together make us say that we are awake. The absence of all this evolution is the characteristic of sleep and therefore it is nearer to pure consciousness than the waking state.
>
> But one should not therefore desire to be always in sleep. In the first place it is impossible, for it will necessarily alternate with the other states. Secondly, it cannot be the state of bliss in which the *jnani* is, for his state is permanent and not alternating. Moreover, the sleep state is not recognised to be one of awareness by people; but the sage is always aware. Thus, the sleep state differs from the state in which the sage is established.
>
> Still more, the sleep state is free from thoughts and their impression to the individual. It cannot be altered by one's will because effort is impossible in that condition.

Although nearer to pure consciousness, it is not fit for efforts to realise the Self.

The incentive to realise can arise only in the waking state and efforts can also be made only when one is awake. We learn that the thoughts in the waking state form the obstacle to gaining the stillness of sleep. 'Be still and know that I am God'. So, stillness is the aim of the seeker. Even a single effort to still at least a single thought even for a trice goes a long way to reach the state of quiescence. Effort is required and it is possible in the waking state only. There is the effort here; there is awareness also; the thoughts are stilled; so there is the peace of sleep gained. That is the state of the *jnani*. It is neither sleep nor waking state but intermediate between the two. There is awareness of the waking state and the stillness of sleep. It is called *jagrat-sushupti* [waking sleep]. Call it wakeful sleep or sleeping wakefulness or sleepless waking or wakeless sleep. It is not the same as sleep or waking separately. It is *atijagrat* [beyond wakefulness] or *atisushupti* [beyond sleep]. It is the state of perfect awareness and perfect stillness combined. It lies between sleep and waking; it is also the interval between two successive thoughts. It is the source from which thoughts spring; we see that when we wake up from sleep. In other words thoughts have their origin in the stillness of sleep. The thoughts make all the difference between the stillness of sleep and the turmoil of waking. Go to the root of the thoughts and you reach the stillness of sleep. But you reach it in the full vigour of search, that is, with perfect awareness.[6]

**17** What problem is there for you to remain established in the blissful sleep of *swarupa*, eating the food that comes to you effortlessly through *prarabdha*?

**Question:** What is the meaning of being in sleepless sleep?
**Bhagavan:** It is the *jnani's* state. In sleep our ego is submerged and the sense organs are not active. The *jnani's* ego has been killed and he does not indulge in any sense activities of his own accord or with the notion that he is the doer. So, he is in sleep. At the same time he is not

unconscious as in sleep but fully awake in the Self; so his state is sleepless. This sleepless sleep, wakeful sleep, or whatever it may be called, is the *turiya* [fourth] state of the Self, on which, as the screen, all the three *avasthas,* the waking, dream and sleep, pass, leaving the screen unaffected.[7]

**18** In order to make the mind, which whirls like a top, be still, become the one who sleeps in the Heart, and realise the truth.
**19** Subside and merge in the Heart in such a way that you are asleep to the world and awake to the Self.
**20** The compassionate *Padam* lovingly says: 'See the light of being here and now and sleep in the Heart.'
**21** Destroying the waking state [and transforming it into] the 'distinguished sleep' [the state of waking-sleep] is subduing and destroying the sleep of delusion.
**22** In the glorious state wherein the mind has died, even deep sleep will become God-consciousness.

*Guru Vachaka Kovai*, verse 461, *Pozhippurai*: Only in an intellect that has developed a desire for the waking state will the eminent state of deep sleep, which is all bliss, be classified as a state of ignorance: 'I did not know anything during sleep.' By failing to enquire into and realise the true experience that is existing and shining in the same way forever, one gets deluded and thinks, 'I am the one who woke up'. If that powerful sheath of the intellect, the ignorance that is experienced in the waking state, is destroyed by the sword of *jnana* [that leads to the knowledge] 'I am not the one who woke up,' then the eminent state of sleep will shine, remaining as pure bliss, its ignorance destroyed.

*Guru Vachaka Kovai*, verse 457: Classifying sleep as a *kosa* [a sheath] is just a consequence of the foolishness of Self-forgetfulness which makes one regard the waking state as a state of knowledge [*prajna*]. If the concept that the waking state is a worthy and true state of knowledge [*prajna*] is lost, then sleep itself will shine as the unique, non-dual reality.

*When Sadhu Natanananda visited Bhagavan for the first time in*

*1917 and asked for his grace, Bhagavan advised him to convert the ignorant state of sleep into a full experience of the Self:*

> **Bhagavan:** It is not the body that desires to obtain the grace. Therefore it is clear that it is the awareness that shines here as 'you'. To you who are the nature of awareness there is no connection during sleep with the body, the senses, the life force [*prana*] and the mind. On waking up you identify yourself with them, even without your knowledge. This is your experience. All that you have to do hereafter is see that you do not identify yourself with them. In the states of waking and dream try to remain as you were in the state of deep sleep. As you are by nature unattached, you have to convert the state of ignorant deep sleep, in which you were formless and unattached, into conscious deep sleep. It is only by doing this that you can remain established in your real nature. You should never forget that this experience will come only through long practice. This experience will make it clear that your real nature is not different from the nature of God.[8]

### *Turiya* and *turiyatita*

*The three states of waking, dreaming and sleeping appear in the underlying state of* turiya, *which means 'the fourth'. Some systems of thought say that underlying* turiya *there is another state,* turiyatita, *which means 'transcending the fourth'. When Bhagavan spoke on this subject, he usually maintained that there was only one state, and that, from the standpoint of the Self, divisions and distinctions such as* turiya *and* turiyatita *were unsustainable.*

**23** *Turiya*, which is beyond the reach of *suttarivu*, will merge in a Heart in which the antics of the mischievous mind have completely ceased.

**24** The *turiya* that pervades as the unique primal state when the three *avasthas* of waking, sleep and dream end, becoming false, is itself *atita* [the transcendental state].

> **Bhagavan:** There is no difference between dream and the waking state except that the dream is short and the waking long. Both are the result of the mind. Because the

waking state is long, we imagine that it is our real state. But, as a mater of fact, our real state is what is sometimes called *turiya* or the fourth state which is always as it is and knows nothing of the three *avasthas,* waking, dream or sleep. Because we call these three *avasthas* we call the fourth state also *turiya avastha.* But it is not an *avastha,* but the real and natural state of the Self. When this is realised, we know it is not a *turiya* or fourth state, for a fourth state is only relative, but *turiyatita,* the transcendent state called the fourth state.[9]

**25** It is the sleep of deep peace, existing as one's nature, that is extolled by the unknowing as *turiyatita*.

**26** The truth of oneself, which shines as the nearest of the near, is itself the *atita* [the transcendental state] that is beyond the uttermost beyond.

**27** Those who dwell in the transcendental state will surpass even the gods and will exercise their rule over the all-pervading, resplendent kingdom of heaven [*parandama*].

**28** The state in which firm *jnana* has been attained, in which *turiya* has become *atita*, is pure *mauna*.

# Practice

The unique ray that shines within the *jiva* as 'I' exists as the clue. If the *jiva* unflaggingly traces the source of that ray to the Heart, it will discover the supreme and its bondage will cease.[1]

Know that the wondrous *jnana vichara* is only for those who have attained purity of mind by softening and melting within. Without this softening and melting away of the mind, brought about by thinking of the feet of the Lord, the attachment to the 'I' that adheres to the body will not cease to be.[2]

Since it is through forgetfulness, which those who are strong in mind fear like death, that the illusion of birth ensnares us, what other means are there to abolish that birth other than the powerful enquiry into one's own true nature?[3]

If we perform *sadhana* to the limit of our abilities, the Lord will accomplish for us that which is beyond our capabilities. If we fail to do even that which is within our capabilities, there is not the slightest fault in the grace of the Lord.[4]

# Liberation and Silence

## Bondage, liberation and delusion are unreal

1 In the *paramartha swarupa*, which shines as reality, delusion is not real; it is just imagined.

Paramartha *means 'the highest truth'. According to Bhagavan, the highest truth is that no one is unenlightened since individual beings and their assorted imaginary problems do not really exist. The best-known formulation of this position is a verse by Gaudapada. Bhagavan translated it from Sanskrit into Tamil and had it included in his* Collected Works.

> There is no creation, no destruction, none bound, none seeking, striving, gaining freedom. Know that this is the supreme truth.[1]

2 In the *paramartha swarupa*, which is the space of grace, bondage, which thrives on ignorance, is a defect of the mind.
3 In the experience of one's own true *jnana swarupa* the ideas of bondage and liberation do not exist.
4 Except in one's imagination [*bhavana*], there is no attainment of liberation from bondage in the ultimate state of supreme truth.

> **Bhagavan:** All questions relating to *mukti* [liberation] are inadmissible because *mukti* means release from bondage, which implies the present existence of bondage. There is no bondage and therefore no *mukti* either.
> **Question:** The *sastras* speak of it and its grades.
> **Bhagavan:** The *sastras* are not meant for the wise because they do not need them; the ignorant do not want them. Only the *mumukshus* [those aspiring for liberation] look up to the scriptures. That means that the *sastras* are neither for wisdom nor for ignorance.[2]

**Bhagavan:** We are all in reality *sat-chit-ananda*. But we imagine we are bound and are having all these pains.
**Questioner:** Why do we imagine so? Why does this ignorance or *ajnana* come to us?
**Bhagavan:** Enquire to whom has this ignorance come and you will find it never came to you and that you have always been that *sat-chit-ananda*. One performs all sorts of penances to become what one already is. All effort is simply to get rid of this *viparita buddhi*, this mistaken impression that one is limited and bound by the woes of *samsara*.[3]

**Question:** Do not Hindu *sastras* speak of *mukti*?
**Bhagavan:** *Mukti* is synonymous with the Self. *Jivanmukti* [liberation while alive] and *videhamukti* [liberation after the body falls] are all for the ignorant. The *jnani* is not conscious of *mukti* or *bandha* [bondage]. Bondage, liberation and orders of *mukti* are all said for an *ajnani* in order that ignorance might be shaken off. There is only *mukti* and nothing else.[4]

**5** The *jivas'* habit of wandering and struggling on many paths and attaining liberation arises from the delusion of bondage.

**Bhagavan:** Our real nature is *mukti*. But we are imagining we are bound and are making various strenuous attempts to become free, while we are all the while free. This will be understood only when we reach that stage. We will be surprised that we were frantically trying to attain something that we have always been and are. An illustration will make this clear. A man goes to sleep in this hall. He dreams he has gone on a world tour, is roaming over hill and dale, forest and country, desert and sea, across various continents and after many years of weary and strenuous travel, returns to this country, reaches Tiruvannamalai, enters the ashram and walks into the hall. Just at that moment he wakes up and finds he has not moved an inch but was sleeping where he lay down. He has not returned after great effort to this hall, but is and always has been in the hall. It is exactly like that. If it is asked, why being free do we imagine we are bound, I answer, 'Why being in the hall did you imagine you were on a world adventure, crossing hill and dale, desert and sea?' It is all mind or *maya*.[5]

6 Thoughts such as bondage and liberation, which are essentially non-existent, appear in the state of *pramada* [forgetfulness of the Self].

Ulladu Narpadu *verse 39:*

> Only so long as one thinks like a madman 'I am a bound one' will thoughts of bondage and liberation remain. But, seeing oneself, 'Who is this bound one?' the eternally liberated and ever-attained Self alone will exist. When the thought of bondage cannot remain, can the thought of liberation still remain?[6]

7 If bondage and liberation are creations of the mind, all the experiences and states manifested through *suttarivu* are likewise concepts.

8 The origin of the concepts of bondage and liberation is in the ego, the deception that is the cause of the pairs of opposites.

Dwandha buddhi, *the pairs of opposites, generally refer to such pairings as heat and cold, joy and misery, and so on. Here, it would also include bondage and liberation.*

9 It is because the mind, the vain ego, is habituated to the thought of bondage that enthusiastic efforts to attain liberation arise.

10 Separation and union exist only through the ignorance of the *jiva*. They do not exist in the nature of the real, which is *jnana* only.

11 If you enquire into the Self and come to know it, in that vision of the Self the age-old primal illusion of bondage will become a story long-forgotten.

> **Question:** Is it possible to attain *moksha* [deliverance] while still in this body?
> **Bhagavan:** What is *moksha?* Who attains it? Unless there is bondage, how can there be *moksha?* Who has that bondage?
> **Question:** Me.

**Bhagavan:** Who really are you? How did you get the bondage? And why? If you first know that, then we can think of attaining *moksha* while in this body.[7]

## Liberation is ever-attained

**12** In the hearts of those who have investigated and come to know reality as it actually is, liberation in all its clarity is eternally attained.

**13** What is always natural to everyone is liberation, which is bliss. Bondage is delusion of mind, a false sensation.

**Bhagavan:** It is only if bondage is real that liberation and the nature of its experiences have to be considered. So far as the Self [*Purusha*] is concerned it has really no bondage in any of the four states [the three states of waking, dreaming and sleeping and the underlying state of *turiya*]. As bondage is merely a verbal assumption, according to the emphatic proclamation of the Vedanta system, how can the question of liberation, which depends upon the question of bondage, arise when there is no bondage? Without knowing this truth, to enquire into the nature of bondage and liberation, is like enquiring into the non-existent height, colour, etc., of a barren woman's son or the horns of a hare.
**Question:** If that is so, do not the descriptions of bondage and release found in the scriptures become irrelevant and untrue?
**Bhagavan:** No, they do not. On the contrary, the delusion of bondage fabricated by ignorance from time immemorial can be removed only by knowledge, and for this purpose the term 'liberation' [*mukti*] has been usually accepted. That is all. The fact that the characteristics of liberation are described in different ways proves that they are imaginary.
**Question:** If that is so, are not all efforts such as hearing, reflection, etc., useless?
**Bhagavan:** No, they are not. The firm conviction that there is neither bondage nor liberation is the supreme purpose of all efforts. As this purpose of seeing boldly, through direct experience, that bondage and liberation do not exist,

cannot be achieved except with the aid of the aforesaid practices, these efforts are useful.

**Question:** Is there any authority for saying that there is neither bondage nor liberation?

**Bhagavan:** This is decided on the strength of experience and not merely on thc strength of the scriptures.

**Question:** If it is experienced how is it experienced?

**Bhagavan:** 'Bondage' and 'liberation' are mere linguistic terms. They have no reality of their own. Therefore they cannot function of their own accord. It is necessary to accept the existence of some basic thing of which they are the modifications. If one enquires, 'For whom is there bondage and liberation?' it will be seen, 'They are for me'. If one enquires, 'Who am I?', one will see that there is no such thing as the 'I'. It will then be as clear as an *amalaka* fruit in one's hands that what remains is one's real being. As this truth will be naturally and clearly experienced by those who leave aside mere verbal discussion and enquire into themselves inwardly, there is no doubt that all realised persons uniformly see neither bondage nor liberation so far as the true Self is concerned.[8]

**14** The ego alone is bondage, and one's own *swarupa*, free of the contagion of the ego, is liberation.

**15*** There is no greater deception than [believing that] liberation, which is ever present as one's own nature, will be attained at some later stage.

**16** Even the desire for liberation is the work of delusion. Therefore, remain still [*summa iru*].

**Bhagavan:** Liberation is our very nature. We are that. The very fact that we wish for liberation shows that freedom from all bondage is our real nature. That has not got to be freshly acquired. All that is necessary is to get rid of the false notion that we are bound. When we achieve that, there will be no desire or thought of any sort. So long as one desires liberation, so long, you may take it, one is in bondage.[9]

**17** If you enquire into and realise *Atma-swarupa*, the reality, as it actually is, it will be clearly known that liberation is eternally attained.

**18** The true *mukti* that banishes the tormenting triple miseries [*tapatraya*] is abandoning everything, not attaining something.

*The triple miseries are those caused by oneself, those brought about by natural events and those that occur as a result of destiny.*

> **Question:** We have come here and are staying here for the same purpose [of attaining *moksha*]. We do not want anything more. It is enough if you give us *moksha*.
> **Bhagavan:** If you renounce and give up everything, what remains is only *moksha*. What is there for others to give you? It is there always. That *is*.
> **Question:** We do not know all that. Bhagavan himself must give us *moksha*. [The questioner then left the hall.]
> **Bhagavan:** I should give them *moksha*, they say. It is enough if *moksha* alone is given to them. Is that not itself a desire? If you give up all the desires that you have, what remains is only *moksha*.[10]

### Knowing consciousness is liberation

**19** The way to liberation is knowing consciousness and abiding there without slipping from consciousness.

**20** That which abides [in the Heart] is liberation, the true and unlimited supreme bliss. Only through that being-consciousness will you attain redemption.

**21** The excellence of peace, which is the clarity of consciousness, is alone the greatness of intensely blissful liberation.

**22** The experience of pure consciousness, one's own *swarupa*, is the bliss of liberation. The misery of bondage is total ignorance.

**23** Unless ignorance, the delusion, is completely destroyed by *jnana*, it is certain that there will be no liberation.

**24** The cessation of the feeling of bondage, which arises from the I-am-the-body delusion, is sovereignty over [the world of] liberation, the freedom of the Self, pure consciousness, the supreme.

## *Summa Iru*

*The title of this section,* Summa Iru, *means 'be still', 'remain still', or 'just be'. It was one of Bhagavan's most famous instructions. Muruganar himself has stated that his own enlightenment was brought about by Bhagavan giving him this instruction.*

**25*** Supreme liberation will shine as *Atma-swarupa* if one remains still.

*This verse is introduced by the word* 'amma', *which indicates that Bhagavan is expressing surprise in this statement, possibly at the thought that anyone could think otherwise.*

**26*** Through his gentle smile, radiant *Padam* joyfully declares: 'Why this distress? Be happy by just remaining still.'

> **Bhagavan:** Your duty is to be, and not to be this or that. 'I am that I am' sums up the whole truth; the method is summarized in 'Be still'.
>
> And what does stillness mean? It means 'Destroy yourself'; because, every name and form is the cause of trouble. 'I-I' is the Self. 'I am this' is the ego. When the 'I' is kept up as the 'I' only, it is the Self. When it flies off at a tangent and says 'I am this or that, I am such and such', it is the ego.
>
> **Question:** Who then is God?
>
> **Bhagavan:** The Self is God. 'I am' is God. If God be apart from the Self, He must be a selfless God, which is absurd. All that is required to realise the Self is to be still. What can be easier than that? Hence *Atma-vidya* [Self-knowledge] is the easiest to attain.[11]

**27** Since becoming established in the state of the Self is both the means and the goal to be attained, remain still.

*Though it was Bhagavan's highest and simplest* upadesa, *he conceded that for many people, it was an impossible command to execute:*

> **Question:** What should one do in order to remain free from thoughts as advised by you? Is it only the enquiry 'Who am I?'
>
> **Bhagavan:** Only to remain still. Do it and see.
>
> **Question:** It is impossible.

**Bhagavan:** Exactly. For the same reason the enquiry 'Who am I?' is advised.[12]

**Bhagavan:** All the age-long *vasanas* carry the mind outward and turn it to external objects. All such thoughts have to be given up and the mind turned inward. For that, effort is necessary for most people. Of course everybody, every book says, '*Summa iru*,' i.e., 'Be quiet or still'. But it is not easy. That is why all this effort is necessary. Even if we find one who has at once achieved the *mauna* or supreme state indicated by '*Summa iru*' you may take it that the effort necessary has already been finished in a previous life.[13]

**28** The wonderful meaning of the one supreme word [*summa iru*] is to know and rest in the *Atma-swarupa* through the enquiry 'Who am I?'

**29** Except by remaining still [*summa iruttal*] by what great *tapas* can the *Atma-swarupa* be attained in the Heart?

**Bhagavan:** People seem to think that by practising some elaborate *sadhana* the Self will one day descend upon them as something very big and with tremendous glory, giving them what is called *sakshatkaram* [direct experience]. The Self is *sakshat* [direct] all right, but there is no *karam* or *kritam* about it. [That is, there is no one who performs actions, and no actions being performed.] The word '*karam*' implies doing something. But the Self is realised not by doing something but by refraining from doing anything, by remaining still and being simply what one really is.[14]

**30** It will be impossible to merge with the feet of Lord Sonachala [Arunachala], unless one remains still, with the mind consumed and annihilated.

**Bhagavan:** Stillness is total surrender without a vestige of individuality. Stillness will prevail and there will be no agitation of mind. Agitation of mind is the cause of desire, the sense of doership and personality. If that is stopped there is quiet.[15]

31 By shining motionlessly, which is meditation on the Self, all manner of excellent benefits accrue.

32 To remain still, without thinking about that which is other than the Self, is to offer the mind to the Self.

33 Being still is the experience of *swarupa jnana*. Whatever is perceived by the senses is a false, illusory appearance.

34 To rest, remaining still as consciousness, is union [*sayujya*], the abundance of peace.

35 Knowing That is only abiding as That. Therefore, shine, remaining still without objectifying.

## Liberation through *mauna*

*This can be regarded as a continuation of the previous section since* mauna, *silence, can be equated with 'being still'.*

36 In the ecstasy of devotion one may sing and one may dance, but it is *mauna* that is useful for liberation.

37 To subside in the state of liberation, Siva *swarupa*, transcending the surface of the mind, is *mauna*.

38 *Mauna*, which shines alone as consciousness of being, possesses the glory of being the highest and most potent *tapas*.

39 *Mauna* – which is not only the means to liberation but also that which abides as the very nature of liberation itself – has a matchless magnificence.

40 If you adhere to that path of *mauna*, the means to liberation, there will be no suffering of any kind.

41 The supreme reality that is liberation is experienced only by perfect *mauna*. Indulging in thoughts drives it away.

42 To attain liberation, the door to which is *mauna*, the ego that rises as a separate 'I' should be completely destroyed.

## Lady Mauna

43 The loving, lustrous smile of that divine Lady Mauna, the lady of liberation, will dispel the darkness of bondage.

44 Whatever labours you have to undergo, cherish as pure gold your worship of that blissful Lady's lustrous feet.

45 Through her propitious grace-bestowing glance, the delusions of wealth, property and family ties will cease to be.

46 To joyfully worship that ever-youthful maiden is the most fitting of all *dharmas*.
47 Cherish as the most lofty *brahmacharya* this householder's life of living blissfully in union with the Lady Mauna.

Brahmacharya *generally denotes celibacy, but Bhagavan frequently noted that it also had a higher connotation – that of abiding in* Brahman.

48 In the presence of that divine Lady Mauna do not raise your head as 'I'.
49 If you raise your head even a little as 'I', that lady will not display to you even the smallest fraction of her face.
50 If you naturally remain in submission to her authority, she will unite you with the realisation of the state of Siva.
51 Harmoniously and with delight live forever in your Heart, embracing that tender Lady.
52 Let your life, in which you live in the state of blissful oneness, beguiled by her charms, stand as a delightful example to others.
53 With you yourself as she, and she herself as you, becoming one, merge together within the Heart.
54 This householder's *dharma*, which is nothing but bliss, is the good *dharma*. Abide as *Sivam*, true love.

## Peace

### The greatness of peace

55 The golden crown that deserves to be worn by *sadhus* on their heads is only the tranquillity that is peace.
56 Through that noble virtue [peace] they will attain the benefit of a life that possesses the greatness of supreme bliss.

> *Guru Vachaka Kovai*, verse 796: There is no fortune greater than peace; there is no force greater than peace; there is no excellent *tapas* greater than peace; there is no immortal life greater than [living in] peace.
> *Vilakkam*: What is here called peace is the state of stillness of mind. This can be achieved only by unceasing enquiry. When the mind knows that in truth there is nothing to

reject or to accept, it will lose its movements and will abide in supreme peace. Since such peace is the seed of the natural state, it is therefore extolled as 'immortal life'.

## Abiding as peace

**57** If one knows reality by uniting with it, a powerful and firm peace will abound.

**58** Why pine for another enjoyment, losing that peace, wherein one is united with the transcendent ambrosia?

**59** If you abide in the Heart, realising your true state, your peace will never cease.

**60** Knowing that inner peace with which you have merged to be your own real nature, abide as that peace and, with determination, drown in it.

## Attaining peace

**61** Bathe and refresh yourself in the broad waters of peace, which dispel the cravings that are fed by the noxious flames of intoxication with the senses.

**62** Whatever else you may gain or lose, firmly establish peace in your mind.

**63** In order to attain immutable peace, your obsessive indulgence in worldly activities should be abandoned.

**64** Only by merging with the truth of oneself, the one Self, will the blissful life of peace surge abundantly in the Heart.

> **Bhagavan:** *Shanti* [peace] is the original state. If what comes from outside is rejected what remains is peace. What then is there to dissolve or merge? Only that which comes from outside has to be thrown out. If people whose minds are mature are simply told that the *swarupa* itself is *shanti,* they get *jnana.* It is only for immature minds that *sravana* [hearing] and *manana* [reflection] are prescribed but for mature minds there is no need of them.[16]

**65** Do not suffer through chasing after the world and its ways, but attain peace by running along the straight path to the Heart.

### The experience of peace

**66** The peace experienced by many simple devotees in their hearts is the divine wealth that possesses great distinction.
**67** To experience peace by eliminating desire and aversion from the Heart is to attain the exalted state of divine dispassion.

> **Question:** Swamiji! How does the soul attain peace?
> **Bhagavan [laughing]:** What! What is peace for the soul?
> **Question:** No, no! I mean for the mind.
> **Bhagavan:** Oh! For the mind! The mind attains peace if the *vasanas* are suppressed. For that, one must enquire and realise who one is. How can one get peace by merely saying, 'I want peace, I want peace!' without first enquiring what is peace? First make efforts to recognise and realise what already exists.[17]

### Wanting and holding onto peace

**68** It is harmful to desire something other than peace, and to pay attention to it in such a way that it becomes firmly imprinted upon the mind.
**69** Whatever you may happen to lose, firmly hold onto peace, which is bliss, and cherish it now itself.
**70** Those who have gained peace have gained all else along with it. But those who have lost that peace, have lost everything.

### Lady Shanti

**71*** Lustrous *Padam* revels in union with the auspicious lady who is praised all the time by *jnanis* as Shanti.
**72** That deep peace is endowed with a presence that can transform an arid desert into an ocean of ambrosia.
**73** Enjoy the supreme, felicitous bliss of peace, the beautiful divine lady, by remaining still.
**74** May you who have married Shanti, the beautifully jewel-bedecked daughter begotten by me, flourish in the supreme enjoyment.
**75** To attain bliss, unite with her, the queen among women, in the Heart, [regarding her] as your dearest companion.
**76** Enjoying in your heart the bliss of Lady Shanti's tight embrace, completely forget all else.

77 What the *jnanis* honour and praise as endless supreme bliss is nothing other than the bliss of that beautiful woman, Shanti.

78 She is beautifully calm, has an extremely comely form, is worthy of reverence, and is boundlessly captivating.

79 Offer yourself as *dakshina* to her. Embrace her. Unite with that lady who is an unsurpassed ocean of magnificent and noble qualities.

80 If you have the good fortune to marry that Fair One [Shanti], your life will be enriched. It will be as though you have discovered buried treasure.

81 *Siddhas* will greatly revere and honour her, keeping their attention firmly fixed on her feet, just waiting to be of service to her.

82 Whosoever becomes the target of her glance of grace will experience an immeasurable bliss.

83 If she becomes your queen, under her reign you will attain unmatched glory.

84 She is a tender young lady whose form is the absolute and utterly perfect, distilled bliss of *Brahman*.

85 Those who are living in the presence of that blissful Lady Shanti will not even deign to look at the blissful realms of the gods.

86 For those who have come into possession of the distinguished way of living in union with that Lady Shanti, a life of living with [other] beautifully decorated women will appear abhorrent.

# Self-enquiry

## The necessity of self-enquiry

1 Unless you enquire, within yourself, through yourself, into yourself, it will be impossible for you to become one with your own Self.

2 Except for true *jnana-vichara* [self-enquiry], there is no other effective means of attaining the state of supreme bliss.

3 Until one enquires into and knows one's own real nature, the agitation experienced by the mind will not cease.

4 Those who do not realise their real nature by careful enquiry cannot gain bliss, the *prasad* of the mind.

5 For your true state to merge in your Heart as your own nature, you must enquire and know that true state. This is the only way.

6 Those who leave the path of self-enquiry, the way of liberation, and wander off along the myriad forest tracks, will encounter only confusion.

*The 'myriad forest tracks' are all the other spiritual practices except self-enquiry.*

7* The state of the Self is reached by going back the way one came. Whichever other path one travels on, it has to take you here and take refuge here.

*The word 'here' in this verse can refer either to the Self or to the path of self-enquiry. Bhagavan said on many occasions that 'going back the way one came' is self-enquiry, meaning, the mind has to return to the source via the route it rose through. He also noted that all other spiritual paths eventually merge into enquiry. This is implied in the words 'Whichever other path one travels on'.*

> **Bhagavan:** This path [attention to the 'I'] is the direct path; all others are indirect ways. The first leads to the

Self, the others elsewhere. And even if the latter do arrive at the Self it is only because they lead at the end to the first path which ultimately carries them to the goal. So, in the end, the aspirants must adopt the first path. Why not do so now? Why waste time?[1]

## The rising 'I'

8* That from which the 'I'-thought, the first thought, rises is the Heart, the Self, consciousness of being.

9 Pursue in the Heart the enquiry 'Who is this "I" that is the source for the manifestation of the ego and all the rest?'

*The first quote is from Bhagavan's essay version of* Who am I?*:*

That which arises in the physical body as 'I' is the mind. If one enquires, 'In what place in the body does this "I" first arise?' it will be known to be in the Heart [*hridayam*]. That is the birthplace of the mind. Even if one incessantly thinks 'I, I', it will lead to that place. Of all thoughts that arise in the mind, the thought 'I' is the first one. It is only after the rise of this [thought] that other thoughts arise. It is only after the first personal pronoun arises that the second and third personal pronouns appear. Without the first person, the second and third persons cannot exist.

**Bhagavan:** The Heart is used in the *Vedas* and the scriptures to denote the place whence the notion 'I' springs. Does it spring only from the fleshy ball? It springs within us somewhere right in the middle of our being. The 'I' has no location. Everything is the Self. There is nothing but that. So the Heart must be said to be the entire body of ourselves and of the entire universe, conceived, as 'I'. But to help the practiser [*abhyasi*] we have to indicate a definite part of the universe, or of the body. So this Heart is pointed out as the seat of the Self. But in truth we are everywhere, we are all that is, and there is nothing else.[2]

10 Why do you now rise as 'I' and languish, losing the bliss of the Self that is experienced in the sleep state?

**11** Do not ruin yourself by repeatedly rising and subsiding as the thinking 'I'. Attain true life by abiding as the being 'I'.

**Question:** This 'I'-thought rises from me. But I do not know the Self.
**Bhagavan:** All these are only mental concepts. You are now identifying yourself with a wrong 'I', which is the 'I'-thought. This 'I'-thought rises and sinks, whereas the true significance of 'I' is beyond both. There cannot be a break in your being. You, who slept, are also now awake. There was not unhappiness in your deep sleep. Whereas it exists now. What is it that has happened now so that this difference is experienced? There was no 'I'-thought in your sleep, whereas it is present now. The true 'I' is not apparent and the false 'I' is parading itself. This false 'I' is the obstacle to your right knowledge. Find out wherefrom this false 'I' arises. Then it will disappear. You will be only what you are – i.e. absolute being.
**Question:** How to do it? I have not succeeded so far.
**Bhagavan**: Search for the source of the 'I'-thought. That is all that one has to do. The universe exists on account of the 'I'-thought. If that ends there is an end of misery also. The false 'I' will end only when its source is sought.[3]

**12** Prevent and stop the 'I'-thought from arising and attaching itself to any *upadhi* [false identification].

**Bhagavan:** As a spark proceeds from fire, individuality emanates from the Absolute Self. The spark is called the ego. In the case of the *ajnani,* the ego identifies itself with some object simultaneously with its rise. It cannot remain without such association with objects.

This association is due to *ajnana,* whose destruction is the objective of one's efforts. If this tendency to identify itself with objects is destroyed, the ego becomes pure and then it also merges into its source. The false identification of oneself with the body is *dehatma-buddhi* or I-am-the-body idea. This must go before good results can follow.[4]

**13** To remain naturally merged in the Heart, without rising as 'I', is the proper *dharma*.

14 Sulking, pretending you are an independent being, and saying 'I', is empty, futile and captious.

**I am**

15 *Padam* declares: 'To enquire and know oneself properly, nothing except the consciousness 'I am' is necessary.'

**Bhagavan:** Self-enquiry by following the clue of *aham-vritti* [the 'I'-thought] is just like the dog tracing its master by his scent. The master may be at some distant unknown place, but that does not stand at all in the way of the dog tracing him. The master's scent is an infallible clue for the animal, and nothing else, such as the dress he wears, or his build and stature etc., counts. To that scent the dog holds on undistractedly while searching for him, and finally it succeeds in tracing him.

Likewise in your quest for the Self, the one infallible clue is the *aham-vritti*, the 'I-am'-ness which is the primary datum of your experience. No other clue can lead you directly to Self-realisation.[5]

**Question:** When I read Sri Bhagavan's works I find that investigation is said to be the one method for realisation.
**Bhagavan:** Yes, that is *vichara* [enquiry].
**Question:** How is that to be done?
**Bhagavan:** The questioner must admit the existence of his self. 'I am' is the realisation. To pursue the clue till realisation is *vichara*. *Vichara* and realisation are the same.
**Question:** It is elusive. What shall I meditate upon?
**Bhagavan:** Meditation requires an object to meditate upon, whereas there is only the subject without the object in *vichara*. Meditation differs from *vichara* in this way...
**Question:** Will *vichara* alone do in the absence of meditation?
**Bhagavan:** *Vichara* is the process and the goal also. 'I am' is the goal and the final reality. To hold to it with effort is *vichara*. When spontaneous and natural it is realisation.[6]

**Bhagavan:** To enable the *sadhaka* to steer clear of possible doubt, I tell him to take up the 'thread' or the clue of 'I'-ness or 'I-am'-ness and follow it up to its source. Because, firstly, it is impossible for anybody to entertain any doubt about his 'I'-notion; secondly whatever be the *sadhana* adopted, the final goal is the realization of the source of 'I-am'-ness which is the primary datum of your experience.

If you, therefore, practise *atma-vichara* you will reach the Heart, which is the Self.[7]

**16** Taking the underlying consciousness ['I am'] as the one unique refuge for your attention, live your life.

**Bhagavan:** 'I exist' is the only permanent, self-evident experience of everyone. Nothing else is so self-evident [*pratyaksha*] as 'I am'. What people call self-evident viz., the experience they get through the senses, is far from self-evident. The Self alone is that. *Pratyaksha* is another name for the Self. So, to do self-analysis and be 'I am' is the only thing to do. 'I am' is reality. I am this or that is unreal. 'I am' is truth, another name for Self. 'I am God' is not true.[8]

**Bhagavan:** Although the concept of 'I'-ness or 'I-am'-ness is by usage known as *aham-vritti*, it is not really a *vritti* [modification or activity of the mind] like the other *vrittis* of the mind. Because, unlike the other *vrittis*, which have no essential inter-relation, the *aham-vritti* is equally and essentially related to each and every *vritti* of the mind. Without the *aham-vritti* there can be no other *vritti*, but the *aham-vritti* can subsist by itself without depending on any other *vritti* of the mind. The *aham-vritti* is therefore fundamentally different from other *vrittis*.[9]

**17** The awareness of being, 'I am' [*sat-bodha*], which shines as the source of the intellect, is the divine grace that enables the attainment of true *jnana*.

### The method

**18** If it is peace you seek, abide in *jnana samadhi* by enquiring only into the 'I'.

**Question:** Please say how I shall realise the 'I'. Am I to make the *japa* [repetition of the phrase] 'Who am I?'
**Bhagavan:** No *japa* of the kind is meant.
**Question:** Am I to think 'Who am I?'
**Bhagavan:** You have known that the 'I'-thought springs forth. Hold the 'I'-thought and find its *moola* [source].
**Question:** May I know the way?
**Bhagavan:** Do as you have now been told and see.
**Question:** I do not understand what I should do.
**Bhagavan:** If it is anything objective the way can be shown objectively. This is subjective.
**Question:** But I do not understand.
**Bhagavan:** What! Do you not understand that you are?
**Question:** Please tell me the way.
**Bhagavan:** Is it necessary to show the way in the interior of your own home? This is within you.[10]

**19** Your truth should be experienced by enquiring, holding onto the one true path, the path of *vichara*.

**Question:** You say one can realise the self by a search for it. What is the character of this search?
**Bhagavan:** You are the mind or think that you are the mind. The mind is nothing but thoughts. Now behind every particular thought there is a general thought which is the 'I', that is yourself. Let us call this 'I' the first thought. Stick to this 'I'-thought and question it to find out what it is. When this question takes strong hold on you, you cannot think of other thoughts.
**Question:** When I do like this and cling to my self, i.e., the I-thought, other thoughts do come and go, but I say to myself 'Who am I?' and there is no answer forthcoming. To be in this condition is the *sadhana*. Is it so?
**Bhagavan:** This is a mistake that people often make. What happens when you make a serious quest for the Self is that the 'I'-thought as a thought disappears, something else from the depths takes hold of you and that is not the 'I' which commenced the quest.
**Question:** What is this something else?
**Bhagavan:** That is the real Self, the import of 'I'. It is not the ego. It is the supreme being itself.[11]

**20** Stop thinking and know by careful investigation only the reality that is within your Heart as your own nature.

**21** Letting go of external objects, turn your back on them, and realise through keen enquiry the effulgent truth that shines in the Heart.

> **Question:** You have often said that one must reject other thoughts when one begins the quest, but the thoughts are endless; if one thought is rejected, another comes and there seems to be no end at all.
> **Bhagavan:** I do not say that you must go on rejecting thoughts. If you cling to yourself, say the I-thought, and when your interest keeps you to that single idea, other thoughts get rejected, automatically they vanish.
> **Question:** And so rejection of thoughts is not necessary?
> **Bhagavan:** No. It may be necessary for a time or for some. You fancy that there is no end if one goes on rejecting every thought when it rises. No. There is an end. If you are vigilant, and make a stern effort to reject every thought when it rises, you will soon find that you are going deeper and deeper into your own inner self, where there is no need for your effort to reject the thoughts.
> **Question:** Then it is possible to be without effort, without strain!
> **Bhagavan:** Not only that, it is impossible for you to make an effort beyond a certain extent.
> **Question:** I want to be further enlightened. Should I try to make no effort at all?
> **Bhagavan:** Here it is impossible for you to be without effort. When you go deeper, it is impossible for you to make any effort.[12]

**I-I**

**22** The answer to the question 'Who am I?' is only the silent *jnana* that shines as 'I-I' in the Heart.

*Bhagavan explained, in verse thirty of* Ulladu Narpadu, *how the 'I-I' experience is a consequence of self-enquiry:*

> Questioning 'Who am I?' within one's mind, when one reaches the Heart, the individual 'I' sinks crestfallen, and

at once reality manifests itself as 'I-I'. Though it reveals itself thus, it is not the ego 'I' but the perfect being, the Self Absolute.[13]

*Bhagavan gave a more detailed explanation in* Vichara Sangraham:

Therefore, leaving the corpse-like body as an actual corpse and remaining without even uttering the word 'I' by mouth, if one now keenly enquires, 'What is it that rises as "I"?' then in the Heart a certain soundless *sphurana*, 'I-I', will shine forth of its own accord. It is an awareness that is single and undivided, the thoughts which are many and divided having disappeared. If one remains still without leaving it, even the *sphurana* – having completely annihilated the sense of the individuality, the form of the ego, 'I am the body' – will itself in the end subside, just like the flame that catches the camphor. This alone is said to be liberation by great ones and scriptures.[14]

**23** Regard it [the question 'Who am I?'] as the axe that cleanly severs the doubts that beset you now, and are that bound to do so in the future.

**24** That which shines as 'I-I' in the Heart, *mauna*, the real nature of true *jnana*, is itself liberation.

### The experience of the true 'I'

**25** Do not imagine that there are two 'I's and suffer and lament as a consequence. By consolidating yourself in the Self, know and enjoy the 'I' as one.

**26** The experience of *ahamkara* [the ego] devoid of '*kara*' is the sharp and strong sword of *jnana*.

*In Sanskrit* kara *is a particle which, when compounded with nouns and prepositions, means 'the doing of' or 'the practice of'.* Ahamkara *can therefore mean 'regarding oneself as the performer of actions'. It is more commonly translated as 'ego'. It is the* kara *suffix that transforms the real 'I' (*aham*) into the ego (*ahamkara*).*

**Bhagavan:** The original name is always going on spontaneously without any effort on the part of the individual. That name is *aham* – 'I'. But when it becomes manifest it manifests as *ahamkara* – the ego.[15]

**27** Do not perish amidst all your troubles but recognise your target to be the truth of the Self that dwells as 'I' within your Heart; cling to it and attain the bliss of consciousness.

### There is no duality or conflict on the path of *vichara*

**28*** The truth that becomes two on any other path [except *vichara*] will shine as one if one enquires into oneself.

*Bhagavan maintained that on every other spiritual path except* vichara *there was an artificial duality between the person who was meditating and the object that was being meditated on. True self-enquiry means abiding as the subject 'I', completely free of all associations and objects.*

> **Bhagavan:** You must learn to realise the subject and object as one, and in the meditating on an object, whether concrete or abstract, you are destroying that sense of oneness, and creating duality. Meditate only on the Self.[16]

> **Question:** Why should self-enquiry alone be considered the direct means to *jnana?*
> **Bhagavan:** Because every kind of *sadhana* except that of *Atma-vichara* presupposes the retention of the mind as the instrument for carrying on the *sadhana*, and without the mind it cannot be practised. The ego may take different and subtler forms at the different stages of one's practice, but is itself never destroyed....
> The attempt to destroy the ego or the mind through *sadhanas* other than *Atma-vichara,* is just like the thief turning out a policeman to catch the thief, that is, himself. *Atma-vichara* alone can reveal the truth that neither the ego nor the mind really exists, and enable one to realise the pure, undifferentiated being of the Self or the Absolute.[17]

**29** Because reality is only one, true *jnana*-yoga is the direct path. Because there is no duality, there is no other path.

**30** In the shortcut of *swarupa vichara* no fear or confusion arises because of the non-dual nature of the Self.

> *Guru Vachaka Kovai*, verse 393, *Pozhippurai*: Those who have entered the excellent, straight and direct path, the *jnana-vichara* 'Who am I?', never get confused and lose their way. The reason is this: that path possesses a straightness, like the light of the sun, that will reveal its straightness to those who have taken to it.
> *Vilakkam*: Because of the non-dual nature of the Self, enquiry, unlike other paths, has the rectitude of always moving towards the Self, taking that Self alone as the target. Moreover, it does not branch out, giving scope for confusion. Because of this it has been described as the straight and direct path.
>
> However much one progresses along the other paths, they enable the aspirant to reach the Self only by causing *vichara*, at least for a brief moment. Hence, in order to bring out the superiority of *vichara* over all the other paths, it has been described here as the excellent path.
>
> Take the Self to be the sun, and *vichara* to be the sunlight.

**31** How can the mind go insane or lose its powers on the path of *vichara* that leads to the clarification of consciousness and the attainment of tranquillity?

> *Guru Vachaka Kovai*, verse 745: This you should know: to say that someone who practised faultless Self-abidance by clinging to the Self, the God whose very nature is consciousness, became confused, mad and ruined is just like saying that someone died by drinking immortalising ambrosia.

**32** In the path of *jnana vichara*, which is enquiring into and knowing reality as it actually is, impediments, which are flaws, are non-existent.

**Enquiry cannot be undertaken through studying books**

**33** Leaving aside the *Vedas* and the *Agamas*, enquire with focused attention into your real nature, pure consciousness.

34 Out of all the [teachings of] the *Vedas* and *Agamas*, only merging with the Self possesses the majesty that deserves to be attained.

*Guru Vachaka Kovai*, verse 146: Only those adepts in enquiry who, abandoning the vast *Vedas* and *Agamas*, take being-consciousness as their guide and enquire within themselves, will, through the shining of being, completely cut off the desire for the sapless sense objects.
*Vilakkam*: Put aside completely the extremely extensive *Vedas* and *Agamas* because their true benefit is getting established in the enquiry of diving within oneself. Why? Because they are apart from oneself, and because their essence is only the attainment of *swarupa*. Since the Self is obtained within oneself, if one wants to know the Self, it is pointless to search in the non-Self. Only those who, in this way, have obtained the fortune of the Self through *vichara* have truly conquered desire at its very root.

35 That trustworthy *vichara* exists neither in book learning nor in learning from others but only in one's own sense of 'I' [*aham*].

*Guru Vachaka Kovai*, verse 391: Those who do not, through enquiry, enter the Heart and see the Self that remains established within the five sheaths but instead, attempt to enquire about it in the famous *jnana sastras* – their enquiry is only scriptural enquiry. Can it be self-enquiry? No.

**Question:** Is reading books any use for those who long for release?
**Bhagavan:** All the texts say that in order to gain release one should render the mind quiescent; therefore their conclusive teaching is that the mind should be rendered quiescent; once this has been understood, there is no need for endless reading. In order to quieten the mind one has only to enquire within oneself what one's self is; how could this search be done in books? One should know one's Self with one's own eye of wisdom. The self is within the five sheaths, but books are outside them. Since the self has to be enquired into by discarding the five sheaths, it is futile

to search for it in books. There will come a time when one will have to forget all that one has learned.[18]

## Neither the Guru nor anyone else can enquire for you

**36** Though my tongue has become weary from repeating instructions over and over again, those whose minds are bewildered have still not abandoned their questioning.

**37** However much instruction the Guru gives, the true support for spiritual aspirants is the enquiry they perform into the nature of their own Self.

**38** You who are wandering around, enquiring, 'What is the nature of the history of other people?' not enquiring who *you* are is a mistake.

**39** One should enquire within oneself, 'Who am I?' What is the use of asking others?

**Question:** Should I go on asking 'Who am I?' without answering? Who asks whom? Which *bhavana* [attitude] should be in the mind at the time of enquiry? What is 'I', the self or the ego?

**Bhagavan:** In the enquiry 'Who am I?', 'I' is the ego. The question really means, what is the source or origin of this ego? You need not have any *bhavana* in the mind. All that is required is, you must give up the *bhavana* that you are the body, of such and such a description, with such and such a name, etc. There is no need to have a *bhavana* about your real nature. It exists as it always does; it is real and no *bhavana*.[19]

**Question:** Should I not say, 'I am not the mind, intellect, body, etc.'?

**Bhagavan:** You should not give answers to the mind in the course of your enquiry. The reply should be allowed to come from within. The reply of the individual 'I' is not real. Continue to enquire until you get the answer by the method of *jnana-marga* [the path of knowledge.] This enquiry is called meditation. The inactive, peaceful, full-of-knowledge experience that arises from this state is *jnana*.

**Question:** Who am I? From where [am I]? Should one

constantly do *japa* of this with the mind or should one put the question once or twice before the mind, then go deep into the root of 'I' and there stop all thoughts of the world?

**Bhagavan:** One should not do *japa* 'Who am I? Who am I?' Having put the question once before the mind, one should search for the root of the 'I' and stop other thoughts. If a person's name is Desai, it is not necessary for him to repeat 'I am Desai, I am Desai'. Similarly, the repetition of the phrases such as 'I am *Brahman,* I am *Brahman*' is not necessary. In all *sadhanas* the mind has to be kept quiet, but while doing *japa* the mind will not be quiet. Instead of practising like this, the seer of the mind, meaning the witness, should be experienced as the form of *Brahman* and *Brahman* should be experienced as the witness.[20]

## When to enquire

**40** If one carefully determines the most auspicious day to perform [self-enquiry,] the one good action, there is no other day like today.

*Guru Vachaka Kovai*, verse 755: If the *jiva* practises *vichara* without wasting any time, his life will come to possess great excellence. 'I am this wretched body' will cease and the sea of supreme bliss will surge abundantly within him.

*Guru Vachaka Kovai*, verse 518, *Pozhippurai*: Whatever the presiding stars, the planetary positions and the astrological conjunctions may be, and whatever auspicious or inauspicious periods may prevail, they are all good and favourable stars, positions, conjunctions and periods for the worship of God, the light of being that never dims.

*Vilakkam*: All differences in time, such as the ones due to star and planetary positions, can only adversely influence those worldly actions that are governed by the mind. They cannot in the least obstruct the worship of God, who transcends the mind's concepts. It is relevant here to study the verses of devotees such as Jnanasambandhar and Arunagirinatha [which state that star and planetary positions cannot harm devotees]. If they cannot influence the actions of those devotees who are under the sway of His grace, you should know that it is completely impossible for them [the planets] to harm the worship of Him who is distinct from them [the activities that go on in his presence].

**41** If one performs [that self-enquiry] whenever the opportunity arises, without the least lapse of attention, one's life will become solid and fortified.

**Question:** Is it enough if I spend some time in the mornings and some time in the evenings for this *atma-vichara*? Or should I do it always – say, even when I am writing or walking?
**Bhagavan:** Now what is your real nature? Is it writing, walking, or being? The one unalterable reality is being. Until you realise that state of pure being you should pursue the enquiry. If once you are established in it, there will be no further worry.

No one will enquire into the source of thoughts unless thoughts arise. So long as you think 'I am walking,' 'I am writing,' enquire who does it.[22]

**Question:** How long should enquiry be practised?
**Bhagavan:** As long as there are impressions of objects in the mind, so long the enquiry 'Who am I?' is required. As thoughts arise they should be destroyed then and there in the very place of their origin through enquiry. If one resorts to contemplation of the Self unintermittently until the Self is gained, that alone would do. As long as there are enemies within the fortress, they will continue to sally forth; if they are destroyed as they emerge, the fortress will fall into our hands.[23]

**42** Even if you are about to lose your life, you should remain eternally vigilant, never losing your mental grip on that one thing, self-enquiry.

**43** Practise *vichara* ceaselessly while you are awake and destroy the forgetfulness of mind that leads one to the *laya* of sleep.

Laya *is a state in which the mind is temporarily in suspension, such as in trance or sleep.*

> **Bhagavan:** Destruction of mind alone is *tapas*. This alone is one's duty. One who is doing his own work will not pay attention to anyone else's work. One should never give room for swerving from the thought of the Self. However many duties one may have, at all the other times not meant for performing duties, one must perform only self-enquiry. While standing, sitting and taking food one can do *vichara*, can one not? If the mind happens to forget the enquiry 'Who am I?' because of *vasanas*, when it remembers the enquiry, it should try not to lose hold of the enquiry again.[23]

**The benefits of enquiry**

44 Only *vichara* removes the desires for the numerous enjoyments of the senses by revealing them to be insubstantial.
45 Only beneficial *vichara* will confer upon you, as your own form, the limitless expanse of supreme bliss.

Sri Ramana Gita, *chapter 7, verse 6:*

> The result of self-enquiry is freedom from all suffering. This is the highest of all fruits. There is nothing higher than this.

46 Through *jnana vichara*, diving within enquiring 'Who am I?', the delusion of attachment and the I-am-the-body idea will be destroyed.
47 When, through enquiry, one attains clear experience of reality as a result of obtaining true *jnana*, there is nothing further to be attained.
48 Seeking knowledge of the Self through the enquiry 'Who am I?' is the perfect medicinal herb for all ailments.
49 The medicinal herb, *vichara*, will attack and destroy all the different diseases [that stem from] the original disease [ego].

> '...Sri Bhagavan has often remarked... that in contrast to the claim of hatha yogis that yoga practice is necessary to ward off disease from the physical body and make it

pure and healthy to help concentration etc., the enquiry method, if followed strictly as directed with absolute one-pointedness of mind is capable of devouring all the germs of disease wherever and whenever they arise.'[24]

**Question**: Hatha yoga practices are said to banish diseases effectively and are therefore advocated as necessary preliminary to *jnana* yoga.
**Bhagavan**: Let those who advocate them use them. It has not been the experience here. All diseases would be effectively annihilated by continuous self-enquiry.[25]

# Surrender, Love and Devotion

## Self-surrender

1 Offer yourself up unconditionally to the power that is your own source [*adhara sakti*].

> **Bhagavan:** It is enough that one surrenders oneself. Surrender is to give oneself up to the original cause of one's being. Do not delude yourself by imagining such a source to be some God outside you. Your source is within yourself. Give yourself up to it. That means that you should seek the source and merge in it.[1]

*This is a key quote in Bhagavan's teachings on surrender. By saying that one should surrender by seeking the source of the individual self, he is, in effect, equating the practice of self-enquiry with that of surrender. This correlation is mentioned by Bhagavan in the following reply:*

> **Bhagavan:** Surrender can take effect only when it is done with full knowledge as to what real surrender means. Such knowledge comes after enquiry and reflection and ends invariably in self-surrender. There is no difference between *jnana* and absolute surrender to the Lord, that is, in thought, word and deed.[2]

2 To attain the flourishing immortal life in which death is no more, there is no means other than surrender.

Ulladu Narpadu, *second benedictory verse:*

> Mature souls who have an intense inner fear of death reach the feet of the birthless and deathless Supreme Lord as their refuge. Through this surrender of theirs they are

dead. Being now deathless, the eternal, can they again have the thought of death?[3]

3 Since to renounce the ego is to offer up one's self in surrender, cast out the debased ego-mind that proclaims itself to be 'I'.

**Question:** If 'I' also be an illusion, who then casts off the illusion?
**Bhagavan:** The 'I' casts off the illusion of 'I' and yet remains as 'I'. Such is the paradox of Self-realisation. The realised do not see any contradiction in it. Take the case of *bhakti* [devotion]. I approach Iswara and pray to be absorbed in Him. I then surrender myself in faith and by concentration. What remains afterwards? In place of the original 'I', perfect self-surrender leaves a residuum of God in which the 'I' is lost. This is the highest form of devotion [*parabhakti*], *prapatti,* surrender, or the height of *vairagya.*

You give up this and that of 'my' possessions. If you give up 'I' and 'mine' instead, all are given up at a stroke. The very seed of possession is lost. Thus the evil is nipped in the bud or crushed in the germ itself. Dispassion [*vairagya*] must be very strong to do this. Eagerness to do it must be equal to that of a man kept under water trying to rise up to the surface for his life.[4]

4 This destruction of the ego, this loss of individuality – a state in which attachment to the non-Self does not find a foothold – is self-surrender.

5 To be absorbed, through surrender of the self, in the non-dual state of *mauna,* is the supreme truth.

6 That which constitutes offering [oneself] up to the Self is living the life that shines, free of the false delusive mind, known as 'I'.

**Question:** In the opinion of Sri Aurobindo, surrender is the main *sadhana.*
**Bhagavan:** That surrender is also accepted here. But when surrender is complete, there will be no distinction... In surrender one has to give up one's mind, and after that mind is given away, there will be no duality of any kind. He who remains separate from God has not surrendered.[5]

7 'Whatever happens, let it happen; whatever does not happen, let it not happen.' A mind with this attitude will be well established in the Self.

**Surrender to God**

8 Since surrender to God, which bestows eminence on the *jiva*, is something that ought to be done, one should not waste time by neglecting to do it.

> **Bhagavan:** Surrender, and all will be well. Throw all the responsibility on God. Do not bear the burden yourself. What can destiny do to you then?
> **Question:** Surrender is impossible.
> **Bhagavan:** Yes. Complete surrender is impossible in the beginning. Partial surrender is certainly possible for all. In course of time that will lead to complete surrender. Well, if surrender is impossible, what can be done? There is no peace of mind. You are helpless to bring it about. It can be done only by surrender.[6]

9 The hearts of those who have not united with the state of the omnipotent Lord, which is grace, will never attain fullness.
10 *Padam* [God] questions: 'When the burden of this world, created by myself, is for me alone, why should you have that thought?'
11 It is God who manages and protects the many worlds. The imagining of *jivas*, who are just a multitude of reflections, that they are bearing the burden of the world is a farce.

Ulladu Narpadu Anubandham, *verse 17:*

> While God sustains the burden of the world, the spurious ego assumes its burden, grimacing like an image on a tower seeming to support it. If the traveller in a carriage which can carry any weight does not lay his luggage down but carries it painfully on his head, whose is the fault?[7]

12 Banish even the thought 'I am a fit instrument for Him' and remain still [*summa iru*].

*Guru Vachaka Kovai*, verse 471, *Pozhippurai*: Even abidance in union [yoga-*nishta*], the excellent *tapas* performed with the intention 'Let me become an instrument for Siva to redeem the world,' causes an obstacle to complete surrender to the Self, the supreme state of abiding in the service of God.
*Vilakkam*: Though that *tapas*, the abidance in union, possesses inherent excellence, to demonstrate that this excellence is destroyed by the selfish desire of the performer of *tapas*, that *tapas* has been ironically ridiculed as 'excellent' *tapas*.

*Guru Vachaka Kovai*, verse 472: Abidance in *swarupa* is ceasing to exist as a slave; it is remaining without even the thought 'I am a slave' rising; it is egoless *mauna*, utterly still, having no mental movements. The unlimited consciousness that shines in this state is the [true] consciousness.

**13** By offering the good mind at the auspicious feet of God, perfect and never-diminishing bliss will be attained.
**14** Bliss comes to you by sweet grace, through the self-surrender you perform lovingly in the heart.

**Question:** How is grace to be obtained?
**Bhagavan:** Similar to obtaining the Self.
**Question:** Practically, how is it to be for us?
**Bhagavan:** By self-surrender.
**Question:** Grace was said to be the Self. Should I then surrender to my own Self?
**Bhagavan:** Yes. To the one from whom grace is sought. God, Guru and Self are only different forms of the same.
**Question:** Please explain, so that I may understand.
**Bhagavan:** So long as you think you are the individual you believe in God. On worshipping God, God appears to you as Guru. On serving the Guru, he manifests as the Self. This is the rationale.[8]

**15** Possessing a being-consciousness that acts without any desire or opinion of its own is rejoicing in the divine will.

**Question:** Does not total or complete surrender require that one should not have left in him the desire even for liberation or God?

**Bhagavan:** Complete surrender does require that you have no desire of your own, that God's desire alone is your desire and that you have no desire of your own.

**Question:** Now that I am satisfied on that point, I want to know what are the steps by which I could achieve surrender.

**Bhagavan:** There are two ways; one is looking into the source of 'I' and merging into that source. The other is feeling 'I am helpless by myself, God alone is all-powerful and except throwing myself completely on him, there is no other means of safety for me,' and thus gradually developing the conviction that God alone exists and the ego does not count. Both methods lead to the same goal. Complete surrender is another name for *jnana* or liberation.[9]

**16** Those around us who say that withdrawing inwardly, turning towards God, is selfishness are strangers to consciousness.

**17** If it is said that self-surrender, the nature of which is deeply imbued with a great nobility, is selfishness, then that which is speaking is the corrupting ego-mind.

**18** 'Whatever is the will of the divine, let it happen.' The best attitude of mind is the one that earnestly desires this.

**19** It is this attitude that will sever the bond of the rising ego, the impurity, and bestow the state of supreme bliss.

**Bhagavan:** Surrender to Him and abide by His will whether he appears or vanishes; await His pleasure. If you ask Him to do as *you* please, it is not surrender but command to Him. You cannot have Him obey you and yet think that you have surrendered. He knows what is best and when and how to do it. Leave everything to Him. His is the burden; you have no longer any cares. All your cares are His. Such is surrender. This is *bhakti*.

Or, enquire to whom these questions arise. Dive deep in the Heart and remain as the Self. One of these two ways is open to the aspirant.[10]

**20** You will lose your peace and your mind will grieve if you put your trust in anyone other than God.

21 It is joyful to move around, feeling happily surrendered to whatever the grace of the Lord prompts us to do.

**Service to God**

22 Even if they render vast amounts of service to God, the service of those who have no genuine love for him in their hearts is of no use.

23 The benefit obtained from service [to God] will only be proportionate to the genuine love that mingles with that service.

24 Only those who do not become a devoted slave [of God or the Guru] will become enslaved by the ego-ghost, desire, and be tormented by the world.

25 If you have the attitude that you are God's servant, the delusion that arises from the cruel ego will lose its strength.

26 The offerings donated to Iswara, who has the highest qualifications to receive such donations, will accumulate as limitless *punya*.

27 The qualification for those performing service [to attain] divine grace is the complete destruction of the mischief of the deluding five senses.

28* If the sordid attitude of mind that habituates you to the I-am-the-doer idea is completely destroyed, all of your actions will be service to God.

29* In the state in which individuality has been lost, all thoughts are thoughts of God, and all that one does is service to the supreme.

**Worshipping and meditating on the Lord**

30 How does a god benefit by worship directed to him? The benefit is only for the worshipper.

31 To enquire resolutely into one's own real nature in the Heart is to meditate unceasingly upon the feet of the Lord.

32* Only the annihilation of mind that results from the destruction of *vasanas* is proper, unceasing worship of Siva-*Padam*.

33 The worship of divine forms will completely destroy the ego, the I-am-the-body conceit.

Sri Ramana Gita, *chapter 16, verses 5 6, 7:*

**[Bhagavan:]** When the devotee, regarding himself as a

separate, limited individual of poor understanding, and desirous of deliverance from suffering, takes the omnipresent supreme reality to be some deity and worships it, even then he attains in the end That [alone]. O best of men, one who attributes names and forms to the deity, through those very names and forms, transcends all name and form.

*Guru Vachaka Kovai* verse 659: Those people who lack consciousness of being, the natural light [I am], and who consequently come, through ignorance, under the spell of karma and suffer, will have their delusion ended and reach the Self, the supreme reality, through meditation on a divine form that is dear to them.
*Vilakkam*: Those who do not know the natural method of remaining still, contemplating reality by Self-abidance, and who suffer by coming under the spell of ignorance, will get rid of their ignorance by meditation on a form of the divine, the artificial method, and get back to *Atma-swarupa*, the ultimate reality.

**34** Unless the hard mind softens, melts and dissolves, what benefit will chanting [of devotional texts] bestow on the *jiva*?

### Performing *japa* of God's name

**35*** Preventing the accumulation of dark *tamas*, *Padam* engenders bright *sattva* in the hearts of those whose righteous tongues sing the names of God.

**Question:** How should I carry on *nama-japa* [repetition of the name]?
**Bhagavan:** One should not use the name of God mechanically and superficially without the feeling of devotion. To use the name of God one must call upon Him with yearning and unreservedly surrender oneself to Him. Only after such surrender is the name of God constantly with the man.[11]

**36** By mentally holding tightly to the names and forms of the Supreme One, destroy your lowly concepts about names and forms.

*The phrase 'lowly concepts' in this verse refers to names and forms in general, and not the names and forms of God.*

*Bhagavan often taught that* japa, *the repetition of a sacred name or phrase, was a preliminary practice that enabled the practitioner to gain enough mental strength to undertake self-enquiry effectively. The following extract from* Who am I? *exemplifies this attitude:*

> Like breath control, meditation on a form of God, repetition of sacred words and regulation of diet are mere aids for controlling the mind. Through meditation on a form of God and through the repetition of sacred words the mind becomes focused on one point. An elephant's trunk is always moving around, but when a chain is given to it to hold in its trunk, that elephant will go on its way, holding onto the chain instead of trying to catch other things with it. Similarly, when the mind, which is always wandering, is trained to hold onto any name or form of God, it will only cling to that. Because the mind branches out into innumerable thoughts, each thought becomes very weak. As thoughts subside more and more, one-pointedness [of mind] is gained. A mind that has gained strength in this way will easily succeed in self-enquiry.

**37** These things [names and forms] exist only in the sight of the *jiva*. They have no real existence in the Lord, the form of pure consciousness.

*'Names and forms' in this verse could mean either the names and forms of the world, the names and forms of God, or both.*

**38*** Worship directed towards forms [of God] also reaches the realm of the formless Self, *Padam*.

> 'If a man adores God, who is nameless and formless, he will be liberated from the bondage due to names and forms.' Such is the teaching of Sri Ramana.
>
> The man who meditates with devotion on God with a form, being endowed with the divine temperament, will attain that same state [of deliverance] which one attains meditating on Him as formless.[12]

**39** Perform *japa* in your heart with true love until it becomes *ajapa*.

Ajapa, *meaning 'involuntary* japa', *takes place when the word or phrase repeats itself effortlessly in the mind.*

> **Question:** How many times do I have to repeat the mantra in order to attain *siddhi* [realisation]?
> **Bhagavan:** You must go on repeating until the consciousness that you are doing it disappears. Then you realise that you are not repeating the mantra. In that state the mantra repeats itself without your effort. That is *sahaja sthiti* [the natural state]. That is *siddhi*.[13]

*On other occasions Bhagavan pointed out that the true* ajapa *was 'I', 'I' since the Self manifests itself as 'I', 'I' in the Heart.*

> **Bhagavan:** That Self will by itself be repeating always '*aham aham*' ['I', 'I']. That is *ajapa*. To know that aspect is '*ajapa*'; how could that which is repeated by mouth be *ajapa*? The vision of the real Self which performs *japa* of its own accord involuntarily and in a never-ending stream, like the flowing down continuously of ghee, is *ajapa*, *gayatri* and everything.
> **Question:** Is there no benefit at all in doing *japa* with the mouth?
> **Bhagavan:** Who said no? That will be the means for *chitta suddhi* [purifying the mind]. As the *japa* is done repeatedly the effort ripens and sooner or later leads to the right path.[14]

## Chanting '*Sivaya Nama*'

'Sivaya Nama', *meaning 'Obeisance to Siva', is the most powerful and sacred mantra for Saivas. It is sometimes referred to as the* 'panchakshari', *the 'five syllables'.*

**40*** Through grace, *Padam* ensures that there is never any danger to those who remain in their heart, meditating '*Sivaya Nama*'.

**41** The mantra '*Sivaya Nama*' on which you meditate will reveal itself within your heart to be your father and mother.

*In this verse the father implies Siva, who is* sat, *being, while the mother denotes* sakti, *or* chit, *consciousness.*

**42*** The mind that does *japa*, 'Siva, Siva,' will later automatically lose itself in *ajapa*.

*Though Bhagavan rarely gave out mantras, when he did, he generally recommended 'Siva, Siva'. Muruganar himself was given this mantra by Bhagavan, as were several other devotees including Annamalai Swami, the brother of Rangan (who was one of Bhagavan's childhood friends), and an unknown harijan.*

**43** The state in which the heart is firmly established in *Sivam* will arise when the heart dwells unceasingly upon the *panchakshari*.

> **Bhagavan:** Sambanda is a devotee of Siva. He explained in a verse the way to do the *japa* of *panchakshari* of Lord Siva's name. Its meaning is that one should close *navadwaras* [the nine apertures of the human body, i.e. two eyes, two ears, two nostrils, mouth, anus and the organ of generation], lock them and seal them; otherwise the mind will run away. After sealing the nine doors, do *panchakshari japa* [repeating the five letters]. If by controlling the senses, the mind can be controlled, i.e. submerged, that which remains is the Self. One meditates on one's Self and the *japa* becomes one's own Self.[15]

*Jnanasambandhar was a sixth century Tamil saint whose poems and biography now form part of the Saiva canon.*

**Love**

**44** Except in consciousness of truth, it is impossible for a life possessing beauty, the manifestation of true love, to exist.

**45** *Padam*, declaring the majesty of *jnana*, states: 'It is only through *jnana* that the bliss that derives from true love will arise.'

*The Tamil word translated as* jnana *in Bhagavan's statement is* aram. *Though it generally denotes* 'dharma', jnana *is one of its secondary meanings.*

**46** It is only in the field of *jnana* experience that the joy of the Self, which is love, can take root and grow.

**47** In everyone true love towards oneself exists as one's own nature. Therefore, one's true nature is bliss.

**48** Therefore, the duty of those who desire to obtain supreme bliss is to know, through thorough enquiry, their real nature.

**49** Consciousness alone is the experience of true love. Sensory experiences, which are not consciousness, are only a spurious semblance of that love.

**50** Only true love that has taken the form of pure consciousness is the Siva *bhakti* that has attained fullness, true *jnana.*

*Sri Ramana Gita,* chapter 16, verse 4:

> Love flowing like a stream of oil towards the Supreme Lord, even without his desire, takes the mind of a person surely to his true form.

**51*** Until one knows consciousness, it is not possible for anyone to know the nature of devotion, the relationship with true love.

**52*** Only the abandonment of the sense of separation [*vibhakti*] can be termed as rejoicing in the true love that rises in pure *Sivam.*

**53** Because the Self has bliss as its nature, love towards the Self exists in the *jiva* as its very nature.

*A manuscript was read out to Bhagavan in which there was the following statement: 'Only when there is complete devotion, the Lord will respond and take charge of the devotee.' This prompted the following exchange:*

> **Question:** Is it a condition precedent for the Lord showing grace that one must be completely devoted? Would not the Lord naturally in his grace be kind towards all his children whether they are devoted or not?
> **Bhagavan:** How can one help being devoted? Everyone loves himself. That is experience. If the Self were not his dearest object, would one love it? The Self or Lord is not

somewhere else but is inside each of us and in loving oneself, one loves only the Self.[16]

**Muruganar:** Because every being naturally has love flowing towards itself, the Self is *sukha swarupa* [the happiness of one's true nature]. To those who have realised *Atma-swarupa* as it is, devoid of the ego, the Supreme Lord shines as their own Self. Because of the love naturally melting towards that Supreme Lord, *Atma jnana* is called by another name: *parabhakti* [supreme devotion]. Hence, *Parabhakti* and *Atma jnana* are not different.[17]

**54*** Unless one loves the Self as one's own *swarupa*, it is impossible to abide as one really is in the Heart.

**Bhagavan:** Love itself is the actual form of God. If by saying, 'I do not love this; I do not love that', you reject all things, that which remains is *swarupa*, i.e. innate Self. That is pure bliss. Call it pure bliss, God, *Atma* or what you will. That is devotion; that is realisation and that is everything.[18]

## Devotion

**55** The amount of blissful grace that spreads out in your heart will only be in proportion to the amount of true devotion that flows steadily from you to God.

**Question**: Then what is true devotion [*bhakti*]?
**Bhagavan:** Whatever I do or consider myself doing is really the Lord's doing. Nothing really belongs to me. I am here for the service of the Lord. This spirit of service... is really devotion supreme and the true devotee sees the supreme being as the Lord immanent in everything. Worship of Him by name and form leads one beyond all name and form. Devotion complete culminates in knowledge supreme.

Even when *bhakti* is actuated by worldly desires in the beginning, it does not cease when the desires are fulfilled. It increases by an unshakable faith growing perfectly into a supreme state of realisation.[19]

56 To gain the accomplishment of true realisation of the Self, which is the goal to be sought, the appropriate means is devotion to Lord Siva.

57 The state of absorption in the Self, where the ego is destroyed, is alone the clear state of glorious devotion to Lord Siva.

58 Perfect devotion will only arise on seeing the Lord who shines in the Heart as *Atma-swarupa*, whose form is all bliss.

> **Question:** Will *bhakti* lead to *mukti*?
> **Bhagavan:** *Bhakti* is not different from *mukti*. *Bhakti* is being as the Self [*swarupa*]. One is always that. He realises it by the means he adopts. What is *bhakti*? To think of God. That means: only one thought prevails to the exclusion of all other thoughts. That thought is of God, which is the Self, or it is the self surrendered unto God. When He has taken you up nothing will assail you. The absence of thought is *bhakti*. It is also *mukti*.
>
> The *jnana* method is said to be *vichara* [enquiry]. That is nothing but 'supreme devotion' [*parabhakti*]. The difference is in words only.[20]

59 The Siva *bhakti* that accumulates in the Heart through the observance of Siva *dharma* will protect the soul like armour.

60 The one-short-of-ten types of devotion are graduated steps for the experience of the non-dual reality.

*Lakshman Sarma has explained what the 'one-short-of-ten' allusion means in a verse and commentary from* Sri Ramana Paravidyopanishad:

> The wise call by the name 'self-surrender' the offering of oneself to God through devotion. Hence the seeker of deliverance must practise devotion to God, which is described as ninefold, consisting of listening and all the rest.

> Here reference is made to a verse in the *Bhagavatam* [in which the nine types of devotion are listed]:

> > Listening to the tales of God's glory, telling and remembering them, cleaving to his feet, worship,

obeisance, acts of service, cherishing him as a friend, and offering of oneself to Him.[21]

61 If the obstacle of *dehatma buddhi* [I-am-the-body idea] ceases completely, *eka-bhakti* [devotion to the one reality] will come into existence in your Heart as your own nature.

**Bhagavan:** Any kind of meditation is good. But if the sense of separateness is lost and the object of meditation or the subject who meditates is alone left behind without anything else to know, it is *jnana*. *Jnana* is said to be *ekabhakti*. The *jnani* is the finality because he has become the Self and there is nothing more to do. He is also perfect and so fearless '*Dwitiyat vai bhayam bhavati*' – only the existence of a second gives rise to fear. This is *mukti*. It is also *bhakti*.[22]

62 Only the experience of the Self, uninterrupted by any forgetfulness, is true devotion. This, indeed, is behaving in a chaste way in one's relationship with the Lord of the *jiva*, the Self.

# Advice on *Sadhana*

## The necessity of serious *sadhana*

1 In order that your mind should become firm, observe with full attention your duty, which is the practice of *sadhana*.

2 Instead of practising *sadhana* superficially, follow it intensively in such a way that your mind is totally immersed in it.

3 Only the aspiration towards the fair firmament of supreme consciousness, which has no final goal other than *mauna*, is most worthy endeavour.

4 Grace will not combine with a bat-like mentality. Stick with intensity to one [path].

*Bats nibble at one fruit and fly away, looking for another fruit to nibble at. They never stay long enough in one place to finish a single fruit.*

5 All meditation practices are the means that enable the attainment of the strength of mind that is necessary for *Atmanishta*.

> **Question:** How is the mind to be eliminated or relative consciousness transcended?
> **Bhagavan:** The mind is by nature restless. Begin liberating it from its restlessness; give it peace; make it free from distractions; train it to look inward; make this a habit. This is done by ignoring the external world and removing the obstacles to peace of mind.
> **Question:** How is restlessness removed from the mind?
> **Bhagavan:** External contacts – contacts with objects other than itself – make the mind restless. Loss of interest in non-Self [*vairagya*] is the first step. Then the habits of introspection and concentration follow. They are characterised by control of external senses, internal faculties, [*sama*, *dama*, etc.] ending in *samadhi* [undistracted mind].

**Question:** How are they practised?
**Bhagavan:** An examination of the ephemeral nature of external phenomena leads to *vairagya*. Hence enquiry [*vichara*] is the first and foremost step to be taken. When *vichara* continues automatically, it results in a contempt for wealth, fame, ease, pleasure, etc. The 'I' thought becomes clearer for inspection.[1]

## On having the right attitude to *sadhana*

6 If you regard *Brahman*, your own real nature, as something different from you, it will feel shy, separate from you and slip away.

7 Any effort to reach reality, thinking it to be different from oneself, will cause the non-dual experience, wherein one abides as reality, to go extremely far away.

8 Do not falter, even for a moment, believing that you face insurmountable obstacles [on the path], but remain vigilant in the unfailing and guaranteed method you have adopted – that of not forgetting the Self.

**Bhagavan:** All thoughts such as 'attainment is hard,' or 'Self-realisation is far from me,' or, 'I have got many difficulties to overcome to know the reality,' should be given up as they are obstacles; they are created by this false self, ego.[2]

9 It is harmful to regard as important the ecstatic experiences of a mind that has not clearly known reality through the *sakti* of Siva.

## What constitutes effective *sadhana*?

10 The foremost of all *sadhanas* is silence of the mind; this is what true devotees should practise.

**Bhagavan:** Silence is of four kinds: silence of speech, silence of the eye, silence of the ear, and silence of the mind. Only the last is pure silence, and it is the most important.[3]

11 How useful can those paths be that do not clearly reveal the Self,

even though they speak clearly about other things?

12 Your duty is only to pay attention to what is already existing. All other *sadhanas* are just a great dream.

13 The many different *sadhanas* are harmonised when the *sadhaka* first comes to know and discover the truth of his real nature.

14 The most appropriate form of practice, the best *sadhana* that you can do, is enquiring into yourself and remaining steadfastly as the Self.

### The importance of physical silence

15 The first and most important lesson that has to be learned by *sadhakas* is silence.

16 The silence [of not speaking] is the medicine that can change the habit of speaking pointlessly like a mad person.

### The importance of subduing mind-consciousness

17 Curb the restless activity of mind-consciousness. Then, as if you were firmly driving in a nail, destroy and annihilate it in pure consciousness.

18 To whatever extent [that] mind-consciousness dives within, to that same extent will the bliss of the Self spring forth and reveal itself.

> *Guru Vachaka Kovai*, verse 451: To whatever extent you dive within the Heart, to that same extent you will experience the bliss that merges with you as the undivided *Atma-swarupa* that exists and shines with an utterly different nature [to sense enjoyments].
> *Vilakkam*: The bliss of *swarupa* will manifest to the extent that one dives into the Heart. It will be equally appropriate to say, 'to the extent that *suttarivu* is diminished'. Bhagavan says that even when a desired object of enjoyment is attained, bliss is experienced because the mind dives into the Heart. Therefore, as the mind abides more and more in the Heart without *suttarivu*, like a discriminating person who does not leave the shade, the bliss of the Self will shine of its own accord.

19 Unless the mind abides as a mere witness to everything, and

conducts itself in this way, what can all the other [practices] do for a *sadhaka*?

## Giving up distinctions

**20** The reason for the mind's perplexity is the belief that the seductive and addictive pairs of opposites are real.
**21** How can liking and disliking be inherent in the non-dual reality in which it is impossible either to reject or accept.
**22** Give up disputation; give up the distinction 'I' and 'this' that arises from delusion and become gloriously whole.
**23** Destroying the feeling that there are differences [*bheda-buddhi*] is the magnificent accomplishment that is attained through extensive *sadhana*.
**24** Abide, bathing constantly in the cascading waters of unsurpassed bliss, beyond all differentiation.

## Ignoring the non-Self

**25** It is the desire to know something other than consciousness that pushes one into ignorance and delusion.
**26** To cleave, not to consciousness' form, but to that which is foreign to it, that is the astonishing stupidity, which is the very image of intoxication.
**27** Rather than gaining peace by regarding consciousness as reality, why do you fret over things that are foreign [to consciousness], as if they are that reality?
**28** You should know that the primal origin of peace is within oneself, and not in the non-Self.
**29** Unless thoughts about non-Self objects cease, the peace of one's own authentic Self-nature will not be realised in the Heart.
**30** Those deluded ones who do not forsake that which is alien [to the Self] and who do not cleave to their own consciousness' form will become frenzied and be lost.
**31** Though you may come to know in great detail the false principles of the non-Self [*anatma tattvas*], it will all be wasted effort.

**Question:** Is it necessary for one who longs for release to enquire into the nature of the categories [*tattvas*]?
**Bhagavan:** Just as one who wants to throw away garbage has no need to analyse it and see what it is, so one who

wants to know the Self has no need to count the number of categories or enquire into their characteristics; what he has to do is reject altogether the categories that hide the Self. The world should be considered like a dream.[4]

**32** Do not roam around, putting your attention on the non-Self. Abide in the fullness that is your own real nature, which is the bliss of peace.

**Question:** Is renunciation necessary for Self-realisation?
**Bhagavan:** Renunciation and realisation are the same. They are different aspects of the same state. Giving up the non-Self is renunciation. Inhering in the Self is *jnana* or Self-realisation. One is the negative and the other the positive aspect of the same, single truth.[5]

**Question:** What is awareness and how can one obtain and cultivate it?
**Bhagavan:** You are awareness. Awareness is another name for you. Since you are awareness there is no need to attain or cultivate it.

All that you have to do is to give up being aware of other things, that is, of the not-Self. If one gives up being aware of them then pure awareness alone remains, and that is the Self.[6]

**33** Why, abandoning the Self, the supreme truth, do you dally with that which is alien [to it]?
**34** Unless the desire for the non-Self completely ceases, that enduring reality will not be attained.
**35** What can the mind, which knows only the non-Self, do to know the nature of the *Atma-swarupa*?

**Question:** How to find the *Atman*?
**Bhagavan:** There is no investigation into the *Atman*. The investigation can only be into the non-Self. Elimination of the non-Self is alone possible. The Self, being always self evident, will shine forth of itself.[7]

**36** Do not wander about seeking the non-Self, but undertake the task of merging with your own nature, *jnana*.

**37** Those in whose hearts the light of *Padam* has penetrated will not see the non-Self, the cause of misery.

## Yoga

**38** The attainment of hatha yoga is a defective accomplishment since it can be lost. But for the one who has attained *jnana*, the perfect accomplishment, there is never any loss.

*Hatha yoga in this context means 'forced yoga', or yogic accomplishments sustained by effort:*

> **Bhagavan:** Again, people often ask how the mind is controlled. I say to them, 'Show me the mind and then you will know what to do'. The fact is that the mind is only a bundle of thoughts. How can you extinguish it by the thought of doing so or by a desire? Your thoughts and desires are part and parcel of the mind. The mind is simply fattened by new thoughts rising up. Therefore it is foolish to attempt to kill the mind by means of the mind. The only way of doing it is to find its source and hold on to it. The mind will then fade away of its own accord. Yoga teaches *chitta vritti nirodha* [control of the activities of the mind]. But I say *Atma vichara* [Self-investigation]. This is the practical way. *Chitta vritti nirodha* is brought about in sleep, swoon or by starvation. As soon as the cause is withdrawn there is recrudescence of thoughts. Of what use it is then? In the state of stupor there is peace and no misery. But misery recurs when the stupor is removed. So *nirodha* [control] is useless and cannot be of lasting benefit.[8]

**39*** *Padam* graciously bestows the majesty of truth by destroying the enemy, delusion, putting an end to the misery of controlling the breath through hatha yoga.

**40** For those who are attempting to know their real nature, the pure consciousness, through the grace of Bhagavan, the method of *pranayama* [breath control] is a deluding attachment.

*When Bhagavan spoke about the practice of* pranayama, *he was rarely as critical as he is in these two verses. Usually, he would say that* pranayama *could be a useful preliminary aid for devotees who could not otherwise control their minds. He would, though, almost always add that the effect of breath control was always temporary. This is what he had to say on the subject in* Who am I?*:*

> To make the mind subside, there is no adequate means except enquiry. If controlled by other means, the mind will remain in an apparent state of subsidence, but will rise again. For example, through *pranayama* the mind will subside. However, the mind will remain controlled only as long as the *prana* [the breath, the life force in the body] is controlled. When the *prana* comes out, the mind will also come out and wander under the influence of *vasanas*.... *Pranayama* is only an aid for controlling the mind; it will not bring about its destruction.

**Affirmation and negation**

**41** Instead of merging without thought as That, why do you repeatedly think, like a mantra, 'I am That,' and get fatigued?

*Bhagavan distinguished between meditation, which he defined as meditating or concentrating on an object, and self-enquiry, which he defined as seeking the source of the 'I'-thought, or abiding as that source. He would say that thinking about the Self – for example repeating 'I am Siva' or 'I am* Brahman*' or 'I am That' – was an intellectual activity that kept the mind busy instead of taking it back to its source. As he explained in* Who am I?*:*

> Keeping the mind fixed in the Self at all times is called self-enquiry, whereas thinking oneself to be *Brahman*, which is *sat-chit-ananda* [being-consciousness-bliss], is meditation. Eventually, all that one has learnt will have to be forgotten.

> *Guru Vachaka Kovai*, verse 902, *Pozhippurai*: Since the reality, the perfect One, is completely established as the nature of *mauna*, why suffer distress by continuously thinking 'I am That'? When the mind has reached this state of *mauna*, this indeed is establishment in the supreme, which is abidance with the 'I' extinguished. Once

the 'I' has completely died, there is absolutely no possibility of thinking 'I am That'.

*Vilakkam*: 'Why, day and night, shout "I am That" loudly, describing the reality, whose bliss is ineffable. Those who have attained the auspicious Siva-*jnana* say that in the state of true *mauna*, there is no "I".' [Thayumanavar chapter 28, verse 25].

In this verse Thayumanavar beautifully describes *jnana*, the non-dual attainment.

**42** Instead of remaining in blissful Self-abidance, as that which one is, why should one think 'I am this, I am that'?

*The advice given out in this verse, whose theme parallels the previous one, was once queried by a visitor:*

**Question:** Is not affirmation of God more effective than the quest 'Who am I?' Affirmation is positive, whereas the other is negation. Moreover, it indicates separateness.

**Bhagavan:** So long as you seek to know how to realise, this advice is given to find your Self. Your seeking the method denotes your separateness.

**Question:** Is it not better to say 'I am the Supreme Being' than ask 'Who am I?'

**Bhagavan:** Who affirms? There must be one to do it. Find that one.

**Question:** Is not meditation better than investigation?

**Bhagavan:** Meditation implies mental imagery, whereas investigation is for the reality. The former is objective, whereas the latter is subjective.

**Question:** There must be a scientific approach to this subject.

**Bhagavan:** To eschew unreality and seek the reality is scientific.[9]

**Question:** If we think 'I am the real,' will it do?

**Bhagavan:** All thoughts are inconsistent with realisation. The correct state is to exclude thoughts of ourselves and all other thoughts. Thought is one thing and realisation is quite another.[10]

**43*** The truth of one's real nature – which remains alone in the Heart without being known by the intellect – cannot be realised by keenness of intellect alone.

> **Bhagavan:** There is a unity really, but intellect makes the differences. Yet intellect is a power of the Self. But the principle which lies behind the intellect cannot be known by the intellect.[11]

**44** Letting go of the tether of *jnana swarupa*, why are you holding onto the tail, the 'I am Siva' concept?

*The tether in this verse is the rope that goes round a bull's neck and through its nose. The bull is the mind, which can easily be led by its tether. Pulling on its tail, though, will not control the bull.*

**45** Declaring that everything is the Self is only the repetition of the deluded view of the ego that perceives everything.

*In order to say that everything is the Self, there must be an 'I' who perceives the everything. Lakshmana Swamy has explained how statements such as these betray a lack of direct experience:*

> People say that seeing the Self or God everywhere is Self-realisation, but that is not true. To see the Self everywhere there must be an 'I' who sees and while that 'I' exists, the mind will also exist. The *jnani* does not see anything because the seeing entity in him has died. In the Self there is no seeing, only being. When the mind still exists one can reach a stage where one can see the whole world as a manifestation of the Self, but when the mind dies, there is no one who sees the world and no world to be seen.
>
> If you have a mind, then the earth, the sky and the stars will exist and you will be able to see them. When the mind dies there will be no earth, no sky, no stars and no world. The world of objects, names and forms is only the mind, and when the mind dies, the world dies with it. Only the Self then remains.
>
> Seeing everything as the Self gives the impression that the Self is equally distributed everywhere. This is also an

idea in the mind. When the mind finally dies, you realise that there is no distribution and no everywhere.[12]

**46** The true consciousness of the unique supreme will not become fixed and constant merely by thinking about it, but only when the degraded delusion 'I' ceases.

**47** Why do you suffer, thinking 'I, I'? If you remain still as the Self, you will be bliss itself.

*Though Bhagavan in this verse is equating thinking 'I, I' with suffering, on a few occasions he did concede that repeating 'I, I' was a possible way of finding the source of the 'I'. However, he would generally reserve this advice for devotees who found his usual teachings on self-enquiry to be too hard to follow:*

**Question:** I am not learned in the scriptures and I find the method of self-enquiry too hard for me. I am a woman with seven children and a lot of household cares and it leaves me little time for meditation. I request Bhagavan to give me some simpler and easier method.

**Bhagavan:** No learning or knowledge of scriptures is necessary to know the Self, as no man requires a mirror to know himself. All knowledge is required only to be given up eventually as not-Self. Nor is household work or cares with children necessarily an obstacle. If you can do nothing more at least continue saying 'I, I' to yourself mentally as advised in *Who am I?* '...if one incessantly thinks "I, I", it will lead one to that state [the Self].' Continue to repeat it whatever work you may be doing, whether you are sitting, standing or walking. 'I' is the name of God. It is the first and greatest of all mantras. Even *Om* is second to it.[13]

**48** Realise that *buddhi vyabara* [intellectual activity] is also *chitta vyabara* [mental activity]. Since it is a great obstacle, get rid of it completely.

*Though the verse refers to intellectual activity of all kinds, it is also a warning to avoid* sadhanas, *such as affirmation and negation, that attempt to utilise the intellect to realise the Self:*

**Question:** We try to meditate, but there is no progress in our meditation. We do not understand how to realise. Can you kindly help us towards realisation?

**Bhagavan:** How do you meditate?

**Question:** I begin to ask myself 'Who am I?', eliminate the body as not 'I', the breath as not 'I', the mind as not 'I' and I am not able to proceed further.

**Bhagavan:** Well, that is so far as the intellect goes. Your process is only intellectual. Indeed, all the scriptures mention the process only to guide the seeker to know the truth. The truth cannot be directly pointed out. Hence this intellectual process.

You see, the one who eliminates all the '*not* I' cannot eliminate the 'I'. To say 'I am not this' or 'I am that' there must be the 'I'. This 'I' is only the ego or the 'I'-thought. After the rising up of this 'I'-thought, all other thoughts arise. The 'I'-thought is therefore the root-thought. If the root is pulled out all others are at the same time uprooted. Therefore see the root 'I', question yourself 'Who am I?'; find out its source. Then all these will vanish and the pure Self will remain ever.[14]

### Eliminating desires

**49** The divine *Padam* says: 'Desiring something, [imagining it] to be wonderful, is the conduct of the ignorant ego-ghost.'

**50** Those ignorant people who are itching with the desire for this illusory life are whirling in the life of the cremation ground.

**51** Evil desire, a pit that can never be filled, is what plunges your life into a poverty that can never be overcome.

*Guru Vachaka Kovai*, verse 371, *Pozhippurai*: Before attaining a desired object, intense desire makes even an atom appear to be a huge mountain. However, when the desired object is attained, in total contrast, the huge mountain appears to be an atom. As strong desires keep us forever impoverished, we have not seen anywhere a bottomless abyss that is as impossible to fill as avaricious desires, which can never be satisfied.

*Vilakkam*: Tiruvalluvar also says, 'desire whose nature is such that it can never be satisfied'. As true wealth is only contentment of mind, when that contentment is absent, no one can pull himself out of poverty and become wealthy, irrespective of how much money he earns.

**52** A heart in which the *kamya buddhi* [a mind that desires particular results] has departed and which possesses the auspicious and excellent *nishkamya buddhi* [a mind that lacks desires for results] will be the home of bliss.

**53** The state of rest that shines when all desire has ceased is the powerful experience of Vedanta.

**54** If the six illusory enemies, beginning with desire, that mingle in your heart are totally destroyed, the extremely clear light of *jnana* will shine.

*The six enemies are desire, anger, greed, delusion, intoxication and envy.*

**Question:** What is the true meaning of renunciation? Subjugation of lust, passion, greed etc. is common to all and forms the essential, preliminary step for any course. Does not freedom from passions indicate renunciation?...
**Bhagavan:** You have said it all. Your question contains the answer also. Freedom from passions is the essential prerequisite. When that is accomplished, all else is accomplished.[15]

**Question:** How am I to deal with my passions? Am I to check them or satisfy them? If I follow Bhagavan's method and ask, 'To whom are these passions?' they do not seem to die but grow stronger.
**Bhagavan:** That only shows you are not going about my method properly. The right way is to find out the root of all passions, the source whence they proceed, and get rid of that. If you check the passions, they may get suppressed for the moment, but will appear again. If you satisfy them, they will be satisfied only for the moment and will again crave satisfaction. Satisfying desires and thereby trying to root them out is like trying to quench fire by pouring kerosene over it. The only way is to find the root of desire and thus remove it.[16]

55 If you drive out and eliminate the demons of desire and so on, what then becomes one with you is the treasure house of liberation.

**Question:** What is the best way of dealing with desires, with a view to getting rid of them – satisfying them or suppressing them?
**Bhagavan:** If a desire can be got rid of by satisfying it, there will be no harm in satisfying such a desire. But desires generally are not eradicated by satisfaction. Trying to root them out that way is like pouring spirits to quench fire. At the same time, the proper remedy is not forcible suppression, since such repression is bound to react sooner or later into forceful surging up with undesirable consequences. The proper way to get rid of a desire is to find out, 'Who gets the desire? What is its source?' When this is found, the desire is rooted out and it will never again emerge or grow. Small desires such as the desire to eat, drink and sleep and attend to calls of nature, though these may also be classed among desires, you can safely satisfy. They will not implant *vasanas* in your mind, necessitating further birth. Those activities are just necessary to carry on life and are not likely to develop or leave behind *vasanas* or tendencies. As a general rule, therefore, there is no harm in satisfying a desire where the satisfaction will not lead to further desires by creating *vasanas* in the mind.[17]

56 This [vision of the Self] will only be encountered by those who are free of the delusion of desire, and not by those whose corrupted minds are full of desires for sense objects.

*Guru Vachaka Kovai*, verse 149: The non-dual experience will only be attained by those who have completely given up desires. For those with desires, it is extremely far away. Hence it is proper for those with desires to direct their desires towards God, who is desireless, so that through desire for God their deluding desires become extinct.

57 A heart that has been usurped by the demon of powerful desires, which are vile attachments, is a home for miseries that will stream

forth like winged white ants from their hole.

58 If everything is perceived as the one consciousness alone, there will not be even the tiniest amount of yearning in your mind.

> **Question:** How can they [desires] be rendered weaker?
> **Bhagavan:** By knowledge. You know that you are not the mind. The desires are in the mind. Such knowledge helps one to control them.
> **Question:** But they are not controlled in our practical lives.
> **Bhagavan:** Every time you attempt satisfaction of a desire the knowledge comes that it is better to desist. What is your true nature? How can you ever forget it? Waking, dream and sleep are mere phases of the mind. They are not of the Self. You are the witness of these states. Your true nature is found in sleep.[18]

> **Bhagavan:** There is room for *kama* [desire] so long as there is an object apart from the subject, i.e., duality. There can be no desire if there is no object. The state of no-desire is *moksha*. There is no duality in sleep and also no desire. Whereas there is duality in the waking state and desire also is there. Because of duality a desire arises for the acquisition of the object. That is the outgoing mind, which is the basis of duality and of desire. If one knows that bliss is none other than the Self the mind becomes inward turned. If the Self is gained all the desires are fulfilled.[19]

59 The proliferation of desires in life results from the spread of worldly attachments, which is in turn the devastating consequence of forgetting one's true nature.

60 It is a wonder that the *jiva* gets destroyed like a moth in the flame of evil sense objects, with the goal of unlimited desire becoming its ruin.

61 By destroying the concepts of the mind, the desires that accumulate in worldly life – a life that is unnatural and born out of delusion – will be destroyed.

62 A mind that is greatly agitated by the winds of desire will find peace for a while through thinking about God.

## Losing the addiction to sense perceptions

**63** Only consciousness is the perfect reality. All senses and their perceptions, which are not consciousness, are the ignoble imperfections of the false mind.

**64** A mind that runs after pleasure through the five senses, while squashing her Lord in the Heart, is an unchaste woman.

*Guru Vachaka Kovai*, verse 73, *Pozhippurai*: Even on the day that the 'I' rises, this lady, the moon-like sense of individuality, is duty bound to carefully conduct herself in a chaste state in the Heart – the space of consciousness – as the legitimate wife of the Lord, the Self which is the sun of *jnana*. If she forsakes the bliss of the Self, which is in harmony with her *dharma*, and slips from that chaste conduct through infidelity, immersing herself in worldly enjoyment and wallowing in it, this is just a frenzied act of stupidity caused by beginningless, ancient karma.

*Vilakkam*: The *jiva* and the Self have here been called, respectively, the moon and the sun, and their residence has been described as the Heart, the space of consciousness.

'The bliss of the Self': this is the supreme bliss that is one's own nature. In truth, it possesses the eminence of transcending the mind.

'Worldly enjoyment': this is the enjoyment experienced through the five senses – seeing, hearing, tasting, smelling and touching.

These two types of enjoyment [the bliss of the Self and worldly enjoyment] differ in greatness like a mountain and a pit in a river bed. They are, respectively, divine and demonic attainments that are opposed to each other. Because of this it has been said, 'forsakes the bliss of the Self... immersing herself in worldly enjoyment and wallowing in it, this is just a frenzied act of stupidity...'.

Therefore, only the attainment of the experience of the Self can be the hallmark of one possessing wisdom.

**65** The enduring knowledge of reality, the experience of truth, is not possible for those who have gone the way of the false and ignoble senses, having had a lover's tiff with the state of the Self.

66 How can the *ekatma swarupa* [the reality of the one Self] shine in the Heart of those dull-minded people who are excessively deluded?

67 Knowing that the real obstacle to [the attainment of *ekatma swarupa*] is the great addiction to the objects perceived by the five senses, get rid of that addiction.

Once a devotee asked Bhagavan about the significance of fasting. With a benevolent look towards him Bhagavan said, 'If all the activities of the *indriyas* [five senses] are given up, the mind becomes single-pointed. When such a mind gets concentrated on God, it is real *upavasam* [fasting]. '*Upa*' means 'being near'. '*Vasam*' means 'living'. Where is he going to live? He will live in his Self. Desires are the food for the mind. Giving them up is *upavasam*. If there are no desires whatsoever, there is no such thing as mind. What remains then is the Self. One who can fast the mind need not fast the body,' said Bhagavan.[20]

68 Do not allow yourself to be buffeted by the sense perceptions in this world, but become firmly established in the discipline of spiritual practice [*tapas*], and be totally free of misery.

69 Protect your mind by all possible means so that harmful cravings for the sense objects of the world do not cling to it.

70 Do not cherish the five sense perceptions, which are illusory, but know your own consciousness that shines, pervading them all equally.

*From the essay version of* Who am I?*:*

Although *vishaya vasanas* [tendencies to indulge in sense perceptions], which have been recurring down the ages, rise in countless numbers like the waves of an ocean, they will all perish as meditation on one's real nature becomes more and more intense. Without giving room even to the doubting thought 'Is it possible to destroy all these *vasanas* and remain as Self alone?' one should persistently and tightly hold onto meditation on one's real nature. However great a sinner one may be, one should, instead of lamenting, 'Oh I am a sinner! How can I attain liberation?', completely give up even the thought of being a sinner. One steadfast in meditation on one's real nature will surely be saved.

71 The deluded existence of the body and the sense organs will not perish except through a direct experience of Vedanta.

72 The highest and most heroic act of valour is to burn to ashes [in the fire of *jnana*] the evil enemy that takes the form of sense perceptions.

73 The minds of those who grieve, regarding the sense-perceptions as real, cannot merge with the bliss of true *jnana*, abounding in goodness.

74 The reason for desiring the insipid objects perceived by the five senses is non-discrimination [*aviveka*], which is an absence of enquiry into one's real nature.

75 In a mind in which divine consciousness holds sway, the feeling of infatuation for the sordid enjoyments of the senses, which arises in the false, will cease to be.

**Purification of the mind**

76 Since purity of mind is indispensable for any kind of spiritual practice, it possesses an eminence of the highest order.

77 The greatness of *chitta suddhi* [purity of mind] is that it is the mother of all virtuous conduct. Realising this, examine your mind every day.

78 It is natural for a mind that behaves with outstanding rectitude to obtain a firm and focused tranquillity.

79 The melting of the mind [towards God] and the compassion [it exhibits towards creatures] are the means for purifying the mind.

80 Consciousness, one's real nature, is extremely subtle, so subtle that it cannot be known by speech, mind or intellect.

81 It is therefore proper and necessary that they [speech, mind and intellect] should first be reformed through reflecting upon the grace-consciousness of God.

*Vasanas*

82 The nature of thoughts that arise in the mind will be in accordance with the old *vasanas*.

**Bhagavan:** *Vasanas* themselves are the mind. If there are no *vasanas* there is no mind. That which is, is *sat*. *Sat* is *Brahman*. That is self-luminous. That is *Atman*, and that is the Self.[21]

83 The disturbing agitation of mind that occurs when one attempts to get firmly established in *sadhana* is a normal occurrence that is prompted by the rising of *vasanas*.

84 If at that time you hold tightly to the power of the grace of the *parasakti* that has possessed you, the *vasana* that agitates your mind and distresses you will be completely destroyed.

*'The power of the grace of the* parasakti *that has possessed you' is a reference to the inner feeling of 'I am' since this feeling is often referred to in Muruganar's writings as* tiruvarul, *the divine grace that will lead one to the Self.*

85 Unless the destruction of [all] *vasanas* is accomplished, it will not be possible even for Iswara to bestow the state of liberation.

86 The felicitous state of immovable peace that never falters will be attainable only to those who have destroyed the ancient multitude of *vasanas*, putting an end to all attachment.

**Question:** Since realisation is not possible without *vasana-kshaya* [destruction of *vasanas*], how am I to realise that state in which the *vasanas* are effectively destroyed?
**Bhagavan:** You *are* in that state now!
**Question:** Does it mean that by holding on to the Self, the *vasanas* should be destroyed as and when they emerge?
**Bhagavan:** They will themselves be destroyed if you remain as you are.[22]

87 *Pramada* [not keeping one's attention on the Self], whose association with one is detected in the culminating phase of *sadhana*, is the mind's original, deluding *vasana*.

88 Achieving *Atmanishta* through *sadhana* is to arrive at a life that is free from the misery caused by the scorching *vasanas*.

**Bhagavan:** Just as water in the pot reflects the enormous sun within the narrow limits of the pot, even so the *vasanas* or latent tendencies of the mind of the individual, acting as the reflecting medium, catch the all-pervading, infinite light of consciousness arising from the Heart and present, in the form of a reflection, the phenomenon called the mind. Seeing only this reflection, the *ajnani* is deluded into the belief that he is a finite being, the *jiva*.

If the mind becomes introverted through enquiry into the source of *aham-vritti* [the 'I'-thought], the *vasanas* become extinct, and in the absence of the reflecting medium the phenomenon of reflection, the mind, also disappears being absorbed into the light of the one reality, the Heart.

This is the sum and substance of all that an aspirant needs know. What is imperatively required of him is an earnest and one-pointed enquiry into the source of *aham-vritti*.[23]

**89** Destroy the worldly *vasanas*. Sow the *vasana* of *chidakasa* [the expanse of consciousness] in your Heart.

## The destruction of *vasanas*

**90** Expelling the accumulation of evil [*vasanas*] from your Heart, garner in copious quantities the wealth of God [which is grace].

**91** Through the momemtum gained by the practice of *bhakti* yoga, which is loving Iswara, attain the destruction of *vasanas* in your Heart.

**92** Truly, *vasanas* are association [*sanga*]. You should therefore know that their extinction is the total abandonment of all association.

*Guru Vachaka Kovai*, verse 912, *Pozhippurai*: Only the collection of *vasanas* present in the Heart deserves to be despised and discarded by the wise as an association [*sanga*] that constitutes the obstacle to Self-abidance. If one initially remains in solitude, patiently practising Self-abidance, and consequently gets the mind to subside completely, then, in whatever environment the one who possesses the eminence of a *vasana*-free mind may happen to live on account of his *prarabdha*, no blemish will accrue to him.

*Vilakkam*: Unless the *vasanas*, the inner attachments, are already present, the outer attachments cannot pull the mind, making it wander here and there, preventing it from getting established in Self-abidance. Therefore, those who possess the greatness of a stilled mind do not incur any blemish irrespective of the environment they may reside in. The implication is: only inner attachment is truly attachment; outer attachment is not the problem.

**93** Establish yourself in the Self so that the *vasanas*, the impurities, are rooted out and destroyed. That is the true course of action.

**Question:** What are the obstacles which hinder realisation of the Self?
**Bhagavan:** They are habits of mind [*vasanas*].
**Question:** How to overcome the mental habits [*vasanas*]?
**Bhagavan:** By realising the Self.
**Question:** That is a vicious circle.
**Bhagavan:** It is the ego which raises such difficulties, creating obstacles and then suffering from the perplexity of apparent paradoxes. Find out who makes the enquiries and the Self will be found.[24]

**Question:** Can there be Self-realisation before the *vasanas* are entirely destroyed?
**Bhagavan:** There are two kinds of *vasanas*: (1) *bandha hetuh,* causing bondage for the ignorant, and (2) *bhoga hetuh*, giving enjoyment for the wise. The latter do not obstruct realisation.[25]

**94** Like cotton in a fire, everything [meaning all *vasanas*] in the hearts of those in whom the divine grace, the fire of *jnana*, has been kindled will be completely and simultaneously destroyed.

# Grace, Effort and Maturity

## The necessity of grace

1 It is impossible for anyone to get established in the experience of reality, being-consciousness, except through the power of grace, the Mother [*chit-para-sakti*].

2 Other than through grace, the Mother, no one can attain reality, the experience of *Sivam*, which is truth.

*'The Mother' is a reference to* chit-para-sakti, *'consciousness, the supreme power', which is often personified in a female form.*

3 Except through that exalted light, which is the grace of consciousness, the supreme power, it is impossible to transcend the conceptualising power of the mind.

4 The ego can only be destroyed by the power of grace, not by the dark, perverted knowledge [*suttarivu*].

## The operation of grace

5 Self-realisation, which appears very difficult, will be attained very easily through the power of grace.

> *Guru Vachaka Kovai*, verse 512: The attainment of non-dual *jnana* is very difficult. However, if devotion, genuine love, is firmly established towards the feet of Siva, then, through the support of divine grace – the truth and the light that clarifies, destroying delusion – it [*jnana*] becomes extremely easy [to attain].

6 What is termed grace is only the light of pure consciousness that has the power to destroy completely the delusion of ignorance.

7 That which manifests as a flood of grace in the hearts of true devotees is the infinite expanse of consciousness, which is reality.

**Muruganar:** The meaning of grace is Self-knowledge, the substratum that shines naturally when the ego, a superimposition, ceases.

As God, the perfect one, has the form of undivided, pure, non-dual, supreme space, he does not know anything other than himself. That complete fullness, the pure consciousness that is his *swarupa*, is the truth of holy grace.[1]

**Question:** How can I obtain grace?
**Bhagavan:** Grace is the Self. That also is not to be acquired; you only need to know that it exists.

The sun is brightness only. It does not see darkness. Yet you speak of darkness fleeing on the sun's approach. So also the devotee's ignorance, like the phantom of darkness, vanishes at the look of the Guru. You are surrounded by sunlight; yet if you would see the sun, you must turn in its direction and look at it. So also grace is found by the proper approach you make, though it is here and now.[2]

**8** Firmly attaining the meditative experience [of the Self] in the mind, with nothing obstructing it, is the life of grace.

**9** Only the bestowal of tranquillity of mind is God's grace, not the fulfilment of what one desires.

*Guru Vachaka Kovai*, verse 753: Do not conclude that you have attained the exalted grace of God merely on account of the many varieties of worldly riches that you have obtained through virtuous means. Take only the profoundly peaceful clarity of consciousness, a clarity that is devoid of the anxieties that arise through *pramada*, as the indication of God's grace.

**10** Do not wilt and lose heart – walk with abundant faith in divine grace.

**Bhagavan:** When a sparrow was flying, holding its egg in its beak, the egg slipped and fell into the ocean. The sparrow, anxious to retrieve it, repeatedly dipped itself in the ocean, sucked some water through its beak, came to the shore, released the water and fanned its wings. The sage Narada who was passing that way saw this action of the sparrow, enquired, and came to know the reason.

'You stupid sparrow! Is this something you can accomplish?' said Narada.

The sparrow replied, 'I don't care whether it is possible or not. If I persevere tenaciously, beyond that it is in God's hands.'

Narada, delighted with its faith, went to Garuda and told him everything.

Then he said, 'A creature belonging to your bird tribe is exerting itself with so much faith. Is it proper for you to keep quiet? Can you not help?'

After hearing this story Garuda flew quickly to the sparrow. As soon as he flapped his wings there, all the waters of the ocean separated into two, leaving the egg of the sparrow visible. The sparrow immediately picked it up in its beak and flew away.

Similarly, those who meditate on the Self and do good deeds, if they labour hard without feeling 'This is a mammoth task! There is no one to help! Is this possible for me?' then the help of God will come automatically. Will the waters of the ocean get diminished by the sparrow sucking water through its beak and releasing it on the shore? The sparrow performed its task with faith [*sraddha*] and perseverance. Similarly, if anyone makes an effort, it will not fail to bear fruit at some time or other. For all things faith alone is important. For those who engage in good deeds, if they work with faith, the help of God will come, just as it did through Garuda. Until it comes one should work on the job without any faltering of faith, and with utmost exertion.[3]

## Effort and grace

**11** The loss of 'I' can never be fully and perfectly accomplished by *sadhana* alone, the effort of the *jiva*.

*Guru Vachaka Kovai*, verse 648: You should know that the Self becomes evident only through the grace of God that is revealed when one offers oneself with love to the feet of God; but this truth is so very subtle, it cannot be known and realised through the efforts of the intellect of the *jiva*.

**Bhagavan:** As often as one tries to surrender, the ego raises its head and one has to try to suppress it. Surrender is not an easy thing. Killing the ego is not an easy thing. It is only when God Himself by His grace draws the mind inwards that complete surrender can be achieved. But such grace comes only to those who have already, in this or previous lives, gone through all the struggles and *sadhanas* preparatory to the extinction of the mind and killing of the ego.[4]

**12** Without the shining light of grace, what can the insignificant *jivas* do to escape from the net of delusion and gain clarity?

*Guru Vachaka Kovai*, verse 634: In this world, which associates with the *jiva* in the state of ignorance, it is quite impossible, except through God's pure light of grace, for the deluded *jiva* to experience the bliss of reality, the consciousness that shines even in the state of darkness [sleep].
*Vilakkam*: There can be no *darshan* of reality without grace. Bhagavan has said [in *Atma Vidya Kirtanam*] 'Grace too is necessary'. Those who think that *jnana* can be attained by their own might will not attain it until they take refuge in the might of grace.

**13** Because of the ever-present identity [*ekanma-bhava*] between the two [Iswara and the *jiva*, or Guru and disciple], grace and good devotion are not separate from each other.

*From the standpoint of the Self, 'the two' are one and the same. The next verse expounds on a consequence of this identity:*

**14** 'There is therefore no contradiction in saying that either one is the cause of the other.' Thus says the perfect *Padam*, ripe in wisdom.

*'Either one' refers to the question of whether grace is obtained through*

*effort or whether grace prompts one to make the effort.*

**Question:** But isn't the Guru's grace necessary for one's progress in the *vichara*?
**Bhagavan:** Yes. But the *vichara* that you are making is itself the Guru's grace or God's grace.[5]

**Question:** Can I then dispense with outside help and by mine own effort get into the deeper truth by myself?
**Bhagavan:** The very fact that you are possessed of the quest of the Self is a manifestation of the divine grace, *arul*. It is effulgent in the Heart, the inner being, the real Self. It draws you from within. You have to attempt to get in from without. Your attempt is *vichara*, the deep inner movement is grace, *arul*. That is why I say there is no real *vichara* without grace nor is there grace active for him who is without *vichara*. Both are necessary.[6]

**Question:** Is divine grace necessary for attaining realisation, or can an individual's honest efforts by themselves lead to the state from which there is no return to life and death?
**Bhagavan:** Divine grace is essential for realisation. It leads one to God-realisation. But such grace is vouchsafed only to him who is a true devotee or a yogin, who has striven hard and ceaselessly on the path towards freedom.[7]

## Maturity and immaturity

### Immature minds

**15** Of all difficult tasks, the most difficult is to explain to those whose minds are intoxicated [with the pleasures of the senses] the real cause of their joy.

**16** Only after the intoxication [caused by sense pleasures] has somewhat abated will teachings that lead to *jnana* be helpful to such people.

**17** In the face of consciousness, the supreme, which exists as the eternally attained reality, the eyes of those owlish folk whose minds are deluded will go blind.

18 For those people whose minds are withered and deluded, the attainment of a total absence of *sankalpas* [thoughts or intentions] is impossible.

19 Forgetting the lofty purpose of coming [to the *Sadguru*] and developing an obsession for the non-Self is a deception brought about by immaturity in those who are dull-minded.

*Guru Vachaka Kovai*, verse 152, *Pozhippurai*: Through the light of a lamp, the darkness that exists a long distance away departs, but the darkness that is present at the foot of the lamp-post is not removed by the lamp. In the same way, those disciples who stay a long way away from the Guru get redeemed by worshipping in their hearts the *jnana*-Guru who cannot be limited by time or space. Even so, some of those who get the good fortune of staying physically close to the Guru, like his shadow, do not become ripe in *jnana*, losing their ego-darkness, but die ripe only in physical age. This is due to their immaturity. *Vilakkam*: The Guru is the shining sun of the Self who removes inner darkness through his true nature. In truth, he is the space of consciousness that has neither rising nor setting. It has therefore been said, 'the *jnana*-Guru who cannot be limited by time or space'. The point of the verse is this: those who, through rare good fortune, have reached a *jnana*-Guru should not forget the purpose for which they came to him. By focussing their entire attention on it day and night, and by taking his grace as the primary support, they should definitely obtain the good fortune of the Self.

*Naladiyar* says: 'If he who has obtained the good fortune of associating closely with sages, which cannot be bought by any amount of wealth, spends his time wastefully, he is a person of immature mind.'

20 Regarding the marriage ceremony itself as the true state of married, conjugal bliss is an erroneous notion that [just shows] immaturity.

*Guru Vachaka Kovai*, verse 599: A child bride who has not attained puberty will feel happy, believing the marriage ceremony itself to be the experience of union. Similarly, those who have not known the Self by careful investigation, by turning within, will declare their prattle, their book knowledge, to be non-dual *jnana*.

**Qualifications for maturity**

**21** When the mind, through the quality of extreme purity, merges in the Heart, it will attain perfection as peace.

**22** If the mind that has become one-pointed, like the tip of *darba* grass, merges with the Heart, the experience of pure being, seemingly impossible to attain, will be very easily discovered.

**23** Taking a thick fat crowbar [as a needle], it is not possible to stitch together extremely delicate silk cloth using very fine thread.

*Question eleven of* Vichara Sangraham *asks, 'Is Self-experience possible for the mind whose nature is constant change? One part of Bhagavan's answer states:*

> '…It is only by the mind that is impure and is under the influence of *rajas* and *tamas* that reality, which is very subtle and unchanging, cannot be experienced; just as a piece of fine silk cloth cannot be stitched with a heavy crowbar, or as the details of subtle objects cannot be distinguished by the light of a lamp-flame that flickers in the wind…'[8]

**24** Whatever it is, nothing can be attained without the necessary fitness for it.

> I [Balaram Reddy] said, 'There is a teacher and his disciples. The teacher gives the same instruction to all the disciples sitting before him. How is it that some disciples hear the teachings, put them into practice and make quick progress, while others hear and apply the teachings and make little or no progress?'
>
> The Maharshi replied, 'Some must have followed that line of teaching in their previous lives, while others may just have begun. Also, some are born more advanced and fit than others.'[9]

Sri Ramana Gita, *chapter 7, verses 8, 9, 10, 11:*

Who is considered fit for this enquiry? Can one by oneself know one's own fitness?

**[Bhagavan:]** He whose mind has been purified through *upasana* and other means or by merit acquired in past lives, who perceives the imperfections of the body and sense-objects, and feels utter distaste whenever his mind has to function among sense-objects and who realises that the body is impermanent, he is said to be a fit person for self-enquiry.

By these two signs, that is by a sense of the transitoriness of the body and by non-attachment to sense-objects, one's own fitness for self-enquiry can be known.

**Bhagavan:** The aspirant may be *kritopasaka* [one whose worship has culminated in a direct experience of a personal God] or *akritopasaka* [one whose worship has not]. The former is fit to realise the Self, even with the slightest stimulus: only some little doubt stands in his way; it is easily removed if he hears the truth once from the Master. Immediately he gains the *samadhi* state. It is presumed that he had already completed *sravana,* reflection, etc. in previous births; they are no more necessary for him.[10]

**25** Those fickle-minded people who have not done any *sadhana* before cannot gain a clear understanding from instructions alone.
**26** Except for those who have completed everything and who have a mind that is free from desires, remaining still [*summa iruttal*] is not easy.

**Question:** In the practice of meditation are there any signs of the nature of subjective experience or otherwise, which will indicate the aspirant's progress towards Self-realisation?

**Bhagavan:** The degree of freedom from unwanted thoughts and the degree of concentration on a single thought are the measure to gauge the progress.[11]

**Question:** Is it possible for all people to hold on to that path of self-enquiry?

**Bhagavan:** It is true that it is only possible for mature minds, not for immature minds. For the latter, repetition of a prayer or holy name under one's breath [*japa*], worship of images, breath-control [*pranayama*] visualising a pillar of light [*jyotishtoma*] and similar yogic and spiritual and religious practices have been prescribed. By those practices, people become mature and will then realise the Self through the path of self-enquiry.[12]

**Question:** Swami, for gaining realisation, is the enquiry, 'Who am I?' the only way?
**Bhagavan:** Enquiry is not the only way. If one does spiritual practice [*sadhana*] with name and form, repetition of holy names [*japa*], or any of these methods with grim determination and perseverance, one becomes That. According to the capacity of each individual, one spiritual practice is said to be better than another and several shades and variations of them have been given. Some people are a long way from Tiruvannamalai, some are very near; some are in Tiruvannamalai, while some get into Bhagavan's hall itself. For those who come into the hall, it is enough, if they are told as they step in, 'Here is the Maharshi', and they realise him immediately. For others they have to be told which route to take, which trains to catch, where to change, which road to turn into. In like manner, the particular path to be taken must be prescribed according to the capacity of the practiser. These spiritual practices are not for knowing one's own Self, which is all-pervading, but only for getting rid of the objects of desire. When all these are discarded, one remains as one is.[13]

**27** Without maturity [desirelessness] in the mind, the abiding experience of *sahaja samadhi* will not ripen.
**28** Unless one has an extremely pure sattvic mind, it will be impossible to have *darshan* in the Heart of the reality that is *jnana*.
**29*** It is due to maturity of mind [*chitta-paripaka*] that what is very difficult for the many is extremely easy for the very few.

**Bhagavan:** We have to contend against age-long

*samskaras*. They will all go. Only, they go comparatively soon in the case of those who have already made *sadhana* in the past, and late in the case of the others.

**Question:** Do these *samskaras* go gradually or will they suddenly disappear one day? I ask this because, though I have remained fairly long here, I do not perceive any gradual change in me.

**Bhagavan:** When the sun rises, does the darkness go gradually or all at once?[14]

**30** Those very few who realise the Self through *daiva gathi* and get redeemed have minds that are fully mature.

*The following explanation of* daiva gathi *is narrated by Kunju Swami:*

> In those early days of my stay at Skandashram, as I always used to remain close to Sri Bhagavan, I found that I could get all my doubts cleared merely by listening to all the answers to other devotees' questions. Moreover, by listening to all these answers I was able to learn many new aspects of Sri Bhagavan's teachings. I rarely had to ask a question myself. Usually, if I was waiting for an opportune moment to raise a question on some spiritual topic, another devotee would ask Sri Bhagavan that very same question. Sri Bhagavan's answer would then clear the doubts of both of us. This method of acquiring knowledge is known in the scriptures as *daiva gathi*. A good example of *daiva gathi* can be found in *Vasishtam* where it is said that King Janaka got his doubts cleared and attained knowledge by hearing the conversation of some *siddhas*.
>
> In books such as *Vedanta Chudamani* three ways of getting realisation, *daiva gathi*, *viveka gathi* and *viraktha gathi*, have been mentioned. To approach a *Sadguru* and to obtain knowledge by both learning the spiritual texts and by practising discrimination is called *viveka gathi*. *Viraktha gathi* is the instantaneous dawn of knowledge, like a bolt of lightning, irrespective of age and environment. *Jnanis* such as the Buddha, Pattinathar and Sri Bhagavan are examples of this *viraktha gathi*.

*Vasishtam*, an authoritative text, proclaims, 'Like fruit falling unexpectedly from above, true knowledge arises easily'.

A person who goes to have the *darshan* of a realised soul without any desire finds the latter answering the spiritual questions of his disciples. On hearing them, because of past merits, realisation dawns immediately like the lighting up of an electric bulb at the press of a switch. This is known as *daiva gathi*. The great karmas performed in many past births become the cause of attaining knowledge by any of the three ways mentioned above. Many other scriptural texts proclaim the same truth.[15]

# The World and its Creator

The world is like a fiction, played out in space and time and generated by the aggregate of the five senses. For the perplexed souls of men, the only way is to follow the feet of the slayer of death, he whose nature is pure and limitless intelligence.[1]

The appearance of this world, like the illusory appearance of a dream, is merely mental and its truth can be known correctly only by the supreme consciousness that transcends *maya*, the mind.[2]

I researched into where the world had sprung from and realised that it is not from anywhere [outside] but from the 'I' within. I established myself within the Heart and the world disappeared, along with the I-am-the-body idea.[3]

# Creation

## Theories

1 Because of the differences in the nature of those who perceive creation, many differences have accumulated in the theories of creation that have been given in the *sastras*.

> **Bhagavan:** There are so many theories, scriptural and scientific. Have they reached any finality? They cannot...
>
> There may be any number of theories of creation. All of them extend outwardly. There will be no limit to them because time and space are unlimited. They are, however, only in the mind. If you see the mind, time and space are transcended and the Self is realised.
>
> Creation is explained scientifically or logically to one's own satisfaction. But is there any finality about it? Such explanations are called *krama srishti* [gradual creation]. On the other hand, *drishti srishti* [the theory that the world is created by the seer of it] is *yugapad srishti* [simultaneous creation]. Without the seer there are no objects seen. Find the seer and the creation is comprised in him. Why look outward and go on explaining the phenomena which are endless?[1]

2 All ideas about creation and so forth are merely imaginary creations of the mind, which roams around enquiring into them, like a straying bull.

3 Theories of creation have been mentioned in the *sastras* only for those who, forgetting themselves, get bewildered by seeing creation.

*Though Bhagavan taught different theories of creation to different people, his own experience was that creation itself had never occurred except in the imagination of those* jivas *who thought themselves to be unenlightened, and who felt themselves to be part of a physical world:*

**Question:** How has *srishti* [creation] come about? Some say it is due to karma. Others say it is the Lord's *lila* or sport. What is the truth?
**Bhagavan:** Various accounts are given in books. But is there creation? Only if there is creation, we have to explain how it came about. All that, we may not know. But that we exist now is certain. Why not know the 'I' and the present and then see if there is a creation?[2]

**Question:** In the Vedanta of Sri Sankaracharya, the principle of the creation of the world has been accepted for the sake of beginners, but for the advanced, the principle of non-creation is put forward. What is your view in this matter?
**Bhagavan:** *Na nirodha na chotpattir*
*Nabaddho na cha sadhakaha*
*Na mumukshur na vai mukta*
*Ityesha paramarthata*

This *sloka* appears in the second chapter [v. 32, *vaithathya prakarana*] of Gaudapada's *Karika* [a commentary on the *Mandukyopanishad*]. It means really that there is no creation and no dissolution. There is no bondage, no one doing spiritual practices, no one seeking spiritual liberation, and no one who is liberated. One who is established in the Self sees this by his knowledge of reality.[3]

## The process of creation

*When Bhagavan did speak about the way in which the world comes into being, he generally propounded theories of instantaneous creation. The world, he said, is a projection of the mind that sees it. It is an expansion of the 'I'-thought and its* vasanas*:*

**4** The beginningless ego-consciousness, present in the Heart, is the seed of this world.

**5** Manifestation of ancient *vasanas* is creation. Destruction of *vasanas* is the end of creation.

> *Guru Vachaka Kovai*, verse 84: Everything that comes out through the mind and shines, previously existed in the Heart as something buried in the depths. These are the *vasanas*, an ancient tale, that manifest in such a way that they can be seen outside. Know this well.

*Bhagavan often stated that the world is projected outwards by the mind in the same way that cinema pictures are projected onto a screen. In an earlier chapter I quoted verse six of* Arunachala Ashtakam, *a verse Bhagavan composed that explains how the ego and its inherent* vasanas, *animated by the power of the Self, expand and become the whole world and the perceiver of it. Bhagavan was particularly fond of explaining the process that culminates in the manufacture of the world appearance in cinematic metaphors. He sometimes said that if ancient teachers such as Sankara had had cinemas in their day, they too would have used them to explain the projection of the world appearance.*

*Since* vasanas *create the world, it naturally follows that when* vasanas *are destroyed by Self-realisation, the world-picture also disappears as an object of perception:*

6 *Sankalpa* [thought] creates the world. The peace attained on the destruction of *sankalpas* is the [permanent] destruction of the world.

> *Guru Vachaka Kovai*, verse 29, *Pozhippurai*: The world is seen distinctly only in the waking and dream states in which *sankalpas* [thoughts] have emerged. Is it ever seen during sleep, where *sankalpas* do not emerge even slightly? *Sankalpas* alone are the material substance of the world.

## The world as a reflection in consciousness [*chidabhasa*]

*When he went into more detail about the process that culminated in the appearance of a world that was apparently separate from the one who perceives it, Bhagavan would sometimes say that the world is projected onto the screen of consciousness and is seen there in the same way that a projection is seen on a screen. This reflection is known as* chidabhasa; chit *is the underlying consciousness that supports the image, while* abhasa *is the reflected picture that appears in it. This* chidabhasa *is the manifestation of the false, divided consciousness, the* suttarivu, *which projects the world and artificially divides it up into the world and a perceiver of it.*

7 The reflected consciousness [*chidabhasa*], the *suttarivu* that is known as the mind, is an extremely wonderful but false appearance.

> From the Self there arise in succession: [i] *chidabhasa*, which is a kind of luminosity. [ii] *jiva*, the individual consciousness, or the seer of the first concept. [iii] phenomena.[4]

> ...at the moment of rising up, the mind is only light; only afterwards the thought 'I am this' rises up. The 'I'-thought forms the *jiva* and the world.[5]

*For a reflection to take place, there must be a surface for the reflection to bounce off. S. S. Cohen once questioned Bhagavan about this:*

> **Question:** Is the light which gives the 'I'-sense identity and knowledge of the world ignorance or *chit*, consciousness?
> **Bhagavan:** It is only the reflected light of *chit* that makes the 'I' believe itself different from others. This reflected light of *chit* also makes the 'I' create objects, but for this reflection there must be a surface on which the reflection takes place.
> **Question:** What is that surface?
> **Bhagavan:** On realisation of the Self you will find that the reflection and the surface on which it takes place do not actually exist, but that both of them are one and the same *chit*.[6]

8 *Padam* marvels: 'How strange it is that the *jiva* is bewildered by seeing its own reflection!'
9 The reason for this is that it does not know its own nature as the Self well enough to experience bliss.
10 Why, like ignorant children, have a dualistic outlook towards the world, which exists like a reflection of your *swarupa*?

### Removing the reflection

11 *Padam*, the Self, speaks the truth in the following way: 'The union

of *jiva* with *Brahman* is just the removal of the reflected consciousness [*chidabhasa*].'

**Question:** If the *Atman* is without activity at that time, how then does it know itself?
**Bhagavan:** For the *Atman* there is nothing to know or be known. It is the one who has no knowledge who has to make an effort to gain knowledge. This is what takes place in the waking state. *Anatman,* which is the not-Self, which can also be called *chidabhasa,* the reflected consciousness, has the ignorance, so this reflected consciousness has to make an effort for *jnana,* or knowledge. Knowing and not knowing happen in the not-Self. The Self does not have to obtain knowledge, for it is knowledge itself. When the knower, the reflected consciousness, is felt, at that time *ajnana* or ignorance is present. The one who feels this ignorance then makes an effort to attain *jnana,* which is knowledge. When the reflected consciousness gets the knowledge, it no longer remains. This is because the reflected consciousness always remains with ignorance or *mityajnana* [false knowledge]. During sleep there is no reflected consciousness. So, [at that time] the false knowledge is not to be obtained. To know the Self means to know the form of the Self. This [explanation] is all from the point of view of the current conversation. In reality, there is only the *Atman.* Because this is so, there is nothing to know and nothing to be known.[7]

**12** Those fools who seek not the light of consciousness, but set off on the path of the senses, believing in the other light [the *chidabhasa*], will swelter.

**Bhagavan:** To see an object that is in the dark, both the eye and the light of a lamp are required. To see the light only, the eye is enough. But to see the sun, there is no need of any other light. Even if you take the lamp with you, its light will be drowned in the light of the sun. Our intellect or *buddhi* is of no use to realise the Self. To see the world or external objects, the mind and the reflected light, or *chidabhasa*, which always arises with it, are necessary. To see the Self, the mind has simply to be turned inside and there is no need of the reflected light.[8]

**13** The *jiva* that regards its reflected form as itself will forsake its true form, *Padam*, and become bewildered.
**14** Why do you suffer, taking the reflection to be real? Investigate your mind and become peaceful.
**15** The mind-moon, the creator of names and forms, will itself set and be extinguished as a concept in front of the sun of consciousness that is one's real nature.

*Bhagavan taught that the mind, like the moon, has no light of its own. It can only appear to shine when it reflects light that comes from elsewhere. It is the light emanating from the sun of the Heart that illumines the mind-moon.*

Sri Ramana Gita, *chapter 5, verses 14, 15, 16, 17:*

**[Bhagavan:]** As the sun gives light to the moon, even so this Heart gives light to the mind.

A mortal, absent from the Heart, perceives only the mind, just as the light of the moon is perceived at night in the absence of the sun.

Not perceiving that the true source of light is one's own Self, and mentally perceiving objects as apart from oneself, the ignorant one is deluded.

The *jnani* present in the Heart sees the light of the mind merged in the light of the Heart, like moonlight in daylight.

# Seer and Seen

## Seeing creates the seen

1 Every time it [the mind] sees, it is in the act of seeing that the many scenes appear as if real to the seeing consciousness.

Creation is not other than seeing; seeing and creating are one and the same process. Annihilation is only the cessation of seeing and nothing else; for the world comes to an end by the right awareness of oneself.[1]

**Question:** What is the relation between mind and object? Is the mind contacting something different from it, *viz.*, the world?
**Bhagavan:** The world is 'sensed' in the waking and the dream states or is the object of perception and thought, both being mental activities. If there were no such activities as waking and dreaming thought, there would be no 'perception' or inference of a 'world'. In sleep there is no such activity and 'objects and world' do not exist for us in sleep. Hence 'reality of the world' may be created by the ego by its act of emergence from sleep; and that reality may be swallowed up or disappear by the soul resuming its nature in sleep. The emergence and disappearance of the world are like the spider producing a gossamer web and then withdrawing it.[2]

Major Chadwick tried to persuade Bhagavan that the world did have some reality and permanence.

'If the world exists only when my mind exists,' he began, 'when my mind subsides in meditation or sleep, does the outside world disappear also? I think not. If one considers the experiences of others who were aware of the world while I slept, one must conclude that the world existed then. Is it not more correct to say that the world got created and is ever existing in some huge collective mind? If this is true how can one say that there is no world and that it is only a dream?'

Bhagavan refused to modify his position. 'The world does not say that it was created in the collective mind or that it was created in the individual mind. It only appears in our small mind. If your mind gets destroyed, there will be no world.'[3]

## The world and the Self cannot be seen together

2* The sight that sees the non-Self is that which veils the nature of the *Atma-swarupa*.

3 Know through discriminating enquiry that of these two, the world and the supreme, only one abides within the Heart, and embrace [that one].

4 The two do not stay together in the Heart, for one is incompatible with the other. Attempting to keep them together is a result of delusion.

5 Since the one veils the other, one of them is an appearance imagined within the other.

*Guru Vachaka Kovai*, verse 876: Until the false appearance of the snake goes, the underlying truth, the rope, will not shine. Until the false world-appearance becomes non-existent, the underlying reality, the truth, the *swarupa*, will not reveal itself.

*Guru Vachaka Kovai*, verse 877, *Pozhippurai*: Only when knowledge of the world, the differentiated consciousness in which the world appears separate from *Atma-swarupa*, leaves, will the experience of the Self, in which everything shines as the Self, be attained. Only the life of being merged with the shining light of the Self is the natural life for the *jiva*. All other lives, which are associated with differences that are objects for *suttarivu*, are illusory.
*Vilakkam*: Since the word *loka* [the world] means 'that which is seen', the phrase 'knowledge of the world' should be taken to mean the knowledge associated with differences. The word 'light' means the shining of reality,

the attribute-free, pure consciousness. Since the attributes comprising *triputi*-differences are a consequence of delusion, and since that delusion is not real, it has been said that only the life in which one is merged with the shining light of the Self is the natural life. Saying that 'all other lives… are illusory' is a declaration that all knowledge based on differentiation, even that pertaining to divine worlds, is only ignorance.

**6*** Through that true effulgent light, which is the knowledge of the Self, the world will be entirely eclipsed, becoming pure consciousness.

*Bhagavan made the following comments while he was explaining one of his verses on Arunachala:*

**Bhagavan:** The sun illumines the universe, whereas the sun of Arunachala is so dazzling that the universe is obscured and an unbroken brilliance remains. But it is not realised in the present state and can be realised only if the lotus of the Heart blossoms. The ordinary lotus blossoms in the light of the visible sun, whereas the subtle Heart blossoms only before the sun of suns. May Arunachala make my Heart blossom so that his unbroken brilliance may shine all along.[4]

7 The *triputis* and their source, pure consciousness, can, under no circumstances, appear simultaneously. Like the wood and the elephant in a wooden elephant, when one appears, the other will disappear.

*Guru Vachaka Kovai*, verse 46: In a carved statue of a dog, the dog and the stone cannot be seen simultaneously. [Similarly,] the Supreme is concealed when the world is seen; but when the Supreme is seen, the world disappears. Both cannot be seen distinctly at the same time.

**Bhagavan:** Wrong interpretations of the words of old sayings are not uncommon. We often hear, 'Dog seen, stone is not seen; stone seen, dog is not seen'. It is ordinarily understood to mean that one cannot find a brickbat to throw at a stray dog. But this popular saying has a much deeper significance. It is based on a story.

A certain wealthy man's house was closely guarded. It had also a ferocious dog chained to a pillar at the gate. The dog and the chain were however very skilful pieces of art. They were sculptured in stone but appeared life-like. A pedestrian on the road once took fright at the sight of the ferocious animal and hurt himself in his attempt to dodge it. A kindly neighbour took pity on him and showed him that it was not a living dog. When the man passed by it the next time he admired the skill of the sculptor and forgot his old experience. Thus, when he found it to be a dog, he could not see the stone of which it was made; and again when he found it a piece of sculpture, he did not see any dog to hurt him. Hence the proverb. Compare it with [the *Tirumandiram* verse]: 'The elephant hides the wood and the wood hides the elephant'. Here it is a wooden elephant.[5]

## The truth of the seer

**8*** As the seen does not exist without the being-consciousness of the seer, [the being-consciousness of the seer] is the foremost and most self-evident among everything that is self-evident.

**Bhagavan:** Can the world exist without someone to perceive it? Which is prior? The being-consciousness or the rising consciousness? The being consciousness is always there, eternal and pure. The rising consciousness rises forth and disappears. It is transient.
**Question:** Does not the world exist for others even while I am asleep?
**Bhagavan:** Such a world mocks at you also for knowing it without knowing yourself. The world is the result of your mind. Know your mind. Then see the world. You will realise that it is not different from the Self.[6]

**Bhagavan:** People see the world. The perception implies the existence of a seer and the seen. The objects are alien to the seer. The seer is intimate, being the Self. They do not however turn their attention to finding out the obvious seer but run about analysing the seen. The more the mind expands, the farther it goes and renders Self-realisation more difficult and complicated. The man must directly see the seer and realise the Self.

**Question:** So then, it amounts to synthesizing phenomena and finding the one reality behind.

**Bhagavan:** Why do you still consider the phenomena? See who the seer is. Synthesis means engaging the mind in other pursuits. That is not the way to realisation.[7]

**9** The seer's greatness far exceeds the greatness of the 'self-evident' objects that are seen.

**10** Unless the seer sees and knows himself in the Heart, it is not possible to attain the state of possessing the perfect space of consciousness as one's own property.

**11** Until the seer sees, knows and becomes one with the truth of his real nature, he [the seer] cannot attain peace of mind.

**12** The seer, by seeing the truth of his real nature, will get released from the profitless bondage of attachment, which arises from the dense darkness [of ignorance].

**13** Only *darshan* of the true nature of the one who sees possesses real greatness. Other than this, whatever is seen by the one who sees is just an illusory vision.

**14** It is the stupidity of the deluded ego to be fixated on that which looks at that which moves.

*'That which looks' is the perceiver of objects that are witnessed, and 'that which moves' is the world that it sees.*

## Vanquishing the world appearance

**15** For everything that is seen to fade away as a concept of the mind, let your mind subside by observing the one who sees it.

**16** If the obstacle of the ego-impurity is destroyed, the creation [*srishti*] that appeared as the world will become a mere appearance [*drishti*].

**17** Effulgent *Padam* says: 'The conquest of the world is merely the complete destruction of the world vision that results from consciousness of reality in the Heart.'

**18** Through firmness in the practice of renunciation become indifferent to the world, realising it to be unreal, and set it aside.

**19** Seeing all that is seen as the creation of the mind, be free from its confusion, and shine as consciousness alone.

## The infinite eye

*Bhagavan sometimes used the phrase 'the infinite eye' to describe the way in which the* jnani *is aware of himself and the world appearance. When* suttarivu, *the divided consciousness, operates, there is an 'I' who creates and sees an external world, and who then processes information about it through the physical eyes. In* jnana *one sees and knows the world to be an appearance in one's own Self, without cognising it through the eyes in a dualistic way. This 'infinite eye' sees and knows nothing other than itself, and it accomplishes this without the false division of seer and seen. The apparent paradox of this state was brought out in* Aksharamanamalai, *verse 15:*

> Eye of the eye you are, and without eyes you see. Who can see you, O Arunachala?[8]

*When the false distinctions of seer and seen have ended and when one knows oneself to be the substratum on which the world appears, rather than being the witness of it, seeing and being become one and the same:*

> **Bhagavan:** First one sees the Self as objects, then one sees the Self as a void, then one sees the Self as Self; only in this last [state] there is no seeing because seeing is being.[9]

**20** The *jiva* that sleeps without sleeping, with its attention on its real nature, will automatically shine as an eye that is very different from the fleshy eye.

> **Bhagavan:** In reality, saying, 'We must see *Brahman* in everything and everywhere' is also not quite correct. Only that stage is final where there is no seeing, where there is no time or space. There will be no seer, seeing and an object to see. What exists then is only the infinite eye.[10]

**21** In *Sivam*, the eye that is fully open as pure consciousness, a second kind of eyesight cannot exist.

**22** If the eye is the eye of the light of truth, then, to see that eye, another eye will not be necessary.

**23** Seeing with the eye of the Self, the true seer, scorch and destroy the one who pays attention to objectified concepts.

**24** Those who see the seen as having the same nature as their eye [*kan-mayam*] will, abiding as the nature of the space of consciousness, shine without confusion.

*The phrase* kan-mayam *can be taken to be either 'the nature of consciousness' or 'the nature of the eye'. The second option is a reference to an idea that Bhagavan occasionally propounded, most notably in* Ulladu Narpadu *verse four:*

> If one is a form, the world and God will also be so. If one is not a form, who can see their forms and how? Can what is seen be of a different nature to the eye? Self, the eye, is the infinite eye.[11]

*The words in the penultimate sentence of this verse can also be taken to mean 'Without the eye, can there be sight?', a much more commonsense reading, but this was not the meaning Bhagavan intended to convey. Lakshman Sarma once recorded Bhagavan's explanation of this verse. Reading it, it becomes clear that the rendering given above is the one Bhagavan intended:*

> **Bhagavan:** If the eye that sees be the eye of flesh, then gross forms are seen; if the eye be assisted by lenses, then even invisible things are seen to have form; if the mind be that eye, then subtle forms are seen; thus the seeing eye and the objects seen are of the same nature; that is, if the eye be itself a form, it sees nothing but forms. But neither the physical eye nor the mind has any power of vision of its own. The real Eye is the Self; as He is formless, being the pure infinite consciousness, the reality, He does not see forms.[12]

**25** The nature of things seen will be according to the nature of the one who sees.

> **Bhagavan:** It is the same truth that is taught in stanza four of *Reality in Forty Verses*. If you have the idea that

you are something with form, that you are limited by this body, and being within this body, you have to see through these eyes, God and the world also will appear to you as form. If you realise you are without form, that you are unlimited, that you alone exist, that you are the eye, the infinite eye, what is there to be seen apart from the infinite eye? Apart from the eye, there is nothing to be seen. There must be a seer for an object to be seen, and there must be space, time, etc. But if the Self alone exists, it is both seer and seen, and above seeing or being seen.[13]

**26** The *muni* who has merged with liberation, in which the infinite eye is one's own nature, is the supremely blissful one who never knows any despondency.

***Jnana drishti***

Jnana drishti *is the true seeing that takes place when one abides in the state of* jnana. *It is therefore intimately associated with 'the infinite eye'.*

**27** Both in *nishta* and true *jnana drishti* the objectification that sees scenes as other [than oneself] is totally non-existent.

*In the state of Self-abidance (*nishta*) there is no one who sees, nor are there objects that are seen. There is only seeing. The seeing that takes place in this state,* jnana drishti, *is both true seeing and true knowing:*

**Bhagavan:** You are the Self. You exist always. Nothing more can be predicated of the Self than it exists. Seeing God or the Self is only being God or your Self. Seeing is being.[14]

**28*** In *jnana drishti* there is only *jnana swarupa*. Since there is nothing other than this to be seen, this is *Padam*, the expanse [of consciousness].

**Bhagavan:** Whatever state one is in, the perceptions partake of that state. The explanation is that in the waking state [*jagrat*] the gross body perceives gross names and forms; in *swapna* [the dream state] the mental body perceives the mental creations in their manifold forms and names; in the *sushupti* [deep dreamless sleep], the identification with the body being lost, there are no perceptions; similarly in the transcendental state identity with *Brahman* places the man in harmony with everything, and there is nothing apart from his Self.[15]

**29** As *swarupa* is non-dual *jnana*, the vision of *swarupa* is merely abidance as *swarupa*.

**30** True vision is that which is known through steadfast abidance in consciousness of being, which shines when *suttarivu* is abandoned.

**31** In the state of true *jnana drishti*, wherein one is firmly and continuously established in Self-abidance, everything is always of the nature of consciousness.

**Bhagavan:** See with the *oona kan* [the physical eye] and you see the world. See with the *jnana kan* [the eye of *jnana*] and everything appears as *Brahma mayam* [comprising *Brahman* alone].[16]

**32** Only when the tangled knot of *chid-jada* has been destroyed will *jnana-drishti*, abidance as the vast expanse of consciousness, be possible.

**33** First root out the confusion in your own mind. Then, seeing with the eye of *jnana*, know everything to be the one pure consciousness.

**34** 'The vision of reality', 'knowledge of reality', 'becoming reality' – all these denote unflagging abidance as *Atma-swarupa*, the reality.

*This is probably derived from an English statement Muruganar heard Bhagavan make: 'To see is to know; to know is to become; to become is to be.'*[17]

**35** The vision of reality that is obtained through the revelation of grace will completely dispel the delusion of differentiating thoughts.

**36** The benefit of complete and perfect *jnana*-experience is merely the cessation of the duality that perceives 'I' and 'this'.

**37*** In the hyperactive vision [of the ego] *Padam* appears as the many different sense objects; in *jnana drishti* it is the expanse of grace.

**38** The vision of reality is only for those in whom the experience of sense pleasures – consisting of enjoyment of the same experiences again and again – has become bitter, and who can therefore give them up.

**39** Only those devotees who possess the power – the light that flourishes, conquering the world through true seeing – are kings.

# The Reality of the World Appearance

## The unreality of the world appearance

1 Since the world ceases to appear when the body is absent, the world is not other than the body.

2 Regarding the world that is seen as different from the mind that sees it, and attributing an abundance of being to it, is illusion.

> **Question:** It is said that the world and the objects that we see are all unreal, like the snake in the rope. It is also stated in other places that the seer and the seen are the same. If the seer and the seen are the same, then how can we say that the seen is unreal?
>
> **Bhagavan:** All that is meant is that the seen regarded as an independent entity, independent of the Self, is unreal. The seen is not different from the seer. What exists is the one Self, not a seer and seen. The seen regarded as the Self is real.[1]

*The following extract is from the essay version of* Who am I? *In the question-and-answer version the equivalent answer is part of a sequence of replies that deals with realisation, the mind, and the world-appearance:*

> … There is no such thing as 'the world' independent of thoughts. There are no thoughts in deep sleep, and there is no world. In waking and dream there are thoughts, and there is also the world. Just as a spider emits the thread of a web from within itself and withdraws it again into itself, in the same way the mind projects the world from within itself and later reabsorbs it into itself. When the mind emanates from the Self, the world appears. When the world appears, the Self is not seen, and when the Self appears or shines, the world will not appear.

3 The world appears within your own Self, very much as the colour blue appears in the sky.

4 What a false pretence to say that this world, an impermanent reflection consisting of sense perceptions, is real!

5 Oh, why do the dull-witted and mad people of the world wander about aimlessly, paying attention to the empty and useless creations of the mind?

6 Regarding mirage-water as water that is in a pond full of blossoming lotuses, and then attempting to get water from it, is foolish ignorance.

7 Separate from the real nature of the Self, the non-dual reality, what dualistic scenes can appear, and how?

8 If the world is real, then it will be incorrect to claim that the consciousness that perceives the world is a delusory one.

**Understand the nature of the world by knowing the Self**

9 [Work] ceaselessly to establish your mind in the Self, the supreme space and, perceiving the external world as a mere appearance, conduct yourself accordingly.

10 All that appears is merely a manifestation of *Atma-swarupa*. To gain this firm conviction, know the nature of the Self well.

*From the essay version of* Who am I?*:*

> If the mind, which is the cause of all knowledge and all actions, subsides, the perception of the world will cease. [If one perceives a rope, imagining it to be a snake] perception of the rope, which is the substratum, will not occur unless the perception of the snake, which has been superimposed on it, goes. Similarly, the perception of one's real nature [*swarupa*], the substratum, will not be obtained unless the perception of the world, which is a superimposition, ceases.

11 If the unique truth that shines within oneself is known first, the truth of the world can then be known completely.

**Question:** What is the reality of this world?
**Bhagavan:** If you know your reality first, you will be able

to know the reality of the world. It is a strange thing that most people do not care to know about their own reality, but are very anxious to know about the reality of the world. You realise your own Self first and then see if the world exists independently of you and is able to come and assert before you its reality or existence.[2]

**12** If you sink and remain withdrawn within your own *swarupa*, becoming extremely tranquil, the entire world will at once be contained within you.

**Question:** What will it be like when one achieves Self-realisation?
**Bhagavan:** The question is wrong. One does not realise anything new.
**Question:** I do not get you, swami.
**Bhagavan:** It is very simple. Now you feel that you are in the world. Then you feel that the world is in you.[3]

**13** Is it not through your real nature, which exists and shines, that the world comprising the *triputis* arises?

*The light of the Self exists and shines prior to the functioning of the* suttarivu, *the objectifying consciousness that divides manifestation into the seer and what is seen. The existence of the light of the Self can therefore be regarded as an immediate cause of the* triputis *– in this case the seer, seeing and what is seen – coming into existence. The same idea appears in the next verse:*

**14** Is it not because of the existence and shining of the one known as 'I' that this world appears before our eyes?

**Bhagavan:** The world is your thought. Thoughts are your projections. The 'I' is first created and then the world. The world is created by the 'I', which in turn rises up from the Self. The riddle of the creation of the world is solved if you solve the creation of the 'I'. So I say, find yourself....There is no creation in the state of realisation. When one sees the world, one does not see oneself. When one sees the Self, the world is not seen. So, see the Self and realise that there has been no creation.[4]

15 This false world vision will exist only until one enquires within and realises the reality as it is.

> **Question:** Is the appearance of the differentiated universe true or untrue?
> **Bhagavan:** It depends on how we regard the terms true and untrue. If we look at *Brahman,* there is no universe.
> **Question:** Then why does the universe appear?
> **Bhagavan:** Appear to whom? The universe does not say 'I am'. Is there any evidence to say that the universe appears? To whom does this universe appear?
> **Question:** To me.
> **Bhagavan:** Who are you? Find out who you are. Then afterwards tell me if there is a universe.[5]

16 Until everything attains subsidence in consciousness, the various scenes one associates with will [appear to] be real.

17 It is fitting that you should first attain knowledge of your real nature. Only then, if everything [*sarvam*] still exists, you may attend to and cherish it.

18 It is ignorance to cling to the shadow-like world that appears to be defective only when one slips from the state of the Self.

## *Sivam* and *sakti*

*In this section creation and the reality of the world appearance will be explained in terms of* Sivam *and* sakti. *In* Sivam, *the pure consciousness that is Siva's true nature, there is no creation at all, not even as a false appearance. However, when* sakti, *the dynamic and creative aspect of* Sivam, *arises, all manifestation appears. This* sakti, *which is regarded as being the presence of Siva, is the energy that enables the projection of the world appearance to take place.*

19* The series of illusory, mental images that appear in consciousness through erroneous superimposition does not exist in *Sivam.*

20 If it is true that, though she [*sakti*] has given birth to the many worlds, she is still a virgin, the truth of the world must be extremely marvellous.

*This is a reference to a Saiva philosophical idea that is encapsulated in* Sivajnana Siddiyar, *2:77:*

> Siva gave birth to Sakti, and Sakti gives birth to Siva. The two join together with delight, giving birth to the world and all beings. Despite this, Siva is a *brahmachari* and Sakti is a virgin. This truth will be known only to *jnanis* who have obtained the grace of Siva through *tapas*.

**21** All forms are only forms of *sakti*. There is no form for the Lord, *Sivam*.

**22** The eight forms [*asta murtam*] are all forms of *sakti*. For *Sivam*, *Atma-swarupa*, there is no form, not even a trace.

*The eight forms are the five elements, the sun, the moon and the individual soul.*

**23*** She [Sakti] does not exist apart from Him [Siva]; and likewise, He does not exist apart from Her.

**24** *Padam*, speaking the truth, warns: To separate Him and Her from each other is wrong.

**25** If the world and *Sivam* are different entities, why then do *jnanis* declare the world to be Siva-*swarupa*?

*These three verses introduce a new aspect of Bhagavan's teachings. Since* sakti *is an inseparable part of* Sivam, *it is also possible to say that the world is an appearance in* Sivam. *As such, it can be said to be real. Though Bhagavan generally taught that the world is unreal, he occasionally remarked that it can be regarded as real if it is known to be a manifestation or appearance within the Self, rather than a real, external, physical entity that is perceived by the senses.*

> **Question:** 'The Supreme Spirit [*Brahman*] is real. The world [*jagat*] is illusion,' is the stock phrase of Sri Sankaracharya. Yet others say, 'The world is reality'. Which is true?
>
> **Bhagavan**: Both statements are true. They refer to different stages of development and are spoken from different points of view. The aspirant [*abhyasi*] starts with the definition, 'that which is real exists always'; then he eliminates the world as unreal because it is changing. It

> cannot be real; 'not this, not this!' The seeker ultimately reaches the Self and there finds unity as the prevailing note. Then, that which was originally rejected as being unreal is found to be a part of the unity. Being absorbed in the reality, the world also is real. There is only being in Self-realisation, and nothing but being.[6]

*When the world is known and experienced to be an indivisible appearance in the underlying substratum of the Self, its nature is correctly known. The world is not real to the* jnani *because it appears physically; it is real because its inherent nature is inseparable from the underlying reality of the Self.*

Ulladu Narpadu, *verse 18:*

> To those who have not known [the Self] and to those who have known [the Self], the world in front of us is real. But to those who have not known [the Self] the reality is limited to the measure of the world, whereas to those who have known [the Self] the reality shines devoid of form as the substratum of the world. Know that this is the difference between these two.[7]

Sri Ramana Gita, *chapter 1, verse 11:*

> The *jnani* takes his stand in his Self at all times, absolute, fearless. He does not think of the universe as unreal nor does he see it as different from himself.

*If the* jnani *knows that the world is ultimately real, why does he usually tell questioners that it is not? Bhagavan provides his own answer to this:*

> **Bhagavan:** In the *sadhak* stage [the stage of being a spiritual seeker] you have got to say that the world is an illusion. There is no other way. When a man forgets he is *Brahman*, who is real, permanent and omnipresent, and deludes himself into thinking that he is a body in the universe which is filled with bodies that are transitory, and labours under that delusion, you have got to remind him that the world is unreal and a delusion. Why? Because

his vision which has forgotten its own Self is dwelling in the external material universe. It will not turn inwards into introspection unless you impress on him that all this external material universe is unreal. When once he realises his own Self, and also that there is nothing other than his own Self, he will come to look upon the whole universe as *Brahman*.[8]

**26*** If the world is seen in the experience in which consciousness has become *Brahman*, then the world too is *Brahman*.

**27** Why is another means necessary for redemption, once the world is known as the sport of the divine?

**28** If you enquire and realise, then the entire world will be the nature of *Sivam*. [Apart from that] where has *samsara* spread?

**29** Only by realising that the real nature of *sakti* [the mind] is *Sivam*, is the most eminent state of being attained.

### *Maya*

Maya, *the power that creates the illusion that there is an external, real world is really* sakti *masquerading under a different name. As such, the conclusions reached in the previous section are equally applicable here. In the Self* maya *does not and cannot exist, but at the same time* maya *mysteriously arises from within the Self and brings into being the apparent reality of the world:*

**30** The power of *maya* is a false, shadow-like power, which is not inherent in the nature of the Self.

*Guru Vachaka Kovai*, verse 597: That which exists is only the Heart, perfect consciousness. Since this is so, is not the great *maya* unreal? Isn't it wonderful the way the *jiva* is bewildered by being bitten by that snake – the false *maya*, the mind?

**31** All the activities, subdivided into creation [sustenance, destruction, veiling and grace], exist only as attributes of that [*maya*].

*In the next three verses, which are a continuation of the previous two, Bhagavan asserts that, abiding as the unmanifest Self, he has no connection with or even cognisance of* maya *and its operations:*

**32** This powerful phenomenon [*maya*], this indescribably potent illusion, has absolutely no connection with myself, none whatsoever.

**33** It is the ego mind that declares it to be real and connects it with me.

**34** Even the ego mind that declares in this way is trapped within that harmful *maya*. Realise the truth of this definitive conclusion in the mind-free state.

**35** As only that which is shines as the Heart in the Heart, the deceitful mind-*maya* is just a concept.

**36** *Maya vada* [the doctrine of illusion] means regarding the non-existent *maya* as real. It does not mean calling *maya* 'illusory'.

Maya *is traditionally defined as 'illusion', and by extension, the power that makes and sustains the illusion. Bhagavan often questioned this traditional definition, preferring instead to regard* maya *as something that does not exist, rather than something real that created illusion.*

> **Bhagavan:** When Sankara is called *mayavadi* [a follower or propounder of the theory of *maya*] it may be retorted, 'Sankara says *maya* does not exist. He who denies the existence of *maya* and calls it *mithya* or non-existent cannot be called a *mayavadi*. It is those who grant its existence and call its product, the world, a reality who should rightly be called *mayavadis*.'[9]

> **Question:** When the *Upanishads* say that all is *Brahman*, how can we say, like Sankara, that this world is *mithya* or illusory?
> **Bhagavan:** Sankara also said that this world is *Brahman* or the Self. What he objected to is imagining that the Self is limited by the names and forms that constitute the world. He only said that the world does not exist apart from *Brahman*. *Brahman* or the Self is like the screen and the world is like the pictures on it. You can see the picture only so long as there is a screen. But when the seer himself becomes the screen only the Self remains. *Kaivalya Navaneeta* has asked and answered six questions about *maya*. They are instructive.

The first question is: What is *maya*? And the answer is: It is *anirvachaniya* or indescribable.

The second question is: To whom does it come? And the answer is: To the mind or ego who feels that he is a separate entity, who thinks: 'I do this' or 'this is mine'.

The third question is: Where does it come from and how did it originate? And the answer is: Nobody can say.

The fourth question is: How did it arise? And the answer is: Through non-*vichara,* through failure to ask: 'Who am I?'

The fifth question is: If the Self and *maya* both exist does not this invalidate the theory of *advaita?* The answer is: It need not, since *maya* is dependent on the Self as the picture is on the screen. The picture is not real in the sense that the screen is real.

The sixth question is: If the Self and *maya* are one, could it not be argued that the Self is of the nature of *maya*, that is, illusory? And the answer is: No, the Self can be capable of producing illusion without being illusory. A conjuror may create for our entertainment the illusion of people, animals and things, and we see all of them as clearly as we see him; but after the performance he alone remains and all the visions he had created have disappeared. He is not a part of the illusion but is real and solid.[10]

**37** The power of the mind, the illusion that makes minute shadows appear as the multiple, colossal worlds is very impressive indeed!

**38** Is it not because one forgets one's truth, the light of consciousness, that one gets caught in the net of *maya*, from which one doesn't know how to escape?

**39** The power of *maya* is that it causes the *jiva* to do over and over again that which it has already done.

**Reality of other worlds**

**40** To whatever extent this world is real, to that same extent are other worlds real.

**41** 'Only this much can be said about heaven and hell without giving rise to arguments.' So says *Padam*, the Lord.

*Guru Vachaka Kovai*, verse 178: Don't argue and quarrel among yourselves about the reality of other worlds that are said to begin with heaven [and include the *deva* and *asura* realms]. As long as and to whatever extent this world is real, till then and to that extent all other worlds, beginning with heaven, are also real.

**Question:** People talk of Vaikunta, Kailasa, Indraloka, Chandraloka [the heavenly realms of the Hindu gods], etc. Do they really exist?
**Bhagavan:** Certainly. You can rest assured that they all exist. There also a swami like me will be found seated on a couch and disciples will also be seated around him. They will ask something and he will say something in reply. Everything will be more or less like this. What of that? If one sees Chandraloka, one will ask for Indraloka, and after Indraloka, Vaikunta and after Vaikunta, Kailasa, and so on, and the mind goes on wandering. Where is *shanti* [peace]? If *shanti* is required, the only correct method of securing it is by self-enquiry. Through self-enquiry Self-realisation is possible. If one realises the Self, one can see all these worlds within one's Self. The source of everything is one's own Self, and if one realises the Self, one will not find anything different from the Self. Then these questions will not arise. There may or may not be a Vaikunta or a Kailasa but it is a fact that you are here, isn't it? How are you? Where are you? After you know about these things, you can think of all those worlds.[11]

**Question:** Are the gods Iswara or Vishnu and their sacred regions Kailasa or Vaikunta real?
**Bhagavan:** As real as you are in this body.
**Question:** Do they possess a *vyavahara satya,* i.e., phenomenal existence, like my body? Or are they fictions like the horn of a hare?
**Bhagavan:** They do exist.
**Question:** If so, they must be somewhere. Where are they?
**Bhagavan:** Persons who have seen them say that they exist somewhere. So we must accept their statement.
**Question:** Where do they exist?
**Bhagavan:** In you.

**Question:** Then it is only idea – that which I can create and control?
**Bhagavan:** Everything is like that.
**Question:** But I can create pure fictions e.g., hare's horn or only part truths, e.g. mirage, while there are also facts irrespective of my imagination. Do the gods Iswara or Vishnu exist like that?
**Bhagavan:** Yes.[12]

**42** The appearance of every one of the worlds is merely a dream of the sordid mind, which is the storehouse of conceptualising power [*kalpana-sakti*].

**Question:** What about Kailas and all the other worlds? Do they really exist?
**Bhagavan:** All are the concoctions of *maya*.[13]

**Bhagavan:** What is meant by *moksha*? Do the heavenly world and heavenly bliss exist somewhere in the sky? Are these to be experienced in some other body and in some other world after leaving this world and this body? The supreme world is only the Heart. Tranquillity in the form of supreme silence is supreme bliss, the happiness of liberation. Cessation of worries is the attainment of the supreme state. Through the state of being-consciousness, the life of supreme bliss can be attained at all times and in all states in this very world and in this very body.[14]

# Iswara and Destiny

*In the theory of simultaneous creation that Bhagavan generally expounded, Iswara, the personal God, has a significant but subsidiary role. The process that brings the world into existence simultaneously brings Iswara into being:*

> **Bhagavan:** At the moment of rising up, the mind is only light; only afterwards the thought 'I am this' rises up. The 'I'-thought forms the *jiva* and the world. The first light is the pure mind, *chidakasa* [the expanse of consciousness], or Iswara. Its modes manifest as objects.[1]

*However, although Iswara is merely a projection within the Self, once He has appeared, He becomes, through His* sakti*, responsible for much of the subsequent manifestation:*

1. Iswara is responsible for the five-fold activities in the same way that the sun is responsible for the activities of the world.
2. Other than through the *sakti* connection, Iswara has no direct relationship with the world.

*In* Who am I? *Bhagavan wrote the following words in response to the query, 'Is not everything the work of God?'*

> In the mere presence of the sun, which rises without desire, intention or effort, the magnifying glass emits hot light, the lotus blossoms and people begin, perform and cease their work. In front of a magnet a needle moves. Likewise, through the mere influence of the presence of God, who has no *sankalpa* [intention to accomplish anything], souls, who are governed by the three or five divine functions, perform and cease their activities in accordance with their respective karmas. Even so, He [God] is not someone who has *sankalpa*, nor will a single

act ever touch him. This can be compared to the actions of the world not touching the sun, or to the good and bad qualities of the elements [earth, water, fire and air] not affecting the immanent space.

Sankalpa *means 'resolve', 'will', or 'intention'. God has no personal* sankalpa. *That is to say, He does not decide or even think about what He should do. Though mature devotees 'bloom' on account of His presence, it is not because Iswara has decided to bestow His grace on these fortunate few. His presence is available to all, but only the mature convert it into realisation. The other beings also become more mature, but not to the point where the veiling can be removed.*

*The three divine functions are creation, sustenance and destruction. The five divine functions are these three plus veiling and grace. According to many Hindu scriptures, God creates, preserves and eventually destroys the world. While it exists, He hides His true nature from the people in it through the veiling power of* maya, *illusion, while simultaneously emanating grace so that mature devotees can lift the veils of illusion and become aware of Him as He really is.*

*However, although Bhagavan taught that Iswara is responsible for the affairs of the world, he also taught that Iswara is, from the standpoint of absolute reality, an unreal entity that ultimately has to be transcended:*

Iswara the personal God, the supreme creator of the universe, really does exist. But this is only true from the relative standpoint of those who have not realised the truth, those people who believe in the reality of individual souls. From the absolute standpoint the sage cannot accept any other existence than the impersonal Self, one and formless.

Iswara has a physical body, a form and a name, but it is not so gross as the physical body. It can be seen in visions in the form created by the devotee. The forms and names of God are many and various and differ with each religion. His essence is the same as ours, the real Self, being one and without form. Hence, forms he assumes are only creations or appearances.

Iswara is immanent in every person and every object throughout the universe. The totality of all things and beings constitutes God. There is a power out of which a small fraction has become all this universe, and the remainder is in reserve. Both this reserve power plus the manifested power as the manifested world together constitute Iswara.

Iswara, God, the creator, the personal God, is the last of the unreal forms to go. Only the absolute being is real. Hence not only the world, not only the ego but also the personal God are of unreality.[2]

3 You should know that the veiling [*tirodana*] that makes *jivas* forget [the events of past lives] is an act of supreme compassion by Iswara towards them.

4 If these memories are not absent, *jivas* will not attain *malaparipaka* [a mature state in which impurities are ready for destruction], and the lives of *jivas* will get shattered and ruined.

*The fourth of Iswara's divine functions – veiling – is generally regarded to mean hiding his true nature from devotees through the power of* maya, *but it also includes concealing from* jivas *knowledge of their previous lives:*

*Guru Vachaka Kovai*, verse 116: The particulars about the past history [of the *jiva*], which are full of [details about] the suffering he inflicted on others and the suffering inflicted on him by others in innumerable past lives, do not remain in the *jiva's* consciousness. Know clearly that this complete forgetfulness, a veiling, is an act of grace by God towards the *jivas*.

*Guru Vachaka Kovai*, verse 117: Even the limited memory, which prompts in the mind the rising of thoughts about a few incidents from this one life, makes the life of the *jiva* miserable. Because of this, forgetfulness alone deserves to be greatly desired.

**Bhagavan:** No one knows about his previous birth. People forget, and that forgetfulness is good. In this one life alone, we are sometimes terribly worried over what had happened in the past; could we bear such worries if we knew all about our previous births? Knowing the facts of previous births means knowing one's own Self. If that is known this birth and the previous births will be seen to be of the mind and its desires [*sankalpa*] only.[3]

## The divine ordinance and destiny

5 Although those who do not know consciousness find fault with things that happen in the world, all events that occur do so in accordance with a unique divine ordinance.

*The 'divine ordinance' originates with Iswara, as Bhagavan makes clear in the following comment on the first verse of* Upadesa Saram*:*

**Question:** In '*Karthuragnaya prapyathe phalam*' [action bears fruit by the ordinance of God] who is the *karta* [God]?
**Bhagavan:** *Karta* is Iswara. He is the one who distributes the fruits of actions to each person according to his karma. That means He is *saguna Brahman* [*Brahman* with attributes]. The real *Brahman* is *nirguna* [without attributes] and without motion. It is only *saguna Brahman* that is named Iswara. He gives the *phala* [fruits] to each person according to his karma. That means that Iswara is only an agent... Without that *sakti* of Iswara, this karma will not take place.[4]

*Elsewhere Bhagavan has explained how the allocation of destiny, or* prarabdha *karma, takes place:*

**Bhagavan:** A man might have performed many karmas in his previous births. A few of them alone will be chosen for this birth and he will have to enjoy the fruits in this birth. It is something like a slide show where the projectionist picks a few slides to be exhibited at a performance, the remaining slides being reserved for another performance.[5]

**Bhagavan:** Individuals have to suffer their karmas but Iswara manages to make the best of their karmas for his purpose. God manipulates the fruits of karma but he does not add or take away from it. The subconscious of man is a warehouse of good and bad karma. Iswara chooses from

> this warehouse what he sees will best suit the spiritual evolution ... of each man, whether pleasant or painful. Thus, there is nothing arbitrary.[6]

6 The truth of that unique ordinance – which conducts all affairs while remaining neutral, without a trace of partiality – cannot be known by *jivas* who are caught up inside creation.

7* True devotees are firmly convinced in their hearts that everything that occurs happens only for the best.

> **Muruganar:** Human beings, who possess insignificant power, do not even have the power to change their own minds, which are supposedly under their control. This being so, trying to alter the events of the external world, which are under the strong control of the powerful Iswara, can be classified as ignorance. Unless such efforts are aligned with what Iswara has already ordained, (in which case, success is a coincidence, like a fruit falling off a tree when a crow alights on a branch) they usually end in failure. Such attempts only lead to disappointment.[7]

8 'Whatever is due to be experienced will not fail to come whether one desires it or not.' *Padam* says this repeatedly.

*Sivaprakasam Pillai recorded one of Bhagavan's statements on destiny in* Irangal, *one of his unpublished poems:*

> 'We have somehow become embodied. Whatever good and bad has been ordained to come, it will certainly come. It will not remain without coming. There is only one way to be free from suffering. That is to turn the mind within.' So said Ramana.[8]

> **Question:** In the early stages would it not be a help to a man to seek solitude and give up his outer duties in life?
> **Bhagavan:** Renunciation is always in the mind, not in going to forests or solitary places or giving up one's duties. The main thing is to see that the mind does not turn outward but inward. It does not really rest with a man whether he goes to this place or that or whether he gives up his duties or not. All that happens according to destiny.

All the activities that the body is to go through are determined when it first comes into existence. It does not rest with you to accept or reject them. The only freedom you have is to turn your mind inward and renounce activities there...

If you want to go to fundamentals, you must enquire who you are and find out who it is who has freedom or destiny. Who are you and why did you get this body that has these limitations?[9]

**9** What is to come to you will automatically come. What is not, will not come. [Therefore,] remain in your blissful natural state.

**Question:** Has man any free will or is everything in his life pre-destined and pre-ordained?
**Bhagavan:** Free will holds the field in association with individuality. As long as individuality lasts, there is free will. All the *sastras* are based on this fact and they advise directing the free will in the right channel.

Find out to whom free will or destiny matters. Abide in it. Then these two are transcended. That is the only purpose of discussing these questions. To whom do these questions arise? Find out and be at peace.[10]

Ulladu Narpadu, *verse 19:*

The argument as to which wins, fate or free will, which are different from each other, is only for those who do not have knowledge of the root of fate and free will. Those who have known the [ego] self, which is the one base of fate and free will, have given them up. Say, will they get entangled in them again.[11]

**10** The steadfast *jnani* will completely consume, without any fear, the *prarabdha* that began with the present body.
**11** In the blissful experience of *jnana,* the Self, those *prarabdha* experiences will not cling to the 'I'.

*Guru Vachaka Kovai*, verse 698, *Pozhippurai*: *Prarabdha,* which, like a whirlwind, relentlessly agitates and spins the mind that has shrunk through *dehatma buddhi*, cannot

even slightly stir the adjunct-free mind that shines as the extremely clear space of pure consciousness when the ego-impurity is destroyed by self-enquiry.
*Vilakkam*: Since a mind shining as the infinite expanse of consciousness is perfect, there is no agitation.

**12** Nothing happens except that which is divinely ordained. Consequently, it is pointless for people [who want the world to be different] to experience anxiety and to be debilitated by distress.

*Guru Vachaka Kovai*, verse 1191, *Pozhippurai*: No one can do anything that is opposed to the ordinance of the Supreme Lord who possesses unlimited power and who can do anything. Therefore, to end the anxiety of the deceptive mind, which engenders an evil discontent, the proper course is to remain under the spell of supreme consciousness, which arises from meditating on the divine feet, with the mischief of the ego subdued.

# Right Attitude, Right Knowledge, Right Behaviour

The boat may remain in water, but if water enters the boat, it will bring great catastrophe. [Likewise,] a man may live in the world, which is surrounded by the seas, but if the world enters the man, his whole life will be miserable.[1]

Just as the goat's beard wanders and wags for nothing, people roam about merrily but in vain, performing activities for the fulfilment of their worldly desires, while despising the disciplines that lead to eternal *moksha* in the Self. Ah, what a pitiable spectacle is the condition of these worldly people.[2]

Though the good *dharmas* [righteous acts] are said to be many, just as the golden ornaments are many, the sole reality of all those *dharmas* is sacrifice of the self, just as the sole reality of all ornaments is gold.[3]

# Religions and Religious Knowledge

## Religious doctrines

1 The doctrines of all religions contradict each other. They wage war, collide with each other, and finally die.

2 On this battlefield all the religions retreat defeated when they stand before *mauna*, which abides beneficently, sustaining them all.

3 The rare and wonderful power of *mauna* is that it remains without enmity towards any of the religions.

4* The many different religions are appropriate to the maturity of each individual, and all of them are acceptable to reality.

> *Guru Vachaka Kovai*, verse 342: Various religions that bring about clarity have come into existence to suit the various levels of mental maturity. It is therefore most wise to have a harmonious outlook towards these religions, which deserve to be practised.

> *Guru Vachaka Kovai*, verse 989: Since *mauna*, the culmination of knowledge, is their common nature, all religions are acceptable as a means to advaitic truth, which shines unique and pure. They are therefore not opposed to the wonderful Vedanta.

*Bhagavan quoted Thayumanavar on this subject in* Day by Day with Bhagavan, *21st November, 1945:*

> Shining Supreme! If we scrutinise all the religions that look so different, we find no contradiction in their purpose. They are all your sport. Just as all rivers discharge into the sea, they all end in the ocean of *mauna*.

5 Abandoning vain disputation, which only deludes and torments

the mind, accept the doctrine of the *mauna* religion, which always remains undisturbed.

**Bhagavan:** The conflict of teachings is only apparent, and can be resolved if one practises self-surrender to God; this will lead to the Self, to which everyone must come back in the end, because that is the truth. The discord among the creeds can never be got rid of by discussing their merits; for discussion is a mental process. The creeds are mental – they exist in the mind alone, while the truth is beyond the mind; therefore the truth is not in the creeds.[1]

**Religious tolerance**

**6** Only as long as the mind survives will there be religion. When the mind attains silence, religion will also cease.

*Guru Vachaka Kovai*, verse 993: So long as mind survives, religion will also exist. No such religion can survive in the abundantly peaceful silence that results from the mind merging in the Heart as a result of turning within and examining itself.

7 In the peaceful state the mind will reach the Heart – the harmonising light of the path of being – and reality will shine forth.

*'Harmonising' here refers to the harmonising of the differing tenets of apparently contradictory religious faiths.*

**8** Feeling anger and hatred in the mind on account of a blind fanaticism towards one's own religion is a cruel and ignoble deed.

*Guru Vachaka Kovai*, verse 991: Instead of turning outwards, arguing against other religions on account of your attachment to your own, turn inwards and practise whichever religion you have faith in with genuine love.

**Bhagavan:** Therefore the aspirant should, with a mind at peace, cease from hatred of other faiths and from all disputation and engage in *sadhana* as taught by his own faith, intent on winning deliverance.[2]

9 On seeing this treachery, both Iswara and true devotees feel ashamed and deem it no better than the act of an ignorant harlot.

10 Instead of condemning another's [path], destroying your clarity, learn one method. Observe it and cherish it in your heart.

'On many occasions, when the subject of religion arises,' he [Bhagavan] remarked, 'men cannot understand their own errors. In many places the ego comes up in the form of saying, "My religion should be embraced by all".'

I [Madhava Tirtha] saw a good example of the Maharshi's disinclination to impose Hindu ideas on people who would not appreciate them when a group of devout Muslims came to see him.

One of them asked, 'What is the best aim of human life?'

Sri Maharshi replied, 'It is Islam, which means, "to remain at the feet of God". And as a consequence one gets *salaam*, which means peace.'[3]

## Religious observances

11* The numerous spiritual practices performed by followers of the many religions serve the sole purpose of merging with the Self, which is consciousness, the supreme.

12 Why so many teachings? Direct your attention towards the attainment of the Self, which is pure consciousness.

13 The state of abiding as *swarupa*, which is the pure and vast true consciousness, is an obligation that should be firmly observed by all the beings in the world.

14 All the various *sadhanas* of the many religions bow to the *jnana-samadhi*, abidance in *Atma-swarupa*, saying, 'You are our refuge'.

15 The vision of mere being, the *Atma-swarupa* that shines as a result of the enquiry ['Who am I?'], is, out of all sacrificial offerings, the foremost and most eminent one.

16 *Swadharma* [one's own duty] is abidance in the pure Self only. All other [perceived] duties are worthless.

**Question:** What am I to do? What is my duty?

> **Bhagavan:** Now you have nothing to do. Enquire 'Who am I?' Then, [when you have found out who you are] if there is still duty, it may be done.[4]

## *Saivam* and *Saktam*

**17** *Saivam* is the excellence of the pure, supreme light of *mauna*. *Saktam*, though, belongs to the category of creation, [preservation, destruction] and so on, which are associated with the mind.

Saivam *means 'pertaining to Siva'. It is the religion of those who worship Siva.* Saktam *is the religion that is primarily focused on the worship of the Divine Mother. However, I would not take this sequence of verses to be a critique of the Sakta faith. I think* Saivam *refers to* Sivam, *the consciousness of Siva, and* Saktam *to the* sakti *that is his power or presence. As the next verse makes clear,* sakti, *the power that brings the mind and manifestation into existence, eventually subsides, leaving the 'grandeur' of 'pure* Sivam'.

**18** *Saktam*, which flourishes in the manifestation of [*maya*] *sakti*, will come to an end in the grandeur of liberation, the pure *Sivam*.

## Scriptures

**19** For all the myriad religious scriptures, the essential truth is only the supreme reality of consciousness.

**20** The true love of the *Vedas*, the mother who declares your real nature to be 'You are That', is the bridge for you [to cross *samsara*].

> **Bhagavan:** Each one knows the Self but is yet ignorant. The person is enabled to realise only after hearing the *mahavakya*. Hence the upanishadic text is the eternal truth to which everyone who has realised owes his experience. After hearing the Self to be *Brahman*, the person finds the true import of the Self and reverts to it whenever he is diverted from it. Here is the whole process of realisation.[5]

**21** Learning the *jnana sastras* is only an incidental cause for travelling the path to *samadhi*. You should understand that its value is limited.

**22** It is the nature of the ignorant to feel proud and superior by mastering scriptural knowledge that consists of pretentious verbiage.

23 The rare benefit that accrues from the *jnana sastras* will only come to the *jiva* that possesses a longing to know the truth. Not for others.

24 Hoping to get a revelation of *jnana* through scriptural knowledge is like resolving to cross the ocean on an insignificant blade of grass.

25 The truth of the one who reads books is not in the books themselves. It is in the experience of [that] vedantic knowledge.

> **Question:** Bhagavan, I have read much of the *Vedas* and the *sastras* but no *Atma jnana* [Self-knowledge] has come to me. Why is this?
> **Bhagavan:** *Atma jnana* will come to you only if it is there in the *sastras* [scriptures]. If you see the *sastras, sastra jnana* [knowledge of the scriptures] will come. If you see the Self, Self-knowledge will shine.[6]

### True learning

26 When the mind, one-pointed and fully focused, knows the supreme silence in the Heart, this is [true] learning.

27 As a result of the knowledge obtained from this true learning, all false misery will fall away, and a profound peace will flourish.

28 Bear in mind that the benefit of scholarship is prompting the mind to turn about, enabling it to be captivated by the light of the Self.

29 The benefit of learning is simply to become established within the Heart, in the concept-free state of reality, which is your own nature.

30 As long as the holy feet do not touch and come to rest squarely upon the head [of the *jiva*] what benefit can scholarship give?

*This verse is speaking obliquely of* saktipata, *the power that is transmitted by the Guru to the disciple.*

> **Question:** *Saktipata* is said to occur in *karmasamya,* i.e., when merit and demerit are equal.
> **Bhagavan:** Yes. *Malaparipaka* [a mature state in which impurities are ready for destruction], *karmasamya* and

*saktipata* mean the same. A man is running the course of his *samskaras*; when taught he is the Self, the teaching affects his mind and imagination runs riot. He feels helpless before the onrushing power. His experiences are only according to his imagination of the state 'I am the Self', whatever he may conceive it to be. *Saktipata* alone confers the true and right experience.

When the man is ripe for receiving the instruction and his mind is about to sink into the Heart, the instruction imparted works in a flash and he realises the Self all right. Otherwise, there is always the struggle.[7]

**31*** Only the learning of *akhanda-vritti* [unbroken experience], one's truth, the substratum, is true learning.

## The true purpose of scriptural knowledge

**32** Mere scholarship derived from copious learning, without putting it into practice, will harm the well being of the *jiva*.

**Bhagavan:** Ancients have said that the superabundance of book knowledge is the cause of the rambling of the mind. That will not carry you to the goal. Reading of *sastras* and becoming pandits may give fame to a person but they destroy the peace of mind which is necessary for the seeker of truth and deliverance. A *mumukshu* [a seeker of deliverance] should understand the essence of the *sastras* but should give up the reading of *sastras* as that is inimical to *dhyana* [meditation]. It is like accepting the grain and discarding the chaff. There will be many big almirahs [cupboards] with many books. How many of them can be read? There are so many books and religions that one life is not enough to read all the books relating to even one religion. Whenever then is the time for practice? The more you read, the more you feel like reading further. The result of all this is to go on discussing with other people who have books and spend time thus but that will not lead to deliverance. What books had I seen and what Vedanta discourses had I heard except to close my eyes and remain peaceful and quiet during the first two years of my coming here?[8]

**33** Even if one has huge amounts of book knowledge, it is of no use unless the inner attachment [the ego] is destroyed.

**34** The excellence of the subtle intellect is only its ability to enter the Heart – that which possesses great nobility – not its ability to research and understand anything.

**Question:** Bhagavan, I would like to read books and find out a path whereby I can attain *mukti* but I do not know how to read. What shall I do? How can I realise *mukti?*
**Bhagavan:** What does it matter if you are illiterate? It is enough if you know your own Self.
**Question:** All people here are reading books but I am not able to do that. What shall I do?
**Bhagavan:** What do you think the book is teaching? You see yourself and then see me. It is like asking you to see yourself in a mirror. The mirror shows only what is on the face. If you see the mirror after washing your face, the face will appear to be clean. Otherwise the mirror will say there is dirt here, come back after washing. A book does the same thing. If you read the book, after realising the Self, everything will be easily understood. If you read it before realising the Self, you will see ever so many defects. It will say, 'First set yourself right and then see me'. That is all. First see your Self. Why do you worry yourself about all that book learning?[9]

**35** Everything that one has learned is total falsehood if it does not become a means for [mind-] consciousness to subside within the Self.

*Guru Vachaka Kovai*, verse 143, *Pozhippurai*: The knowledge of scriptures should prompt one to reach the Heart, the source of the ego, by taking the grace of God to be the primary support in such a way that the ego ceases to be. If it does not [help in this way] the knowledge borne as a burden by those who behave as if they are the body, the illusory lump of flesh, is nothing but the swinging, fleshy beard of the goat.
*Vilakkam*: The grace of God is that which springs forth naturally in every being all the time. Since knowledge that does not help one to reach the Heart is totally useless,

it has been compared to a goat's fleshy beard. Until one reaches the Heart, the ego will not cease. Hence it has been said, 'To reach the Heart in such a way [that] ... the ego ceases to be'. Any effort to reach the Heart that relies primarily on ego-consciousness will be utterly futile. This is why it has been said, 'by taking the grace of God to be the primary support'.

**36** The benefit of learning should be nothing less than to dwell upon the gracious feet of the one whose form is the wealth of pure consciousness.

**Pandits and scholars**

**37** Only those who are dwelling in the land of *Atma-swarupa*, which is consciousness, the supreme, are scholars. The rest are madmen.

**38** Even though they have acquired knowledge of other things, what have those lowest of people really gained, they who have not learned to enquire into and know the state of the Self in a fitting manner?

**39** He who sees an object as separate from consciousness cannot be a pandit who has known consciousness.

*Guru Vachaka Kovai*, verse 132, *Pozhippurai*: Why do many of you who have moved with me call me a pandit? The indispensable mark that should be present as a characteristic of the true pandit is only knowing the one who has studied, right from the beginning, all the arts and sciences that are apart from himself in such a way that they cease, being known to be ignorance.

*Guru Vachaka Kovai*, verse 133, *Pozhippurai*: By enquiring deeply within oneself, 'Who is the one who has known all the arts and sciences?' the ego that says 'I am a knowledgeable one' ceases immediately, without raising its head. Along with it, the knowledge of arts and sciences that was known by the ego also ceases. Only he who has unerringly known, as it really is, his true state, the Self that remains after this enquiry, is a pandit. How can someone with an ego, who has not known the *Atma-swarupa*, become a pandit?

**40** What can be accomplished by intellectual mastery, which overcomes opponents through clever arguments, humbling them and preventing them from opening their mouths?

**41** Even if one studies and knows in minute detail the subtlest of books, unless there is [*nishkamya*] *punya* it will be impossible for the mind to enter the Heart.

'Punya' *here refers to the merits that come from spiritual practices performed without any thought of a reward.*

# Death and Suffering

## Death

1 In a mind in which *pramada* has departed, birth and death will become mere words.

2 The mind slipping, through bewilderment, from the truth that is never defective – this is what roams around as the god of death [Yama].

**Bhagavan:** The great teachers say that forgetfulness is the root of all evil, and is death for those who seek release, so one should rest the mind in one's Self and should never forget the Self.[1]

**Bhagavan:** Forgetfulness of your real nature is the present death; remembrance of it is the rebirth. It puts an end to successive births. Yours is eternal life.[2]

**Bhagavan:** If a man considers he is born he cannot avoid the fear of death. Let him find out if he has been born or if the Self has any birth. He will discover that the Self always exists, that the body which is born resolves itself into thought and that the emergence of thought is the root of all mischief. Find wherefrom thoughts emerge. Then you will abide in the ever-present inmost Self and be free from the idea of birth or the fear of death.
**Question:** How to do it?
**Bhagavan:** The thoughts are only *vasanas* accumulated in innumerable births before. Their annihilation is the aim. The state free from *vasanas* is the primal state and eternal state of purity.[3]

3 The ego that binds one to the false, perishable body is indeed the death that makes one a prey to Yama.

**Dead or alive?**

4 Those who have even a trace of the feeling of 'I' in the body, which becomes corpse-like in sleep, are really dead, even though they may appear to be living.

> **Bhagavan:** We are now living in death. Those who have limited the unlimited Self have committed suicide by putting on such limitations.[4]

5 In that state where you [the ego] die, the life of the Self, which is beyond all description, will become manifest in your Heart.

6 That which makes the deathless Self appear as something that dies is the ego that regards the perishable body as 'I'.

> **Bhagavan:** Is there death for you? For whom is death? The body which dies, were you aware of it, did you have it, during sleep? The body was not when you slept, but you existed even then. When you awoke, you got the body and even in the waking state you exist. You existed both in sleep and waking. But the body did not exist in sleep and exists only in waking. That which does not exist always, but exists at one time and not at another, cannot be real. You exist always and you alone are therefore real.[5]

7 People who are subject to the vain intoxication of the ego's demented arrogance will die over and over again, a thousand times a day.

8 Only those whose minds are dead truly live. Those who have a living mind, which is a delusion, are those who are truly dead.

> **Bhagavan:** There is really no such thing as a dead or a living body. That which does not move we call dead, and that which has movement we call alive. In dreams you see any number of bodies, living and dead, and they have no existence when you wake up. In the same way this whole world, animate and inanimate, is non-existent. Death means the dissolution of the ego, and birth means the rebirth of the ego. You exist whether the sense of ego is there or not. You are its source, but not the ego-sense. Deliverance [*mukti*] means finding the origin of these

births and deaths and demolishing the ego-sense to its very roots. That is deliverance. It means death with full awareness. If one dies thus, one is born again simultaneously and in the same place with *aham sphurana* known as '*Aham, Aham* ["I", "I"]'. One who is born thus, has no doubts whatsoever.[6]

9 The upside-down life in which the perishable, useless and false body has become the *swarupa* is indeed death.

## Immortality

10 Those whose hearts have been penetrated by the ever-present existence of *Atma-swarupa* are immortals.

11 Your close association with that negligent inattention [*pramada*] is the death that haunts you, striking fear into the heart.

12 If, after great struggles, you uproot and cast aside that *pramada*, you will attain immortal life.

13 Those who[se egos] have died have reached the state of immortality. Those ignorant ones with inflated egos are truly dead.

> *Guru Vachaka Kovai*, verse 227: Death is nothing but the delusion that rises as 'The alien body is "I"'. Immortality is merely the bliss of the Self, the difference-free consciousness that becomes one with you when that delusion, the identification with the ego, is destroyed.

14 The deathless state is attained only by *tyaga* [giving up everything]. It is impossible to get by any kind of yoga.

15 Those who have in this world itself obtained true *jnana* in their Heart, which is beyond the knowledge of the senses, are immortals.

## Grief

16 People lamenting and crying over the deaths of others is merely a reflection crying over the disappearance of a reflection.

> **Bhagavan:** If the man dies while alive, if he dies the death which is not death, by the extinction of the ego – he would not grieve for anybody's death.[7]

17 The mental disturbance of feeling sad over the death of friends and relatives is an act of ignorance.

News of someone's death was brought to Sri Bhagavan. He said, 'Good. The dead are indeed happy. They have got rid of thc troublesome overgrowth – the body. The dead man does not grieve. The survivors grieve for the man who is dead. Do men fear sleep? On the contrary sleep is courted and on waking up every man says that he slept happily. One prepares the bed for sound sleep. Sleep is temporary death. Death is longer sleep. If the man dies while yet alive he need not grieve over others' deaths. One's existence is evident with or without the body, as in waking, dream and sleep. Then why should one desire continuance of the bodily shackles? Let the man find out his undying Self and die and be immortal and happy.[8]

**Bhagavan:** By turning the mind inwards one can overcome the worst of griefs. Grief is possible only when one thinks of oneself as a body. If the form be transcended, one will know that the Self is eternal – that there is neither birth nor death; it is the body that is born and dies, not the Self; the body is a creation of the ego, which however is never perceived apart from a body. One should consider that in sleep one was not aware of a body; one will then realise that the body is not real. On waking from sleep the ego arises; then thoughts. Find out to whom the thoughts belong. Ask wherefrom they arise. They must spring from the Self, which is consciousness. Apprehending this truth even vaguely helps towards extinction of the ego; and thereafter the one infinite existence will be realised; in that state there are no individuals – only that one being. Hence there is no ground for even the *thought* of death.

If one thinks oneself to have been born, one cannot escape the thought of death. Let one therefore question whether one was born at all. One will then find that the real Self is ever-existent and that the body is only a thought – the first of all thoughts, the root of all mischief.[9]

# Suffering

## The cause of suffering

18 Those who through mental confusion perceive as real that which is not real will suffer in their minds and be ruined.

A couple of days back a devotee who was with Bhagavan continuously for several years passed away all of a sudden. All who knew him felt much [grief] when Sri Bhagavan remarked, 'That which is not real [the body] you take as real, and anguish is the only result.'[10]

19 The reason why one experiences misery is that one does not first come to know the real nature of that primal entity, the source.

20 The afflictions experienced by the beings of the world do not exist except in the outlook of those in whom enquiry is absent.

**Question:** Bhagavan, all through my life I have been experiencing nothing but suffering. Is it due to the sinful karma of my previous births? I once asked my mother whether I had been happy in her womb. She told me that she had suffered a great deal at that time. How is it that I have acquired so many sins? Why do I suffer so much?
**Bhagavan:** We could say that it is due to *purva* karma [past karma]. But instead of thinking that this *purva* karma is due to the karma of, for example, the incarnation previous to the last, find out to whom this present incarnation has come. If this body is what has taken birth, let it ask the question. You say that you are always experiencing suffering. That is only your thought. Happiness alone exists. What comes and goes is suffering.[11]

**Bhagavan:** Misery is due to objects. If they are not there, there will be no contingent thoughts, and so misery is wiped off. 'How will objects cease to be?' is the next question. The *srutis* and the sages say that the objects are only mental creations. They have no substantive being. Investigate the matter and ascertain the truth of the statement. The result will be the conclusion that the objective world is in the subjective consciousness. The Self is thus the only reality which permeates and also envelops the world. Since there is no duality, no thoughts will arise to disturb your peace. This is realisation of the Self. The Self is eternal and so also its realisation.[12]

**21** The great mountain of anxieties is an unreal accumulation of fictions bundled together by the imagining mind.

**Question:** Worries of worldly life trouble me much and I do not find happiness anywhere.
**Bhagavan:** Do these worries trouble you in sleep?
**Question:** No.
**Bhagavan:** So it proves that the worries do not belong to you.[13]

**22** Nothing that is worth grieving over ever happens to you. Examine your real nature.

*Guru Vachaka Kovai*, verse 953: Since one's own reality, the sun of *jnana* that has never seen the darkness of delusion, itself shines as happiness, the mental distress of misery appears only because of ego-consciousness. In truth, no one ever experiences misery at all.

**23** For those who are distressed, the distressing mind that associates with them is indeed a self-created evil.
**24** When enduring true bliss exists and fills the heart to the brim, it is an error of the ego to feel distress.

*Guru Vachaka Kovai*, verse 969, *Pozhippurai*: The *jivas* remain immersed unceasingly in the ambrosial-flood of God's grace. The anxious distress and the mental grief they experience by coming under the sway of delusion is like someone who, despite living all the time in the midst of the River Ganga, whose waters rush against the shore, does not know the way to quench his tormenting thirst and, through stupidity, suffers as if he were dying.
*Vilakkam*: As grace is the very nature of God, it is present everywhere. The *jivas*' suffering through the misery of

birth, even as they remain immersed in [grace], without ever leaving it, is nothing but ignorance.

**25** The whirling of the mind that spins like a top in the Heart which, like, sleep, is free from thought, is misery.

**26** Why indeed does the *jiva* feel aggrieved and suffer by forgetting *swarupa*, its real nature, which surges as the vast expanse of supreme bliss?

**27** The mind, imagining a cause for the transcendent reality, and growing weary, will be rewarded only with suffering.

**28** The foundation for all miseries is the impure *vasana*, the belief that holds the body to be 'I'.

*Guru Vachaka Kovai*, verse 954: If one examines one's own real nature, which is auspicious bliss, there will be no misery at all in one's life. One suffers because of the idea that the body, which is never the Self, is 'I'. It [misery] is all due to this evil, deluding connection.

**29** Only those people who do not know the way to destroy the *vasanas* suffer increasing misery.

**30** Since you have created all your miseries through the degraded attitude of mind [that thinks I-am-the-body], why do you rail against God as though he were the cause of your suffering?

**Question:** If God is all why does the individual suffer for his actions? Are not the actions prompted by Him, for which the individual is made to suffer?
**Bhagavan:** He who thinks he is the doer is also the sufferer.
**Question:** But the actions are prompted by God and the individual is only His tool.
**Bhagavan:** This logic is applied only when one suffers, but not when one rejoices. If the conviction prevails always, there will be no suffering either.
**Question:** When will the suffering cease?
**Bhagavan:** Not until individuality is lost. If both the good and bad actions are His, why should you think that the enjoyment and suffering are alone yours? He who does good or bad, also enjoys pleasure or suffers pain. Leave it there and do not superimpose suffering on yourself.[14]

**31** Know that suffering is only in the bewildered vision of the *jiva* that has been grabbed by the stupidity of becoming attached to the false ego.

> *Guru Vachaka Kovai*, verse 952: One's own reality, which shines within everyone as the Heart, is the ocean of unalloyed bliss. Therefore, like the unreal blueness of the sky, misery exists merely in the imagination, not in reality.

**32** If the harmful ego rises, an endless chain of miseries will manifest for a long, long time.

**33** If the *jiva* slips from the true state, its real nature, the Self, a life full of misery, like the unceasing waves [of the ocean], will associate with it.

### The ending of suffering

**34** Since you are intent on driving out suffering, you should know that your real nature is bliss alone.

**35** Confusion and agitation are erroneous superimpositions upon consciousness, within which they have no real existence.

**36** For all the many distressful diseases the peerless medicine is definitely the certainty of the real nature of the Self.

**37** Why do you become distressed and suffer to no purpose over things that are not worthy of your concern? Let go of the mind's anxieties.

**38** Those adepts who have perfected their *sadhana* will not become dejected and perturbed when they are beset by trials and tribulations.

**39** In what way do lamentations benefit the *jiva*? The sensible policy is to terminate the tyrannical insurgency of the mind.

**40** Until you enquire into your real nature, seeing and abiding as it, the triple miseries experienced by you will not cease.

*The triple miseries are those caused by oneself, those caused by the physical world, and those caused by destiny.*

**41** Subside in the Heart, the seat of the soul where the bliss of *swarupa* surges, so that you are not afflicted by misery.

**42** Seeking within the Heart and knowing oneself as the expanse of consciousness is total fulfilment, but to suffer, imagining the contemptible body to be 'I', is poverty.

# Right Behaviour, Right Attitude

## *Siddhis*

1 Directing the mind towards *siddhis* [supernatural powers] is a stumbling block that inhibits progress towards the supreme state of liberation.

*Guru Vachaka Kovai*, verse 222: If those *sadhakas* who are striving on the path of liberation direct their minds towards various *siddhis*, their ego-root will swell up more and more, making the bondage that adheres to them stronger and stronger.

2 Excepting *jnana siddhi*, all the many other *siddhis* are merely concepts of the mind.

Ulladu Narpadu, *verse 35:*

To know and to be, with the mind subsided, the reality that is ever attained is the [true] attainment. All other *siddhis* are *siddhis* that are acquired in a dream. When one wakes up, will they be real? Will they who, by abiding in the true state, are rid of the false be deluded? Know and be yourself.[1]

### Omniscience

3 That which is termed omniscience is associated with delusion because in reality no kind of objectified knowing exists.

*Guru Vachaka Kovai*, verse 926, *Pozhippurai*: Because one does not know any being other than oneself, *Atma-swarupa*, only the pure, attribute-free consciousness that shines as fullness, without any limitation, is in truth the omniscience that is unequalled; it is not the other knowledge of simultaneously and completely knowing the three times [past, present and future] and the three worlds.

*Vilakkam*: Since everything is pure consciousness alone, and since that pure consciousness is one's own real nature, the truth is, apart from oneself, no other being exists. Because divided and particularised knowledge ceases in that Self-state, having no room to exist, only the attribute-free consciousness, the reality that shines undivided, free from the act of knowing, is, in truth, omniscience.

*Guru Vachaka Kovai*, verse 927: In those minds that have not subsided, all the afflictions arising from the delusion existing within them have already accumulated through their limited knowledge. If they gain omniscience, the already-existing darkness of delusion will become more dense, but there will be no benefit whatsoever to the *jivas*.

*Guru Vachaka Kovai*, verse 930, *Pozhippurai*: The *Vedas* loudly proclaim that God is omniscient only for the sake of those who are confused, thinking that they possess limited knowledge. When carefully examined, [it will be known that] God does not at any time know anything because in His very nature he is the fullness of being [*unmai pooranam*].

4 Only knowledge of reality is omniscience. If omniscience is different from knowledge of reality, it will become defective, false knowledge.

5 Since, in reality, nothing apart from consciousness exists, omniscience is ignorance because its nature involves differences.

*Guru Vachaka Kovai*, verse 928: In truth, one is that which is, but through self-bewilderment one imagines oneself to be a knower and sees a few illusory scenes. Only to such a one will omniscience be real. For the *jnani*, who is without that bewilderment, omniscience is only deranged knowledge.

6 Omniscience pertaining to the *triputi*-differences [can exist] only

until [one] realises correctly one's real nature, consciousness, the supreme.

*Guru Vachaka Kovai*, verse 929, *Pozhippurai*: Instead of knowing oneself to be mere being, when one gets bewildered on account of regarding oneself as being someone whose nature is to know other things as objects, one feels mentally distressed, feeling, 'I possess only limited knowledge'. When one clearly knows the truth of oneself, the characteristic of knowing objects becomes incongruous and departs. Therefore, in the state of supreme truth [*paramartika*] omniscience, becoming unreal, will also cease and perish along with limited knowledge.

7 If omniscience exists in objectified knowing, then it too is limited knowledge by virtue of having a fragmented nature.

## Good and bad habits

### Pride, honour and praise

**8** Though respect and honour are esteemed in the world, realise in your heart that they are flawed, and disregard them.

Ulladu Narpadu Anubandham, *verse 38:*

Without thinking of oneself as apart from others, without swerving from one's true state, if one abides always in one's Self, who is there alien to one? What does it matter what people say of one? What does it matter if one praises or blames oneself?[2]

**9** Do not get caught up in the pride that causes you to practise deception in your heart. Shine by living an open life.

**10** To take pride in boasting about oneself is the mark of an empty and insignificant person, a mere husk.

**11** Even if someone praises you, to delight in it with relish is wrong. Only someone who is totally useless speaks in praise of himself.

**12** Self-praise, an enemy posing as a friend, will delude one and push one into a dark pit from which it will be difficult to escape.

13 An even more disgraceful fault than feeling pride by speaking in praise of oneself is gossiping about the minor defects of others.

## Fame

14 Protect yourself from the mental agitation that stems from being caught up in the net of praise and fame, which only deceives you.

> *Guru Vachaka Kovai*, verse 623: Being praised engenders, through *pramada*, the fault of changing oneself – who is in truth the supreme – into the totally profitless body. The wise should, with firm determination, totally detest it. It is not a worthy thing to desire.

15 The egotistical who are ensnared by the empty desire for fame are not different from those who have been ensnared by harlots.

16 If in your mind there arises a desire for fame, which is worthless and more harmful than a harlot, that mind will become an irredeemable slave to it.

17 You should know that a desire for fame runs contrary to the great glory exhibited by my true devotees. Keep away from people [who have that desire], or leave their company.

## Traditional rules of conduct

18 Lustrous *Padam* frequently speaks of the benefits of virtuous behaviour [*achara*], advising devotees not to forsake traditional rules of conduct, but to cherish and observe them.

> *Guru Vachaka Kovai*, verse 791: Since the moral and religious observances that have been laid down protect the *sadhaka* for a long distance [along the path], they deserve to be appropriately observed, but if they obstruct the practice of the excellent and true *jnana vichara*, then give them up as deficient.

Sri Ramana Gita, *chapter 7, verses 12, 13, 14:*

> **[Question:]** When one is fit for self-enquiry by one's non-

attachment to sense objects and by discrimination, are ceremonial baths, morning and evening prayers, repetition of mantras, oblations poured into the fire, chanting of *Vedas*, worship of gods, *bhajans*, pilgrimages, sacrifice, giving in charity, and observance of special spiritual practices, are these of any use or are they a waste of time?
**[Bhagavan:]** For competent beginners with waning attachments all these aids will make the mind increasingly pure.

Ramanadeva! You gave me [Sivaprakasam Pillai] a small bag containing *vibhuti* and asked me to keep it all the time. You also told me that giving up traditional disciplines is harmful.[3]

**19** This disgraceful aberration known as 'the mind' will not depart simply by observing *achamana* and *agamarshana*.

Achamana *is the ritual sipping of water while uttering mantras and* agamarshana *is a mantra that is uttered during ritual immersion. Bhagavan's comment can be taken to apply to all similar rituals.*

**20** The splendorous condition, the state in which the vile ego is abolished, is indeed the sum of the many and various vedic sacrifices that confer spotless purity.

**21** Since *charya* [devotion and detachment] alone sustains *sadhana*, observe and cherish it in an appropriate way, without ever slackening.

*Guru Vachaka Kovai*, verse 826 *Pozhippurai*: A heavy building raised on foundations that have not been strongly laid will collapse in devastation, to the ridicule of all. It is therefore the duty of striving *sadhakas* to first thoroughly practise by any means devotion and detachment.
*Vilakkam*: The effort to restrain the activities [*vrittis*] of the mind is indispensable. If beginners act as if they are free, this will, ultimately, lead to disappointment.

*In a note to the* Guru Vachaka Kovai *verse Muruganar explains that* charya *means devotion and detachment. I have therefore added these words in the* Padamalai *verse and used them as a translation of* charya *in the* Pozhippurai.

**22** Observe the disciplines of external conduct [*achara*], knowing in your heart their real object by properly reflecting on their inner meaning.

Some of those who came for Maharshi's *darshan* used to perform *ashtanga namaskaram* in the traditional way. It was their belief that this practice, done devoutly, was indispensable for those who wanted the grace of the *Sadguru*.

In order to drive home the point that in spiritual life mere mechanical observance of any *sadhana*, without knowing its inner meaning and without experiencing its fruit, will not make one blessed, Sri Bhagavan, addressing one such devotee, said, 'The benefit of performing *namaskaram* to the Guru is only the removal of the ego. This is not attained except by total surrender. Within the Heart of each devotee the gracious Guru is giving *darshan* in the form of consciousness. To surrender is to offer fully, in silence, the subsided ego, which is a name-and-form thought, to the *aham-sphurana* [the effulgence of "I"], the real holy feet of the gracious Guru. Since [this is so], Self-realisation cannot be attained by a bowing of the body, but only by a bowing of the ego.'

In this way Sri Bhagavan explained the truth of *namaskaram* and further explained that if spiritual practices are to yield their fruits without fail, they should be observed with a full awareness of their purpose.[4]

**23*** Unless one is a *jnani* whose consciousness has become calm and clear, it is not possible to enquire and know the underlying subtle principles of *dharma* [the true meanings of practices].

**24** The Self-abidance that flourishes when one realises one's true nature is the supreme *dharma* of *sat-achara*.

*Though* achara *generally denotes some form of behaviour or a code of conduct that one must adhere to, the 'supreme* dharma *of* sat-achara' *is just abiding as* sat, *being.*

25 The clear, true *jnana*, the propitious observance, should be more dearly cherished within the Heart than life itself.

## Fear

26 *Padam* shines in the Heart, saying, 'In *Atma-swarupa* what remains either to desire or be afraid of?'
27 Since nothing exists outside the Self, which is one's own nature, what foolishness it is to be frightened!
28 Know that there are never any circumstances and never any cause for you to get bewildered and frightened in your heart.

> **Question:** How to uproot weariness, fear and anxiety that arise during meditation?
> **Bhagavan:** Find out to whom these questions occur. By conducting this enquiry these things will disappear. These things are impermanent. Do not pay attention to them. When there is knowledge of duality, fear arises. Fear only comes when you think that there are others apart from you. If you direct your mind towards the Self, fear and anxiety will go away. In your present state, when the mind is agitated, if you remove one kind of fear, another will rise up and there will be no end of them. It is a laborious task to pluck the leaves off a tree one by one. The 'I' feeling is the root of all thoughts. If you destroy the root, the leaves and branches will wither away. Instead of forming bad habits and taking medicine for them, it is better to see that such bad habits are not formed.[5]

29 Unless one realises one's non-dual real nature, the desire and fear that are caused by delusion will not cease.
30 Instead of enjoying bliss, established in the state of the Self, why this desire in you for the world, which frightens the mind?
31 With the help of divine grace, destroy your fear, end your suffering and attain the state of bliss.

## Deceitfulness

32 The modern 'civilised' behaviour of covering a deceitful heart with sweet and seductive words is very fine, very fine indeed!

33 Save yourself by eschewing the modern 'civilised' life, whose nature is to practise deception, which is just like smearing ambrosia over the top of poison.

34 The soul that has consumed this poison, this life of deception, will experience misery and distress in the mind, and will perish.

35 An existence dominated by the cunning and deceitful mind will eventually attack the heart like a powerful poison, and torment it.

**Question:** Some people put on all sorts of false appearances to deceive the world.
**Bhagavan:** Yes. Not some, but many. What of that? If people put on false appearances, it is their own minds that get troubled ultimately. They begin to be afraid of what others would think of them and so their minds become their own enemies. If people think of deceiving others by putting on false appearances they themselves get deceived ultimately. They think, 'We have planned and have deceived others and thereby have shown more cleverness'. With pride they practise more and more deceptions. The consequences of their actions will be realised only when the deceptions are discovered. When the time comes, they will collapse as a result of their own deceits.[6]

36 Since Iswara abides as your own Self, it is impossible to deceive him, no matter what you do.

37 Deceitful conduct, like the root-maggot, will undermine and topple the great [tree of] *tapas*, which is the striving for redemption.

38 To an evil heart that is full of deceitfulness, the profound peace that is free from agitation is far, far away.

39 Those fools involved in deceitful worldly life will beg others when overwhelmed by problems, but when others beg from them, they will behave arrogantly.

40 By indulging in improper conduct the *jiva* will swelter and suffer in the burgeoning fire of sordid sense objects.

## Diet

41 To abstain from the disgusting habit of eating flesh is the first rule observed by those whose conduct is impeccable.

42 That flesh food itself will destroy those true devotees who have entered the path of grace, diverting them onto the path of delusion.

43 For those who have undertaken the task of abolishing the dominion of the ego, which is rooted in the fleshy body, fattening flesh by eating flesh is improper.

44 Be moderate in food, activities and sleep. In some way or other set a limit to them.

> **Question:** What must I do to avoid sleep during my meditation?
>
> **Bhagavan:** Meditators must not work too much, nor should they fill their stomachs with excessive food. The more one fills the stomach, the lower one's mental state becomes. If the stomach is mostly empty, one will go higher spiritually. One should not tighten the strings of the *veena* [a large, stringed, musical instrument] either too much or too little. The body must be kept like that.
>
> Likewise with sleep. One third of the night has been allotted for sleep. That is, one must go to bed at 10 p.m. and wake up at 2 a.m. One should not sleep during the day time. There is another system also. One should get up whenever one wakes up and one should sleep whenever sleep comes. But one should not think, 'I slept' or 'I woke up'.[7]

*On other occasions Bhagavan was less insistent about this somewhat extreme regime of four hours sleep a night:*

> **Bhagavan:** When the body and mind are engaged in the ordinary pursuits of life, the body reels if you give up food and sleep. Therefore it must be said that limitation of food and movement is very necessary for the elevation of the soul. Great people restrict their sleep to the barest minimum so that they may not waste their time but use it for the performance of selfless good deeds. Some say that it is healthy to go to bed at 10 p.m. and wake up at 2 a.m. That means that four hours' sleep is enough. Some say that four hours' sleep is not enough, but that it should be six hours. It amounts to this, that sleep and food should not be taken in excess. If you want to cut off either of

them completely, your mind will always be directed towards it. Therefore the *sadhaka* should do everything in moderation.[8]

**Question:** What diet is prescribed for a *sadhaka*?
**Bhagavan:** Sattvic food in limited quantities.
**Question:** What is sattvic food?
**Bhagavan:** Bread, fruits, vegetables, milk, etc.[9]

**Question:** Why are such restrictions for food given?
**Bhagavan:** Your present experience is due to the influence of the atmosphere you are in. Can you have it outside this atmosphere? The experience is spasmodic. Until it becomes permanent, practice is necessary. Restrictions of food are aids for such experience to be repeated. After one gets established in truth the restrictions drop away naturally. Moreover, food influences the mind and it must be kept pure.[10]

**45** Food eaten when one feels hungry will be useful, but food eaten before hunger has set in will cause harm to the soul.

**Bhagavan:** The rule regarding food is that one should allow time enough for the belly to recuperate, and after that, when hunger has come, should eat measured and sattvic food.[11]

**46** Cure the disease of hunger with the medicine of food obtained through begging and live without any desire in your mind.

*This particular piece of advice should not be taken as being applicable to everyone. Several of Bhagavan's devotees, including Muruganar himself, used to beg for their food in Tiruvannamalai. However, Bhagavan never insisted that everyone should adopt this particular lifestyle. On many occasions he refused permission to devotees who wanted to renounce their family obligations and take to the life of a begging monk. Bhagavan sometimes gave permission to beg to people who had no worldly responsibilities, but those with jobs and families were expected to obtain their food in more conventional ways.*

*This is what Bhagavan had to say about the period of his life when he himself lived on* bhiksha, *food obtained by begging:*

**Bhagavan:** It used to be an exhilarating experience in those days. When I was going out for *bhiksha,* I used to take the alms in the palms of my hands and go along the street eating it. When the eating was over I used to go on licking my hands. I never used to care for anything. I used to feel shy to ask anyone for anything. Hence that *karathala bhiksha* [taking alms in the palms of one's hands] used to be very interesting. There used to be big pundits this side and that; sometimes big government officials also used to be there. What did I care who was there? It would be humiliating for a poor man to go out for *bhiksha,* but for one who has conquered the ego and become an *advaiti,* it is great elevation of the mind. At that time, he would not care if an emperor came there. In that way, when I went out for *bhiksha* and clapped my hands, people used to say 'Swami has come,' and give me *bhiksha* with fear and devotion. Those who did not know me used to say, 'You are strong and sturdy. Instead going out like this as a beggar, why don't you go out to work as a coolie?' I used to feel amused. But I was a Mouna Swami and did not speak. I used to laugh and go away feeling that it was usual for ordinary people to talk like that. The more they talked like that the more exhilarated I felt. That was great fun.[12]

**47** Accept with great joy whatever is obtained without desiring it. Regard it as sufficient and offer it to the body.

## Bad habits

**48** *Padam* admonishes, saying: 'It is a serious error for the good mind to have a keen interest in fictional stories about the world, which are merely mental creations.'

**49** It is proper for *sadhakas* to keep under control the addiction for intercourse with the opposite sex, which is the cause of much shame.

**50*** Realising that desire for women leads to one's death, the wise ones firmly hold onto *Padam* to free themselves from that desire.

**Question:** Is not *brahmacharya* [celibacy] necessary for realisation of the Self?

**Bhagavan:** *Brahmacharya* is 'living with *Brahman*'. It has no connection with celibacy as commonly understood. A real *brahmachari,* that is one who lives in *Brahman*, finds bliss in *Brahman*, which is the same as the Self. Why then should you look for other sources of happiness? In fact the emergence from the Self has been the cause of all the misery.
**Question:** Celibacy is *sine qua non* for yoga?
**Bhagavan:** So it is. Celibacy is certainly an aid to realisation among so many other aids.
**Question:** Is it then not indispensable? Can a married man realise the Self?
**Bhagavan:** Certainly, it is a matter of fitness of mind. Married or unmarried, a man can realise the Self, because that is here and now. If it were not so, but attainable by some efforts at some other time, and if it were new and something to be acquired, it would not be worthy of pursuit. Because what is not natural cannot be permanent either. But what I say is that the Self is here and now and alone.[13]

**Question:** How to root out sexual impulse?
**Bhagavan:** By rooting out the false idea of the body being the Self. There is no sex in the Self.
**Question:** How to realise it?
**Bhagavan:** Because you think you are the body, you see another as the body. Difference in sex arises. But you are not the body. Be the real Self. Then there is no sex.[14]

**51** Jealousy will distress the hearts of those who have kept company with it, dispelling their inner peace.
**52** Even a trace of the tendency to hoard is an enemy of perfect renunciation, the fullness of the Heart.
**53** It is foolish to harbour a deep hatred for the non-Self, which is perceived in consciousness through confusion.

*Guru Vachaka Kovai*, verse 488: Noble people should not, in a state of revulsion, hate enemies even slightly, no matter how bad they may be. For aversion, just like desire, deserves to be curbed.

**Bhagavan:** The mind should not be allowed to wander towards worldly objects and what concerns other people. However bad people may be, one should bear no hatred for them. Both desire and hatred should be eschewed.[15]

54 Wherever you may go and search, it is rare to come across people who have the honesty to see their own mistakes.

55 The reason for refusing to accept one's own defects is the identification with the false ego, the reflection.

## Behaviour towards others

56 In your behaviour keep in mind that it is proper conduct to treat oneself and others in an identical way.

57 When, in the first place, your mind has ceased to be under your control, what is the point of speaking about the inconsistent nature of others?

58 To be afraid, effervescing with frenzied anger, is the very picture of those whose base mind is filled with self-conceit.

59 To go looking for imperfections is the fault of the twisted mind since one's real nature flourishes as the fullness of consciousness.

60 Do not analyse the objective world saying 'This is good, this is bad,' but seek the reality of the one Self that abides within your own Heart.

61 If you manifest love through your mind, speech and body then for your beloved soul there will never be any enmity.

62 Those who desire to become the recipients of God's grace will not think harmful thoughts about anyone else.

63 Only those who have learned to conduct themselves with a deep respect for the sensibilities of others can be said to have learned civilised behaviour.

64 To err is human, but to forgive others' faults with love flourishing in the heart is distinguished and godly behaviour.

## Performing actions

65 *Padam* decrees: 'Whatever work you undertake, you should do it with your attention fixed one-pointedly upon it.'

Sri Bhagavan used to go to the kitchen at 4 a.m. to

start cutting the vegetables. One or two of us would join him and help. Sometimes the amount of vegetables to be prepared used to startle us. Sri Bhagavan managed to cut much more and more quickly than the rest of us. One time, faced with a mountain of work, I looked up at the clock because I was impatient to finish the job. Actually, I wanted to go back to sleep and have another short nap.

Sri Bhagavan sensed my impatience and asked, 'Why are you looking at the clock?'

I tried to bluff him by saying, 'If I could only complete the work before five, I could go and meditate for an hour'.

Sri Bhagavan retorted, 'The allotted work has to be completed in time. Other thoughts are obstacles, not the amount of work. Doing the allotted work in time is itself meditation. Go ahead and do the job with full attention.'

In this way Sri Bhagavan taught us the importance of right, honest work.[16]

**66** If it is necessary to perform a particular task, then it is fitting to do it in a proper manner.

**67** It is wisdom to abandon all activities other than those that are indispensable, being caused by nature.

**68** Live your life without getting agitated, performing only those worldly activities that are unavoidable.

**69** Surrender your mind to the Lord and play your part in the drama of worldly life with great skill, without getting caught up in the world.

**70** If you are thinking of performing a good deed, do it well, and in appropriate measure.

**71** However good an action may be, if performing it spoils and destroys your equanimity of mind, what is the benefit of it?

*Guru Vachaka Kovai*, verse 574: Only those actions that are performed whole-heartedly, with tranquillity, and from a virtuousness that comes from purity of mind, are good actions. All actions performed with oppressive agitation and through the contaminating desires of the mind, fall under the category of sinful actions.

**72** Not doing the things that should be done, and doing the things that should not be done – these are errors that arise simultaneously in the state of great delusion.

## Reforming the world

**73** The way to reform the world is to reform oneself in such a way that reality shines in the Heart.

**74** Before attempting to enquire into and know the way to reform the world, subjugate and destroy your insurgent mind.

**75** Without first filling your own heart [with Self-knowledge], what aid can you give, and to whom?

**76** Those who do not have the power to redeem themselves cannot render genuine service to the beings of the world.

**77** The non-existent *maya* can deceive the good sense [of a *sadhaka*] by showing itself as compassion to other beings.

> **Bhagavan:** A seeker should recognise it as a future bondage when some action presents itself which makes him feel that he wishes to do it because the doing of it is an act of human kindness and sympathy; and so he is tempted into doing it. He does not realise that the act will be the cause of future bondage. He thinks that, by being a non-doer [*akarta*] and by being detached [*asanga*], the fulfilment of the desire will not affect him and he can therefore do the act. He will become bound all the same and will be freed from the bondages only after several more births. That future bondages result in rebirths is authoritatively stated in the scriptures.[17]

## Avoiding bad company

**78** Association with those demonic people whose minds are dishonest and whose morals are debased deserves to be totally shunned.

**79** The fundamental cause of all miseries is friendship with dishonourable, deluded and depraved people.

**80** Rather than closely associating with those whose nature is incompatible with your own, it is better to avoid their company, without speaking badly of them.

**81** Those useless people who have lost their peace by getting over-excited are harmful not only to others but also to themselves.

**82** Get rid of the foolish excitement, the wild, turbulent frenzy that belongs exclusively to the worthless.

**Muruganar:** The wise one should not only restrain and control completely his own frenzied emotions, he should also conduct himself with extreme care towards those who are under the sway of their own emotions. If not, it may be a cause of pointless regret later. Therefore, one can even say that to whatever extent it is possible, it is better to avoid such people.[18]

**83** It is wise to shun those ego-crazed people who have not learned to attain peace by placing their attention upon consciousness alone.

## Right attitude

### *Udaseena* [indifference]

**84** In relationships with the world, any attitude other than indifference [*udaseena*] will only lead to suffering.

**Question:** We are told to practise indifference [*udaseena*] which is possible only if the world is unreal.
**Bhagavan:** Yes. *Oudasinyam abhipsitam.* Indifference is advised. But what is it? It is absence of love and hatred. When you realise the Self on which these phenomena pass, will you love or hate them? That is the meaning of indifference.
**Question:** That will lead to want of interest in our work. Should we do our duty or not?
**Bhagavan:** Yes – certainly. Even if you try not to do your duty you will be perforce obliged to do it. Let the body complete the task for which it came into being.

Sri Krishna also says in the *Gita*, whether Arjuna liked it or not he would be forced to fight. When there is work to be done by you, you cannot keep away; nor can you continue to do a thing when you are not required to do it, that is to say, when the work allotted to you has been done. In short, the work will go on and you must take your share in it – the share which is allotted to you.

**Question:** How is it to be done?
**Bhagavan:** Like an actor playing his part in a drama – free from love or hatred.[19]

85 Ascend to the summit of the mountain of indifference [*udaseena*], which shines without desire or aversion, and remain established there.
86 Realising that there is no state apart from you, maintain an attitude of indifference in your heart towards everything that appears different from you.

## Equanimity of mind

87 Know that *sama-chitta* [equanimity of mind] is when both praise and blame appear to be identical.
88 Those who have seen in their heart that God is their refuge will not swerve from the state of impartiality.
89 The attitude of mind that retains equanimity in the midst of the pairs of opposites will not be engendered in anyone who does not possess the clarity of grace.
90 To the exalted ones who possess the wealth of grace, the mental feeling 'enough' is true exhilaration, being devoid of the thought 'I am poor'.
91 A mind overflowing with joy through having the feeling 'enough' is a divine and magnificent treasure-trove. This treasure is only attained by [*nishkamya*] *punya*.
92 If they are enquired into and known, [it will be discovered that] the innumerable feelings and emotions are not in the least separate from the *santa-rasa* [the peaceful taste] of the Self.

*Guru Vachaka Kovai*, verse 945, *Pozhippurai*: Whatever experiences are gained by any being, from any object in any place, if they are enquired into, they [the experiences] will be known to be really fractions of the experience of the Self.
*Vilakkam*: 'Any place' and 'any being' refer respectively to the many different worlds and their rulers.

**Muruganar:** It is only the bliss of the Self, whose nature is peace and which permeates the many different sense objects, that is experienced by everyone. However, only *jnanis* who have attained perfect peace know this truth. Those who run frenziedly after sense objects cannot know it.[20]

**93** The divine perspective, clarity of mind, is the proper means for salvation.

**94** *Padam* declares with conviction: 'Only if the mind attains bliss through contentment will it attain tranquillity.'

## Humility

**95** A humble attitude of mind will give you redemption, transporting you to the world of the immortals. Without humility, you will drown in the pitch blackness of Hell.

*This* Padamalai *verse is a rendering of* Tirukkural, *verse 121.*

*Guru Vachaka Kovai*, verse 494, *Pozhippurai*: The position of human beings will improve to the extent that they behave with humility towards others. Is not the cause of God's supremacy, the reason why the whole world bows to Him, His distinction of not having a deluded ego that rises, even inadvertently?

**96** Humility will destroy the powerful and difficult-to-vanquish enemy [the ego] and will bestow on the *jiva* the great fortune [of liberation].

**Bhagavan:** The power of humility, which bestows immortality, is the foremost among powers that are hard to attain. Since the only benefit of learning and other similar virtues is the attainment of humility, humility alone is the real ornament of the sages. It is the storehouse of all other virtues and is therefore extolled as the wealth of divine grace. Although it is a characteristic befitting wise people in general, it is especially indispensable for *sadhus*. Since attaining greatness is impossible for anyone except by humility, all the disciplines of conduct such as *yama* and *niyama*, which are prescribed specifically for aspirants on the spiritual path, have as their aim only the attainment of humility. Humility is indeed the hallmark of the destruction of the ego. Because of this, humility is especially extolled by *sadhus* themselves as the code of conduct befitting them.

Moreover, for those who are residing at Arunachala, it is indispensable in every way. Arunachala is the sacred place where even the embodiments of God, Brahma, Vishnu and Sakti, humbly subsided. Since it has the power to humble even those who would not be humbled, those who do not humbly subside at Arunachala will surely not attain that redeeming virtue anywhere else. The Supreme Lord, who is the highest of the high, shines unrivalled and unsurpassed only because he remains the humblest of the humble. When the divine virtue of humility is necessary even for the Supreme Lord, who is totally independent, is it necessary to emphasise that it is absolutely indispensable for *sadhus* who do not have such independence? Therefore, just as in their inner life, in their outer life also *sadhus* should possess complete and perfect humility. It is not that humility is necessary only for devotees of the Lord; even for the Lord it is the characteristic virtue.[21]

## Wealth and poverty

**97** What benefit do those who have lost their minds [to the world] gain even if they obtain enormous wealth?

**98** Worldly riches are never a matter of importance to those true devotees who have in their hearts an abundance of the wealth of grace.

**99** To true devotees who are leading a life that abounds in the wealth of grace, a life replete with earthly riches is insignificant.

**100** For true devotees, the only benefit worth attaining is the blissful wealth of grace. All other kinds of wealth are of no consequence.

**101** The heart can only attain fullness through the wealth that is grace, never through material wealth.

**102** Only when possessions and possessor become one and the same will peace abide.

**103** As long as one's possessions or the possessor of them remain different [from each other], it is impossible for the mind to become still.

104 In times of great wealth the quality that will be the greatest blessing is humility of heart.

105 In poverty's straitened circumstances, the quality that should shine out is a loftiness of mind that confers inner fortitude.

*Bhagavan is here quoting* Tirukkural, *verse 963.*

106 If you disregard your worldly setbacks and have no interest in them, a joyful life will automatically be obtained in the heart.

107 Reversals of fortune in outer life come only to turn one within towards the Self.

## Giving up attachments

108 By attaining perfection in the way of abiding without any attachments, the mind and the intellect will obtain great eminence.

109 Attachments originating in the ego, which display themselves as 'love', will deceive and ruin you, pushing your heart into the deepest abyss.

110 Examine your heart so that you do not get destroyed by getting trapped in the net of attachments which, originating in the ego, only deceive.

111 The proper way to attain the blissful supreme is to weed out the thoughts of the mind that cling to wife, children and wealth.

112 Removing and destroying the long-standing attachment that is born out of the obsession for the non-Self is said to be realising the *Atma-swarupa*.

113 Since the ego is everything, the unattached state is not attained except by the cessation of the ego.

114 Noble ones should learn and practise as the supreme yoga a life that is lived without attachments.

# *Padam's* Grace Towards Muruganar

Since all praised him as one of unbounded liberality, I came to him expectantly, and with joy. The bounteous 'giver' looked at me and stealthily plundered my very self! Great indeed is the liberality of this bountiful giver![1]

Even as I grieved, thinking thoughts I should not think, he became my Lord, spreading his radiance within my Heart so that I tasted the sweet nectar of his bliss. He is the heavenly one who fills my sight with his form, which is pure consciousness. He is Mount Arunachala's exalted Guru Ramana.[2]

Amongst your devotees there is none so worthless as myself. Yet, through dwelling on you constantly in the Heart, I gained the pure, undivided experience of *Brahman*. Not one among those who resort to you goes to waste.[3]

Feeling [concerned] that it was difficult for me to bite and chew sugarcane, he merged with me as sugarcane juice itself. My Lord, the rare Supreme, has so much true love towards me. My Lord's very form is grace.[4]

# *Padam's* Grace Towards Muruganar

*In this final chapter Muruganar speaks of the experiences he had as a result of Bhagavan's grace. In all these verses* Padam *denotes Bhagavan himself.*

**Preliminary comments**

1 Due to the perfect oneness of its nature, *Padam*, *Atma-swarupa* abiding in the Heart, does not desire words of praise.

2 I am afraid that if I say words of praise about *Padam,* this will create a sense of difference [between us], making my praise turn into blasphemy.

***Padam* made me sing his praise**

3 Golden *Padam,* the source of fragrant Tamil, ascended onto my tongue and stood there, making words of grace originate [from it] as if I were possessed.

4 *Padam* caused me to prattle, like ambrosia at a feast, child-like words in the precious Tamil tongue on the greatness of his noble and pre-eminent feet.

5 *Padam* empowered me to sing as worship songs of grace in great abundance.

6 Bestowing upon me an understanding suffused with his grace, *Padam* caused me to sing his immaculate praises, making this my pastime.

7 Making my tongue a channel for hymns of grace, *Padam* diverted it from songs of delusion.

8 *Padam,* most bounteous in his grace, granted that I should speak in praise of nothing else whatsoever, save his glory alone.

*In the years before he came to Bhagavan in 1923, Muruganar composed poetry on a wide variety of topics. After his first meeting with Bhagavan, he took a vow that he would never again compose verses on any subject other than Bhagavan and his teachings. He kept his promise, and in the succeeding fifty years he composed over 20,000 verses on these subjects. In* Padamalai *Muruganar has recorded two statements by Bhagavan himself that indicate that a poetic talent should not be wasted on praising ordinary people:*

1580 A poetic talent should sing of the glory of God. If, instead, it degenerates and sinks to glorifying ignoble human beings, this is only prostitution caused by the delusion of a mind inflated by pomposity.

2172 What a shame that poets lose the proper habit of singing in praise of the supreme and then suffer, [having degenerated into] glorifying lowly mortals!

**9** *Padam* made me illustrious as the Lord of Poetic Wealth, which shines through the grace of God.

**10** Though I was unfit to speak of his glory, *Padam* enabled me to praise his majesty with my own mean intellect.

**11** *Padam* gave me a tongue of ambrosial savour and sweetness, making me exclaim, 'What more could I desire other than this?'

**12** For this humble servant's consciousness there exists no sensory faculty that is doing anything other than holding onto *Padam* and singing his praises.

## *Padam* enjoyed and corrected my words

**13** To make clear everything that I write in a babbling way, *Padam* graciously and thoroughly corrects [me].

*Many of Muruganar's verses came to him spontaneously, as natural manifestations of his devotional fervour. When he showed them to Bhagavan, the latter would go through them very thoroughly, making revisions and corrections wherever appropriate. When I was cataloguing the Ramanasramam archives about twenty years ago, I came across a proof copy of the first edition of* Guru Vachaka Kovai *that contained a huge number of corrections and revisions in Bhagavan's own handwriting. As the following two verses indicate, Bhagavan took Muruganar's poetic outpourings very seriously and went to endless trouble to put them into a proper form.*

14 *Padam* is highly pleased to accept as excellent worship my praise of his majesty in all possible ways.
15 Golden Guru *Padam*, deciding that everything I uttered was a delight-bestowing garland, adorned himself [with it].
16 *Padam*, grace, delighted even in the insane babbling of a madman such as I, as though it were an exposition of the essence of the wisdom of Vedanta.

### *Padam* ended my bad behaviour

17 I realise now that my disrespectful vilification of *Padam*, the grace-form that never leaves [me], was ignorance.

*I would take 'vilification of* Padam*' to mean ignoring it, or not believing in its reality. For several years prior to his first meeting with Bhagavan, Muruganar was not convinced that God existed. This attitude led him to believe that righteous behaviour was alone what mattered:*

> Over many *yugas* I went repeatedly through the eighty-four *lakh* forms of life in which, with the indescribable, intense suffering of embodied existence, I longed for the multifarious miseries that itch and eat one away. Moving up the many steps [of animate life forms] in the ordained manner, I came to a human birth, a birth fit for attaining the clarity of *jnana*. Though I had such a birth, and though my mind had attachment to the Supreme, the nature of the Supreme was not realised. I came to the conclusion that, since the entity known as God might be either real or an unreal imagination, what really conferred benefit on my soul was good conduct and character. Convinced of this, I practised [righteous] behaviour, but though I tried, I frequently failed.
>
> The supreme being Siva, having no body-delusion, abides as the real nature of one's own Self. Shining within the intellect, illuminating it, it cannot be reached by those indulging in fallacious arguments. Tolerating my immature conduct and treating me as if I had attained freedom from impurities, [Siva] considered admitting me to the group of his companions.[1]

18 I was a boor, acting in a perverse manner, but *Padam* showed me

forbearance, forgiving me my faults a hundredfold.

**19** [Even] as I wallowed in imaginary appearances, *Padam* immersed me in the clarity of its supreme space of consciousness.

**20** *Padam* led me to conduct myself in conformity with the ways of the world, making me ashamed of the foolishness that made me think I had withdrawn from it.

**21** I was like an empty vessel, acting boisterously and playing the fool, until *Padam* filled me full, bringing peace and contentment to my heart.

**22** If I miss the benefit of the bliss of union with *Padam*, it is entirely my fault, and not the fault of the upright *Padam* of supreme, refreshing grace.

### *Padam* saved this sinner

**23** Instead of scorning me, profligate that I was, with a gesture of contempt, *Padam* took pity on me, bestowing grace in abundance.

**24** Not shunning me, *Padam*, the sugar-sweet experience of *jnana*, entered my Heart, sinner that I was.

**25** Having destroyed the deluding ignorance of me, a heretic, gracious *Padam*, the light of supreme bliss, held me under his sway as his favourite.

**26** *Padam* accepted me into his service, totally converting me from the evil-doer that I was into a servant who sang his praises.

**27** *Padam* is the lodestone of grace that drew to itself and stole away the evil mind of this ignorant sinner who lacked even one good quality.

**28** Fool that I was, condemned by my own lack of knowledge, *Padam*, whose form is grace-consciousness, expunged my sinfulness.

### *Padam* protects me

**29** *Padam* gave protection to my soul with the armour of consciousness of being, which shines as Siva-*sakti*.

**30** *Padam* gave me shelter in the Heart, preventing me from becoming involved in the pantomime of the bustling and deceitful world.

**31** As I flew in dread to him for protection, *Padam*, the fear-free refuge, merged with my Heart and rejoiced, uttering words of comfort.

**32** Preventing me, wretch that I was, from deviating from the state of the Self and falling into that which is alien to it, gracious *Padam* flourished, casting its radiance all around.

**_Padam_ rules over me, having become my Lord**

**33** *Padam* shines in my Heart in such a way that I rejoice intensely here, dwelling constantly with love on the gracious nobility with which he has governed me.

**34** Hearing my call 'Save me!', *Padam*, saying 'What's the problem?' took pity on me and came down and governed me with relish, becoming my father who gave me birth in *jnana*.

**35** Even though *Padam*, the Supreme, is the mother and father of all beings, he abides with me as my very own Lord in the Heart.

**36** *Padam*, the supreme light of bliss, became my Lord, sheltering me at the feet of the adepts of *jnana* who have attained the Self.

**37** Enthroned within the Heart of this guileless person, as upon a lion-throne, *Padam* exercises his rule over the entire, vast world.

Sinhasana, *'the lion-throne' is a Virasaiva term that denotes the place in the Heart from where God exercises his rule and dominion over both the soul and the physical world. Allama Prabhu, one of the great Virasaiva saints, once described his experience of the Self as 'sitting on the* sinhasana *of emptiness'.*

**38** Deeply ignorant as I was, auspicious *Padam* ruled over me, focusing my mind, flooding me with light so that I could enter the Heart.

**39** As surely as *Padam* first entangled me in worldly existence, just as surely did he later restrain me through his grace and become my Lord, putting an end to my wretchedness.

*Prior to his first meeting with Bhagavan, Muruganar was a married man who earned his living as a teacher and as a member of a prestigious committee that was compiling the definitive Tamil dictionary. Bhagavan's* darshan *affected him so fundamentally, in the months that followed he abandoned most of his family and worldly responsibilities. After his mother died in 1926, he spent the remainder of his life living as a* sadhu, *begging his food and writing verses on Bhagavan and his teachings.*

**40** Effulgent *Padam*, bounteous in his grace, placed me under the rule of his feet so that *mauna* remained firmly established as [my own] nature in my Heart.

41 Becoming my Lord by making me sink within the Heart, *Padam* became the absolute measure of extreme liberality.

**_Padam_ transformed my destiny and attitude**

42 *Padam* made me worship it through the Siva-*puja* that surges naturally in a mind in which *vasanas* have perished.

43 *Padam*, through the power of *swarupa*, the pure being-consciousness, totally eradicated the powerful mischief of Kama from my Heart.

*Kama is the god of desire or lust. In a famous puranic incident Siva burned him to ashes while he was attempting to arouse in Siva a desire for Parvati.*

44 Virtuous, golden *Padam* intensified my surging desire so that my mind is naturally established totally in his feet.

45 *Padam*, the enjoyment I have found, is experiencing, as the *prasad* of Siva, clarity of mind.

46 My existence craves for nought save the pure expanse of the Self in which everything exists and shines as *Sivam*.

47 I realised clearly that in everything that is not the supreme reality, immutability does not exist, not even in the slightest degree.

48 *Padam* reformed my understanding [making me realise] that the nature of bondage and liberation depends on the nature of one's outlook.

49 Through the feeling of fullness brought about by grace gushing in my Heart, I, his devotee, rejoiced in *Padam* without any pining for other things.

50 Keeping me from the way of falsehood, *Padam* set me upon the straight path of the Heart, the path upon which the truth flourishes.

51 *Padam* made me realise in my Heart that all paths, other than the path of *jnana* [*vichara*], are defective paths of the mind.

52 *Padam* destroyed the power of *prarabdha* and firmly established me in the Heart so that I do not lose my mind to prosperity or poverty.

53 My Lord, golden *Padam*, guides me well with the attitude of mind that all is God's doing.

54 *Padam* walks sweetly within me such that its divine will flourishes well within my Heart.

55 Gracious *Padam* delightfully bestowed upon me the attitude of mind that whatever it does, it is all to my liking.

## *Padam* abolished my actions and their fruit

56 'What is the problem for you? Just be!' Speaking in this way *Padam* ensured that there is not even a single activity for me.

57 'When I have taken on your responsibilities, what is lacking for you?' Speaking in this way, *Padam* embraces me in the Heart in eternal rejoicing.

58 *Padam* is the consciousness, the supreme, in which I have no responsibilities to think about since every responsibility is his alone.

59 Even as I suffered through the delusion of regarding myself as the actor, true *Padam* caused me to shine as the enduring stage.

*'Stage' refers to a theatre stage, rather than a period or a stage of life. Muruganar is saying that Bhagavan made him aware that he was the permanent screen of the Self, rather than the transient images that are projected onto it.*

60 *Padam* destroyed my sense of doership so that, through the peace of *jnana*, a life free from evil flourished within the Heart.

61 The golden *Padam* shines in my Heart in such a way that neither my deeds, their consequences nor any thought about them exist for me.

## *Padam* made me lazy

62 The golden *Padam* completely abolished my wandering around as a wicked one and made me shine as a perfect idler.

*Both Muruganar and Bhagavan occasionally spoke ironically of realisation being a lazy state of inactivity. However, unlike ordinary laziness, it is the culmination of extreme effort. Muruganar puts this apparently perverse comment in context in verse 773 of* Guru Vachaka Kovai*, and then follows it (verse 774) with an explanation from Bhagavan:*

773 What our Lord [Ramana] firmly teaches us to take as the greatest and most powerful *tapas*, is only this much: '*Summa iru* [Be still].' There is no other duty for the mind and its thoughts.

774 The lazy state of just being and shining is the state of Self, and that is the highest state that one can attain. Revere as the most virtuous those who have attained that lazy state which cannot be attained except by very great and rare *tapas*.

**63** *Padam* subdued me, making it impossible for me to do anything other than eat and sleep.

**64** Even the actions I perform, believing them to be my own, are in reality the actions of *Padam*, the complete and absolute truth.

### *Padam* ended my attachment to the body

**65** *Padam* gave me this knowledge: 'The tormenting bondage is only body-consciousness. It is not the body form itself.'

**66** *Padam*, whose *swarupa* is intense *jnana*, destroyed my body consciousness, ensuring the elimination of all my karma.

**67** *Padam*, my own true form, taught me to investigate and know [the truth], preventing my soul's purity from being defiled by the filthy body.

**68** In order that I rejoice in intimacy with it, *Padam*, the sun of true *jnana*, shone in my Heart, destroying identification with the body through right action.

### *Padam*, my Guru

**69** If form truly exists for the Lord, I took that form to be the form of the Guru, making it the focus of my attention.

**70** Divine *Padam* took birth and came before me as the *jnana*-Guru *Padam* so that all my suffering died completely and disappeared.

**71** Becoming the solar orb, bright *Padam*, the grace-bestowing *jnana*-Guru, destroyed the pitch darkness of ignorance, refined my heart and brought me under his sway.

**72** Coming in the form of the Guru and infusing the beautiful light of grace, golden *Padam* [Bhagavan] revealed the grandeur of divine *Padam* [the Self] in my Heart.

**73** Golden *Padam* manifested as the Guru so that a life that

transcended mind and speech abounded within my Heart.
74 *Padam* led me to reflect upon and realise as the *jnana*-Guru the truth of the Self, so that I, a faithful follower, did not fall into confusion.

*The phrase 'a faithful follower' implies in the original someone who tries sincerely but doesn't succeed.*

**Padam's grace**

75 Just as its bounty lent radiance to my tongue, *Padam*, grace, filled my Heart to overflowing with the boon of realisation.
76 Lacking in love [for it] as I was, *Padam* afforded me its refreshing grace, accepting all my deeds as its service.
77 Firmly convincing me in the Heart, 'This is the state of being,' grace-*Padam* brought me under the sway of his feet and made me his very own.
78 *Padam* granted me his own true nature such that for myself, as his devotee, no other state of being remained except that of grace, the supreme.
79 Gentle, golden *Padam*, victorious in his grace, cured the deadly wound of the mind, so that I am no longer tormented by thoughts of 'tomorrow'.
80 *Padam*, who will transmute venom into pure ambrosia, established my mind as the vast heaven of its grace.

*The venom is probably the mind, while the ambrosia is the Self. In a similar metaphor Bhagavan, in* Aksharamanamalai *verse 64, equates 'venom' with* maya*:*

> Before the venom of the serpent called *maya* mounts to my head and kills me, grant me your grace, the ambrosia of immortality, and save me, O Arunachala.[2]

81 As I wandered, I know not where, fair *Padam*, supreme bliss, brought me here to his feet through his sweet grace and brought me salvation.
82 *Padam* gave me the emotion that makes my body soften and melt every time I think of the true, cool grace that it bestowed on me.
83 *Padam* in its grace ripened within me a feast of unbroken and ever-present *jnana*.

**_Padam's_ glance of grace**

84 Through its glance, golden *Padam* dammed up in my Heart the ocean of Siva-*ananda* – that which cannot be dammed up.

85 *Padam* is the eye of grace that looked upon me in such a way that the open expanse of that grace, which cannot be contained, was confined within my very Heart.

86 The light of *mauna* illumined my face as golden *Padam* dispensed the grace of *jnana* through his radiant gaze.

87 Through his grace-filled glance, golden, bewitching *Padam* destroyed my infatuation with the ego-mind, scooping me up and consuming me with relish.

88 The grace-bestowing gaze of *Padam* shot forth, granting me, in the form of deep absorption, the victorious sword of exalted *swarupa-jnana*.

89 Having abolished the defect of the poison-like delusive ego by looking at me with his *jnana*-bestowing eye, *Padam* resides within my Heart.

*These verses may all refer to a particular incident that took place shortly after Muruganar came to Bhagavan:*

> Muruganar had a strong desire to have Bhagavan wholly to himself, at least for a short while. Muruganar never mentioned this yearning to anybody. But can anybody hide anything from Bhagavan? Muruganar's secret wish was fulfilled in a totally unexpected way. In those days Bhagavan and his devotees used to collect leaves from the trees in the forest to make leaf plates. Once, while a party was getting ready to go into the forest, Bhagavan gave Muruganar a very significant glance. Interpreting this look as a signal to follow him, Muruganar hurried after Bhagavan. By the time the others entered the forest, Bhagavan and Muruganar had disappeared into the woods.
>
> Bhagavan led Muruganar deep into the forest. At one place Bhagavan sat down on a log and asked Muruganar to sit beside him. Muruganar sat, but no words were exchanged. Bhagavan looked directly into his eyes and Muruganar felt the power of Bhagavan's grace flowing through him like an electric current. He lost all perceptions

of time and space and experienced a joy beyond description. Immersed in this state of bliss, Muruganar was oblivious to the passage of time; it was only when he regained his senses that he realised that he must have remained in this state of bliss for hours together.[3]

*Muruganar himself has mentioned this incident in one of his verses:*

He took me to the forest with him on the pretext of plucking leaves to make leaf-plates. There, with great delight, he destroyed my mind's restlessness by bestowing his glance on me. In the middle of the night he subdued my divided individual consciousness, granting me the experience of the undivided reality.[4]

**Marrying *Padam's* grace**

**90** *Padam* infused my mind with love so that a marriage took place between my mind, the bride, and the bridegroom, his grace.

**91** While I was practising being a faithful wife, *Padam* caused chaste conduct to spring forth within me as my own nature so that it [chaste conduct] never became defiled.

*The wife is the mind and the chaste conduct is not letting her attention stray to anything except her husband,* Padam. *Muruganar is saying that while he was performing this practice through effort,* Padam *united with him to such an extent that absorption in* Padam *became natural and effortless.*

**92** *Padam* ensnared me in the bright radiance of consciousness' wondrous power of enlightenment, that skilled mistress of grace.

**93** Here on this earth the auspicious *Padam* united that Lady [Shanti] with me as my fortunate destiny, binding me to her in a blissful marriage.

**94** *Padam*, the supreme reality, the wealth of grace, attracted and kept me at his side so that I am benevolently redeemed in this birth.

***Padam's* love towards me**

**95** Through the boundless nature of its true grace, *Padam*, the jewel of my eye, stealthily united with me in love's embrace.

**96** Through its true love, which dwells in my Heart, the soft and tender red lotus blossom, *Padam*, speaks softly to my soul with no hint of harshness.

**97** Pursuing me since time immemorial and becoming my Lord, *Padam*, grace, the supreme consciousness, the true state of love, abides within my Heart.

**98** *Padam* shines within my Heart, making it melt at the true love of its coming as the grace-bestowing Guru.

**99** Through his love, golden *Padam*, the bewitching *Sivam*, zealously exercised his goodly rule over me so that I was not in the least overwhelmed and terrified continuously by one thought after another.

**100** Taking my Heart as a temple, *Padam* carefully nurtures me so that I no longer struggle helplessly like a motherless child.

**101** Having completely destroyed the embattled existence of the wicked ego-mind, *Padam* fondles and caresses my Heart.

### *Padam* gave me peace and bliss

**102** Golden *Padam* shines brightly with the fair hue of red coral so that the fullness of bliss wells up, and I rejoice in the Heart.

**103** Luminous *Padam*, the Self, free of all dependency, fills my Heart with a supreme bliss, free of all cares.

**104** Through the feeling 'enough', golden *Padam* bestowed upon me in my Heart the prosperity of utterly peaceful bliss.

**105** *Padam*, the truth, enduringly shines its inner light, making peace well up within me so that I do not suffer ruin and die, bewildered by a life lived through the treacherous mind.

**106** *Padam*, the light of peace, brought about in a fitting manner within my Heart the blissful, unceasing state of absorption.

**107** In my Heart, where peace flourished like the cool light of the moon, *Padam* in its grace conferred upon me the condition of thought-free bliss.

**108** In order that I should not pine, thinking of bliss, the golden *Padam* caused bliss to blaze forth as my own nature.

### Padam consumed and devoured me

**109** The gracious *Padam*, Siva-*jnana*, swallowed up my ego-consciousness in such a way that I did not know any world other than *Padam*.

110 Like ice melting in water, *Padam* dissolved my beloved soul into its own state, whose form is love, turning me into itself.

Aksharamanamalai, *verse 101:*

As snow in water melts, let me dissolve as love in you
who are all love, O Arunachala.[5]

111 The vast emptiness, golden *Padam*, wildly dances with elation, full of joy, having swallowed up my soul.

112 *Padam*, the state of the Self, remained as a bright effulgence, consuming my soul in its fire, so that the giddying infatuation, objective consciousness, was destroyed.

113 *Padam*, the truth, drowned me, a vile one, in the Heart, making bondage, liberation, and so on, mere concepts.

114 Swallowing me up in its vast expanse, *Padam*, the Heart, remains shining as the light that is filled with the truth of the pure Self.

115 Like fire that consumes all else but itself, *Padam* entered my Heart, spreading its sweetness, the delightful ambrosia of its grace.

116 *Padam*, [despite] remaining as the *swarupa*, the bliss of supreme liberation, hungrily consumed true devotees as if he were the powerful Yama.

*Yama is the god of death who consumes all souls at the end of their physical lives. The phrase 'the bliss of supreme liberation' in this verse can also be translated as 'food'. This links it to the next verse. In the preceding verse it is the food that becomes hungry; in the following one it is the water that becomes thirsty. A similar idea can be found in* Aksharamanamalai, *verse 28: 'To feed on you I came, O Arunachala, but I have become your food and am now at peace.'*[6]

117 When *Padam* adopted and swallowed my dear soul, it was as if a great, ambrosial spring of water, which gives satisfaction when drunk, itself became thirsty.

### ***Padam* removed my ego**

118 *Padam* embraced my Heart and stood saying, 'Do not be afraid!',

making the illusory existence of the ego-ghost, the deceitful mind, depart.

> Once I [Devaraja Mudaliar] criticised Muruganar in Bhagavan's presence, saying to him: 'You poets allow yourselves all kinds of licence and say anything you choose. Is it true that Bhagavan ever told you "Have no fear"? You have written in *Ramana Sannidhi Murai*, "The Master who saved me, saying 'Fear not'". Elsewhere in the same book [you wrote] "He who uttering by his lips 'Fear not, fear not,' removes the anxiety". I ask you, did Bhagavan ever tell you "Have no fear"?'
>
> Muruganar replied rather spiritedly: 'His look is like that to me. His look tells me "Have no fear".'
>
> I said: 'I accept the explanation and have no further criticism to make.'
>
> I did not say this to please Muruganar or even Bhagavan. I said it because it was true. Bhagavan's mere look on many an occasion said eloquently, 'I give you refuge. Don't worry any more.'[7]

**119** *Padam*, the sun of supreme *jnana*, presided over me with such delight that in its presence the waxing and waning moon-mind, the perceiving ego, drew back in shame.

**120** *Padam* granted me salvation as I languished, having lost my inner peace amidst the throng of false concepts that appear in the treacherous mind of the ghost-ego.

**121** Radiant *Padam* destroyed my ego, demolishing it over and over again. It wore it down and down, smaller and smaller, to the size of an atom, until it became one with itself.

*This is a reference to an experience of Manikkavachagar, recorded in* Tiruvachakam, *that Bhagavan frequently quoted: 'Approaching and approaching, getting worn down to an atom and finally becoming one, O Siva residing in Tirupperundurai.'*

### *Padam* showed me the true 'I'

**122** In order that I should not pine away, thinking myself to be a sinner, grace-bestowing *Padam* fashioned [my] 'I' as the supreme.

**123** I realised that it was through the grace of *Padam*, and not through my ego consciousness, that the 'I' came to know its [true] support and was redeemed.

124 Through the majesty of the Self in which 'I' exists as 'He', *Padam* shines out so that there is never any place for 'I' and 'mine'.

125 Whilst causing others to dance the dance of 'I and mine', within my own Heart the dancer *Padam* performs the dance of 'I am that I am'.

126 *Padam* is the sacred hall of the Self that, as the eternal supreme reality, performs the dance of 'I-I' within my Heart.

### *Padam* destroyed my mind

127 Having risen up as the pure expanse [of consciousness], yea, the exalted destroyer of all my actions' fruit, *Padam*, the truth that exists and shines, became the destroyer also of my very self.

128 Grace-*Padam* seized my mind, like a great fiend who would not let go its grip, and destroyed it, transforming it into its own deathless form.

129 *Padam* shattered and threw away my mind so that it became the vast expanse, with not even the slightest scope for darkness.

130 Through the Self, the perfection that transcends even thought, *Padam*, the truth, shone forth, refuting my mind, the base defect.

131 Through the divine light of the Self, distilled consciousness, *Padam* put a final end to my vile *maya*, the three *gunas*.

Gunas *are the three alternating qualities of the mind and of manifestation in general:* sattva *(harmony, clarity),* rajas *(activity, excitability) and* tamas *(torpor, inertia).*

132 *Padam*, the truth, the supreme, shines in my life as spotlessly pure consciousness such that worldly bondage, the condition of being a *jiva*, is annihilated.

133 *Padam* [whose nature is] wholeness, overpowered my consciousness, restraining and destroying it, so that the delusion based on distinctions was destroyed.

### *Padam* opened my Heart, revealing himself to me

134 Through its majesty that confers the Self in the form of grace, *Padam*, the overflowing clear expanse, succeeded in unsheathing my Heart.

**135** Manifesting fully within my Heart, transcending comparisons, *Padam*, the Self, shines as joyful splendour, without clinging to anything.

**136** As a recompense for stealing me, the peaceful, effulgent *Padam* revealed itself in the Heart.

**137** *Padam*, the light in my Heart, showed me the true vision of the expanse of consciousness everywhere I went, [enabling me] to praise it every day.

**138** Through the light of his countenance, *Padam*, grace, bewitched my mind, and through the light of the Heart, which suffused me inwardly, subjugated my soul.

**139** *Padam* opened up my Heart, revealing to me with perfect clarity the experience of the one Self, in which there is no place for a second.

### *Padam* established me in the Heart

**140** *Padam* established the truth of the Self within my Heart as firmly as a nail driven into soft, green wood.

**141** Golden *Padam* established permanently within my Heart the shining red mountain of the real [Arunachala], unfailing in its splendour.

**142** *Padam*, the Self, remains established within my Heart, as clear as a glorious mountain standing against the open sky.

*This is a reference to a Tamil idiom. If something is self-evident, Tamils may say that it is as clear as a large mountain that stands against the sky.*

**143** By shining as fullness within my Heart, *Padam* became formless, omnipresent effulgence.

**144** *Padam* offered dancing and singing to others, but it targeted me only for merging in the Heart.

**145** *Padam*, the light of supreme *jnana*, actively rises up within me so that the experience of supreme bliss wells up, embracing me in the Heart.

**146** *Padam* bestows within my Heart the fullness of truth, abolishing the poverty of thought that results from deceitful illusion.

**147** *Padam*, as the open sky of grace, completely encompassed me in the Heart and destroyed the power of the idea of 'I' that flourishes in ignorance.

**148** Declaring that the content-free consciousness of a mind that has become clear is the attainment of the most exalted supreme, *Padam*, in its grace, established that consciousness within my Heart.

### *Padam* now dwells in my Heart

**149** *Padam* is the beauteous supreme, the one Self that shines within my Heart, having destroyed my infatuation for the world.

**150** Driving away the black cloud of ignorance, *Padam* rejoices, dwelling delightedly within my Heart.

**151** Extinguishing the flames of desire and aversion, along with the other evil dispositions that constitute *samsara*, *Padam*, with its refreshing coolness, dwells within my Heart.

**152** The welling up of the Self, *Padam*, whose nature is all pervading, exists within the place of my Heart.

**153** *Padam* dwells within my Heart so that I gain the might of the true state of the Self, which cannot be acquired through the mastery of arts and sciences.

**154** Radiant *Padam* dwells within my Heart so that the state of blissful absorption in the real obtains there, free from any trace of thought.

**155** Through the true enquiry 'What is my *swarupa*?' *Padam* shines, abiding in the Heart as the immutable pole star.

**156** *Padam* is the felicitous state of the Self, whose form is consciousness, that flourishes within my Heart in such a way that there is not the minutest trace of any thought that is foreign to it.

**157** *Padam*, grace, dwells in the makeshift shrine of my Heart as if it were a rich and permanent temple.

*When renovation work is taking place in temples, gods are often moved to temporary locations ('the makeshift shrine') and returned to the permanent one once the work is over.*

**158** Appropriating the title deed to my Heart, effulgent *Padam* resides there, keeping me from falling under the power of the *vasanas*, the enemies.

### *Padam* liberated me

**159** The bottle gourd that *Padam* lovingly served up [for me] is the sweet dish of the supreme bliss of liberation, not a picture of it drawn on paper.

*Guru Vachaka Kovai,* verse 531: The supreme *jnana* that destroys deceptive delusion will be born only out of a true enquiry in the form of attention towards that which exists as reality in the Heart. Know that mere book knowledge about enquiry, even though learnt from clear scriptures, will be like a picture-gourd drawn on a sheet of paper, which is useless for cooking.

*Guru Vachaka Kovai,* verse 532: Is it possible to appease one's hunger by eating food cooked by a painted picture of a blazing fire? Likewise, an end to the miseries of life and the enjoyment of the bliss of the Self cannot be achieved by mere verbal knowledge but only by the experiential knowledge of the Self, which is obtained by extinguishing the ego in the Heart. Thus you should know.

**160** *Padam* routed with his lion's roar the rutting elephant of my dream, abolishing my confusion.

**161** Ignorant fool that I was, blinded by a mind as obdurate as a tree-stump, yet did golden *Padam* grant me enlightenment.

**162** *Padam* conferred upon [me] the realisation: 'You are that which remains when all else has been rejected as "not this, not this".'

**163** *Padam* made me realise that the arising births are only dreams that became associated [with me] through the delusive power of the mind.

**164** Attaining in full measure in the Heart the wealth of *Sivam,* the Self, so that nought else remains, I exult in *Padam.*

**165** *Padam,* absolute oneness, presided over me, putting an end to my forgetfulness of *swarupa,* making this my final birth.

**166** *Padam* is that fiery third eye that dried up with his scorching heat the desolate ocean of the long succession of births, which is so hard to cross over.

*When Siva opens his third eye, which is located in the centre of his forehead, whatever it alights on is burnt to ashes.*

## *Padam* made me still

**167** *Padam* made it possible for us to know the deeply subtle experience of the Self, which is to remain still.
**168** Saying, 'Enough of dancing, now be still,' *Padam* bestowed on me the state of true *jnana* that exists forever in my Heart as my own nature.
**169** *Padam* drew me into the shade of his beautiful and glorious feet, the experience of the Self that shines when one keeps still.
**170** The sovereign grace of *Padam* completed my *sadhana* with the words 'Be still'. What a wonder is this!

## *Padam* gave me true *jnana*

**171** *Padam* immersed me, who possessed a mind deluded by forgetfulness, in the flood of grace that is *jnana*.
**172** Like the golden sun rising over the ocean in the early morning, *Padam* is the bright radiance [of *jnana*], the golden lustre that rises up within my body.
**173** By establishing me in *Atma-swarupa*, making my mind slip away, *Padam* convinced me that *jnana* is the very nature [*swarupa*] of the Self; it is not merely an attribute of the Self.
**174** *Padam* is the bliss that has settled as the essence of *jnana* within my Heart so that I have not the least desire for, nor awareness of, other essences.
**175** While [for others] it remains concealed as an illusory expanse, *Padam* became manifest in my Heart as the expanse of *jnana*.
**176** Resplendent *Padam* wells up within my Heart so that it clings to nought save the goodly life of Siva *jnana*.
**177** Destroying and putting a final end to my delusion, *Padam* is the form of true *jnana* that is the supreme benefit for the soul.
**178** Performing yoga-*sadhana* for my sake, *Padam* helped me [to attain] the benefit of true *jnana*.
**179** *Padam* gave me the knowledge that, except for the victory of *jnana*, all other victories are flawed victories arising from dishonourable delusion.
**180** Rejecting arid renunciation, *Padam*, through the power of true *jnana*, made renunciation merge with me as my own nature.
**181** *Padam* gave me *jnana* as the distilled essence of the sweet syrup, *Tiruvachakam*.

Tiruvachakam *is a famous 9th century anthology of devotional poetry composed by the Tamil poet-saint Manikkavachagar. The poems all praise Siva, Manikkavachagar's God and Guru. On Muruganar's second visit to Tiruvannamalai in 1923, Bhagavan suggested that he write poetry in the same style as Manikkavachagar's famous work. Muruganar initially felt that he was not spiritually competent to follow this advice, but with Bhagavan's encouragement he eventually produced a work,* Sri Ramana Sannidhi Murai, *that closely follows the style and presentation of* Tiruvachakam. *While Manikkavachagar had praised Siva in his work, Muruganar reserved his praises exclusively for Bhagavan.*

*When Muruganar states that Bhagavan has given him the 'distilled essence' of* Tiruvachakam, *he means that he has given him oneness with* Sivam.

*Bhagavan himself had a very high regard for* Tiruvachakam, *and frequently referred to it. On the night that his mother passed away, he initiated a reading of the whole work that only concluded at 4 a.m. the next morning. Muruganar recorded Bhagavan's statements and views on* Tiruvachakam *in the following* Padamalai *verses:*

> Manikkavachagar's *Tiruvachakam* expresses in words the exuberant, graceful experience of *Sivam*, which transcends speech.
>
> *Tiruvachakam* is a work that deserves to be experienced. The meaning of its sweet verses is beyond intellectual knowledge.
>
> When asked by others about the meaning of the *Tiruvachakam*, the great and saintly Manikkavachagar pointed at the subtle *chidakasa* [space of consciousness] and merged in it.
>
> The *Tiruvachakam* is a sea of divine honey expressing the God-experience that puts an end to the birth-misery of getting caught in the womb.[8]

*Elsewhere in the same work Muruganar reveals that Bhagavan gave him the same experience that forms the core of* Tiruvachakam's *essence and meaning:*

> *Padam* made me merge in the essence of the *Tiruvachakam*, [revealing it to be] the ultimate conclusion of the *Vedas*.[9]

*Bhagavan himself felt that* Sri Ramana Sannidhi Murai, *Muruganar's version of* Tiruvachakam, *was a major literary and spiritual accomplishment. The following story conveys the extent of Bhagavan's admiration for both the work and its author:*

> On one occasion Bhagavan happened to overhear some people in the ashram making disparaging remarks about Muruganar.
>
> He at once remarked, 'The very day that *Sannidhi Murai* and *Guru Vachaka Kovai* came out, Muruganar became one among the very foremost of devotees'.
>
> In commenting on this statement Michael James (*Ramana's Muruganar*, p. 93) has stated: 'By the words "the very foremost of devotees" Sri Bhagavan was referring to [poet] saints such as Appar, Sundarar, Sambandhar, Manikkavachagar…'
>
> This interesting interpretation finds support in a verse Bhagavan himself composed in the following circumstances.
>
> Shortly before *Sri Ramana Sannidhi Murai* was published, a manuscript version was being read out to Bhagavan. A devotee, Viswanatha Swami, spontaneously exclaimed, in appreciation, 'Mugavapuri Murugan'. Mugavapuri is another name of Ramanathapuram, the birthplace of Muruganar. Bhagavan then challenged Viswanatha [Swami] to compose his own verse, incorporating these two words. When Viswanatha [Swami] was unable to do so, he asked Bhagavan to compose the verse himself. Bhagavan responded with the following lines. They were composed as if Muruganar himself was the poet.
>
>> 'Arunachala Ramana, who dwells on the Heart-lotus, smiled and looked fixedly, poured forth grace in abundance and completely annihilated my soul.' Singing in this way, so that the people of the world might be saved, Mugavapuri Murugan composed *Sannidhi Murai*, which is equal to *Tiruvachakam*.

The *Tiruvachakam*, Manikkavachagar's *magnum opus*, is one of the most famous and widely admired collections of Tamil devotional poetry. In this one verse Bhagavan gave a public confirmation of two things: Muruganar's elevated spiritual status and his right to be ranked alongside the all-time greats of Tamil devotional poetry.[10]

### *Padam* gave me true learning and knowledge

**182** *Padam* gave me this true knowledge: 'In the splendour of true *jnana* all the glory of scientific knowledge becomes ignorance.'

**183** *Padam*, the truth, shines within my Heart as the awareness of consciousness, making all other types of knowledge depart, having become flawed.

**184** The moment that the darkness of the false disappeared, radiant *Padam* shone forth within my intellect [*buddhi*] as my true form.

> **Question:** In verse 266 of *Vivekachudamani* Sri Sankaracharya says that *Brahman* can be realised by *buddhi*, the subtle intellect, which means that the intellect can be of great help; in fact, indispensable for realisation.
> **Bhagavan:** The word '*buddhi*' is rightly translated as the subtle intellect, but here it means the cave of the Heart... [reads aloud verse 266:]
>
> In the cave of the *buddhi* there is the *Brahman*, distinct from gross and subtle, the existence, absolute, supreme, the one without a second. For one who lives in this cave as *Brahman*, O beloved, there is no more entrance into a woman's womb.[11]

**185** In no time at all, *Padam* revealed within me the secrets of the *Vedas*, whose lofty goal is grace, impossible to know [with the mind].

**186** Saying: 'May you learn that which cannot be learnt,' golden *Padam* spoke without speaking, illuminating my Heart.

### *Padam* gave me *mauna*

**187** Especially for me, *Padam* distilled and gave me to drink, as the juice of the ripe fruit of *jnana*, the supreme state of *mauna*.

**188** Splendorous *Padam* caused my target [the Self] to blaze forth in *mauna*, which is the peace granted by the power of his being.

**189** *Padam* declared that my offering myself to the *mauna*, the profound peace conferred [by *Padam*], is itself the recompense.
**190** *Padam* played upon me the trick of its abundance, making me expire in the embrace of *mauna*, the divine first cause.
**191** *Padam* completely destroyed my life of religious observances by uniting me [with itself], enabling me to attain *mauna*, the *sat-achara*.

Achara *usually means 'code of conduct'. In this context* sat-achara *means 'the observance of abiding as* sat, *the reality'.*

### *Padam* revealed my *swarupa*

**192** *Padam* bestowed on me true life by showing to me, as conspicuously as a mountain, *swarupa*, that subtle essence which no book can convey.
**193** With nothing above it *Padam* is itself the highest of the high. It is my *swarupa*, the unique Heart for me.
**194** *Padam* caused my own truth to shine out within me as the pure consciousness that shines by itself merely as its own being.
**195** Clarifying [my] consciousness and making it still, *Padam* enabled me to realise the undivided *Atma-swarupa*.
**196** Radiant *Padam* shines out within me as the Self – formless, subtle, and eternally free from defilement.
**197** *Padam* redeemed me in my *swarupa* so that I did not roam around like a herd of deer that wanders in the forest, mistaking a mirage for water.
**198** *Padam*, the glorious light, brought me to that state of deep peace, known as *samadhi*, making it unite with me and blaze forth as my own nature.
**199** Wherever I flee, attempting to live apart from *swarupa*, *Padam* pursues me, refusing to let me go.

### *Padam* united me with itself as itself

**200** Non-dual *Padam* is such that in no way whatsoever do I exist apart from it, nor it apart from me.
**201** *Padam*, the expanse [of consciousness] that is impossible to see not only by those who have not experienced it but also by those who have, became very close to me, becoming my own existence.

**202** There is no likeness of anything upon this earth to describe the harmony that reigns between *Padam* and myself.

**203** Just like Sakti delighting in Siva, *Padam* caused my mind to immerse itself in being-consciousness.

**204** *Padam* established my Heart in the life of union with Siva so that the affliction caused by the disease of birth [and death] disappeared.

**205** *Padam* is *mauna*, the beingness of Siva that unites with my Heart's inner character through its own sweet nature, like milk mixed with honey.

**206** *Padam*, the real, existing and shining as my own source, remains also established as its own source.

**207** Though *Padam* appears as two of us, when I enquire into my real nature, it is the one reality [*eka-swarupa*].

**208** Manifesting as the ultimate supreme within the Heart, *Padam* united with me, shining its light by day and by night.

**209** *Padam* is a great, good fortune to me because, though it is hard to embrace, I merged with it well, moving intimately [with it] through love.

**210** *Padam* bestowed on me the true realisation that the reality, which from time immemorial had appeared to be different from me, had always been one with me.

**211** *Padam* is the *sahaja* [state] that exists without departing from the Heart in such a way that it is not possible for me to separate from it.

**212** *Padam* is the clarity of truth that shines within my Heart as the perfection of praiseworthy union.

**213** *Padam* is in harmony with my every word, my every deed, with every thought I think.

### *Padam* gave me *Sivam*

**214** *Padam*, *Sivam*, shines as endless space within my Heart, as my very existence, beyond the reach of objective knowledge.

**215** Indivisible, all-pervasive *Sivam* itself entered my Heart, that refuge that could not be entered, shining as *Padam*, the truth.

**216** *Padam* caused my true nature to flourish as the golden form of *Sivam*, the Self, grace-consciousness, driving away my wretched defilement.

**217** Golden *Padam* bestowed upon me, as an endowment within my

Heart, the blissful heaven of *Sivam*, which is both absolute emptiness and absolute fullness.

**218** Like a father, *Padam*, grace, revealed and gave to me in the Heart a gift, that rich hoard of hidden treasure which is *Sivam*, perfect contentment of mind.

**219** *Padam* in its grace granted within my Heart, even here in this birth, the purity of a life lived in the state of *Sivam*.

**220** *Padam* established my mind in the *tapas* of true *jnana*, wherein the mind disports itself within *Sivam*.

## Seeing and knowing only *Padam*

**221** Wherever I look, all that I see is *Padam*, the light of the expanse of consciousness that never dims.

> Once a group of people made preparations for a pilgrimage. They came to Muruganar and asked him whether he would be interested in joining them.
>
> Muruganar replied, 'The moment I set eyes on Bhagavan, who is the sun of Self-awareness, my eyes became blinded by the brilliance of his form. Now I cannot see anything or anybody other than my Bhagavan. This being the case, of what use would a pilgrimage be for me?'[12]

**222** Since I hold his [Bhagavan's] *Padam* as my very eye, *Padam*, the real, sprouts and shines by itself as the leading light of all my sense perceptions.

**223** *Padam* opened my Heart in such a way that the exalted essence that could not be seen anywhere came to be seen everywhere.

**224** The effulgent, peaceful *Padam* surges as the vast sea of bliss in such a way that there is no room for foreign thoughts in my Heart.

## The benefit of studying this work

**225** *Padam* bestows grace upon those who recite, praise and adorn him with this *Padamalai*, uniting them permanently with the *Atma-swarupa* that forever remains one with them in their hearts.

# References

At the beginning of each chapter, before the footnote references begin, there will be a sequence of pairs of numbers. The first item of the pair, printed in bold, is the verse number in this book. The second number, after the colon, gives the verse number in the Tamil original.

**Introduction**

1 'Tiruvandappahudi', *Sri Ramana Sannidhi Murai*, cited in *The Power of the Presence*, part two, p. 98.

**Bhagavan *Padam* (title page)**

1 *Sri Ramana Anubhuti*, volume two, verse 2.
2 *Non-Dual Consciousness – the Flood Tide of Bliss*, *Sri Ramana Anubhuti*, verse 252.
3 *Sri Ramana Anubhuti*, volume two, the *dhyana* verse printed below the frontispiece.

**Bhagavan *Padam* (chapter)**

**1**:1962, **2**:2098, **3**:75, **4**:938, **5**:71, **6**:732, **7**:675, **8**:2180, **9**:389, **10**:2866, **11**:1192, **12**:329, **13**:2593, **14**:145, **15**:175, **16**:218, **17**:738, **18**: 1253, **19**:1713, **20**:1923, **21**:466, **22**:1103, **23**:1949, **24**:2695, **25**:1485, **26**:2031, **27**:2648, **28**:1508, **29**:1509, **30**:123, **31**:470, **32**:857, **33**:1840, **34**:1493, **35**:2652, **36**:416, **37**:1287, **38**:1354, **39**:2978, **40**:2684, **41**:2509, **42**:375, **43**:469, **44**:561, **45**:291, **46**:1722, **47**:2439, **48**:33, **49**:2093, **50**:1717, **51**:528, **52**:909, **53**:1917, **54**:2614, **55**:1365, **56**:674, **57**:2813, **58**:2696, **59**:1603, **60**:1038, **61**:1500, **62**:290, **63**:2446, **64**:468, **65**:3015, **66**:2217, **67**:2982, **68**:2090, **69**:289, **70**:1505, **71**:550, **72**:2321, **73**:1242, **74**:1263, **75**:723, **76**:1866, **77**:2365, **78**:241, **79**:944, **80**:2396, **81**:2007, **82**:1741, **83**:refrain.

1 *Ninaivil Niraindavai*, p. 199.
2 *Day by Day with Bhagavan*, 8th October, 1946.
3 *The Power of the Presence*, part three, p. 133.
4 *Bhagavan Sri Ramana, a Pictorial Biography*, p. 74.
5 *The Mountain Path*, 1968, p. 236.
6 *Cherished Memories*, p. 144.
7 *Sri Ramana Paravidyopanishad*, verse 562, cited in *The Power of the Presence*, part three, p. 189.

8 *Living by the Words of Bhagavan*, p. 191.
9 *The Power of the Presence*, part three, pp. 133-4.
10 *The Power of the Presence*, part two, p. 91, 93.
11 *The Power of the Presence*, part two, p. 159.
12 *Living by the Words of Bhagavan*, pp. 33-4.
13 *Day by Day with Bhagavan*, 27th June, 1946.
14 *Letters from Sri Ramanasramam*, 26th October, 1947.
15 *The Power of the Presence*, part two, p. 65.
16 *Ramana Maharshi and the Path of Self-Knowledge*, p. 127.
17 *Self-Realization*, p. 66.
18 *The Power of the Presence*, part two, p. 94.
19 *The Power of the Presence*, part three, p. 33.
20 *Letters from Sri Ramanasramam*, 17th January, 1946.
21 *Living by the Words of Bhagavan*, pp. 86-7.
22 *Letters from Sri Ramanasramam*, 16th February, 1949.
23 *Living by the Words of Bhagavan*, p. 95.
24 *Letters from Sri Ramanasramam*, 7th April, 1947.
25 *Living by the Words of Bhagavan*, p. 72.
26 *Living by the Words of Bhagavan*, pp. 70-71.
27 *Living by the Words of Bhagavan*, p. 29.
28 *The Power of the Presence*, part two, p. 51.

**Bhagavan's Promises and Declarations**

**1**:149, **2**:525, **3**:916, **4**:994, **5**:367, **6**:368, **7**:995, **8**:996, **9**:1661, **10**:1662, **11**:230, **12**:371, **13**:360, **14**:1045, **15**:1619, **16**:2253, **17**:236, **18**:237, **19**:238, **20**:1656, **21**:262, **22**:521, **23**:522, **24**:1313, **25**:914, **26**:915, **27**:523, **28**:524, **29**:366, **30**:450, **31**:347, **32**:348, **33**:978, **34**:143, **35**:598, **36**:599, **37**:600.

1 *Ulladu Narpadu*, p. 142, 1979 ed.
2 *Day by Day with Bhagavan*, 24th June, 1946.
3 *The Power of the Presence*, part one, p. 234.
4 *The Power of the Presence*, part two, pp. 84-5.
5 *The Power of the Presence*, part one, pp. 114-5.
6 *Talks with Sri Ramana Maharshi*, talk no. 543.
7 *Sri Ramana Darsanam*, p. 11.

**The Self (title page)**

1 *Guru Vachaka Kovai*, verse 901.
2 *Sri Ramana Jnana Bodham*, volume 9, verse 15 of *Bodha Arut Porul Vanakkam*.
3 *Sri Ramana Jnana Bodham*, volume 9, verse 3 of *Bodha Arut Porul Vanakkam*.

***Padam***

**1**:1810, **2**:1529, **3**:2932, **4**:957, **5**:2849, **6**:2019, **7**:1502, **8**:1701, **9**:2727, **10**:2147, **11**:2628, **12**:2186, **13**:1043, **14**:1652, **15**:1079, **16**:2471, **17**:2686, **18**:1248,

**19**:2763, **20**:1208, **21**:2834, **22**:3021, **23**:2257, **24**:870, **25**:76, **26**:1486, **27**:2860, **28**:1921, **29**:1827, **30**:1080, **31**:1997, **32**:2756, **33**:496, **34**:1213, **35**:2473, **36**:2503, **37**:954, **38**:166, **39**:92, **40**:267, **41**:2510, **42**:1044, **43**:585, **44**:512, **45**:2181, **46**:2677, **47**:492, **48**:2258, **49**:2551, **50**:1993, **51**:1982, **52**:1783, **53**:1372, **54**:2582, **55**:1544, **56**:576, **57**:1028, **58**:950, **59**:1605, **60**:2896, **61**:2897, **62**:2447, **63**:2448, **64**:272, **65**:1602, **66**:2979, **67**:2735, **68**:887, **69**:108, **70**:2313, **71**:2311, **72**:2774, **73**:2312, **74**:2681, **75**:1859, **76**:146, **77**:3010, **78**:945, **79**:2069, **80**:1309, **81**:1086, **82**:1087, **83**:2157, **84**:32, **85**:2654, **86**:20, **87**:551, **88**:3022, **89**:1977, **90**:2153, **91**:2998, **92**:2452, **93**:3035, **94**:955, **95**:1224, **96**:38, **97**:951, **98**:2624, **99**:494, **100**:2451, **101**:1426, **102**, 952, **103**:953, **104**:2552, **105**:1346, **106**:205, **107**:1650, **108**:2050, **109**:2377, **110**:2701, **111**:2127, **112**:2693, **113**:2990, **114**:83, **115**:288, **116**:21, **117**:164, **118**:2758, **119**:1262, **120**:153, **121**:2403, **122**:1751, **123**:1874, **124**:2862, **125**:294, **126**:2971, **127**:407, **128**:1191, **129**:867.

1 *The Power of the Presence*, part three, p. 252.
2 *Spiritual Instruction, The Collected Works of Sri Ramana Maharshi*, pp. 55-6.
3 *Maha Yoga*, p. 241.
4 *Spiritual Instruction, The Collected Works of Sri Ramana Maharshi*, p. 57.
5 Unpublished translation by Sadhu Om.
6 *The Power of the Presence*, part one, p. 269.
7 *Sat Darshana Bhashya*, p. xxxi.
8 *Sat Darshana Bhashya*, p. xxxii.
9 *Talks with Sri Ramana Maharshi*, talk no. 529.
10 *The Collected Works of Sri Ramana Maharshi*, p. 80-1.
11 *Sri Ramana Reminiscences*, p. 37.
12 *Talks with Sri Ramana Maharshi*, talk no. 143.
13 *Letters from Sri Ramanasramam*, 30th October, 1947.
14 *The Power of the Presence*, part one, p. 261.
15 *Maharshi's Gospel*, p. 52.
16 *Talks with Sri Ramana Maharshi*, talk no. 208.
17 *Talks with Sri Ramana Maharshi*, talk no. 349.
18 *Letters from Sri Ramanasramam*, 22nd August, 1946.
19 *The Power of the Presence*, part one, p. 29.

**The Self**

**1**:805, **2**:707, **3**:219, **4**:2413, **5**:1275, **6**:2412, **7**:2535, **8**:2131, **9**:2156, **10**:2294, **11**:842, **12**:900, **13**:851, **14**:1438, **15**:1021, **16**:2238, **17**:609, **18**:736, **19**:1114, **20**:1115, **21**:896, **22**:997, **23**:2964, **24**:2437, **25**:312, **26**:932, **27**:513, **28**:332, **29**:653, **30**:310, **31**:923, **32**:2101, **33**:514, **34**:2160, **35**:571, **36**:918, **37**: 908, **38**:1108, **39**:305, **40**:2663, **41**:1180, **42**:311, **43**:2102, **44**:1724, **45**:1725, **46**:1174, **47**:165, **48**:991, **49**:617, **50**:2212, **51**:1930, **52**:1773, **53**:2940, **54**:2431, **55**:635, **56**:2821, **57**:2299, **58**:1276, **59**:917, **60**:1944, **61**:364, **62**:1095, **63**:875, **64**:1462, **65**:1672, **66**:594, **67**:223, **68**:689, **69**:1155, **70**:1451, **71**:1576, **72**:1847, **73**:2388, **74**:852, **75**:152, **76**:1575, **77**:740, **78**:965, **79**:2254, **80**:335, **81**:1889, **82**:1795, **83**:1754, **84**:925, **85**:2625, **86**:2151, **87**:3039, **88**:420, **89**:1636, **90**:465,

**91**:708, **92**:2318, **93**:1304, **94**:275, **95**:2387, **96**:802, **97**:2302, **98**:2304, **99**:1852, **100**:2425, **101**:2633, **102**:439, **103**:265, **104**:607, **105**:1201, **106**:1842, **107**:1215, **108**:676, **109**:1601, **110**:1163, **111**:1143, **112**:1475, **113**:170, **114**:299, **115**:473, **116**:1600, **117**:1113, **118**:228, **119**:569, **120**:556, **121**:629, **122**:1608, **123**:1540, **124**:1541, **125**:1832, **126**:2915, **127**:649, **128**:1121, **129**:308, **130**:555, **131**:2256, **132**:1127, **133**:1513, **134**:1515, **135**:700, **136**:547, **137**:1027, **138**:2418, **139**:1937, **140**:1176, **141**:1768, **142**:989, **143**:1390, **144**:1391, **145**:1392, **146**:2988.

1 *Ulladu Narpadu – Kalivenba, The Mountain Path*, 1981, p. 221.
2 *Day by Day with Bhagavan*, 22nd March, 1946.
3 *Ulladu Narpadu – Kalivenba, The Mountain Path*, 1981, pp. 218-9.
4 *Conscious Immortality*, 1984 ed., p. 181.
5 *Day by Day with Bhagavan*, 9th January, 1946.
6 *Talks with Sri Ramana Maharshi*, talk no. 551.
7 *Talks with Sri Ramana Maharshi*, talk no. 372.
8 *Guru Ramana*, p. 63.
9 *Talks with Sri Ramana Maharshi*, talk no. 289.
10 *Maharshi's Gospel*, 1994 ed., p. 48.
11 *Talks with Sri Ramana Maharshi*, talk no. 197.
12 *Talks with Sri Ramana Maharshi*, talk no. 122.
13 *Talks with Sri Ramana Maharshi*, talk no. 251.
14 *Sri Ramana Paravidyopanishad*, verse 166, *The Call Divine*, vol. V, p. 563.
15 *Living by the Words of Bhagavan*, pp. 218-9.
16 *Letters from Sri Ramanasramam*, 28th January, 1947.
17 *Talks with Sri Ramana Maharshi*, talk no. 589.
18 *My Reminiscences*, p. 75.
19 *Talks with Sri Ramana Maharshi*, talk no. 98.
20 *Day by Day with Bhagavan*, 21st July, 1946.
21 *Talks with Sri Ramana Maharshi*, talk no. 30.
22 *The Power of the Presence*, part one, p. 246.
23 *Talks with Sri Ramana Maharshi*, talk no. 626.
24 *Talks with Sri Ramana Maharshi*, talk no. 591.
25 *Talks with Sri Ramana Maharshi*, talk no. 433.
26 *Day by Day with Bhagavan*, 19th October, 1945.
27 *Talks with Sri Ramana Maharshi*, talk no. 406.
28 *Talks with Sri Ramana Maharshi*, talk no. 152.
29 *Talks with Sri Ramana Maharshi*, talk no. 202.
30 *The Power of the Presence*, part one, p. 242.
31 *Talks with Sri Ramana Maharshi*, talk no. 294.
32 *Sat Darshana Bhashya*, p. ix.
33 *Conscious Immortality*, 1984 ed., p. 118.
34 *Self Enquiry, Collected Works*, p. 27.
35 *Conscious Immortality*, p. 117.
36 *Talks with Sri Ramana Maharshi*, talk no. 294.
37 *Talks with Sri Ramana Maharshi*, talk no. 406.
38 *Letters from Sri Ramanasramam*, 22nd January, 1949.

39 *Sadakarkuriya Sattana Nerigal*, no. 73.
40 *Maharshi's Gospel*, pp. 39-40.
41 *Day by Day with Bhagavan*, 18th October, 1945.
42 *Talks with Sri Ramana Maharshi*, talk no. 106.
43 *Letters from Sri Ramanasramam*, 18th May, 1947.
44 *Living by the Words of Bhagavan*, pp. 245-6.
45 *Talks with Sri Ramana Maharshi*, talk no. 627.

### Consciousness

**1**:3020, **2**:1826, **3**:1969, **4**:2803, **5**:3036, **6**:317, **7**:2190, **8**:2953, **9**:1893, **10**:2958, **11**:825, **12**:278, **13**:2058, **14**:788, **15**:2651, **16**:636, **17**:686, **18**:687, **19**:1218, **20**:1219, **21**:1220, **22**:505, **23**:1173, **24**:1804, **25**:1805, **26**:1340, **27**:2484, **28**:2782, **29**:1480, **30**:1534, **31**:552, **32**:460, **33**:2047, **34**:2300, **35**:1911, **36**:2104, **37**:1152, **38**:843, **39**:943, **40**:508, **41**:1165, **42**:631, **43**:568, **44**:2656, **45**:679, **46**:680, **47**:681, **48**:1743, **49**:724, **50**:2260, **51**:1024, **52**:1025, **53**:1026, **54**:2887, **55**:1772, **56**:1730, **57**:1638, **58**:2130, **59**:1315, **60**:2282, **61**:970, **62**:1237, **63**:338, **64**:247, **65**:1211, **66**:1845, **67**:1892, **68**:2618, **69**:517.

1 *Talks with Sri Ramana Maharshi*, talk no. 289.
2 *Day by Day with Bhagavan*, 19th November, 1946.
3 *Letters from Sri Ramanasramam*, 30th October, 1947.
4 *Talks with Sri Ramana Maharshi*, talk no. 82.
5 Unpublished translation from Annamalai Swami's diary. A partial translation of this answer is contained in *Living by the Words of Bhagavan*, p. 252.
6 *Day by Day with Bhagavan*, 22nd November, 1945.
7 *Letters from Sri Ramanasramam*, 9th April, 1947.
8 *The Power of the Presence*, part one, pp. 263-4.

### Other Synonyms for the Self

**1**:1617, **2**:186, **3**:562, **4**:1212, **5**:2632, **6**:543, **7**:1831, **8**:779, **9**:2272, **10**:404, **11**:1547, **12**:434, **13**:1119, **14**:1245, **15**:422, **16**:633, **17**:1727, **18**:1817, **19**:984, **20**:630, **21**:453, **22**:983, **23**:454, **24**:1530, **25**:650, **26**:651, **27**:1286, **28**:974, **29**:2106, **30**:1118, **31**:1130, **32**:1175, **33**:1285, **34**:476, **35**:1549, **36**:2056, **37**:1377, **38**:833, **39**:2042, **40**:2848, **41**:2122, **42**:1919, **43**:421, **44**:2080, **45**:1395, **46**:1482, **47**:632, **48**:1267, **49**:1834, **50**:1099, **51**:1100, **52**:2315, **53**:841, **54**:545, **55**:2515, **56**:1512, **57**:684, **58**:1069, **59**:1144, **60**:1581, **61**:596, **62**:1076, **63**:1077, **64**:930, **65**:931, **66**:2904, **67**:2154, **68**:2226, **69**:634, **70**:2332, **71**:874, **72**:2669, **73**:1774, **74**:2262, **75**:2366, **76**:1112, **77**:1971, **78**:1078, **79**:1250, **80**:1251, **81**:240, **82**:1151, **83**:1536, **84**:2995, **85**:2571, **86**:2767, **87**:2339, **88**:232, **89**:233, **90**:721, **91**:418, **92**:1798, **93**:2338.

1 *Be As You Are*, p. 12.
2 *Day by Day with Bhagavan*, 16th September, 1945.
3 *Day by Day with Bhagavan*, 31st January, 1946.
4 *Talks with Sri Ramana Maharshi*, talk no. 238.

5 *Maharshi's Gospel*, p. 66.
6 *Talks with Sri Ramana Maharshi*, talk no. 27.
7 *Talks with Sri Ramana Maharshi*, talk no. 99.
8 *Ulladu Narpadu – Kalivenba, The Mountain Path*, 1981, p. 219.
9 *Talks with Sri Ramana Maharshi*, talk no. 450.
10 *The Collected Works of Sri Ramana Maharshi*, p. 118.
11 *Sri Ramana Darsanam*, pp. 8-9.
12 *Day by Day with Bhagavan*, 18th April, 1946.
13 *Talks with Sri Ramana Maharshi*, talk no. 244.
14 *Talks with Sri Ramana Maharshi*, talk no. 68.
15 *Talks with Sri Ramana Maharshi*, talk no. 273.
16 *Talks with Sri Ramana Maharshi*, talk no. 450.
17 *Self Enquiry, Collected Works*, pp. 32-3.

**The Guru (title page)**

1 *Sri Ramana Jnana Bodham*, vol. 7, verse 916.
2 *Sri Ramana Jnana Bodham*, vol. 3, verse 842.
3 *Guru Vachaka Kovai*, verse 321, cited in *The Power of the Presence*, part one, p. 110.

**The Guru (chapter)**

**1**:666, **2**:662, **3**:663,**4**:1056, **5**:1839, **6**:665, **7**:1188, **8**:1323, **9**:3014, **10**:346, **11**:695, **12**:696, **13**:697, **14**:698, **15**:699, **16**:625, **17**:626, **18**:1766, **19**:668, **20**:669, **21**:670, **22**:664, **23**:2229, **24**:2408, **25**:1880, **26**:830, **27**:1878, **28**:1879, **29**:1881.

1 *Letters from Sri Ramanasramam*, 26th February, 1947.
2 Taken from a Tamil essay by Muruganar on Bhagavan's life, entitled 'Sri Ramana', which appeared in appendix six of volume nine of *Sri Ramana Jnana Bodham*.
3 *Sadakarkuriya Sattana Nerigal*, no. 27.
4 *Sri Ramana Darsanam*, pp. 38-9.
5 *The Power of the Presence*, part one, p. 230.
6 *Letters from and Recollections of Sri Ramanasramam*, p. 26.
7 *Maharshi's Gospel*, p. 33.
8 *Talks with Sri Ramana Maharshi*, talk no. 31.
9 *Sadakarkuriya Sattana Nerigal*, no. 50.
10 *Sri Ramana Darsanam*, p. 35.
11 *Letters from Sri Ramanasramam*, 24th April, 1947.
12 *Talks with Sri Ramana Maharshi*, talk no. 68. I have amended the Sanskrit quotation a little since the original citation was incomplete.
13 *Talks with Sri Ramana Maharshi*, talk no. 246.
14 A more detailed account of this exchange between Bhagavan and Muruganar can be found in *The Mountain Path*, 1982, pp. 11-12.
15 *Spiritual Instruction, The Collected Works of Sri Ramana Maharshi*, p. 50.

16 *Talks with Sri Ramana Maharshi*, talk no. 282.

### The *Jnani*

**1**:1138, **2**:2598, **3**:2609, **4**:1708, **5**:2429, **6**:1040, **7**:713, **8**:1660, **9**:1704, **10**:1950, **11**:2402, **12**:1705, **13**:2201, **14**:919, **15**:920, **16**:1436, **17**:1437, **18**:1618, **19**:639, **20**:2307, **21**:2245, **22**:1676, **23**:1134, **24**:714, **25**:1979, **26**:2739, **27**:2650, **28**:1980, **29**:958, **30**:1205, **31**:1272, **32**:1815, **33**:1816, **34**:2219, **35**:2833, **36**:2295, **37**:685, **38**:1427, **39**:784, **40**:354, **41**:1048, **42**:2337, **43**:2470, **44**:939, **45**:2330, **46**:1495, **47**:785, **48**:2713, **49**:405, **50**:2892, **51**:1649, **52**:992, **53**:1709, **54**:780, **55**:2273, **56**:2163, **57**:2111, **58**:3023, **59**:781, **60**:2291.

1 *Talks with Sri Ramana Maharshi*, talk no. 204.
2 *Sri Ramana Darsanam*, p. 25.
3 *Maha Yoga*, p. 230.
4 *The Power of the Presence*, part one, p. 231.
5 *Talks with Sri Ramana Maharshi*, talk no. 210.
6 *Talks with Sri Ramana Maharshi*, talk no. 20.
7 *Letters from Sri Ramanasramam*, 17th May, 1947.
8 *Talks with Sri Ramana Maharshi*, talk no. 155.
9 *Living by the Words of Bhagavan*, pp. 220-1.
10 *Day by Day with Bhagavan*, 16th July, 1946.
11 *My Recollections of Bhagavan Sri Ramana*, pp. 30-32. The first quote is from *Brahma Gita* and the second from *Jnana Vasishta*.
12 *Letters from Sri Ramanasramam*, 3rd June 1946, p. 65.
13 *The Power of the Presence*, part one, p. 193.
14 *Talks with Sri Ramana Maharshi*, talk no. 449.
15 *The Power of the Presence*, part one, p. 245.
16 *Maharshi's Gospel*, p. 81.
17 *Conscious Immortality*, 1984 ed., p. 69.
18 *Sat Darshana Bhashya*, p. xx.
19 *Sri Ramana Paravidyopanishad*, verse 565, cited in *The Power of the Presence*, part three, p. 190.
20 *Day by Day with Bhagavan*, 21st January, 1946.

### The Mind and its Creations (title page)

1 *Guru Vachaka Kovai*, verse 187.
2 *Guru Vachaka Kovai*, verse 188.
3 *Sri Ramana Jnana Bodham*, vol. 8, verse 588.
4 *Sri Ramana Jnana Bodham*, vol. 8, verse 417.

### The Nature of the Mind

**1**:702, **2**:1531, **3**:1630, **4**:1036, **5**:1050, **6**:456, **7**:2487, **8**:2137, **9**:988, **10**:2419, **11**:1643, **12**:2876, **13**:2533, **14**:1109, **15**:1631, **16**:794, **17**:795, **18**:796, **19**:797,

**20**:798, **21**:799, **22**:800, **23**:801, **24**:1364, **25**:2629, **26**:313, **27**:315, **28**:935, **29**:2094, **30**:2906, **31**:1472, **32**:1953, **33**:716, **34**:1644, **35**:1458, **36**:2329, **37**:1189, **38**:1283, **39**:3003, **40**:1190, **41**:2894, **42**:2579, **43**:2577, **44**:1073, **45**:1074, **46**:2335, **47**:1292, **48**:2148, **49**:1759, **50**:458, **51**:704, **52**:705, **53**:504, **54**:582, **55**:455, **56**:1164.

1 *Sadakarkuriya Sattana Nerigal*, no. 55.
2 *Day by Day with Bhagavan*, 8th November, 1945.
3 *Day by Day with Bhagavan*, 11th January, 1946.
4 *Talks with Sri Ramana Maharshi*, talk no. 26.
5 *Talks with Sri Ramana Maharshi*, talk no. 195.
6 *Sadakarkuriya Sattana Nerigal*, no. 43.
7 *Talks with Sri Ramana Maharshi*, talk no. 99.
8 *Crumbs from his Table*, p. 27.
9 *Sadakarkuriya Sattana Nerigal*, no. 19.
10 *Talks with Sri Ramana Maharshi*, talk no. 195.

### *Suttarivu*

**1**:1129, **2**:1096, **3**:2472, **4**:1124, **5**:2375, **6**:1363, **7**:1128, **8**:2287, **9**:1011, **10**:1386, **11**:2239, **12**:575, **13**:1097, **14**:1005, **15**:807, **16**:502, **17**:808, **18**:574, **19**:1574, **20**:2479, **21**:1671, **22**:1474, **23**:1202, **24**:2589, **25**:787, **26**:2361, **27**:246, **28**:677, **29**:678, **30**:1102, **31**:2532, **32**:2564, **33**:946, **34**:947, **35**:1308, **36**:912, **37**:1158, **38**:2539, **39**:314, **40**:1457, **41**:1784, **42**:962, **43**:457, **44**:1094, **45**:986, **46**:2881, **47**:1178, **48**:2020, **49**:2398, **50**:1968, **51**:1684, **52**:845, **53**:216, **54**:1582.

1 *The Collected Works of Sri Ramana Maharshi*, p. 116.
2 *Talks with Sri Ramana Maharshi*, talk no. 323.
3 *Guru Ramana*, p. 46.
4 *Talks with Sri Ramana Maharshi*, talk no. 445.
5 *Ulladu Narpadu – Kalivenba, The Mountain Path*, 1981, p. 219.
6 *Day by Day with Bhagavan*, 18th March, 1946.

### Individual Identity

**1**:1710, **2**:2637, **3**:1460, **4**:1374, **5**:2384, **6**:2541, **7**:1091, **8**:692, **9**:693, **10**:203, **11**:2249, **12**:1447, **13**:2077, **14**:980, **15**:1927, **16**:435, **17**:1006, **18**:327, **19**:2660, **20**:2059, **21**:2649, **22**:2742, **23**:2129, **24**:2426, **25**:2639, **26**:2927, **27**:1181, **28**:2103, **29**:1378, **30**:440, **31**:1136, **32**:1229, **33**:718, **34**:2211, **35**:1385, **36**:1799, **37**:2526, **38**:1484, **39**:835, **40**:836, **41**:837, **42**:838, **43**:701, **44**:1473, **45**:1667, **46**:2830, **47**:1449, **48**:2342, **49**:1252, **50**:2659, **51**:1538, **52**:1070, **53**:2885, **54**:441, **55**:878, **56**:442, **57**:1227, **58**:688, **59**:1305, **60**:1235, **61**:1312, **62**:1376, **63**:2992, **64**:1268, **65**:929, **66**:579, **67**:580, **68**:581, **69**:583, **70**:1459, **71**:1020, **72**:1736, **73**:893, **74**:560, **75**:879, **76**:1015, **77**:2875, **78**:2916, **79**:725, **80**:1606, **81**:690, **82**:691, **83**:1014, **84**:2459, **85**:2264, **86**:148, **87**:1469, **88**:614,

**89**:615, **90**:715, **91**:1145, **92**:2761, **93**:2297, **94**:1221, **95**:1137, **96**:2888, **97**:1707, **98**:167, **99**:2128, **100**:1714, **101**:1685, **102**:1042, **103**:1375, **104**:2298, **105**:1290, **106**:2544, **107**:849, **108**:298, **109**:743, **110**:744, **111**:745, **112**:1243, **113**:1206, **114**:2874, **115**:2040, **116**:1046, **117**:2415, **118**:2416, **119**:2268, **120**:372, **121**:3029, **122**:515, **123**:516, **124**:1244.

1 *Sri Ramana Paravidyopanishad*, cited in *The Power of the Presence*, part three, p. 174.
2 *Five Hymns to Arunachala*, tr. Prof. K. Swaminathan, p. 68.
3 *Self Enquiry, The Collected Works of Sri Ramana Maharshi*, pp. 33-4.
4 *Sri Ramana Darsanam*, pp. 49-50.
5 *Five Hymns to Arunachala*, tr. Prof. K. Swaminathan, p. 125.
6 *Talks with Sri Ramana Maharshi*, talk no. 612.
7 *Talks with Sri Ramana Maharshi*, talk no. 146.
8 *Ulladu Narpadu – Kalivenba, The Mountain Path*, 1981, p. 220.
9 *Maharshi's Gospel*, pp. 47-8.
10 *Day by Day with Bhagavan*, 2nd November, 1945.
11 *Maharshi's Gospel*, pp. 80-1.
12 *The Collected Works of Sri Ramana Maharshi*, p. 118.
13 *Talks with Sri Ramana Maharshi*, talk no. 383.
14 *Talks with Sri Ramana Maharshi*, talk no. 404.
15 *Talks with Sri Ramana Maharshi*, talk no. 503.
16 *Day by Day with Bhagavan*, 3rd January, 1946.
17 *Spiritual Instructions*, *Collected Works*, pp. 63-4.
18 *Letters from Sri Ramanasramam*, 3rd June, 1946.
19 *Talks with Sri Ramana Maharshi*, talk no. 565.

**The *Avasthas***

**1**:2961, **2**:1448, **3**:2082, **4**:628, **5**:2168, **6**:1686, **7**:1761, **8**:1673, **9**:1700, **10**:971, **11**:972, **12**:973, **13**:566, **14**:567, **15**:274, **16**:771, **17**:227, **18**:553, **19**:554, **20**:273, **21**:1913, **22**:2267, **23**:1573, **24**:2107, **25**:772, **26**:826, **27**:1273, **28**:2108.

1 *Maharshi's Gospel*, pp. 83-4.
2 *Day by Day with Bhagavan*, 11th January, 1946.
3 *Talks with Sri Ramana Maharshi*, talk no. 609.
4 *Maharshi's Gospel*, pp. 25-6.
5 *Sri Ramana Paravidyopanishad*, verse 32, *The Call Divine*, vol. IV, p. 530.
6 *Talks with Sri Ramana Maharshi*, talk no. 609.
7 *Day by Day with Bhagavan*, 21st November, 1945.
8 *The Mountain Path*, 1969, pp. 108-9.
9 *Day by Day with Bhagavan*, 5th January, 1946.

**Practice (title page)**

1 *Sri Ramana Jnana Bodham*, vol. 8, verse 462.
2 *Sri Ramana Jnana Bodham*, vol. 7, verse 340.

3 *Sri Ramana Jnana Bodham*, vol. 1, verse 683.
4 *Sri Ramana Jnana Bodham*, vol. 8, verse 192.

**Liberation and Silence**

**1**:1698, **2**:2061, **3**:1744, **4**:894, **5**:895, **6**:610, **7**:548, **8**:2205, **9**:2405, **10**:1503, **11**:1000, **12**:1255, **13**:913, **14**:475, **15**:2877, **16**:2184, **17**:1439, **18**:2570, **19**:1716, **20**:834, **21**:1988, **22**:1888, **23**:694, **24**:2580, **25**:2221, **26**:2399, **27**:1217, **28**:2328, **29**:2114, **30**:2261, **31**:2436, **32**:1511, **33**:2240, **34**:2457, **35**:1924, **36**:839, **37**:1833, **38**:2432, **39**:748, **40**:749, **41**:1345, **42**:877, **43**:750, **44**:752, **45**:753, **46**:754, **47**:758, **48**:762, **49**:763, **50**:764, **51**:765, **52**:766, **53**:767, **54**:768, **55**:1646, **56**:1647, **57**:846, **58**:406, **59**:937, **60**:936, **61**:979, **62**:1976, **63**:820, **64**:1941, **65**:452, **66**:577, **67**:401, **68**:436, **69**:437, **70**:438, **71**:2548, **72**:751, **73**:761, **74**:769, **75**:770, **76**:809, **77**:810, **78**:811, **79**:812, **80**:813, **81**:814, **82**:815, **83**:816, **84**:817, **85**:818, **86**:819.

1 *The Garland of Guru's Sayings*, verse 'Bhagavan 28', p. 234.
2 *The Power of the Presence*, part three, pp. 132-3.
3 *Day by Day with Bhagavan*, 22nd November, 1945.
4 *Talks with Sri Ramana Maharshi*, talk no. 266.
5 *Day by Day with Bhagavan*, 5th January, 1946.
6 *Ulladu Narpadu – Kalivenba*, verse 39, *The Mountain Path*, 1981, p. 220.
7 *Letters from Sri Ramanasramam*, 20th February, 1946.
8 *Spiritual Instruction, The Collected Works of Sri Ramana Maharshi*, pp. 72-3.
9 *Day by Day with Bhagavan*, 24th December, 1945.
10 *Letters from Sri Ramanasramam*, 8th January, 1946.
11 *Maharshi's Gospel*, pp. 31-2.
12 *Talks with Sri Ramana Maharshi*, talk no. 322.
13 *Day by Day with Bhagavan*, 11th January, 1946.
14 *The Power of the Presence*, part three, pp. 131-3.
15 *Talks with Sri Ramana Maharshi*, talk no. 354.
16 *Letters from Sri Ramanasramam*, 19th July, 1947.
17 *Letters from Sri Ramanasramam*, 28th March, 1947.

**Self-enquiry**

**1**:1770, **2**:1668, **3**:1193, **4**:321, **5**:821, **6**:300, **7**:2879, **8**:1342, **9**:934, **10**:424, **11**:2105, **12**:459, **13**:425, **14**:892, **15**:276, **16**:518, **17**:1055, **18**:337, **19**:304, **20**:706, **21**:504, **22**:640, **23**:641, **24**:642, **25**:344, **26**:234, **27**:1216, **28**:2921, **29**:998, **30**:356, **31**:1938, **32**:999, **33**:301, **34**:302, **35**:622, **36**:741, **37**:742, **38**:829, **39**:277, **40**:295, **41**:296, **42**:720, **43**:727, **44**:620, **45**:621, **46**:2280, **47**:643, **48**:2368, **49**:2369.

1 *Conscious Immortality*, p. 176.
2 *Talks with Sri Ramana Maharshi*, talk no. 29.
3 *Talks with Sri Ramana Maharshi*, talk no. 222.
4 *Maharshi's Gospel*, pp. 24-5.
5 *Maharshi's Gospel*, pp. 78-9.

6 *Talks with Sri Ramana Maharshi*, talk no. 390.
7 *Maharshi's Gospel*, p. 77.
8 *Day by Day with Bhagavan*, 22nd March, 1946.
9 *Maharshi's Gospel*, p. 79.
10 *Talks with Sri Ramana Maharshi*, talk no. 486.
11 *Sat Darshana Bhashya*, p. iii.
12 *Sat Darshana Bhashya*, p. iv.
13 *Truth Revealed*, v. 30, 1982 ed.
14 Question three of *Vichara Sangraham*, translated by Sadhu Om, taken from page 98 of *The Mountain Path*, 1982. The word order has been slightly changed in this version.
15 *Talks with Sri Ramana Maharshi*, talk no. 591.
16 *Conscious Immortality*, 1984 ed., p. 54.
17 *Maharshi's Gospel*, p. 47.
18 *Who am I?, The Collected Works of Sri Ramana Maharshi*, p. 44.
19 *Day by Day with Bhagavan*, 3rd January, 1946.
20 *The Power of the Presence*, part one, pp. 236-7.
21 *Talks with Sri Ramana Maharshi*, talk no. 596.
22 *Who am I?, The Collected Works of Sri Ramana Maharshi*, p. 42.
23 *The Power of the Presence*, part one, p. 56.
24 *Crumbs from his Table*, 1969 ed., pp. 46-7.
25 *Crumbs from his Table*, 1969 ed., pp. 35-6.


**Surrender, Love and Devotion**

**1**:2766, **2**:2389, **3**:646, **4**:1246, **5**:623, **6**:2449, **7**:109, **8**:2346, **9**:1706, **10**:235, **11**:904, **12**:231, **13**:1110, **14**:659, **15**:2202, **16**:445, **17**:447, **18**:448, **19**:449, **20**:1970, **21**:2378, **22**:1972, **23**:1973, **24**:352, **25**:1120, **26**:1058, **27**:1853, **28**:2775, **29**:3013, **30**:683, **31**:1394, **32**:2442, **33**:1785, **34**:2317, **35**:510, **36**:1835, **37**:1836, **38**:2867, **39**:2263, **40**:1765, **41**:831, **42**:2481, **43**:2581, **44**:1331, **45**:2925, **46**:403, **47**:1170, **48**:1171, **49**:2314, **50**:1762, **51**:2259, **52**:2814, **53**:2316, **54**:2383, **55**:1126, **56**:1882, **57**:1446, **58**:1049, **59**:1389, **60**:2176, **61**:1614, **62**:1516.


1 *Talks with Sri Ramana Maharshi*, talk no. 208.
2 *Maharshi's Gospel*, pp. 22-3.
3 *Ulladu Narpadu – Kalivenba, The Mountain Path*, 1981, p. 217.
4 *Talks with Sri Ramana Maharshi*, talk no. 28.
5 *The Power of the Presence*, part one, p. 244.
6 *Talks with Sri Ramana Maharshi*, talk no. 244.
7 *The Collected Works of Sri Ramana Maharshi*, p. 125.
8 *Talks with Sri Ramana Maharshi*, talk no. 271.
9 *Day by Day with Bhagavan*, 1st March, 1946.
10 *Talks with Sri Ramana Maharshi*, talk no. 450.
11 *Maharshi's Gospel*, p. 22.
12 *Sri Ramana Paravidyopanishad*, vv. 232, 233, *The Call Divine*, vol. VI, p. 60.
13 *The Power of the Presence*, part three, p. 125.
14 *Letters from Sri Ramanasramam*, 23rd May, 1947.

15 *Letters from Sri Ramanasramam*, 2nd May, 1948.
16 *Day by Day with Bhagavan*, 7th January, 1946.
17 *Sadakarkuriya Sattana Nerigal*, no. 12.
18 *Letters from Sri Ramanasramam*, 26th April, 1948.
19 *Sat Darshana Bhashya*, p. vi.
20 *Talks with Sri Ramana Maharshi*, talk no. 650.
21 *Sri Ramana Paravidyopanishad*, verse 18, *The Call Divine*, vol. IV, p. 18.
22 *Talks with Sri Ramana Maharshi*, talk no. 650.

**Advice on *Sadhana***

**1**: 1551, **2**:889, **3**:172, **4**:336, **5**:2635, **6**:1528, **7**:2115, **8**:888, **9**:1844, **10**:2352, **11**:1179, **12**:1022, **13**:850, **14**:1455, **15**:656, **16**:655, **17**:248, **18**:249, **19**:868, **20**:1813, **21**:911, **22**:443, **23**:1679, **24**:345, **25**:1362, **26**:169, **27**:1639, **28**:637, **29**:638, **30**:2303, **31**:824, **32**:1117, **33**:2096, **34**:966, **35**:2394, **36**:1161, **37**:1811, **38**:924, **39**:56, **40**:2213, **41**:2144, **42**:1388, **43**:2230, **44**:1116, **45**:2374, **46**:1931, **47**:1146, **48**:1241, **49**:860, **50**:2385, **51**:884, **52**:2341, **53**:1234, **54**:357, **55**:423, **56**:1001, **57**:1133, **58**:2125, **59**:2255, **60**:255, **61**:2360, **62**:542, **63**:2248, **64**:2138, **65**:1771, **66**:1225, **67**:1226, **68**:977, **69**:1085, **70**:396, **71**:1952, **72**:1569, **73**:1172, **74**:1548, **75**:2290, **76**:2074, **77**:863, **78**:1747, **79**:1149, **80**:1257, **81**:1258, **82**:2081, **83**:1270, **84**:1271, **85**:1682, **86**:2301, **87**:2497, **88**:1098, **89**:358, **90**:520, **91**:658, **92**:2467, **93**:2468, **94**:2556.

1 *Talks with Sri Ramana Maharshi*, talk nos. 26, 27.
2 *Conscious Immortality*, 1984 ed., p. 58.
3 *The Power of the Presence*, part three, p. 145.
4 *Who am I?, The Collected Works of Sri Ramana Maharshi*, p. 44.
5 *Day by Day with Bhagavan*, 2nd January, 1946.
6 *Day by Day with Bhagavan*, 24th July, 1946.
7 *Talks with Sri Ramana Maharshi*, talk no. 78.
8 *Talks with Sri Ramana Maharshi*, talk no. 485.
9 *Talks with Sri Ramana Maharshi*, talk no. 338.
10 *Talks with Sri Ramana Maharshi*, talk no. 30.
11 *Conscious Immortality*, 1984 ed., p. 200.
12 *No Mind – I am the Self*, p. 103.
13 *Day by Day with Bhagavan*, 28th June, 1946.
14 *Talks with Sri Ramana Maharshi*, talk no. 197.
15 *Talks with Sri Ramana Maharshi*, talk no. 643.
16 *Day by Day with Bhagavan*, 2nd January, 1946.
17 *Day by Day with Bhagavan*, 12th April, 1946.
18 *Talks with Sri Ramana Maharshi*, talk no. 495.
19 *Talks with Sri Ramana Maharshi*, talk no. 502.
20 *Letters from and Recollections of Sri Ramanasramam*, p. 134.
21 *Letters from Sri Ramanasramam*, 19th December, 1946.
22 *Maharshi's Gospel*, p. 28.
23 *Maharshi's Gospel*, p. 82.
24 *Talks with Sri Ramana Maharshi*, talk no. 13.

25 *Talks with Sri Ramana Maharshi*, talk no. 317.

## Grace, Effort and Maturity

**1**:776, **2**:1830, **3**:251, **4**:2392, **5**:872, **6**:2034, **7**:279, **8**:2214, **9**:2194, **10**:1039, **11**:906, **12**:1539, **13**:1131, **14**:1132, **15**:1061, **16**:1062, **17**:1256, **18**:2242, **19**:2126, **20**:2177, **21**:1259, **22**:1260, **23**:1261, **24**:2751, **25**:2231, **26**:2401, **27**:1063, **28**:1621, **29**:960, **30**:2434.

1 *Sadakarkuriya Sattana Nerigal*, nos. 8, 21.
2 *Maharshi's Gospel*. pp. 35-6.
3 *Letters from Sri Ramanasramam*. This story should have appeared at the end of the letter dated 27th July, 1948, but it was omitted from the English edition. It appears in both the Tamil and Telugu versions of the book.
4 *Day by Day with Bhagavan*, 27th June, 1946.
5 *Crumbs from his Table*, p. 30.
6 *Sat Darshana Bhashya*, p. v.
7 *Talks with Sri Ramana Maharshi*, talk no. 29.
8 *Self-Enquiry, The Collected Works of Sri Ramana Maharshi*, p. 12.
9 *My Reminiscences*, p. 3.
10 *Talks with Sri Ramana Maharshi*, talk no. 249.
11 *Talks with Sri Ramana Maharshi*, talk no. 427.
12 *Letters from Sri Ramanasramam*, 12th September, 1947.
13 *Letters from Sri Ramanasramam*, 29th November, 1947 (volume 2, letter 22).
14 *Day by Day with Bhagavan*, 31st March, 1945.
15 *The Power of the Presence*, part two, pp. 13-14.

## The World and its Creator (title page)

1 *Non-Dual Consciousness – The Flood Tide of Bliss, Sri Ramana Anubhuti*, verse 256.
2 *Guru Vachaka Kovai*, verse 55.
3 *Sri Ramana Jnana Bodham*, vol. 5, verse 128.

## Creation

**1**:2244, **2**:417, **3**:2243, **4**:1396, **5**:2274, **6**:897, **7**:1123, **8**:1965, **9**:1966, **10**:1017, **11**:608, **12**:1357, **13**:1829, **14**:565, **15**:844.

1 *Talks with Sri Ramana Maharshi*, talk no. 388.
2 *Day by Day with Bhagavan*, 17th February, 1946.
3 *The Power of the Presence*, part one, p. 240.
4 *Spiritual Instruction, The Collected Works of Sri Ramana Maharshi*, p. 58.
5 *Talks with Sri Ramana Maharshi*, talk no. 589.
6 *Guru Ramana*, p. 56.
7 *The Power of the Presence*, part one, p. 262.
8 *Day by Day with Bhagavan*, 21st November, 1945.

**Seer and Seen**

**1**:1197, **2**:136, **3**:1871, **4**:1872, **5**:1873, **6**:2331, **7**:397, **8**:1010, **9**:309, **10**:1317, **11**:2587, **12**:2588, **13**:1670, **14**:898, **15**:224, **16**:1321, **17**:2463, **18**:1851, **19**:414, **20**:729, **21**:2333, **22**:2334, **23**:717, **24**:1307, **25**:969, **26**:519, **27**:1068, **28**:2443, **29**:1196, **30**:1198, **31**:1320, **32**:1344, **33**:1990, **34**:2161, **35**:1945, **36**:1910, **37**:2856, **38**:1939, **39**:1693.

1 *Sri Ramana Paravidyopanishad*, v. 147, *The Call Divine*, vol. V, p. 438.
2 *Talks with Sri Ramana Maharshi*, talk no. 25.
3 *Living by the Words of Bhagavan*, p. 236.
4 *Talks with Sri Ramana Maharshi*, talk no. 442.
5 *Talks with Sri Ramana Maharshi*, talk no. 566.
6 *Talks with Sri Ramana Maharshi*, talk no. 53.
7 *Talks with Sri Ramana Maharshi*, talk no. 427.
8 *Five Hymns to Arunachala*, tr. Prof. K. Swaminathan, p. 23.
9 *Day by Day with Bhagavan*, 21st July, 1946.
10 *Day by Day with Bhagavan*, 10th April, 1946.
11 Unpublished translation by Sadhu Om and Michael James.
12 *Maha Yoga*, 1973, p. 72.
13 *Day by Day with Bhagavan*, 18th April, 1946.
14 *Day by Day with Bhagavan*, 17th October, 1946.
15 *Talks with Sri Ramana Maharshi*, talk no. 2.
16 *Day by Day with Bhagavan*, 21st November, 1945.
17 *Aksharamanamalai Vritti Urai*, p. 103.

**The Reality of the World Appearance**

**1**:1894, **2**:1895, **3**:1016, **4**:2068, **5**:985, **6**:886, **7**:774, **8**:1200, **9**:394, **10**:341, **11**:1052, **12**:221, **13**:1399, **14**:967, **15**:2283, **16**:2804, **17**:339, **18**:168, **19**:2664, **20**:2791, **21**:871, **22**:873, **23**:2141, **24**:2142, **25**:1194, **26**:3006, **27**:2903, **28**:498, **29**:2143, **30**:601, **31**:602, **32**:603, **33**:604, **34**:605, **35**:557, **36**:885, **37**:1067, **38**:1053, **39**:2722, **40**:1012, **41**:1013, **42**:1254.

1 *Day by Day with Bhagavan*, 19th March, 1945.
2 *Day by Day with Bhagavan*, 19th October, 1945.
3 *Ramana Smrti Souvenir*, 'Tales of Bhagavan', no. 18.
4 *Talks with Sri Ramana Maharshi*, talk no. 455.
5 *Living by the Words of Bhagavan*, p. 222.
6 *Talks with Sri Ramana Maharshi*, talk no. 33.
7 *Ulladu Narpadu – Kalivenba, The Mountain Path*, 1981, p. 219.
8 *Letters from Sri Ramanasramam*, 24th August, 1946.
9 *Day by Day with Bhagavan*, 7th April, 1946.
10 *Day by Day with Bhagavan*, 29th May, 1946.
11 *Letters from Sri Ramanasramam*, 31st January, 1946.
12 *Talks with Sri Ramana Maharshi*, talk no. 30.
13 *The Power of the Presence*, part one, p. 27.

14 *Sri Ramana Darsanam*, p. 62.

**Iswara and Destiny**

**1**:1007, **2**:1009, **3**:1030, **4**:1031, **5**:398, **6**:399, **7**:2869, **8**:1867, **9**:987, **10**:921, **11**:922, **12**:2070.

1 *Talks with Sri Ramana Maharshi*, talk no. 589.
2 *Conscious Immortality*, pp. 10, 180-1.
3 *Letters from Sri Ramanasramam*, 21st November, 1947.
4 *Letters from Sri Ramanasramam*, 11th August, 1946.
5 *The Mountain Path* 1982, p. 23.
6 *Conscious Immortality* p. 135.
7 *Sadakarkuriya Sattana Nerigal*, no. 78.
8 *The Power of the Presence*, part one, p. 47.
9 *Day by Day with Bhagavan*, 1st June, 1946.
10 *Talks with Sri Ramana Maharshi*, talk no. 426.
11 *Ulladu Narpadu – Kalivenba*, verse 19, *The Mountain Path*, 1981, p. 219.

**Right Knowledge, Right Behaviour, Right Attitude (title page)**

1 *Guru Vachaka Kovai*, verse 822.
2 *Guru Vachaka Kovai*, verse 71.
3 *Guru Vachaka Kovai*, verse 849.

**Religions and Religious Knowledge**

**1**:1032, **2**:1033, **3**:1034, **4**:2838, **5**:1035, **6**:537, **7**:538, **8**:539, **9**:540, **10**:1665, **11**:128, **12**:964, **13**:2045, **14**:2235, **15**:2117, **16**:2250, **17**:777, **18**:778, **19**:1846, **20**:2395, **21**:1140, **22**:558, **23**:1932, **24**:1054, **25**:1535, **26**:244, **27**:245, **28**:501, **29**:648, **30**:905, **31**:3008, **32**:2089, **33**:1233, **34**:1571, **35**:1210, **36**:1204, **37**:1355, **38**:1669, **39**:2783, **40**:2359, **41**:1141.

1 *Maha Yoga*, p. 220.
2 *Sri Ramana Paravidyopanishad*, verse 61, *The Call Divine*, vol. IV, p. 586.
3 *The Power of the Presence*, part one, p. 271.
4 *Living by the Words of Bhagavan*, p. 218.
5 *Talks with Sri Ramana Maharshi*, talk no. 647.
6 *Living by the Words of Bhagavan*, p. 217.
7 *Talks with Sri Ramana Maharshi*, talk no 275.
8 *Letters from Sri Ramanasramam*, 2nd July, 1949.
9 *Letters from Sri Ramanasramam*, 1st February, 1946.

**Death and Suffering**

**1**:2478, **2**:1750, **3**:1461, **4**:1059, **5**:782, **6**:2266, **7**:1071, **8**:1060, **9**:1857, **10**:1111, **11**:611, **12**:612, **13**:1823, **14**:1293, **15**:2039, **16**:2382, **17**:993, **18**:2038, **19**:968,

**20**:2095, **21**:546, **22**:564, **23**:2617, **24**:1604, **25**:1680, **26**:1002, **27**:2110, **28**:1951, **29**:1681, **30**:1004, **31**:595, **32**:618, **33**:3007, **34**:1162, **35**:1122, **36**:597, **37**:563, **38**:712, **39**:1998, **40**:990, **41**:890, **42**:1387.


1 *Self-Enquiry, The Collected Works of Sri Ramana Maharshi*, p. 30.
2 *Talks with Sri Ramana Maharshi*, talk no. 396.
3 *Talks with Sri Ramana Maharshi*, talk no. 80.
4 *Talks with Sri Ramana Maharshi*, talk no. 435.
5 *Day by Day with Bhagavan*, 9th March, 1946.
6 *Letters from Sri Ramanasramam*, 11th September, 1947.
7 *Maha Yoga*, p. 228.
8 *Talks with Sri Ramana Maharshi*, talk no. 64.
9 *Maha Yoga*, pp. 227-8.
10 *Sri Ramana Reminiscences*, p. 110.
11 *Living by the Words of Bhagavan*, p. 238.
12 *Talks with Sri Ramana Maharshi*, talk no. 485.
13 *The Power of the Presence*, part one, p. 265.
14 *Talks with Sri Ramana Maharshi*, talk no 420.


**Right Behaviour, Right Attitude**

**1**:901, **2**:2296, **3**:2400, **4**:2493, **5**:2494, **6**:2568, **7**:3004, **8**:1975, **9**:343, **10**:2738, **11**:773, **12**:2233, **13**:2234, **14**:419, **15**:1203, **16**:1593, **17**:1594, **18**:511, **19**:703, **20**:1228, **21**:297, **22**:899, **23**:2714, **24**:606, **25**:1359, **26**:2575, **27**:1492, **28**:616, **29**:1974, **30**:1821, **31**:722, **32**:2228, **33**:1801, **34**:1802, **35**:1358, **36**:342, **37**:963, **38**:657, **39**:2573, **40**:2225, **41**:791, **42**:792, **43**:793, **44**:1655, **45**:1341, **46**:1029, **47**:1023, **48**:486, **49**:790, **50**:2943, **51**:1849, **52**:1572, **53**:2709, **54**:927, **55**:928, **56**:862, **57**:1989, **58**:1177, **59**:2189, **60**:340, **61**:1683, **62**:2008, **63**:351, **64**:2006, **65**:487, **66**:1075, **67**:1915, **68**:710, **69**:711, **70**:215, **71**:2555, **72**:2453, **73**:2591, **74**:400, **75**:444, **76**:446, **77**:2721, **78**:1466, **79**:1467, **80**:982, **81**:3002, **82**:1166, **83**:709, **84**:2292, **85**:395, **86**:728, **87**:981, **88**:682, **89**:1150, **90**:1658, **91**:627, **92**:1967, **93**:1148, **94**:541, **95**:260, **96**:2072, **97**:2021, **98**:1310, **99**:1657, **100**:1153, **101**:2780, **102**:1837, **103**:1838, **104**:975, **105**:976, **106**:1088, **107**:2220, **108**:462, **109**:535, **110**:536, **111**:559, **112**:853, **113**:1294, **114**:1659.


1 *Ulladu Narpadu – Kalivenba, The Mountain Path*, 1981, p. 221.
2 *The Collected Works of Sri Ramana Maharshi*, p. 128.
3 *The Power of the Presence*, part one, p. 49.
4 *Sri Ramana Darsanam*, pp. 40-1.
5 *The Power of the Presence*, part one, p. 234.
6 *Letters from and Recollections of Sri Ramanasramam*, p. 88.
7 *Living by the Words of Bhagavan*, p. 244.
8 *Letters from Sri Ramanasramam*, 6th April, 1947.
9 *Talks with Sri Ramana Maharshi*, talk no. 22.
10 *Talks with Sri Ramana Maharshi*, talk no. 24.
11 *Guru Ramana Vachana Mala*, verse 178.
12 *Letters from Sri Ramanasramam*, 20th June, 1947.
13 *Talks with Sri Ramana Maharshi*, talk no. 17.

14 *Talks with Sri Ramana Maharshi*, talk no. 169.
15 *Who am I?, Collected Works*, p. 41.
16 *The Power of the Presence*, part two, pp. 65-6.
17 *Letters from Sri Ramanasramam*, 26th September, 1947.
18 *Sadakarkuriya Sattana Nerigal*, no. 49.
19 *Talks with Sri Ramana Maharshi*, talk no. 653.
20 *Sadakarkuriya Sattana Nerigal*, no. 72.
21 *Sri Ramana Darsanam*, pp. 77-8.

**_Padam's_ Grace Towards Muruganar (title page)**

1 *Sri Ramana Jnana Bodham*, volume 7, verse 851.
2 *Non-Dual Consciousness – the Flood Tide of Bliss, Sri Ramana Anubhuti*, verse 248.
3 *Sri Ramana Jnana Bodham*, vol. 4, verse 1541.
4 *Sri Ramana Jnana Bodham*, vol. 3, verse 1398.

**_Padam's_ Grace Towards Muruganar (chapter)**

**1**:2513, **2**:2514, **3**:252, **4**:1586, **5**:200, **6**:2703, **7**:199, **8**:2149, **9**:431, **10**:2150, **11**:201, **12**:1653, **13**:2433, **14**:229, **15**:526, **16**:2279, **17**:2507, **18**:386, **19**:1554, **20**:155, **21**:382, **22**:1347, **23**:1794, **24**:578, **25**:413, **26**:3049, **27**:2705, **28**:1065, **29**:2949, **30**:258, **31**:1591, **32**:44, **33**:1291, **34**:2308, **35**:1790, **36**:1690, **37**:1789, **38**:1860, **39**:3040, **40**:1824, **41**:1371, **42**:1696, **43**:2800, **44**:1302, **45**:2905, **46**:2634, **47**:2572, **48**:361, **49**:2779, **50**:409, **51**:1607, **52**:157, **53**:3048, **54**:2733, **55**:243, **56**:586, **57**:2277, **58**:3042, **59**:2702, **60**:584, **61**:587, **62**:120, **63**:121, **64**:256, **65**:1891, **66**:2698, **67**:1299, **68**:1864, **69**:2704, **70**:2795, **71**:1336, **72**:2121, **73**:119, **74**:1776, **75**:362, **76**:2719, **77**:647, **78**:2818, **79**:2590, **80**:318, **81**:482, **82**:2119, **83**:1404, **84**:334, **85**:2899, **86**:588, **87**:2227, **88**:1370, **89**:2465, **90**:78, **91**:194, **92**:477, **93**:755, **94**:2210, **95**:1413, **96**:1522, **97**:1561, **98**:2216, **99**:2720, **100**:2785, **101**:355, **102**:3050, **103**:268, **104**:2777, **105**:2754, **106**:1442, **107**:1417, **108**:2430, **109**:1419, **110**:1348, **111**:1300, **112**:2323, **113**:28, **114**:2771, **115**:464, **116**:2270, **117**:2271, **118**:1731, **119**:506, **120**:1719, **121**:379, **122**:490, **123**:1350, **124**:2674, **125**:531, **126**:530, **127**:2789, **128**:2116, **129**:2409, **130**:1843, **131**:26, **132**:2179, **133**:264, **134**:2585, **135**:2825, **136**:1414, **137**:1408, **138**:2945, **139**:115, **140**:1316, **141**:106, **142**:2428, **143**:1418, **144**:2574, **145**:2986, **146**:2586, **147**:2929, **148**:187, **149**:2691, **150**:333, **151**:2464, **152**:2805, **153**:1775, **154**:1440, **155**:591, **156**:2155, **157**:1899, **158**:2755, **159**:1453, **160**:427, **161**:1746, **162**:2438, **163**:942, **164**:2746, **165**:941, **166**:1568, **167**:384, **168**:1222, **169**:1640, **170**:471, **171**:1406, **172**:99, **173**:1702, **174**:2983, **175**:1589, **176**:2984, **177**:1303, **178**:2626, **179**:1918, **180**:1777, **181**:2018, **182**:2363, **183**:2973, **184**:2435, **185**:2411, **186**:463, **187**:156, **188**:667, **189**:757, **190**:1553, **191**:1525, **192**:2826, **193**:2694, **194**:2954, **195**:1527, **196**:412, **197**:2816, **198**:393, **199**:377, **200**:570, **201**:17, **202**:374, **203**:2170, **204**:2841, **205**:2175, **206**:127, **207**:2901, **208**:1402, **209**:2707, **210**:2364, **211**:1403, **212**:2489, **213**:2345, **214**:2604, **215**:2631, **216**:2810, **217**:2612, **218**:2715, **219**:1479, **220**:2215, **221**:1125, **222**:1435,

**223**:2716, **224**:1563, **225**:3059.

1 'Potri Tiruvahaval', *Sri Ramana Sannidhi Murai*, cited in *The Power of the Presence*, part two, p. 146.
2 *Five Hymns to Arunachala*, tr. Prof. K. Swaminathan, p. 60.
3 *Cherished Memories*, p. 154.
4 'Keerti Tiruvahaval', *Ramana Sannidhi Murai*, cited in *The Power of the Presence*, part two, p. 113.
5 *Five Hymns to Arunachala*, tr. Prof. K. Swaminathan, p. 96.
6 *Five Hymns to Arunachala*, tr. Prof. K. Swaminathan, p. 31.
7 *My Recollections of Bhagavan Sri Ramana*, pp. 110-11.
8 *Padamalai*, vv. 1296, 1295, 1324, 1325.
9 *Padamalai*, verse 1565.
10 *The Power of the Presence*, part two, pp. 127-8.
11 *Guru Ramana*, p. 80.
12 *Cherished Memories*, p. 143.

## *Guru Vachaka Kovai* references

These are all the *Guru Vachaka Kovai* verses that appear in the commentary to *Padamalai*. The first number in **bold** is the *Guru Vachaka Kovai* verse. The second number in the pair indicates the page number on which the verse begins.

**29**:264, **46**:270, **55**:261, **62**:169, **71**:296, **73**:244, **84**:264, **100**:50, **116**:291, **117**:291, **132**:304, **133**:304, **143**:303, **146**:210, **147**:35, **149**:242, **152**:255, **178**:287, **187**:138, **188**:138, **204**:93, **207**:116, **221**:131, **222**:315, **227**:308, **310**:116, **317**:26, **321**:109, **332**:130, **342**:297, **356**:179, **371**:240, **391**:210, **393**:209, **417**:92, **426**:64, **451**:232, **457**:183, **461**:183, **471**:219, **472**:219, **488**:326, **494**:332, **512**:250, **518**:212, **531**:353, **532**:353, **547**:85, **553**:178, **555**:178, **570**:174, **574**:328, **597**:284, **599**:255, **623**:318, **634**:253, **646**:159, **648**:252, **656**:112, **659**:222, **668**:174, **698**:294, **705**:134, **745**:209, **753**:251, **755**:212, **759**:87, **760**:180, **765**:75, **773**:343, **774**:343, **791**:318, **796**:196, **804**:120, **822**:296, **826**:319, **837**:171, **849**:296, **876**:269, **877**:269, **885**:146, **887**:65, **901**:32, **902**:236, **912**:248, **920**:143, **926**:315, **927**:316, **928**:316, **929P**:317, **930**:316, **945**:331, **947**:153, **952**:313, **953**:311, **954**:312, **965**:47, **966**:30, **969**:311, **989**:297, **991**:298, **993**:298, **1026**:82, **1028**:158, **1124**:167, **1158**:130, **1159**:131, **1168**:132, **1169**:132, **1170**:132, **1191**:295, **1192**:77, **1237**:55, **1238**:55.

# Bibliography

*Aksharamanamalai Vritti Urai*, by Muruganar, pub. Sri Ramanasramam, Tiruvannamalai, 1984.

*Be As You Are*, ed. David Godman, pub. Penguin, London, 1992.

*Bhagavan Sri Ramana, a Pictorial Biography*, comp. Matthew and Joan Greenblatt, pub. Sri Ramanasramam, Tiruvannamalai, 1981.

*Call Divine, The*, journal, published from various addresses in Bombay, starting 1952.

*Cherished Memories*, by T. R. Kanakammal, pub. Sri Ramanasramam, Tiruvannamalai, 2002.

*Collected Works of Sri Ramana Maharshi, The*, by Ramana Maharshi, pub. Sri Ramanasramam, Tiruvannamalai, 2002.

*Conscious Immortality*, by Paul Brunton, pub. Sri Ramanasramam, Tiruvannamalai, 1984.

*Crumbs from his Table*, by Ramanananda Swarnagiri, pub. Sri Ramanasramam, Tiruvannamalai, 1969.

*Day by Day with Bhagavan*, comp. Devaraja Mudaliar, pub. Sri Ramanasramam, Tiruvannamalai, 1977.

*Five Hymns to Arunachala*, by Ramana Maharshi, tr. Prof. K. Swaminathan, pub. Sri Ramanasramam, Tiruvannamalai, 2001.

*Garland of Guru's Sayings, The*, by Muruganar, tr. Prof. K. Swaminathan, pub. Sri Ramanasramam, Tiruvannamalai, 1990.

*Guru Ramana Vachana Malai*, by 'Who' (Lakshman Sarma), pub. Sri Ramanasramam, Tiruvannamalai, 1998.

*Guru Ramana*, by S. S. Cohen, pub. Sri Ramanasramam, Tiruvannamalai, 1980.

*Guru Vachaka Kovai* (Tamil), by Muruganar, pub. Sri Ramanasramam, Tiruvannamalai, 1998.

*Kaivalya Navaneeta,* Tandavaraya Swami, pub. Sri Ramanasramam, Tiruvannamalai, 1974

*Letters from and Recollections of Sri Ramanasramam*, by Suri Nagamma, pub. Sri Ramanasramam, Tiruvannamalai, 1992.

*Letters from Sri Ramanasramam*, by Suri Nagamma, pub. Sri Ramanasramam, Tiruvannamalai, 1985.

*Living by the Words of Bhagavan*, 2nd ed., by David Godman, pub. Sri

Annamalai Swami Ashram Trust, Tiruvannamalai, 1995.

*Maha Yoga*, by 'Who', (Lakshman Sarma), pub. Sri Ramanasramam, Tiruvannamalai, 1974, 2002.

*Maharshi's Gospel*, pub. Sri Ramanasramam, Tiruvannamalai, 1994.

*Mountain Path, The*, journal, pub. Sri Ramanasramam, Tiruvannamalai.

*My Recollections of Bhagavan Sri Ramana*, by Devaraja Mudaliar, pub. Sri Ramanasramam, Tiruvannamalai, 1992.

*My Reminiscences*, by Balaram Reddy, pub. Sri Ramanasramam, Tiruvannamalai, 1996.

*Ninaivil Niraindavai* (Tamil), by T. R. Kanakammal, pub. Sri Ramanasramam, Tiruvannamalai, 1995.

*No Mind – I am the Self*, by David Godman, pub. Bhanumathy Ramanadham, Gudur, A. P., 1988.

*Non-Dual Consciousness – the Flood Tide of Bliss, Sri Ramana Anubhuti*, by Muruganar, tr. Robert Butler, pub. Ramana Maharshi Centre for Learning, Bangalore, 1998.

*Power of the Presence, The*, parts one, two and three, edited by David Godman, pub. David Godman, Boulder, Colorado, USA, 2001, 2002.

*Ramana Maharshi and the Path of Self-Knowledge*, by Arthur Osborne, pub. B. I. Publications, New Delhi, 1970.

*Ramana Smrti Souvenir*, pub. Sri Ramanasramam, Tiruvannamalai, 1980.

*Sadakarkuriya Sattana Nerigal* (Tamil), by Muruganar, pub. Sri Ramana Mandiram, Madurai, 1996.

*Sat Darshana Bhashya*, by 'K' (Kapali Sastri), pub. Sri Ramanasramam, Tiruvannamalai, 1975.

*Self-Realization*, by B. V. Narasimha Swami, pub. Sri Ramanasramam, Tiruvannamalai, 1993.

*Sri Ramana Anubhuti*, volume two, (Tamil), by Muruganar, pub. Dharmalaya Publications, Madras, 1961.

*Sri Ramana Darsanam*, by Sadhu Natanananda, pub. Sri Ramanasramam, Tiruvannamalai, 2002.

*Sri Ramana Gita*, by Ganapati Muni, pub. Sri Ramanasramam, Tiruvannamalai, 1998.

*Sri Ramana Jnana Bodham* (Tamil), nine volumes, by Muruganar, pub. New Delhi Ramana Kendra, New Delhi, 1978 to 1996.

*Sri Ramana Reminiscences*, by G. V. Subbaramayya, pub. Sri Ramanasramam, Tiruvannamalai, 1967.

*Talks with Sri Ramana Maharshi*, comp. Munagala S. Venkataramiah, pub. Sri Ramanasramam, Tiruvannamalai, 1984.

*Truth Revealed*, by Ramana Maharshi, pub. Sri Ramanasramam, Tiruvannamalai, 1982.

*Ulladu Narpadu* (Tamil), by 'Yaar' (Lakshman Sarma), pub. Sri

Ramanasramam, Tiruvannamalai, 1979.
*Who am I?* by Ramana Maharshi, unpublished translation based on one done by Sadhu Om and Michael James, and edited by David Godman.

# Glossary

Many of the technical terms in this book are explained or defined when they appear. The following list comprises terms that do not have definitions on the page on which they occur.

*Agamas* – Saiva scriptures that primarily describe the rules and procedures for ritual worship.

*aham* – generally means 'I'. See page 37 for other possibilities.

*ajnana* – ignorance; more specifically, ignorance of the true knowledge that expresses itself as a direct experience of the Self.

*ajnani* – an unenlightened person; someone who has not experienced *jnana*.

*ananda* – bliss; the bliss that is a consequence of experiencing the Self.

*Atma swarupa* – The real nature of one's own Self. See page 33 for a brief explanation of how this term has been used in this book.

*Atman* – the Self. It is also occasionally spelled without the final 'n' when it appears in compounds with other terms.

*avasthas* – the three alternating states of waking, dreaming and sleeping.

*bhajan* – devotional song addressed to a Hindu deity or Guru.

*bhakta* – a devotee.

*bhakti* – devotion to God.

*Brahman* – The impersonal absolute reality of Hinduism.

*chidabhasa* – the unreal reflection in consciousness that displays the pictures of the world that the mind has projected onto it. See page 264.

*chit* – consciousness; this is not the antonym of unconsciousness, it is unmediated Self-awareness.

*chit-jada* - 'literally, 'consciousness-inert'; it is the unreal bond that ties or limits consciousness to the body. See page 166.

*dakshina* – a monetary gift traditionally given to a Guru by a disciple.

*darshan* – to see or be seen by a Guru or God.

*dharma* – there are several shades of meaning that depend on the context. It may mean right action, moral duty, divine law, or religious tradition.

*dhyana* – meditation; when Ramana Maharshi uses this term he is generally referring to meditation that consists on concentration on a form or a particular thought.

*gayatri* – a vedic mantra, an invocation to the sun, that is recited daily by many Hindus.

*gunas* – the three fundamental qualities that make up the mind and physical manifestation. See page 144 for more details.

*idam* – 'this'; used in this book to denote objects that are seen or thought of by *aham*, the perceiving 'I'.

*japa* – the repetition of God's name or of any other combination of sacred words or syllables.

*jiva* – the soul; the individual self. See page 34.

*jivanmukta* – a liberated being; sometimes this term implies someone has realised the Self while still alive, rather than someone who attains liberation at the moment of death.

*jnana* – true knowledge; direct knowledge of the reality that is the Self.

*jnani* – one who has a direct awareness of himself as *jnana*; an enlightened person.

*Kali Yuga* – a *yuga* is an immensely long period of Hindu cosmology which is subdivided into four smaller units, of which the Kali Yuga is the last. We are currently in a Kali Yuga period.

*lingam* – a vertical column of stone with a rounded upper end. Installed in the inner shrines of all Siva temples, it is regarded by devotees as a physical manifestation of the deity.

*mahavakyas* – 'great statements'; specifically four key upanishadic statements that declare the nature of reality and one's identity with it.

*mauna* – 'silence'; one of Ramana Maharshi's favourite synonyms for the thought-free experience of the Self. See page 95.

*maya* – illusion; the power that makes the unreal world appear to be real.

*moksha* – liberation; more specifically, liberation from the cycle of birth and death.

*mukta* – someone who has attained liberation.

*mukti* – spiritual liberation; the state of enlightenment.

*nishkamya punya* – the spiritual merit that accumulates from doing good deeds that are performed without any particular motive.

*niyama* – see *yama*.

*Padam* – literally 'the foot'; a synonym for the Self. In this particular work it is also an epithet that Muruganar uses to describe or designate Ramana Maharshi.

payasam – a sweet porridge usually made from milk, sugar, cereal, and other flavouring ingredients.

*Pozhippurai* – a prose rendering of a verse; see page 30 for more details.
*pramada* – forgetfulness; more specifically, the forgetfulness of one's Self.
*prarabdha* karma – the destined acts and experiences that one has to undergo in one's life; the God-given script for a particular incarnation.
*prasad* – a consecrated offering; anything offered to a deity or Guru becomes *prasad* when some or all of it is returned to the donor or distributed publicly.
*puja* – ritual worship of a Hindu deity.
*punya* – the merit accumulated by performing good deeds. See also *nishkamya punya*.
*rajas* – activity, excitability; one the of the three *gunas*. See page 144 for more details.
*Sadguru* – a fully enlightened Guru who is established in *sat*, the underlying being or reality.
*sadhana* – spiritual practice; the means by which liberation is attained.
*sadhus* – full-time spiritual seekers who have renounced worldly responsibilities in order to seek enlightenment.
*sahaja* – 'natural'; used by Ramana Maharshi to designate the permanent and highest level of experiencing the Self. See page 89.
*Saiva* – a follower or worshipper of Siva; an adjective meaning 'pertaining to Siva'. Saivism is the term used to denote the branch of Hinduism that regards Siva as the ultimate deity.
*sakti* – 'power'; more specifically, the power through which the universe is created and sustained. This power is often personalised as a female deity.
*samadhi* – a direct but temporary experience of the Self, usually in a trance-like condition in which there is no outer awareness of either the body or the world; the term is also used to describe the tomb of a saint.
*samsara* – the continuous round of birth and death to which the *jiva* is subjected until it attains liberation; also, more generally, worldly life.
*samskaras* – mental tendencies and habits, often those that have been brought forward from a previous birth.
*sastras* – scriptures.
*sat* – being, reality, truth.
*sat-chit-ananda* – being-consciousness-bliss.
*sattva* – purity, harmony; one of the three *gunas*. See page 144.
*satvam* – see *sattva*.
*shanti* – peace, the peace that one experiences when one is directly experiencing the Self.

*siddha* – one who has attained; a realised being.
*siddhi* – attainment; more specifically, the attainment of Self-realisation.
*siddhis* – supernatural powers.
*Sivam* – the true consciousness of Siva; the Self. See page 105.
*sphurana* – a throbbing, a pulsation; Ramana Maharshi generally associated it with '*aham*', the 'I', (*aham-sphurana*), in which context it means the continuously experienced emanation of the real 'I', the Self.
*summa iru* – 'be quiet'; 'be still'.
*suttarivu* – the false consciousness that divides itself into someone who sees and objects that are seen. See page 148 for more details.
*swarupa* – one's true nature; one's true form; the Self. See page 33.
*tamas* – sloth, torpor; one of the three alternating *gunas* that comprise the mind and manifestation. See page 144 for more details.
*tapas* – arduous spiritual practice, often involving bodily mortification. Its aim is to burn off spiritual impurities. See page 36.
*tattva* – truth; the essence of a thing; in Saivism, there are innumerable subdivisions called '*tattvas*' which describe and categorize the nature of reality.
*triputis* – the trinities of seer-seeing-seen and knower-knowing-known.
*upadesa* – a teaching; usually a teaching given by a Guru to a disciple.
*upasana* – meditation on a form of God.
*vairagya* – dispassion; non-attachment.
*vasanas* – mental tendencies; the latent desires and feelings that compel one to behave in a particular way. See page 35.
*Vedas* – the ultimate scriptural authorities for Hindus. They include the *Upanishads*, which are the original texts upon which Vedanta philosophy is based.
*vichara* – enquiry; when Ramana Maharshi used this term he is referring specifically to the practice of self-enquiry.
*Vilakkam* – an explanation. See page 30 for more details.
*yama* – *yama* and *niyama* are codes of conduct for dealing with the world and with other people.
*yugas* – see *Kali Yuga*.

# Index

The subheadings listed on the Contents pages give a fairly exhaustive list of the themes and ideas that comprise this book. This index is primarily an alphabetical listing of proper nouns and technical terms that appear in the text.

B



C

H



I



J

**K**



**L**

**M**



**N**



**O**

W



Y